Minds, Brains, Computers

For Csilla

Minds, Brains, Computers

An Historical Introduction to the Foundations of Cognitive Science

Robert M. Harnish

BLACKWELL
Publishers

The right of Robert M. Harnish to be identified as author of this work has been
asserted in accordance with the Copyright, Designs and Patents Act 1988.

First published 2002

2 4 6 8 10 9 7 5 3 1

Blackwell Publishers Inc.
350 Main Street
Malden, Massachusetts 02148
USA

Blackwell Publishers Ltd
108 Cowley Road
Oxford OX4 1JF
UK

Library of Congress Cataloging-in-Publication Data

Harnish, Robert M.
Minds, brains, computers: an historical introduction to the foundations of cognitive
science/Robert M. Harnish.
p.   cm.
Includes bibliographical references and index.
ISBN 0-631-21259-0 (alk. paper)—ISBN 0-631-21260-4 (pbk.: alk. paper)
1. Cognitive science—History.   I. Title.
BF311 .H339   2001
153'.09—dc21
00-052929

British Library Cataloguing in Publication Data

A CIP catalogue record for this book is available from the British Library.

Typeset in 10.5 on 12.5 pt Ehrhardt
by Best-set Typesetter Ltd, Hong Kong
Printed in Great Britain by T.J. International, Padstow, Cornwall

This book is printed on acid-free paper.

Contents

List of Figures

Preface

Cognitive science is the scientific study of cognition, drawing contributions from such diverse fields as psychology, computer science, neuroscience, linguistics, and philosophy. The idea that holds most of this research together is that the brain (neuroscience) is a kind of computational device (computer science), and cognition (psychology) studies its software – the programs running on the brain. The present work is an *historical* introduction to the *foundations* of cognitive science. Each of these notions is important. It is historical in that we trace the history of central concepts from mainly the nineteenth century (but occasionally back to Aristotle) to the present. It is foundational in that it is concerned mainly with the general (computational) framework for the study of the mind-brain in contemporary cognitive science, and not with the details of particular competing theories or experimental results predicted by those theories. And as cognitive science is currently practiced it is interdisciplinary, in that we survey the contributions of philosophy, psychology, neuroscience, and computer science in some detail.

Introduction: what is cognitive science describes the broad and narrow conceptions of the discipline, then offers a combined view.

Part I: historical background traces some of the contributions of philosophy, psychology, and neuroscience to what would become cognitive science, up to the point of the development of the digital computer about 1950.

Part II: the digital computational theory of mind looks at a particular artificial intelligence demonstration project SHRDLU, then surveys some digital architectures, and some standard knowledge representation formats. With this computational material in place we look at the theory of mind these developments suggested as well as some of the most important problems with it.

Part III: the connectionist computational theory of mind follows the same pattern for connectionist machines. It looks at a pair of connectionist computational demonstration projects, Jets and Sharks and NETtalk. Then we survey some connectionist architectures, learning procedures and representational schemes. With this material in place we turn to the theory of mind these developments suggest, as well as some of its significant problems.

Coda: Computation for cognitive science, or what IS a computer, anyway? outlines two dominant conceptions of a computer and computation, then tries to reconcile them and show that the resulting characterization applies equally well to digital and connectionist models.

Acknowledgments

This book grew out of lecture notes as the result of many years of teaching, and talking, cognitive science. The hundreds of students who endured earlier incarnations of this material must be the first to be thanked. Without their patience and good sense not only wouldn't this work be as it is, it wouldn't be. I was also aided in these courses by a string of excellent teaching and research assistants: Peter Graham, Laleh Quinn, Bongrae Seok, Jack Lyons, Scott Hendricks, and Brad Thompson, who compiled the index. Thanks are due to teachers who introduced me to cognitive science, though it was not called that then, and subsequently influenced my views (in chronological order): Bert Dreyfus and John Searle at Berkeley, Jerry Fodor and Ned Block (then) at MIT. Integrating what I learned from them has proven to be a challenge. Various colleagues here at the University of Arizona and elsewhere read portions of this work and provided useful feedback including (alphabetically): Kent Bach, Tom Bever, Ned Block, András Bocz, Dick Carter, Dave Chalmers, Ken Forster, Merrill Garrett, Alvin Goldman, Bill Ittelson, Tom Larson, Shaughan Lavine, Chris Maloney, Lynn Nadel, and Rich Zemel. Jason Barker helped with some of the figures, and Ágnes Pásztor secured the rights to the cover print. The University of Arizona has proven to be extremely hospitable for the pursuit of interdisciplinary work such as this, and I am grateful to Merrill Garrett, director of cognitive science, for providing such an environment. I want to thank Csaba Pléh, for an invitation to present this material at the University of Budapest (ELTE), and the Rockefeller Foundation, for a month at the Bellagio Study and Conference Center, which provided just the right opportunity to give the manuscript a rewriting. Finally, my wife Csilla Pásztor is beyond thanking – I dedicate this work to her.

A note regarding quotations: all are from the items mentioned in the bibliography and suggested readings, but in the interest of readability, only some (amusing, contentious, important, unbelievable) have been attributed.

I

Introduction: What is Cognitive Science?

Cognitive science, as an institutionalized field of study, emerged in the mid 1970s in response to a perceived gap in the fabric of existing research areas. As central to research and education as cognition is, there was no science of cognition, no systematic exploration of central questions in the domain of thought: how is knowledge acquired? how is it represented in the mind? how is knowledge then utilized in thought and action? How can the acquisition and utilization of knowledge be enhanced and how can disabilities in these areas be overcome? Like computer science, which started at some institutions as a special program uniting electrical engineering and applied mathematics, "cognitive science" emerged as a self-conscious discipline when the problems and methods of researchers in various fields, such as psychology, neuroscience, computer science, linguistics, anthropology, and philosophy began to overlap. In the late 1970s and early 1980s a remarkable convergence appeared among researchers concerned with understanding cognition, and "cognitive science" established itself as a discipline. Three landmarks in this process were:

1977	Journal *Cognitive Science* founded
1978	Sloan Foundation Report: State of the Art in Cognitive Science
1979	Cognitive Science Society: first meeting La Jolla, CA

It has since become plausible that this is a "natural" domain of investigation, and it has become clear that researchers will profit from being in systematic contact with others also interested in understanding cognition from their own point of view. There are at present two main construals of "cognitive science" – what we will call, for want of better terms, a *broad* conception and a *narrow* conception. Since we will adopt a specific way of putting these two construals together, we should say what each is, and what its strengths and weaknesses are.

I.1   Broad Construal

As a first approximation, cognitive science, broadly construed, is the scientific study of cognition. It is basically a *domain* of investigation plus a set of *procedures* for investigating that domain – a "discipline." A good example of this conception is Norman (1981:1): "Cognitive Science is a new discipline, created from a merger of interests among those pursuing the study of cognition from different points of view. The critical aspect of Cognitive Science is the search for understanding of cognition, be it real or abstract, human or machine. The goal is to understand the principles of intelligent, cognitive behavior. The hope is that this will lead to better understanding of the human mind, of teaching and learning, of mental abilities, and of the development of intelligent devices that can augment human capabilities in important and constructive ways." Given the domain of cognition, the central sciences (philosophy comes later) have been: (1) cognitive psychology, (2) cognitive neuroscience, (3) computer science, (4) linguistics and (5) anthropology.

Cognitive psychology gives us many detailed theories of various cognitive capacities and works out experimental paradigms for assessing these theories (see Bower and Clapper, 1989).

Cognitive neuroscience gives us analyses of those portions of the nervous system subserving cognitive capacities. It tells us how systems with specific neural features have the cognitive functions they have.

Computer science gives us our most complete understanding of how a complicated (intelligent?) capacity can be realized in a physical system – how software is related to hardware. The study of various architectures, algorithms, and data structures offer potential theoretical insights into how animate systems might be organized.

Linguistics' role in cognitive science is historically direct, but by subject matter indirect. In the late 1950s and early 1960s linguists such as Chomsky led the charge against behaviorism and influenced a whole generation of psychologists (such as George Miller) and philosophers (such as Hillary Putnam) who later contributed directly to cognitive science. Chomsky's version of transformational grammar postulated rich cognitive structures, and many cognitive scientists have been exploring these ideas. Language processing is an important cognitive capacity and it is fortunate to have a whole discipline (linguistics) dedicated to analyzing its input and output.

Anthropology has a unique role to play in cognitive science by exploiting its expertise at investigating cognitive phenomena from a cross-cultural perspective.

Philosophy has a distinctive role in cognitive science. First, it is not a science and so has no "scientific" methodology to offer. But many of the problems now confronting cognitive science are traditional philosophical problems; think of the mind-body problem, the problem of personal identity, consciousness, mental representation, rationality, etc. Because these problems are so fundamental and so general, they do not yield readily to methodologies of the special sciences, which were formulated to deal with much more local issues. Philosophy has been concerned with some of these problems for a long time, and though it has not solved them, it has charted out some of the consequences of accepting various solutions to them. Philosophy's analytical methodology is useful in sophisticating thinking in these areas.

How are these and neighboring disciplines related? One popular proposal is the "cognitive hexagon" of the 1978 Sloan State of the Art Report (see the Appendix to this chapter). On a second approximation, then, the *broad construal* of cognitive science is that it is *the scientific study of cognition as carried out in accordance with the methodologies of these six disciplines*. Of course, mutual admiration does not always reign, and cooperation can break down, as in Dennett's delightful parody:

> Why . . . , ask the people in Artificial Intelligence, do you waste your time conferring with neuroscientists? They wave their hands about "information processing" and worry about *where* it happens, and which neurotransmitters are involved, and all those boring facts, but they haven't a clue about the computational requirements of higher cognitive functions. Why, ask the neuroscientists, do you waste your time on the fantasies of Artificial Intelligence? They just invent whatever machinery they want, and say unpardonably ignorant things about the brain. The cognitive psychologists, meanwhile, are accused of concocting models with *neither* biological plausibility *nor* proven computational powers; the anthropologists wouldn't know a model if they saw one, and philosophers, as we all know, just take in each other's laundry, warning about confusions they themselves have created, in an arena bereft of both data and empirically testable theories. (1995: 254–5).

I.2   Narrow Construal

Construed narrowly, cognitive science is not an area but a *doctrine*, and the doctrine is basically that of the computational theory of mind (CTM) – the mind/brain is a type of computer. Consider the 1978 Sloan Report on Cognitive Science: "what the subdisciplines of cognitive science share ... is a common research objective: *to discover the representational and computational capacities of the mind and their structural and functional representation in the brain*" (1978: 76). Some authors endorse the narrow as opposed to the broad conception explicitly:

> When I speak of cognitive science, I have in mind an ideology ... presupposed by a significant line of work in cognitive psychology and artificial intelligence, and to some extent linguistics and philosophy. Many – and perhaps most – cognitive psychologists do not subscribe explicitly to such a point of view, though most do work that implicitly involves it. Many writers on this topic prefer to use "cognitivism" to refer to the ideology I have in mind, treating "cognitive science" as a neutral disciplinary term. I see "cognitive science" as an ideologically loaded term (as is "sociobiology"), since *the research programs which parade under the banner of cognitive science would not form a field at all without the ideology.* (Block 1983: 521; emphasis added).

There certainly is some justice to this remark. Not every collection of research programs forms a field. But is the underscored reason for denying that cognitive science would form a field without the ideology compelling? Should we agree? Maybe, maybe not. Remember, the alternative to *doctrine* was a *subject matter*, not a "research program." Furthermore, there is no single research program that makes up the "field" of anthropology, or history, or philosophy, or even linguistics – should we demand one of cognitive science?

I.3   Cognition: Broad and Narrow

Although the disciplines under the broad construal give us the relevant notion of "science" ("science" is what these disciplines do), we still do not know which portions of our mental life are *cognitive*. What is it for mental phenomena to be "cognitive"? Like many other important concepts, "cognition" seems to have clear instances, but it lacks a general definition. One way of specifying what is cognitive is by analogy to the broad conception of cognitive science – we just list the clear cases of cognitive phenomena and declare cognition to be the study of them. As inspection of any number of cognitive psychology textbooks will reveal, traditionally the domain of cognition has included such subareas as: attention, memory, learning, reasoning, problem solving, and aspects of motivation theory and action theory. Some would extend this list to aspects of perception and language processing. So we can say that the *broad conception of cognition* is the study of attention, memory, learning, reasoning, problem solving, and aspects of motivation theory, action theory, perception, and language processing. But what do these have in common? How would we know when to add something to the list?

One feature that the members on the list seem to share is that they all involve the mental "manipulation" of mental representations of some sort or other. Let's call this the *narrow conception of cognition*: cognition is the mental "manipulation" (creation, transformation, deletion) of mental representations. For example, percepts typically represent the objects that cause them. Memories (real ones) are based on certain perceptions, including language, and so they come to be about the objects, events, or situations that the perceptions themselves represent. Other cognitive capacities have the same representational feature. One typically reasons "about something," or plans "to do something," and both of these ideas involve representing the way the world is, or the way the world might be, or the way it will become.

What is the relation between the broad and narrow conceptions of cognition? Our *working assumption* will be that the phenomena listed above in the broad conception as cognitive all share the description mentioned in the narrow conception. Of course this could turn out to be wrong (you can read behaviorism as claiming that it is wrong), but there will still be the phenomena to study.

I.4 Computation: Broad and Narrow

Computation *broadly* construed is just what computers do. This of course puts all the weight of specifying the nature of computation on saying what computers do (they do lots of things including give off heat), not to mention saying what a computer is (is your digital watch a computer?). A popular idea is that computers basically input, store and output "information" – they are "information-processing" devices. But what is information processing and what do such devices have in common (even if it is only a family resemblance)? An influential *narrow* conception of computers is Marr's "tri-level" hypothesis: information-processing devices are algorithmic symbol manipulators, which are describable at three importantly different levels, answering three importantly different questions: what problem(s) does the system solve, what algorithm(s) does it use, and how are these algorithms implemented in the physical world (silicon, neural tissue, other)?

I.5   The Working Conception of Cognitive Science

The narrow conceptions of *cognitive science*, *cognition*, and *computation* all go together in the following way: if cognition is the mental manipulation of mental representations, and if these representations are symbols, and this manipulation is automatic, then cognition could be a species of computation, and this is the narrow conception of cognitive science. It is clear that the broad and narrow construals of cognitive science are not equivalent, since cognitive science could be the interdisciplinary scientific study of cognition, but cognition might fail to be computational. It might be a mistake to adopt the narrow conception and thereby put ourselves in the position of being without a subject matter if a certain theory turns out to be wrong. So how should we see the two conceptions as related? Some authors solve this problem by conceiving of the field of cognitive science in *both ways* simultaneously. For instance Gardner (1985: 6) gives the following four central features of cognitive science:

1   In talking about (human) cognitive activities it is necessary to speak about mental representations independently of the biological/ neurological and the sociological.
2   Central to understanding the human mind is the computer; the computer serves as the most viable model of how the human mind functions.
3   Cognitive science de-emphasizes emotions, historical and cultural context.
4   Cognitive science is interdisciplinary.

We see here in item 2 the narrow conception of cognitive science as the discipline which is exploring a computational conception of cognition, and in item 4 the broad conception of cognitive science as the interdisciplinary study of cognition. The relationship between the broad and the narrow construals of cognitive science, which we will call the "working view of cognitive science," assumed by this book, is this: the *domain* of cognitive science is cognition, the *methodologies* of cognitive science are the methodologies of the participating disciplines (see the cognitive hexagon again), and the *central assumption* of the

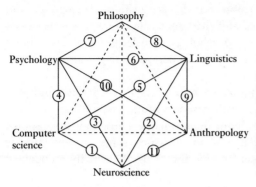

Subdomains of cognitive Science:
(1) cybernetics; (2) Neurolinguistics;
(3) neuropsychology; (4) simulation
of cognitive processes; (5) computational
linguistics; (6) psycholinguistics; (7)
philosophy of psychology; (8) philosophy
of language; (9) Anthropological linguistics; (10) cognitive anthropology; (11)
evolution of brain.

Figure I.1   The cognitive hexagon (from Pylyshyn, 1983: 76)

field is that mental states and processes are computational. In this way we give prominence to the computational notion while ensuring that if it turns out to be false, cognitive science will not self-destruct.

Appendix
1978 Sloan Report (excerpt)

Cognitive science is the study of the principles by which intelligent entities interact with their environments. By its very nature, this study transcends disciplinary boundaries to include research by scholars working in such disciplines as neuroscience, computer science, psychology, philosophy, linguistics, and anthropology. The familiar labels of these disciplines have provided the road map adopted here to explore the state of research in cognitive science.

It is, however, the richly articulated pattern of interconnections among these subdomains which makes explicit the basis for the claim that an autonomous science of cognition has arisen in the past decade. The disciplines contributing to this science, and the major bonds among them, are summarized in figure I.1. Each of the six fields listed is connected to the others by a network of interdisciplinary regimens, some of which represent ancient topics of intellectual concern, others of which raise familiar and important issues which have not yet become the focus of major scholarly effort.

Each of the component fields is tied to two or more of the others by a network of interdisciplinary regimens. Each labeled link represents a well-defined area of inquiry which involves the intellectual and physical tools of the two disciplines it ties together. Thus cybernetics uses the concepts developed by computer scientists to model brain functions elucidated by neuroscientists. Similarly, psycholinguistics joins two fields in its concern for the mental apparatus and operations responsible for the acquisition of language and its production and understanding, and the simulation of cognitive processes has combined computer science and psychology in order to formulate explicit theories of thinking and problem solving. Other pairs share similar sets of concerns.

Each of the 11 solid lines in figure I.1 represents a well-defined and professionally established domain of interdisciplinary inquiry which may be found within one or more traditional academic departments. Those four links shown as dotted lines in the figure identify a set of issues, some already familiar and important, which have not yet become the focus of formally recognized scholarly effort.

It is possible to consider linked sets of the six major disciplines taken three or more at a time. The triad of philosophy, psychology, and linguistics, for example, represents an old area of inquiry concerned with language and the use of language in cognitive tasks. Each such group represents a valid and increasingly active area of research whose practitioners have been trained in two or more of the fields involved. A major concern of this paper is the argument that the network of interacting disciplines shown here should be considered as a whole under the name of cognitive science. That whole cannot yet be integrated successfully, but such an integration is the goal toward which these related groupings are moving.

What the subdisciplines of cognitive science share, indeed, what has brought the field into existence, is a common research objective: *to discover the representational and computational capacities of the mind and their structural and functional representation in the brain.* Cognitive science is already being practiced by workers in the fields and subfields listed above. These workers have accepted the challenge to specify adequate theoretical descriptions of cognitive systems and to test empirically the predictions of these theories.

(Sloan Report: 75–6)

Study questions

What perceived need did the advent of cognitive science fill?

What is the "broad" conception of cognitive science?

What are the major disciplines involved in cognitive science?

What distinctive contribution do each of these disciplines make to cognitive science?

What is the main problem with the broad conception?

What is the "narrow" conception of cognitive science?

What is the main problem with the narrow conception?

What is the broad conception of cognition?

What is the narrow conception of cognition?

What is the broad conception of computation?

What is the narrow conception of computation?

How do the narrow conceptions of cognition and computation fit the narrow conception of cognitive science?

What is the working view of cognitive science?

Suggested reading

Nature of cognitive science

See for instance Pylyshyn (1983) and the commentaries, especially Newell (1983). And for the nature of cognitive scientists, see the enlightening (and entertaining) Baumgartner and Payr (1995).

Introductions to cognitive science

There are numerous good introductions to cognitive science available based on the two conceptions of cognitive science reviewed above. And just browsing through Wilson and Keil (1999) can be a wonderful introduction for the curious. Dunlop and Fetzer (1993) provide a useful, compact volume defining many of the most important notions in cognitive science.

Broad conception

The first text in cognitive science to survey the various disciplines and their contributions to cognitive science is Stillings et al. (1995). It is clearly written and multi-authored, but it has the advantage of reading like a single-authored text. The multiple volume set by Osherson et al. (1990, 1995) has individually written chapters on a variety of topics in cognitive science by well-known authorities in the field.

Narrow conception

One of the first texts written based on the notion of the mind as a computational device is Johnson-Laird (1988). A more recent text based on the same idea, but covering material more similar to ours is von Eckhardt (1993). It contains an extensive discussion of the nature of cognitive science in chapters 1 and 2 (as well as the notion of its "working assumptions"). Likewise, Crane (1995) covers much of our non-historical material in a very readable and lively manner – the nature of representation is the focus of the book. As it is in Thagard (1996), who organizes his introduction around various representational formats used in cognitive science. Dawson (1998) is organized around Marr's "tri-level hypothesis" (see text above).

History of cognitive science

The best-known history of cognitive science to date is the very readable Gardner (1985). Flanagan (1991) also contains interesting historical chapters on some of the people (such as William James) and movements (such as behaviorism) which we discuss, and some (such as Freud, Gestalt theory) which we do not. The first part of Bara (1995) also reviews some cognitive science history, as does part I of Bechtel and Graham (1998), which is the best short history.

Anthologies

An excellent collection of influential original papers can be found in Haugeland (1997), and an excellent collection of theoretical papers on the foundations of cognitive science can be found in Posner (1989). Collins and Smith (1988) focuses on psychology and artificial intelligence. Garfield (1990) contains selections from a variety of sources with emphasis on philosophical issues. Goldman (1993c) is a wide-ranging collection of articles emphasizing the impact of cognitive science on philosophy. Thagard (1998) is a useful companion to Thagard (1996), and Cummins and Cummins (1999) is relevant and up-to-date, as is Lepore and Pylyshyn (1999).

Related disciplines

Virtually all of *cognitive psychology* is relevant to cognitive science, so we will make no attempt to survey it. We will mention Barsalou (1992) as a particular attempt to relate the two, Baars (1986) as an overview, and Hinst (1988) as a view from one of cognitive sciences founders. Philosophical discussions of *artificial intelligence* (AI) often overlap with parts of cognitive science. See Copeland (1993b) or the shorter and less technical Moody (1993). The anthology by Boden (1990) contains many of the articles discussed here. Discussions in the *philosophy of mind* also overlap with cognitive science. For texts see Churchland (1988), Sterelny (1990), Kim (1996), Braddon-Mitchell and Jackson (1996), Goldberg and Pessin (1997), and Rey (1997). For anthologies see Block (1981), and Lycan (1990). Goldman (1993d) traces the impact of cognitive science on a number of branches of philosophy, and Guttenplan (1994) is an excellent handbook with many articles directly relevant to cognitive science. In *neuroscience* one might look at P. S.

Churchland (1986) for a survey of neuroscience and its connection to philosophy, and Churchland and Sejnowsky (1992) for an attempt to integrate neuroscience and cognitive science. Gazzaniga (1995) is a monumental compendium of topics, issues, and areas in cognitive neuroscience. Squire and Kosslyn (1998) is a shorter selection of recent articles on major subareas of cognitive neuroscience. For the cognitive side of anthropology one might look at D'Andrade (1989). Glimpses of the scope of current cognitive science can be had by looking at a recent *Proceedings of the Annual Conference of the Cognitive Science Society*.

Part I
Historical Background

Introduction

The computational theory of mind (CTM) emerged first in its "digital" form, then in its "connectionist" form. The purpose of Part I is to survey some of the historical antecedents to this emergence. Not all we will discuss contributed directly (or even indirectly) to the CTM, but it is all relevant to cognitive science, broadly construed. From these larger pictures we will try to extract a sketch of what these fields contributed directly to the CTM. We will see that the influences contributing to the shaping of cognitive science, and especially the computational theory of mind include the following. The connectionist form of the CTM is a descendant of both perceptrons (chapter 4) and associationism (chapter 1). After introducing connectionism we will return to associationism (chapter 12). From associationism and James we have the idea of (i) the conscious mind as an introspectable manipulator (association) of representations (ideas), and (ii) two levels of explanation: the introspective subjective psychological (software) and the objective neurological (hardware). From behaviorism we moved away from just introspection and into laboratory experimentation as practiced by current cognitive psychology. Information processing psychology gave us cognition as information processing, and more specifically in Miller, Galanter, and Pribram, TOTE units for explaining behavior are structured and function like computer programs. From biology we got most importantly the neuron doctrine: the nervous system and especially the idea that the brain is composed of networks of discrete units (neurons, axons, dendrites) joined together at synapses. The neuro–logical tradition, and especially McCulloch and Pitts, argued that the brain is composed of on/off units and circuits of such units that can be associated with the propositions of logic – the brain is equivalent to a machine table of a Turing machine, and if supplemented with unlimited memory is equivalent to a universal Turing machine. Perceptrons demonstrated that a computer hardware organized on the gross anatomy of the brain could be trained to discriminate certain categories of things in a broadly human way.

1

Associationism

1.1 Introduction: What is Associationism?

Associationism is the view that the mind is organized, at least in part, by principles of association. Associationists don't say just what makes a principle "associationist." Rather, they are content to state specific principles and call them "associationist" (the word gained currency with Locke, see below). But the *basic idea* behind associationism seems to be this: *items that "go together" in experience will subsequently "go together" in thought*. Typically, associationists are *empiricists* – they hold that all knowledge comes from experience both in the sense of being causally dependent on experience and in the sense of being justified solely by reference to experience. However, this is about where agreement ends, and each particular empiricist holds a doctrine slightly different from the others.

1.2 Generic Empiricist Associationism

These English psychologists – what do they really want? One always discovers them . . . seeking the truly effective and directing agent . . . in just that place where the intellectual pride of man would least desire *to find it (in the* vis inertiae *of habit, for example, or in forgetfulness, or in a blind and chance mechanistic hooking together of ideas, or in something purely passive, automatic, reflexive, molecular and thoroughly stupid) – what is it really that always drives these psychologists in just* this *direction? Is it a secret, malicious, vulgar, perhaps self-destructing instinct for belittling man?*

(Nietzsche, 1887)

Although empiricists differ in the details of their conception of the structure and operation of the mind, they can all be understood in terms of a common

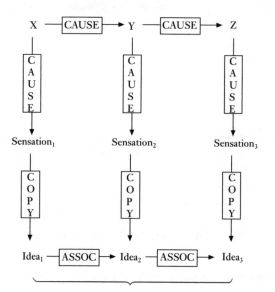

Events in the world

Complex Idea

Figure 1.1   Generic empiricist associationism

overarching framework, one we call "generic empiricist associationism." It fits no particular empiricist exactly, but gives instead a kind of composite photo of the movement (see figure 1.1).

Basic tenets

Figure 1.1 illustrates at least three basic tenets of generic associationism: (i) ideas, for instance (we return to this), are associated in the mind through experience; (ii) ideas can be decomposed into a basic stock of "simple" ideas, and ideas from the basic stock can be composed into more complex ideas; (iii) these simple ideas are derived from sensations. Sensations (sensory data) themselves are *not* governed by principles of association, but rather are caused by something outside the head (Hobbes, Locke, Hume: the world; Berkeley: God).

Author	Date	Contiguity	Similarity	Contrast	Causality
Aristotle	330 BC	X	X	X	
Thomas Hobbes	1651	X			
John Locke	1700	X	X		
George Berkeley	1733	X	X		
David Hume	1739	X	X		(X)*
David Hartley	1749	X			
James Mill	1829	X			
John Stuart Mill	1843	X	X		
Alexander Bain	1855	X	X		
Herbert Spencer	1855	X	X		

*Subsequently reduced to contiguity.

Figure 1.2   Principles of association (from Marx and Hillix, 1963: 106, figure 8; reproduced by permission of MeGraw-Hill Companies)

1.3   Varieties of Associationism

Pure associationism holds that only associationist principles govern the operation of the mind, whereas *mixed* associationism holds that there are non-associationist principles at work as well. For associationists there are different dimensions of "going together." Items can go together by having certain relations in space (e.g. spatial contiguity), they can have certain relations in time (e.g. temporal contiguity). They can go together by having more abstract relations such as cause and effect, similarity, and contrast. Here are some typical associationist principles:

1 *contiguity*: items that are contiguous in space or time are linked by association;
2 *similarity*: items that are similar are linked by association;
3 *contrast*: items that contrast are linked by association;
4 *causality*: items that are linked by cause and effect are linked by association.

Even though associationists provided no principled reason why the list of relations couldn't be extended indefinitely, there was remarkable agreement over the years as to what in fact the operative associationist principles are (see figure 1.2).

Associationist processes

For associationists, there are also three major processes of association. One kind of process involves *which items follow one another in time*, such as recalling something from memory or the temporal order of thoughts. Another kind involves *compounding*, such as taking simpler items and building more complex ones. A final kind of process involves *decomposition* or taking complex items and breaking them down into simpler ones:

1 *sequencing*: associationist principles can govern such processes as: recalling items in memory, and the temporal order of thoughts;
2 *compounding*: complex items can be formed from simple items by (a) mental mechanics, (b) mental chemistry;
3 *decomposition*: complex items can be broken down into their simpler constituents.

With compounding there is a major difference between those who, like Locke, use a kind of "mental mechanics," from those, like J. S. Mill (see below), who argue for a kind of "mental chemistry" as well.

The domain of associationism

Finally, different associationists think that the "items" involved in associations are quite different: memories, ideas, images, thoughts, and things were all suggested, used, and defended candidates.[1] With these general observations in place, let's see how these ideas are played out by two of the most famous associationists.

1.4 Locke and James

At first philosophical and psychological studies of associationism were often hard to distinguish because philosophy and psychology were hard to distinguish. Although some investigations were clearly philosophical in their focus (David Hume) and others were clearly psychological in their focus (William James) there were some who were both (e.g., David Hartley who, like Locke, was both a medical doctor and a philosopher). Muddying the issue is the fact that some philosophers wrote like psychologists and some psychologists wrote like philosophers. However, it seems that with Hartley, associationism changed from being a component of empiricist epistemology to being basically a psychological doctrine on its own. Associationist theorizing has almost the same history as theorizing on the mind up until Hobbes. At about the same time Descartes popularized the doctrine of innate ideas (and relegated associationism to a purely neurological doctrine). Philosophical associationism reached its peak with the British Empiricists (ca. 1700–1850) and although the most extensive associationist theorizing probably occurs in James Mill's (1829) *The Analysis of the Phenomena of the Human Mind*, the most influential discussion of associationism for philosophy was probably David Hume's (1739), *Treatise of Human Nature*. However, contemporary cognitive science seems to owe more to Locke and James than to any of the other players in the associationist tradition.

John Locke, An Essay on Human Understanding

John Locke (1632–1704) was a contemporary (and friend) of Boyle as well as Newton. He studied metaphysics and logic at Oxford, and had an affair there which he said "robbed me of my reason." At the end of the affair his reason seems to have returned; he never married, and went on to produce his famous work on the theory of knowledge (his *Essay*, 1700, took 20 years to write), and political theory (which influenced the Declaration of Independence).

Ideas

For Locke, unlike Descartes (see chapter 3), there are no innate ideas: "Let us then suppose the mind to be, as we say, white paper, void of all character, without any ideas. How comes it to be furnished? . . . I answer, in one word, from *experience*. In that, all our knowledge is founded, and from that it ultimately derives itself" (*Essay*, bk 2, ch. 1, para. 2). Mental contents (ideas) are derived either through external experience, *sensation*, or from internal experience, *reflection*, on the operations of the mind itself. Sensation and reflection yield *simple* ideas upon which mental operations, such as recognizing similarity and differences or abstracting, creates *complex* ideas of substance, relation, etc.

The world

Sensation gives us ideas of qualities of external things and there are two important classes of qualities:

primary qualities (such as solidity, extension, figure, motion, rest, number) are essential to, and dependent on, only their bearers, and are independent of any perceiving mind;

secondary qualities are not essential to their bearers, and are the powers of objects (by configurations of primary qualities) to cause experiences (such as color, sound, taste, smell) in perceiving minds.

Ideas of the world

Locke is sure we believe in an external world and an internal self: "Sensation convinces us that there are solid, extended substances; and reflection, that there are thinking ones; experience assures us of the existence of such beings" (*Essay*: ch. 23, para. 15). But the above picture of our mental contents raises the question, how do we come to know anything about the world (or ourselves)? Locke's metaphor for our predicament, and the direction out of it, is striking: "the understanding is not so much unlike a closet wholly shut from light, with only some little opening left, to let in external visible resemblances, or *ideas* of things without; would the pictures coming into such a dark room but stay there, and lie so orderly as to be found upon occasion, it would very much resemble the understanding of a man in reference to all objects of sight and the *ideas* of them" (*Essay*: ch. 11, para. 17). Note two things (which we will be returning to later): (1) ideas of sensation are analogized to *pictures* and have "visible resemblances" to external things; (2) ideas of sensation are *linked* to what they are about. At this point Locke presses the above distinction in qualities into service: ideas caused by external objects *do resemble primary qualities* – such ideas "are resemblances of them, and their patterns do really exist in the bodies themselves" (*Essay*: ch. 16. para. 16). But ideas caused by external objects *do not resemble secondary qualities* – the world itself contained no sweetness or blueness, only extension in motion. But what kind of link is needed for ideas to be about what they are about? His answer seems to be that it is a *causal* link: "these several appearances being designed to be the marks whereby we are to know and distinguish things which we have to do with, our *ideas* do as well serve us to that purpose and are as real distinguishing characters, whether they be only constant effects [secondary qualities?] or else exact resemblances [primary qualities?] of something in the things themselves: the reality lying in that *steady correspondence* they have with the distinct constitution of real beings . . . it suffices that they are *constantly produced* by them" (*Essay*: ch. 30, para. 2; last two emphases added). So this is how we break out of the dark room of our senses to the world about us – causation and resemblance. We will return to these themes soon, and in depth, in chapters that follow.

We can distinguish in Locke two general concerns: compounding and succession. It is not clear exactly what the domain of association is for Locke (though we will assume it is "ideas"), nor how general and pervasive are its principles. Locke acknowledges three general operations of the mind:

(1) composition, (2) setting ideas next to each other without composition (relations of ideas), and (3) abstraction (general ideas). The first relates especially to association.

Composition and complex ideas

Locke calls composition the process where the mind: "puts together several of those simple ideas it has received from sensation and reflection, and combines them into complex ones" (*Essay*: ch. 11, sect. 6). And in reverse: "All our complex ideas are ultimately resolvable into simple ideas, of which they are compounded and originally made up" (*Essay*: ch. 22, sect. 4). Here we see a kind of "mental mechanics" at work, where complex ideas are built out of simpler ideas like a wall is built out of bricks and mortar. It may be that associative principles such as similarity and contiguity are operative in composition, but if so, they are merely two of many principles and by no means hold sway over the process in general: "The mind . . . arbitrarily unites into complex ideas such as it finds convenient; whilst others that have altogether as much union in nature are left loose, and never combined into one idea, because they have no need of one name. It is evident, then, that a mind, by its free choice, gives a connection to a certain number of ideas, which in nature have no more union with one another than others it leaves out" (*Essay*: bk III, ch. 5, sect. 6). According to Locke, then, complex ideas need not always result from ideas which arrive together, and complex ideas can be formed "arbitrarily" and by "free will" – hardly associationist principles.

Succession of ideas

In the 4th edition of his *Essay*, Locke added a new chapter entitled "Of the association of ideas," thereby giving a name to a doctrine, which name turns out to have been more influential that the original doctrine. His interest in the association of ideas (he also used "connection" of ideas) seems restricted almost completely to the pathological, that is, to mental breakdowns and he never names or formulates explicit principles of association. Like Hobbes before him and Hume after him he distinguishes two types of association of ideas[2] – those that have "a natural correspondence and connexion one with another," and "wholly owing to chance or custom; ideas that in themselves are not at all of kins, come to be so united in some men's minds, that 'tis very hard to separate them, they always keep in company, and the one no sooner at any time comes into the understanding but its associate appears with it." Locke says little here about the first category, but he goes on to make a number of points about the second: (i) the mind makes these combinations either voluntarily or by chance (hence people exposed to the same environment can be very different psychologically); (ii) strength of the first impression or "future indulgence" (positive reinforcement?) can so unite ideas "that they always afterwards kept company together in the man's mind as if they were but one *idea*"; (iii) some antipathies "depend upon our original constitution, and are born with us." Locke's main concern here is a concern with rectifying *wrong* associations – pedagogical, not psychological, analysis. That will change dramatically in the hands of probably the most distinguished and influential associationist, William James.

William James, The Principles of Psychology

The most readable treatment of associationism from within psychology proper was chapter 14: "Association," of William James's *The Principles of Psychology*, a book he contracted in 1878 to publish in two years, but which finally took him twelve years to finish.[3] William James (1842–1910) is probably America's most distinguished psychologist to date. He was ten years younger than Wundt, but the year Wundt went from Zurich to Leipzig, 1875, James got $300 for "physiological" apparatus from Harvard: "It is conventional to say that Wundt founded the world's first psychological laboratory at Leipzig in 1879, although Wundt himself had facilities for experimental demonstration at Leipzig soon after he arrived there in 1875. In short, both James and Wundt had informal demonstrational laboratories (not research laboratories) in 1875 and thereafter" (Boring 1929: 509). At age 19 James entered Lawrence Scientific School of Harvard after schooling abroad and a year of studying art. He studied chemistry and comparative anatomy, and after two years entered Harvard Medical School. At age 23 he accompanied Louis Agassiz on a naturalist expedition to the Amazon. He then went to Germany for a year and a half of medical studies. After that, he had a multi-disciplined career, as befits a contributor to cognitive science. In 1872 he was made instructor of physiology at Harvard College. In 1876 he was made assistant professor of physiology. In 1880 he was made assistant professor of philosophy, and in 1885 professor of philosophy. In 1889 he was made professor of psychology (just in time for his book).

Mental life: thinking

Psychology is the science of mental life, both its phenomena and of their conditions.

(*The Principles of Psychology*)

For the purposes of cognitive science, James's conception of our mental life or "thinking" (James: "I use the word thinking for every form of consciousness indiscriminately") has the following central features:

1 It is conscious. "Consciousness from our natal day is the teaming multiplicity of objects and relations. The only thing which psychology has a right to postulate at the outset is the fact of thinking itself. The first fact for us then as psychologists is that thinking of some sort goes on."

2 It is introspectable. "Introspective observation is what we have to rely on first and foremost and always." However, James, unlike some later writers, did not think introspection was incorrigible: "introspection is difficult and fallible . . . the difficulty is simply that of all observation of whatever kind."

3 It is private. "My thought belongs with *my* other thoughts, and your thought with *your* other thoughts . . . the only states of consciousness that we naturally deal with are found in particular consciousness, minds, selves, concrete particular I's and you's."

4 It "flows like a stream." What one introspects is an unbroken flow of ideas that follow one another according to principles of association: "Consciousness, then, does not appear itself chopped in bits. . . . In talking of it hereafter, let us call it the stream of thought, consciousness, or of subjective life."

5 It is about something ("intentional"). Thoughts have "ideas" as their constituents and ideas are about something or other.

6 It is evolutionary. Higher cognitive functions evolved because of their adaptive value.

Association

Background

Although James speaks occasionally, as the British empiricists did, of the mind compounding idea parts into complex wholes, he was on the whole skeptical of the doctrine of complex ideas. James also, paradoxically, claims explicitly that "objects are associated, not ideas" and he goes on to say: "We shall avoid confusion if we consistently speak as if *association*, so far as the word stands for an *effect* were between things thought of . . . not ideas, which are associated in the mind. . . . And so far as association stands for a *cause*, it is between *processes in the brain*" (*Briefer Course*: 5). This is not completely clear: what exactly is an effect of what here? Maybe we should think of it in the way shown in figure 1.3.

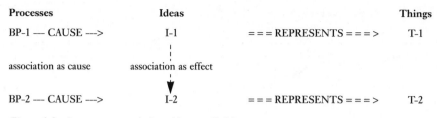

Figure 1.3 James on association, ideas, and things

Brain processes are the basic bearers of association. One brain process (BP-1) *causes* and becomes associated with another brain process (BP-2). But brain processes cause ideas (I) which are about or represent, objects, things (T) in the world that we think about, and by this means these things come to be associated – that is the *effect* of brain processes. Ideas, then, are the intermediary between brain processes and things – ideas both are caused by brain processes and represent these things.

Whatever exactly James meant by his remark, the real issue, he thinks, is accounting for the time course of thought: *how does the mind solve the problem of what to think next?* His general answer is that the sequencing of thoughts is in accordance with principles of association, and he suggests a variety of such principles including contiguity and similarity. But James never rests content with mere *descriptions* of patterns of association. He regularly presses for *explanations* at a deeper neural level. For instance, after formulating association by contiguity he says: "Whatever we name the law, since it expresses merely a phenomenon of mental habit, *the most natural way of accounting for it is to conceive it as a result of the laws of habit in the nervous system; in other words, it is to ascribe it to a physiological cause*" (*Principles of Psychology*: 561–2). "*The psychological law of association* of objects thought of through their previous contiguity in thought or experience *would thus be an effect, within the mind, of the physical fact that nerve currents propagate themselves easiest through those tracts of conduction which have been already most in use*" (*Principles of Psychology*: 563). And true to this explanatory strategy he postulates a pair of important, and prescient, neurological principles, the first for a pair of brain processes, the second for multiple brain processes:

(P1)   When two elementary brain-processes have been active together or in immediate succession, one of them, on reoccurring, tends to propagate its excitement into the other.   (*Briefer Course*: 5)

Principle (P1) is, as we will see in chapter 3, similar to a principle later proposed by Hebb. The second principle is:

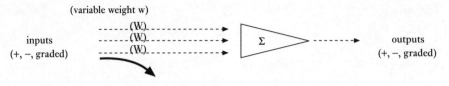

Figure 1.4   A James neuron

(P2)   The amount of activity at any given point in the brain-cortex is the sum
of tendencies of all other points of discharge into it, such tendencies
being proportionate:
1   to the number of times the excitement of each other point may have
accompanied that of the point in question;
2   to the intensity of such excitements; and
3   to the absence of any rival point functionally disconnected with the
first point, into which the discharges might be diverted.

(Briefer Course: 5)

It might be useful here to diagram this second principle in terms of an
imaginary "neuron," which we dub the "James neuron" (see figure 1.4). In
applying his associative principles James divides thought into two categories:
spontaneous thought and *voluntary* thought (see figure 1.5).

Spontaneous trains of thought
Here we find three large categories of phenomena: total recall, partial recall,
and focalized recall (association by similarity).

Total recall
This happens when there is unrestricted association between previous events
and later recall. In James's example a dinner party is followed by a brisk walk:

> If a, b, c, d, e, for instance, be the elementary nerve-tracts excited by the last act
> of the dinner party, call this act A, and l, m, n, o, p be those of walking home
> through the frosty night, which we may call B, then the thought of A must
> awaken that of B, because a, b, c, d, e, will each and all discharge into l through
> the paths by which their original discharge took place. Similarly they will dis-
> charge into m, n, o, and p; and these latter tracts will also each reinforce the
> other's action because, in the experience B, they have already vibrated in unison.
> The lines in Fig. 57 . . . symbolize the summation of discharge into each of the
> components of B, and the consequent strength of the combination of influences
> by which B in its totality is awakened.   (*Briefer Course*: 6).

Spontaneous thought	Voluntary thought

1. Total (impartial) association
   [figures 57, 58]
	1. Recalling a thing forgotten
	   [figure 61]

2. Partial (mixed) association
   habit
   recency
   vividness
   emotional congruity
   [figure 59]
	2. Means–end reasoning
	   [figure 61]

3. Similarity association [figure 60]	3. Generalization to all problem solving

Figure 1.5   James's taxonomy of the succession of thought

"Such processes as we have just described . . . would necessarily lead, if unob-structed, to the reinstatement in thought of the *entire* content of large trains of past experience" (*Briefer Course*: 6). (See figures 1.6(a) and 1.6(b).) Such massive and detailed association is not the norm.

Partial recall
Partial recall (see figure 1.6(c)) is the most common variety of association and in these cases only some of the past experiences have associational con-sequences; "In no revival of a past experience are all the items of our thought equally operative in determining what the next thought shall be. Always some ingredient is prepotent over the rest" (*Briefer Course*: 7). So the question arises as to which ingredient is prepotent and why. James's answer is that "the prepotent items are those which appeal most to our INTEREST" (ibid.) "Expressed in brain-terms, the law of interest will be: *some one brain-process is always prepotent above its concomitants in arousing action elsewhere*" (ibid.). James surveys four principles of "interest" for determining "revival in thought":

(1)   *Habit*   By this James means an association will favor elements that are most *frequent* in past experience: "Frequency is certainly one of the most potent determinants of revival. If I abruptly utter the word *swallow*, the reader, if by habit an ornithologist, will think of a bird, if a physiologist or medical specialist in throat-diseases, he will think of deglutition" (*Briefer Course*: 8).

(2)   *Recency*   James gives the example of a book, which habitually reminds him of the ideas it contains, but upon hearing of the suicide of the author, now remind him of death. He concludes: "Thoughts tend, then, to awaken their most recent as well as their most habitual [frequent] associates" (*Briefer Course*:

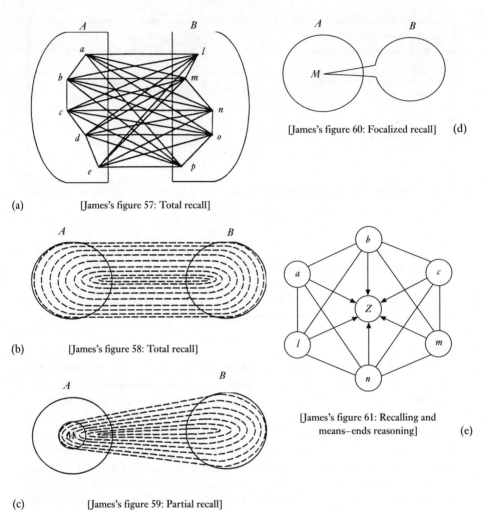

(a)   [James's figure 57: Total recall]

(b)   [James's figure 58: Total recall]

(c)   [James's figure 59: Partial recall]

[James's figure 60: Focalized recall]   (d)

[James's figure 61: Recalling and
means–ends reasoning]   (e)

Figure 1.6   James's figures for the succession of thought (from *Briefer Course*)
        (a)   James's figure 57: Total recall
        (b)   James's figure 58: Total recall
        (c)   James's figure 59: Partial recall
        (d)   James's figure 60: Focalized recall
        (e)   James's figure 61: Recalling and means–ends reasoning

8). And as usual, James tries to account for the phenomena at a lower level: "Excitement of peculiar tracts, or peculiar modes of general excitement in the brain, leave a sort of tenderness or exalted sensibility behind them which takes days to die away. As long as it lasts, those modes are liable to have their activities awakened by causes which at other times might leave them in repose. Hence *recency* in experience is a prime factor in determining revival in thought" (*Briefer Course*: 8–9).

(3) *Vividness* This is the strength or degree of an impression that the original experience carries and "*Vividness* in an original experience may also have the same effect as habit or recency in bringing about likelihood of revival" (*Briefer Course*: 9). For example: "If the word *tooth* now suddenly appears on the page before the reader's eye, there are fifty chances out of a hundred that, if he gives it time to awaken any image, it will be an image of some operation of dentistry in which he has been the sufferer. Daily he has touched his teeth and masticated with them; this very morning he brushed them, chewed his breakfast and picked them; but rarer and remoter associations arise more promptly because they were so much more intense" (ibid.).

(4) *Emotional congruity* As for this, James writes: "A fourth factor in tracing the course of reproduction [in thought] is *congruity in emotional tone* between the reproduced idea and our mood. The same objects do not recall the same associates when we are cheerful as when we are melancholy. Nothing, in fact, is more striking than our utter inability to keep up trains of joyous imagery when we are in depressed spirits. . . . And those of sanguine temperament, when their spirits are high, find it impossible to give any permanence to evil forebodings or to gloomy thoughts" (*Briefer Course*: 9).

James sums up these four factors: "*Habit, recency, vividness, and emotional congruity* are, then, all reasons why one representation rather than another should be awakened by the interesting portion of a departing thought. We may say with truth that *in the majority of cases the coming representation will have been either habitual, recent, or vivid, and will be congruous*" (*Briefer Course*: 9).

Notice that although James *labels* these associational principles (APs), and gives us examples of them, he never explicitly *formulates* them. What might such a principle look like? James never says, but if such principles are supposed to control the time course of thought, they might look like these:

(AP1) If the subject is entertaining the thought A, and A is associated by habit (frequency) with thought B, then the subject will next think thought B – unless this association is overridden by some stronger principle of association.

(AP2)   At any given time, the strongest principle of association is the operative one.

James also does not distinguish the fourth principle (emotional congruity)
from the earlier three, yet it is possible that it is really quite different in that
it does not seem to associate any particular thought (B) with any other particular thought (A). It says that a whole class of thoughts is more likely to be
called up than the rest – the class of thoughts that are similar in emotional
value.

Focalized recall, or association by similarity
This sort of association turns on a similarity between parts of things, shared
qualities or relations (see figure 1.6(d)): "let us suppose that selective agency
of interested attention . . . refined itself still further and accentuates a portion
of the passing thought, so small as to be no longer the image of a concrete
thing, but only of an abstract quality or property. Let us moreover suppose
that the part thus accentuated persists in consciousness (or, in cerebral terms,
has its brain process continue) after the other portions of the thought have
faded. *This small surviving portion will then surround itself with its own associates*
after the fashion we have already seen, and the relation between the new
thought's object and the object of the faded thought will be a *relation of similarity*. This pair of thoughts will form an instance of what is called '*Association by Similarity*.' . . . Similarity, in compounds, is *partial identity*. When the
same attribute appears in two phenomena, though it be their only common
property, the two phenomena are similar in so far forth" (*Briefer Course*: 9–10).
James's example here is first thinking of the moon, then a gas flame (by
similarity of color), then a football (by similarity of shape). Note that the moon
and the football share no relevant associated property themselves.

Voluntary trains of thought
James wants to extend his associationist account of the time course of "spontaneous trains of thought" to "voluntary trains of thought": "Hitherto we have
assumed the process of suggestion of one object by another to be spontaneous.
. . . This is revery, or musing; but great segments of the flux of our ideas consist
of something very different from this. They are guided by a distinct purpose
or conscious interest; and the course of our ideas is then called *voluntary*"
(*Briefer Course*: 11). As usual, James also redescribes this at the physiological
level: "Physiologically considered, we must suppose that a purpose means the
persistent activity of certain rather definite brain-processes. . . . This interest
is subserved by the persistently active brain-tracts we have supposed" (ibid.).
At the physiological level the crucial difference between spontaneous and vol-

untary sequences of thought is that the latter involves persistently active neural processes while the former does not.

Voluntary thought is traditionally a stumbling block for associationist theories since it would seem that here, if anywhere, rational, logical procedures can occasionally prevail over associative links. James approaches the question in two stages. First he tries to account for "recalling a thing forgotten" in associationist terms. Then he tries to extend this account to problem solving. James poses the issue of voluntary thought in terms of problems and their means of solution: "But in the theoretic as well as in the practical life there are interests of a more acute sort, taking the form of definite images of some achievement which we desire to effect. The train of ideas arising under the influence of such an interest constitutes usually the thought of the *means* by which the end shall be attained. If the end by its simple presence does not instantaneously suggest the means, the search for the latter becomes a *problem*; and the discovery of the means forms a new sort of end . . . an end, namely, which we intensely desire . . . but of the nature of which . . . we have no distinct imagination whatever" (*Briefer Course*: 11). Thus problem solving is pictured as predominantly means–end reasoning. James immediately extends this: "The same thing occurs whenever we seek to recall something forgotten" (ibid.). "The desire strains and presses in a direction which it feels to be right, but towards a point which it is unable to see. In short, the *absence of an item* is a determinant of our representations quite as positive as its presence can ever be" (ibid.). As usual, James tries to redescribe this at the physiological level: "If we try to explain in terms of brain-action how a thought which only potentially exists can yet be effective, we seem driven to believe that the brain tract thereof must actually be excited, but only in a minimal and subconscious way" (ibid.). James thinks that both kinds of problem have a common structure: "Now the only difference between the effort to recall things forgotten and the search after the means to a given end is that the latter have not, whilst the former have, already formed a part of our experience" (ibid.).

Recalling a thing forgotten
In the case of recalling a thing forgotten: "The forgotten thing is felt by us as a gap in the midst of certain other things. . . . We recollect the general subject to which it pertains." James schematizes the process of recalling a thing forgotten as shown in figure 1.6(e).

James explains: "Call the forgotten thing Z, the first facts with which we felt it was related a, b, and c, and the details finally operative in calling it up l, m, and n. Each circle will stand for the brain processes principally concerned in the thought of the fact lettered within it. The activity of Z will first be a mere tension; but as the activities in a, b, and c little by little irradiate into l, *m*, and *n*, and as *all* these processes are somehow connected with Z, their combined irradiations upon Z, represented by the centripetal arrows, succeed in rousing Z also to full activity" (*Briefer Course*: 12).

Problem solving: means–end reasoning

James conceives of problem solving as related to recall. Going back to figure 1.6(e) (James's figure 61), he says: "The end here stands in the place of *a*, *b*, *c*, in the diagram. It is the starting point of the irradiations of suggestion; and here, as in that case, what the voluntary attention does is only to dismiss some of the suggestions as irrelevant, and hold fast to others which are felt to be more pertinent – let these be symbolized by *l*, *m*, *n*. These latter at last accumulate sufficiently to discharge all together into Z, the excitement of which process is, in the mental sphere, equivalent to the solution of the problem. The only difference between this case and the last [recalling something forgotten] is that in this one there need be no original sub-excitement in Z, co-operating from the very first" (*Briefer Course*: 12). And James concludes, generalizing (hastily): "*From the guessing of newspaper enigmas to the plotting of the policy of an empire there is no other process than this*. We trust to the laws of cerebral nature to present us spontaneously with the appropriate idea" (ibid.; emphasis added).

James never addresses doubts one might have as to whether all reasoning is means–end reasoning as he described it (nor whether he has described all means–ends reasoning correctly). Consider the problem of balancing one's checkbook: one adds up columns of numbers, subtracts others, compares results, etc. Are these processes like (James's version of) means–ends reasoning? When adding a column of numbers and carrying a "l," do we voluntarily attend to associates and wait for the requisite associate to pop into consciousness? It would seem not. Furthermore, the solution in this case is better described as the end, not the means – the means being the principles of arithmetic. Here again we see Hobbes's early distinction between associative processes and "calculation" at work. Perhaps James's theory is appropriate only for the former, and it was a mistake for him to generalize to all problem solving. Note that James is skeptical about the possibility of a complete account of such reasoning: "It is foreign to my purpose here to enter into any detailed analysis of the different classes of mental pursuit. In scientific research we get perhaps as rich an example as can be found. . . . No rules can be given by which the investigator may proceed straight to his result. . . . But the final stroke of discovery is only prepared, not effected by them [associations]. The brain-tracts must, of their own accord, shoot the right way at last, or we shall grope in darkness . . . we are at the mercy of the spontaneous workings of Similarity in our brain" (*Briefer Course*: 12–13).

James is also skeptical about a complete brain science: "The *elementary* process of revival can be nothing but the law of habit. Truly the day is distant when physiologists shall actually trace from cell-group to cell-group the irra- diations which we have hypothetically invoked. Probably it will never arrive" (*Briefer Course*: 13). James sums up as follows, again returning to the neural level: "To sum up, then, we see that *the difference between the three kinds of asso- ciation reduced itself to a simple difference in the amount of that portion of the nerve-tract supporting the going thought which is operative in calling up the thought which comes*" (ibid.). "The order of *presentation of the mind's materials* is due to cerebral physiology alone" (ibid.). Thus, the overall thrust of James's analysis of the sequencing of thoughts is to *describe* them in terms of associationist principles, then try to *explain* their occurrence in terms of neurological principles.

1.5 The End of Classical Associationism

At least three factors led to the downfall of classical associationism in psy- chology in the late nineteenth and early twentieth centuries. Each factor was away from British empiricists' focus on the introspectable association of ideas. *First*, there was the bankruptcy of the *introspective methodology* itself. By the end of the nineteenth century it came to be characterized by endless squab- bles with no method for resolving them. After the establishment of Wundt's laboratory in Leipzig (1879) psychology was becoming a science and there was little or no perceived place in it for the impressionistic literary style that heaped unverifiable anecdote upon unverifiable anecdote. It was time to close the "bloodshot inner eye" of introspection. *Second*, there was a set of related factors that led eventually to *behaviorism* and *stimulus-response* psychology. Perhaps the initial development was Ebbinghaus's (1885) work on the as- sociation of stimulus and response in learning nonsense syllables. This can be considered one of the first laboratory applications of associationist principles, and at the same time one of the first steps in the creation of a science of exper- imental psychology related to learning, memory, and thought. This was fol- lowed by Thorndike's (1911) work on animal learning, which paved the way for Watson (1913) and the behaviorist movement of the 1930s and 1940s, and for the acceptance of the importance of Pavlov's (1927) work on the condi- tioned reflex (we turn to this in the next chapter). *Third*, there was Hartley's and James's systematic appeals to the *neural* level of explanation for psycho- logical phenomena. This explanatory strategy, coupled with the development of neuroscience (and "physiological psychology"), with its techniques and theories for studying the nervous system (Golgi, Cajal, Sherrington), called into question the desirability of (purely) psychological principles at all (we turn to this in chapter 3). With the demise of introspectionist methodology came the demise of the objects of introspection – ideas. The new elements of mind were stimuli and response, and their neural substrata – not introspectable at all. And as ideas were replaced by stimuli and responses, introspection was replaced with laboratory experimentation. There was also the increased prominence of reinforcements, reward, and conditioning – procedures rarely discussed by the British empiricists.

Notes

1　As we will see, it is William James's official position that it is things (out in the world), not ideas, that are associated.
2　"Ideas" for Locke, unlike Hume later, cover all mental contents: ideas of sensation and of reflection.
3　A shorter version occurs in chapter 16 of William James's *Psychology (Briefer Course)*. Figure numbers are those of the *Briefer Course*.

Study questions

What is associationism?

What is a general statement of what makes a principle "associationist"?

What is "pure" vs. "mixed" associationism?

Are sensations governed by principles of association – why/why not?

What two principles of association did most associationists subscribe to?

What are the two major types of mental processes that associationist principles are supposed to account for?

What is association by contiguity?

What is association by similarity?

What is association by contrast?

What is association by cause and effect?

Locke and James

What were Locke's main contributions to associationism?

What is psychology the study of, according to James?

What six features characterize our mental life, according to James?

What associational process is the main focus of James's work?

What level of explanation is basic for James?

What is James's view on the likelihood of a complete physiological account of thought?

What basic principle governs association involving two brain processes active together?

What basic principle governs association involving multiple brain processes active together?

What does "association as an effect is a relation between things" mean?

What does "association as a cause is a relation between brain processes" mean?

What is the role of interest in spontaneous thought?

What are the labels James gives to the four principles of partial recall?

Give an example (from James) of each.

Try to state these explicitly as associational principles.

What is association by similarity? Give James's example.

What does James mean by saying that similarity is partial identity?

What distinguishes voluntary from spontaneous thought?

Into what two subcategories does James divide voluntary thought?

What is the main difference between recalling something forgotten and means–ends reasoning?

What kind of reasoning seems to pose a problem for James, and why?

What three factors contributed to the end of classical associationism?

Suggested reading

General: The single most complete survey of associationism is Warner (1921), which is obviously a bit dated and which, curiously, does not discuss James. Boring (1929), chapter 10, covers British empiricism, and chapter 12 covers the Mills and Bain. Marx and Hillix (1963), chapter 6, covers both traditional associationism and early behaviorism, which it treats as associations between stimuli and responses. For a more contemporary perspective, see the introduction to Anderson and Bower (1974).

For more on *Locke* see Cummins (1989), chapter 4, and McCulloch (1995), chapter 2, for more on Locke on representation. For more on *James* see Flanagan (1991), chapter 2, contains an excellent discussion of James's philosophy of mind and psychology from a cognitive science perspective, and some of our general remarks follow his. For some *other empiricists* we did not cover: on Hume, Wilson (1992) is a particularly relevant study of Hume (see references therein). On Bain, Young (1970), chapter 3, contains a discussion of Bain from a contemporary point of view. A recent *selection of associationist* writings can be found in Beakley and Ludlow (1992), part IV. Hunt (1993), chapter 3, contains a readable brief survey of empiricist and rationalist psychological doctrine, and chapter 6 contains a general discussion of James.

2

Behaviorism and Cognitivism

2.1 Introduction

So far we have briefly surveyed the rise and fall of associationism. The dominant event between the heyday of associationism and the computational theories of mind (digital and connectionist) was the rise and fall of behaviorism and stimulus-response (S-R) theory, mostly in America, Britain, and Australia (think of it as an English-speaking movement and you won't be far wrong). A number of other movements were afoot during this period: there was Freud's investigations into unconscious processes, the Gestalt investigation into the internal organization of perception, ethological studies of natural animal behavior, and Piaget's work on children's cognitive developmental stages (think of these as mainly European, German-speaking initially, movements and you won't be far wrong). Our goal in this chapter will be to try to understand what motivated behaviorism, what its basic doctrines are, and what led to its demise. We want to see how criticisms of behaviorism set the foundation for cognitivism and information-processing psychology, which eventually led to the computational theory of mind.

2.2 The Rise of Behaviorism and Stimulus-Response Psychology

A new epoch in the intellectual history of man.
(New York Times, 1942)

On the American side of the Atlantic Ocean there was a great gap in research on human complex cognitive processes from the time of William James almost down to World War II. Although the gap was not complete, it is fair to say

*that American cognitive psychology during this period was dominated by
behaviorism, the nonsense syllable, and the rat.*

(Newell and Simon, 1972: 874)

The years 1910–13 were pivotal in the establishment of behaviorism. By 1911
psychology had pretty much abandoned consciousness and introspectable
mental *contents* as the focus of research and had turned to the study of the
effects of mental processes. This led naturally away from introspection as the
attendant methodology. The American Psychological Association meeting of
1911 served as one forum for this shift from consciousness to the explanation,
prediction, and control of behavior. One observer, Angell, commented: "There
is unquestionably a movement on foot in which interest is centered in the *results*
of conscious process, rather than in the *processes* themselves. This is peculiarly
true in animal psychology; it is only less true in human psychology. In these
cases interest is in what may for lack of a better term be called 'behavior'; and
the analysis of consciousness is primarily justified by the light it throws on
behavior, rather than vice-versa" (1911: 47).

I. P. Pavlov

Pavlov (1849–1936) followed in the tradition of (though he was not a student
of) I. Sechenov (1829–1905), "the father of Russian reflexology," whose most
famous work (1863), *Reflexes of the Brain*, attempted to give a purely physiological account of psychological phenomena: "All psychical acts without exception, if they are not complicated by elements of emotion (with which we shall
deal later) are developed by means of reflexes. Hence, all conscious movements
(usually called voluntary), inasmuch as they arise from these acts, are reflex, in
the strictest sense of the word" (1863: 317). Pavlov's work can be seen as
combining the existing traditions of reflexology, which we will see in the next
chapter was pioneered by Descartes, and associationism. Pavlov received the
Nobel Prize in 1904 for his work on digestion, though his most famous, and
popular, contribution was the discovery of classical conditioning, work that
grew out of his Nobel studies on canine salivation.

The paradigm of what is now called "classical conditioning" contains the
following elements: one begins with a natural response such as salivation
(the unconditioned response: UR) to food (the unconditioned stimulus: US).
Then before presenting the US, one also presents, for example, a ringing bell
(the conditioned stimulus: CS). After some pairings the CS will elicit the
formerly unconditioned response (UR), which now becomes the conditioned
response: CR.

food (US) → salivation (UR)
bell (CS) + food → salivation (UR)
bell (CS) → salivation (CR)

Pavlov found a number of principles governing these processes: CRs must precede, not follow, the UR, CRs will occur with stimuli which resemble the original CS – the phenomenon of "generalization." Animals can be conditioned to one stimulus vs. another, the phenomenon of "discrimination." And CRs could be eliminated by continually presenting the CS without the US – the phenomenon of "extinction." If the animal is left alone for a while "spontaneous recovery" will occur and the CS will again elicit the CR. Pavlov thought that all of behavior could be analyzed in terms of innate and acquired reflexes and he set out to catalog the basic inventory of such mechanisms. As he put it: "On the one hand, it is necessary first to establish and systematize all the inborn reflexes as basic and unchanging fundamentals on which is built up the enormous structure of the acquired reflexes. . . . On the other hand, there must be made a study of the laws and mechanisms of the acquired as well as the inborn reflex activity. . . . Only the knowledge of all the separate reflexes will give the possibility of gradually clearing up this chaos of phenomena of higher animal life, which is now at last falling into the order of scientific analysis. . . . We again insist on the necessity of describing and enumerating the elementary inborn reflexes, in order gradually to understand the whole conduct of the animal" (1928: 281–3). Pavlov's general view seems to be that such explanations can be given for all animal (and human) behavior, that "the entire mechanism of thinking consists in the elaboration of elementary associations [such as the above] and in the subsequent formation of chains of association."

J. B. Watson

The year 1913 marked the publication in the *Psychological Review* of Watson's (1878–1958) behaviorist manifesto "Psychology as the behaviorist views it." In 1943 a group of eminent psychologists proclaimed this the most important article ever published in the *Psychological Review*. Watson's early work was on animal behavior, where reports of introspection and consciousness play, naturally, no role. This was congenial to Watson's hostility to the conscious introspection of the psychology of the time (e.g., James and Wundt), and to traditional worries about the relation of mind to matter (the "mind–body problem"): "The time honored relics of philosophical speculation need trouble the student of behavior as little as they trouble the student of physics. The consideration of the mind–body problem affects neither the type of problem selected nor the formulation of the solution of that problem." Watson helped to make the study of rats in a maze one of the central research paradigms in animal laboratory studies and he sought to extend this thinking to human psychology. His opening paragraph marks the first salvo: "Psychology as the behaviorist views it is a purely objective branch of natural science. Its theoretical goal is the prediction and control of behavior. Introspection forms no essential part of its methods, nor is the scientific value of its data dependent on the readiness with which they lend themselves to interpretation in terms of consciousness. The behaviorist, in his efforts to get a unitary scheme of animal response, recognizes no dividing line between man and brute. The behavior of man, with all of its refinement and complexity, forms only a part of the behaviorist's total scheme of investigation" (1913: 158). Here in this single quote we see a number of themes of behaviorism:

1   psychology is an objective natural science, with the methodology of such;
2   the goal of psychology is the prediction and control of behavior;
3   the psychology of humans is continuous with the psychology of animals;
4   introspection and consciousness play no role in psychology.

Like Hartley and James before him, Watson hoped ultimately for physiological explanations. From the behaviorist perspective, "the findings of psychology become the functional correlates of structure and lend themselves to explanation in physico–chemical terms" (1913: 177). Watson originally formulated his theory in terms of "habits," but in 1916 he embraced the conditioned reflex method developed by Pavlov as the correct way of understanding habit units. Some of Watson's views regarding habits strike us as quaint (at best). For instance, he claimed that "thinking" (it is not clear what a behaviorist is referring to with this term) does not involve the brain, but rather consists in "sensori-motor processes in the larynx."

E. Thorndike

Thorndike's (1874–1949) original research interest was in child learning and pedagogy, but because of a shortage of subjects he turned to animal learning and set up shop in William James's basement (Harvard wouldn't give him space for his chickens). His early work, summarized in *Animal Intelligence* (1911), can be seen as early work on operant leaning. His basic apparatus was a "puzzle box." Here the animal (typically a cat) is rewarded (with food) if it makes some response, in this case escaping by stepping on a pedal, and over time it learns that response. But if the response is not rewarded, it gradually disappears. Learning is by trial and error, reward and punishment. Thorndike's description of his aim was to catch animals "using their minds," but his methodology has also been (uncharitably) described as "studying a response that could be readily made accidently by a half-starved cat attempting to escape from the cage in which it was confined" (Hilgard 1987: 190). Early critics of Thorndike, such as Kohler, complained that animals should be studied in their natural settings, and that they seemed not to reason in the laboratory because their situations did not permit it. Thorndike proposed two laws which he thought could explain all animal (and human) behavior: the so-called "law of effect" and the "law of exercise":

Law of effect   Any act which in a given situation produces satisfaction becomes associated with that situation, so that when the situation recurs the act is more likely than before to recur also. Conversely, any act which in a given situation produces discomfort becomes disassociated from the situation, so that when the situation recurs the act is less likely than before to recur (positive and negative reinforcement).

Law of exercise   Any response to a situation will, all other things being equal, be more strongly connected with the situation in proportion to the number of times it has been connected with that situation, and to the average vigor and duration of the connections.

It is not hard to see the influence of William James in the latter law. Later, in *Human Learning* (1929), Thorndike extended and applied these principles to human learning, which he formulated in terms of hierarchies of stimuli (S) and responses (R). Every S-R link has a probability that S would elicit R; learing amounts to increasing that probability and forgetting amounts to decreasing it. Thorndike also developed a neurological theory of learning involving the establishment of new connections at the synapse (made prominent in 1906 by Sherrington). In virtue of this he called himself a "connectionist."

B. F. Skinner

The most famous and influential behaviorist after Watson undoubtedly was B. F. Skinner (1904–90). Skinner rejected all mental states and processes, and even went further, along with the logical positivism of the period, to reject "hypothetical" entities altogether. Early on (1931) he rejected even the reflex as a hypothetical entity and preferred to view it as "a convenient description for a regular correlation between stimulus and response." The goal of psychology, for Skinner, was to experimentally determine the specific environmental causes of behavior. Or to put it more in his preferred vocabulary, to view an organism as a "locus of variables" – a place where antecedent environmental influences or "independent variables" produce behavior or "dependent variables." The analysis of the functional relations between these variables is the domain of psychology, and is independent of physiology – though like James before him, he thought that ultimately physiology would reveal the physical mechanisms underlying these functional relations.

Skinner's first major book *The Behavior of Organisms* (1938)[1] outlined a research program for psychology: the experimental analysis of behavior consists in the systematization of "contingencies of reinforcement" in animal and human operant behavior. The *contingencies of reinforcement* consist of three items: (1) the setting in which the behavior occurs, (2) the reinforced response, and (3) the reinforcer. Skinner's laboratory methodology used what has come to be (often derisively) called the "Skinner Box." It involved (i) placing an animal in a space and reinforcing some spontaneous "voluntary" behaviors, (ii) controlling the variations in the environment, (iii) choosing a simple, unambiguous response (such as pressing a lever or pecking a key), and (iv) recording the rate of response. All of these design choices are meant to simplify the analysis of the contingencies of reinforcement. Skinner distinguished two kinds of learned behavior: (1) reflex (or "respondent") behavior such as the salivation Pavlov studied, and (2) operant behavior, such as the spontaneous lever-pressings or key-peckings. Operant behavior on the individual level parallels natural selection on the species level: the organism does something "novel" that has a positive effect or reward and the probability goes up that it will be repeated (just as a novelty in the "gene pool" which leads to greater reproductive success will up the probability it will be passed on and spread through the population). Skinner's interest was in systematizing the principles governing operant behavior when under the influence of reinforcers. On Skinner's view, all behavior is the result of an individual's reinforcement history plus their genetic endowment.

In 1957 Skinner published his major attempt to test this idea. Since Descartes, language has been viewed as a distinctively human capacity and as such it was a natural candidate to use to test out the scope of his behavioristic principles. However, no new experiments were reported, none even on language. He tried only to establish the plausibility of applying the framework discussed above to language – or more accurately, to speech occurring in a particular environment. As we will see from Chomsky's critique, the project was not a great success, and Skinner's reputation still stands on his animal work.

2.3 Challenges to Behaviorism and Stimulus-Response Psychology

The 1950s mark the end of the dominance of *behaviorism* in American psychology (and related cognitive sciences) and the rise of an alternative *cognitive, information processing*, paradigm. Four things were happening simultaneously. *First*, logical positivism, with its unrealistic and restrictive conception of scientific methodology and theory construction had been mostly abandoned by the philosophical community, and this reaction was spreading to other disciplines. *Second*, behaviorism was professionalizing itself out of existence. Hundreds (thousands?) of articles were being written on problems of interest to no one outside the field. As one psychologist wrote: "a strong case can be made for the proposition that the importance of the psychological problems studied during the last 15 years has decreased as a negatively accelerated function approaching an asymptote of complete indifference" (Harlow, 1953). *Third*, serious criticisms of behaviorism's basic assumptions were launched during this period. The basic point of the critiques we will review is the structured nature of behavior (organization that cannot be explained by traditional behaviorism and S-R psychology) and the contribution of the organism that produces it. *Finally*, an alternative, less restrictive and more exciting research program stated in terms of computation and information was emerging. We now turn to the third point, and in the next section to the final point.

K. Lashley

In 1951 Lashley published an influential article criticizing some basic tenets of behaviorism. The focus of his discussion was behavior involving serial order: "This is the essential problem of serial order; the existence of generalized schemata of action which determine the sequence of specific acts, acts which in themselves or in their associations seem to have no temporal valence" (1951: 122).

On a behaviorist, stimulus-response account, an activity such as rapidly playing a correct sequence of notes from memory on an instrument would involve an associative chain of stimuli and responses, where each response acts as the stimulus for the next response:

S1 → R1/S2 [1st note] → R2/S3 [2nd note] → . . .

Lashley's critique of this idea involves drawing attention to dozens of examples, from the organization of language, to the coordination of movements, to the integration of timing and rhythm, where such associative chains cannot explain the behavior: "Considerations of rhythmic activity and of spatial orientation force the conclusion, I believe, that there exist in nervous organization, elaborate systems of interrelated neurons capable of imposing certain types of integration upon a large number of widely spaced effector elements" (1951: 127). Lashley's (like James's before him) alternative conception is of a nervous system that is always active, not passive as in traditional S-R theories, that has its own principles of organization that it imposes on incoming sensory material: "My principal thesis today will be that the input is never into a quiescent or static system, but always into a system which is already actively excited and organized. In the intact organism, behavior is the result of interaction of this background of excitation with input from any designated stimulus" (1951: 112).

Noam Chomsky

Skinner's most trenchant critic was not another psychologist, nor a physiologist, but the young linguist Noam Chomsky, whose review of Skinner's book *Verbal Behavior* in 1959 is credited with helping to bring down behaviorism as a framework for human psychology, and to inaugurate the new cognitive approach: "Chomsky's review is perhaps the single most influential psychological paper published since Watson's behaviorist manifesto of 1913" (Leahey 1992: 418). Chomsky's (excruciatingly) detailed critique focuses on, but is not limited to, Skinner's analysis of language. Chomsky is also anxious to cast doubt on the adequacy of Skinner's framework for both other forms of human activity and some forms of animal behavior, especially those emphasized by comparative ethologists. Chomsky closes his review by outlining his alternative framework from the point of view of generative grammar.

Critique of Skinner's general framework

After setting out Skinner's notions of stimulus, response ("respondents," "operants") and reinforcement, Chomsky notes that although these are relatively well defined in laboratory settings, Skinner fails to show how to extend them to real-life behavior: "This creates the illusion of a rigorous scientific theory with very broad scope, although in fact the terms used in the description of real-life and of laboratory behavior may be mere homonyms, with at most a vague similarity of meaning" (1959: 30). Chomsky then spends the next three sections of his review substantiating this charge, and by all accounts he succeeds completely.

Critique of Skinner's Verbal Behavior

After setting out Skinner's notions of verbal behavior, verbal "operant," "mand," "tact," etc., Chomsky comments: "The preceding discussion covers all the major notions that Skinner introduces in his descriptive system. My purpose in discussing the concepts one by one was to show that in each case, if we take his terms in their literal meaning, the description covers almost no aspect of verbal behavior, and if we take them metaphorically, the description offers no improvement over various traditional formulations" (1959: 54).

Chomsky's general assessment of Skinner's accomplishment is that it is very modest, limited to certain animals in highly constrained laboratory conditions, and even for animals, concentration on just observable conditions that evoke certain forms of behavior misses much that is needed to understand behavior: "One would naturally expect that prediction of the behavior of a complex organism . . . would require, in addition to information about external stimulation, knowledge of the internal structure of the organism, the ways in which it processes input information and organizes its own behavior" (1959: 27). "Careful study of this book . . . reveals . . . that the insights that have been achieved in the laboratories of the reinforcement theorist, though quite genuine, can be applied to complex human behavior only in the most gross and superficial way. . . . The magnitude of the failure of this attempt to account for verbal behavior serves as a kind of measure of the importance of the factors omitted from consideration, and an indication of how little is really known about this remarkably complex phenomenon" (1959: 28).

Conclusion

One moral of both Lashley's and Chomsky's critique of behaviorism is that while aspects of behavior may be controlled and explained by environmental factors, stimuli and responses, or internal chains of such stimuli and responses, *the explanation of complex behavior in complex organisms will require a careful assessment of the contribution of the organism, its internal organization and principles of operation.* In this respect information theory and the digital computer filled the bill perfectly.

2.4   Cognitivism: Information Processing Psychology

The downfall of behaviorism was aided in part by the rise of a competing paradigm, but one that grew mainly outside of mainstream psychology, from information theory and (what would become) computer science: "In the long run the most important approach to cognition grew out of mathematics and electrical engineering and had little or nothing to do with psychology and its problems" (Leahey, 1992: 397). The digital computational influence will occupy Part II of this book, so we will here be concerned primarily with influential work in the 1950s and 1960s that used or presupposed information-processing notions.

Information

There are a number of notions of information in the literature. To begin with there is the ordinary notion of information that is hard to define (hence the narrow technical notion), but is something like: a purported fact, or proposition that something is the case. It is the sort of thing you find in the *Information Almanac*. On this ordinary notion, the information you are given can be either true or false, and there is no obvious way of measuring it. Sometimes this notion is called "semantic information" because it is "about" something (semantic). Contrasting with this ordinary notion of information is a technical notion developed by Shannon in the early 1940s, which involves the idea that information reduces possibilities, ignorance, or uncertainty. The main concern with this idea is measuring information and the standard measure of information is the *bit* (**binary digit**). One bit of information about a situation reduces the uncertainty or ignorance concerning that situation by one-half, so flipping a normal fair coin would reduce the uncertainty regarding its two possible alternative states (heads, tails) to just one. Two bits of information reduce the uncertainty about a situation involving four possibilities to one (first bit: 4 to 2, second bit: 2 to 1), etc. A *message* (information) travels from a *sender* to a *receiver* over a *channel* which has a specific *capacity* and a certain amount of *noise*.

Pure information theory concerned itself mostly with measuring information and its transmission over various channels with various capacities and levels of noise, whereas in the hands of early information theoretic psychologists the *processing* of information came to predominate. More importantly, early informational psychology as summarized by, for example, Neisser (1967) tended to focus on sensory input (vision and audition) with only one chapter out of eleven devoted to "higher mental processes" such as memory and thought. In part this was because the technical notion of information could be applied fairly directly to sensation: the environment "sends" a "message" through the sensory "channel" against a background of "noise" which must then be received and interpreted by the organism. One of the earliest flow

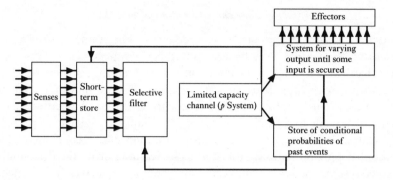

Figure 2.1 One of the first information-processing diagrams (from Broadbent, 1958: 299, figure 7)

charts of this conception makes this clear (see figure 2.1). However, as we move to memory and thought it is not at all clear how to apply the technical notion of information, and so the informal notion surreptitiously began to replace it until finally "information processing" became virtually a pun.

Miller, "The magical number seven, plus or minus two"

George Miller was an early enthusiast of information theory and its application to psychology. His early book *Language and Communication* (1951) and papers, specially "The magical number seven . . ." (1956), "drew attention to limitations on human attention and memory and set the stage for the first wave of research in information-processing psychology" (Leahey 1992: 406). As Miller himself said: "Informational concepts have already proved valuable in the study of discrimination and of language; they promise a great deal in the study of learning and memory" (1951: 42). Miller begins his influential (1956) article remarkably: "My problem is that I have been persecuted by an integer. For seven years this number has followed me around, has intruded in my most private data, and has assaulted me from the pages of our most public journals." In the body of his paper he rehearses about a dozen experiments, and his conclusion is two-fold: "First, the span of absolute judgment and the span of immediate memory impose severe limitations on the amount of information that we are able to receive, process, and remember" (1967: 41). "Second, the process of recoding is a very important one in human psychology and deserves much more explicit attention than it has received" (1967: 42). Let's take a look at each of these in a little more detail.

Absolute judgments of unidimensional stimuli

Miller surveys four studies of absolute judgment. For example, when subjects were asked to identify tones by assigning them numbers, researchers got the result that: "When only two or three tones were used the listeners never confused them. With four different tones confusions were quite rare, but with five or more tones confusions were frequent. With fourteen different tones the listeners made many mistakes" (1956: 18). Similar results are reported for judgments of loudness, saltiness, and spatial location. Miller concludes: "There seem to be some limitations built into us by learning or by the design of our nervous systems, a limit that keeps our channel capacities in this general range. On the basis of the present evidence it seems safe to say that we possess a finite and rather small capacity for making unidimensional judgments and that this capacity does not vary a great deal from one simple sensory attribute to another" (1956: 25). And this capacity, he proposes, is about 7 plus or minus 2.

Recoding

Since our memory span is limited to such a small number of "chunks" of information, one way of getting more into it is to make each chunk worth more bits of information. This process is called "recoding." Miller cites a study of expanding memory of binary digits by recoding them into larger chunks. The author was able, using the 5 : 1 recoding scheme, to repeat back 40 binary digits without error: "The point is that recoding is an extremely powerful weapon for increasing the amount of information that we can deal with" (1956: 40).

Miller's article had a significant influence on the field, coming out as it did at the same time as Chomsky's early critique of structuralist linguistics (as well as his critique of behaviorism). It not only synthesized a wide variety of experimental findings, but it did so by endowing the organism with endogenous information-processing structure – also what Chomsky was proposing in the realm of language.

Miller, Galanter, and Pribram, **Plans and the Structure of Behavior**

We saw earlier that Chomsky (1959) complained that Skinner, and behaviorists in general, ignored "knowledge of the internal structure of the organism, the ways in which it processes input information and organizes its own behavior." Behaviorist and stimulus-response theorists proposed internal S-R chains to "mediate" input stimuli and output response, but as we also saw,

Lashley (1951) and others complained that most interesting behavior needed more structure than this. In particular, the organism needed to have goals, and knowledge, plans, strategies, and tactics to achieve these goals. This requires in part a hierarchical organization, not a linear one. Miller, Galanter, and Pribram in *Plans and the Structure of Behavior* (1960) offered an influential analysis of complex behavior in these terms.

The problem

According to Miller, Galanter, and Pribram (hereafter MGP), one's behavior during a typical day involves two central notions: what one expects or imagines will happen and what one plans to do about it. As they note, these notions cannot be easily analyzed away in behaviorist terms. In fact "the suspicion has been growing in recent years that the reflex idea is too simple, the element too elementary" (1960: 22–3). Against the "reflex theorists" is the "cognitive position": "They [cognitivists] believe that the effect an event will have upon behavior depends on how the event is represented in the organism's picture of itself and its universe. They are quite sure that any correlations between stimulation and response must be mediated by an organized representation of the environment, a system of concepts and relations within which the organism is located. A human being – and probably other animals as well – builds up an internal representation, a model of the universe, a schema, a simulacrum, a cognitive map, an image" (1960: 7). However, even though the gap between knowledge and action is smaller than the gap between stimulus and response, the gap is still there and needs to be filled: "many psychologists, including the present authors, have been disturbed by a theoretical vacuum between cognition and action. The present book is largely the record of . . . how that vacuum might be filled . . . to describe how actions are controlled by an organism's internal representation of its universe" (1960: 11–12).

The solution

MGP's solution to the problem involves five leading ideas: the distinction between molar and molecular levels of analysis, the image, the plan, execution, and the TOTE unit.

The hierarchical structure of behavior

The first step in the solution to the problem is to recognize the "hierarchical organization of behavior." For the purposes of explanation and understanding, most human behavior can and must be analyzed at different, hierarchically organized levels simultaneously: X can be made up of A + B, A can then be made up of a + b, and B made up of c + d + e:

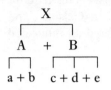

One popular example comes from language: X might be a sentence, A, B phrases, a–e words. We could continue further to words made from morphemes and morphemes made from phonemes. Non-linguistic actions can have such organization as well. X might be starting a car, A is stepping on the gas, B is turning the key, a is moving your leg to the gas pedal, b is pressing down, c is taking your key out of your pocket, d is putting it in the ignition, e is twisting it. Since at least the work of Tolman, psychologists, MGP included, called the larger, higher-level units of behavior "molar" units, and the smaller, lower-level units "molecular" units. Once behavior has been seen to have a potentially complex and multi-leveled organization, we can face the problem of describing and explaining it at both levels with some hope of success.

Image (unfortunate label): this is all the knowledge that the organism has about the world around it, including itself (1960: 17–18).

Plan: this is any hierarchical process in the organism that can control the order in which a sequence of operations is performed (1960: 16).

Execution: a creature is executing a particular plan when that plan is controlling the sequence of operations he is carrying out (1960: 17).

TOTE units

"TOTE" is an acronym for Test, Operate, Test, Exit. It is a unit of analysis that MGP propose to replace the reflex arc of S-R theory. They initially propose it at the neural level: "The neural mechanism involved in reflex action cannot be diagrammed as a simple reflex arc or even as a chain of stimulus-response connections. A much more complex kind of monitoring, or testing, is involved in reflex action than the classical reflex arc makes any provision for" (1960: 25). "The general pattern of reflex action, therefore, is to test the input energies against some criteria established in the organism, to respond if the result of the test is to show an incongruity, and to continue to

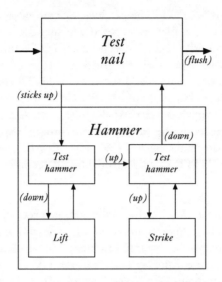

Figure 2.2   A TOTE unit for hammering a nail (from Miller, Galanter, and Pribram, 1960: 36, figure 5; reproduced by permission of the authors)

respond until the incongruity vanishes, at which time the reflex is terminated" (1960: 26).

Although the arrows in a TOTE unit (see below) might represent neural impulses, they could also represent higher-level processes: "The reflex should be recognized as only one of many possible actualizations of a TOTE pattern. The next task is to generalize the TOTE unit so that it will be useful in a majority – hopefully in all – of the behavioral descriptions we shall need to make" (1960: 27). Two such processes MGP discuss in detail are the transmission of *information* and the transfer of *control* – telling the system what to do next. In a standard digital computer, this is done by the program, where control is passed from instruction to instruction, telling the machine what to fetch, what operation to perform, and where to store the result. According to MGP "the TOTE unit . . . is an explanation of behavior in general" (1960: 29). To account for complex hierarchical behavior they suggest that TOTE units be nested inside one another. Plans are to be conceptualized as complex TOTE hierarchies and behavior is explained in terms of the execution of the operations contained in them. The "image" (knowledge of the world) provides conditions which will be tested for when needed. An illustrative example of such a complex TOTE unit is the one for hammering a nail flush to a surface as shown in figure 2.2.

The transition from TOTE hierarchies to computers was a quick and natural generalization: "a plan is to an organism essentially the same as a program for a computer" (1960: 16). Think of TOTE units as fulfilling two functions: representing aspects of the world, and controlling what the system does next. The images of MGP, and the tests of TOTE units, contain representations of the world. The plans of MGP, and the operations of TOTE units control what the system does next. Analogously, the data structures of computers represent aspects of the world, and the program specifies the transfer of control – what the machine is to do next. Furthermore, the nesting of TOTE units within TOTE units is analogous to a computer program calling a subroutine.

By the time of Neisser (1967), the "information processing" approach had reached enough of an orthodoxy to have its first textbook – a book generally regarded as having exerted substantial influence on the direction of the field. Not long after this came Lindsay and Norman (1972), *Human Information Processing: An Introduction to Psychology*, to solidify this tradition, which was to dominate psychology for 10 to 15 years.

Note

1   It was not a bestseller, only 80 copies were sold in four years.

Study questions

What are the elements of "classical conditioning"?

What is the main idea behind Thorndike's "law of effect"?

What is the main idea behind Thorndike's "law of exercise"?

What are four main themes of behaviorism to be found in Watson's (1913) article?

What are the elements of the "Skinner Box"?

What is "operant behavior"?

What four things were happening at the end of behaviorism?

What was Lashley's main point against behaviorism?

What was Lashley's alternative conception of the nervous system?

What is Chomsky's basic criticism of Skinner?

What is one moral of both Lashley's and Chomsky's critique of Skinner?

From what two fields (outside psychology) did the "cognitive" tradition emerge?

What are the ordinary vs. technical notions of information?

How does one measure information (the technical notion)?

What limitation did Miller find on short-term memory?

What, for Miller, Galanter, and Pribram, is the "image," "plan," and "TOTE unit"?

How were TOTE units analogous to computers?

Suggested reading

General

A very readable brief survey of psychology with special emphasis on cognition and its contribution to cognitive science can be found in Gardner (1985), chapter 5. An influential recent general history of psychology is Leahey (1992) – parts III and IV are especially relevant to our present topic. Hilgard (1987) covers some of the same material, focusing on American psychology, and with more biographical information. Hernstein and Boring (1966) has not been improved on as an amazing collection of classics from the history of psychology (and philosophy and physiology). Pavlov (1927) is his classic work.

Behaviorism

Skinner (1976) is an authoritative general introduction. Fancher (1979), chapter 8, covers behaviorism well. An older, but still useful and interesting book is Boring (1957), which focuses on experimental psychology – see chapter 24, "Behavioristics." Marx and Hillix (1963) is a classic, but a bit dated, survey of these views from a theoretical perspective – see chapter 7, "Behaviorism," and chapter 10, "Varieties of S-R Theory." For a more recent discussion of behaviorism, and especially the contribution of Skinner, see Flanagan (1991), chapter 4. Hunt (1993), chapter 9, offers a readable survey of behaviorism, and Smith (1986) is a recent study of behaviorism in relation to logical positivism. Dennett (1995) is a lively discussion of natural selection in general with application to cognition and behaviorism in particular.

Other movements

For a discussion of other schools of the time see Flanagan (1991), chapter 7 on Freud, and chapter 10 on the Gestalt movement.

Cognitivism

Besides the works cited in the text, and the relevant chapters from the general histories mentioned above, see Gardner (1985), the latter parts of chapter 5, Flanagan (1991), chapter 6, and Hunt (1993), chapter 16.

3

Biological Background

3.1 Introduction

The history of neuroscience, from antiquity to the present, can be seen to a large extent as the story of the attempt to map the mind as brain *function* onto brain *structure*, with a subtheme: the constant tension between *localist* and *holist* tendencies. At first the role of the brain itself in thought (broadly construed) and action had to be established. Then the question, of whether it was the brain mass or the holes in the brain mass (ventricles) that supported thought, had to be resolved. Next, gross divisions of the brain, such as the cerebellum vs. the cortex, had to be functionally and anatomically characterized. Then the issue of the functional subdivision of the cortex itself had to be settled, and the basic cellular elements of the nervous system had to be identified. Finally, the fine structure and functioning of these basic cellular parts had to be determined. At each stage, the ability to move on to the next stage was in part determined by available technology, such as microscopic resolution and staining techniques.

3.2　Brain Ventricles vs. Brain Substance

At first the role of the brain itself in thought (broadly construed) and action had to be established. Greek thought, for instance, was divided on the question of the location of the mind (the "seat of the soul"). Some continued to believe that the heart was primarily responsible for mental functions. For example, Empedocles (490–430 BC), who is given the major credit for developing the theory of the four basic elements (earth, air, fire, and water) held the cardio-centric theory of mind. Aristotle (384–322 BC) also held the cardio-centric theory, but with the further refinement that the function of the brain was to serve as a radiator for the "heat and seething" of the heart. On the other hand Anaxagoras (500–428 BC) proposed that the brain was the center of sensation and thought. Democritus (460–370 BC), famous for his "atomic" theory of matter, believed in a "triune" soul: one part was in the head, was responsible for intellectual matters and was immortal. A second part was in the heart and was associated with emotions. A third part was located in the gut, and was associated with lust, greed, desire, and the "lower" passions. These last two parts were not immortal.

Then the question of whether it was the brain mass or the holes in the brain mass (ventricles) that supported thought had to be resolved. Among those who assigned a significant role in thought to the brain were those who located this function in the large cavities (ventricles) vs. the surrounding tissue. One of Galen's (AD 130–200) most influential doctrines was the idea that vital spirits, produced by the left ventricle of the heart, are carried to the brain by the carotid arteries. These were then transformed into the highest spirits in the *rete mirabile* (miraculous net) at the base of the brain. Those spirits were stored in the brain's ventricles. When needed they passed through hollow nerves, to force muscles into action and mediate sensation (he didn't say exactly how). Interestingly, Galen broke the mind into three components: imagination, cognition, and memory, which he suggested should be associated with brain substance (the "encephalon"), but he seems not to have localized the function in that substance. In the fourth and fifth centuries this changed to belief in *ventricular localization*. Nemesius (390), Bishop of Emesa (Syria) localized perception in the two lateral ventricles, cognition in the middle ventricle, and memory in the posterior ventricle. In one form or another this doctrine continued for almost one thousand years.

Descartes

He was the first person since Aristotle to create a new psychology

René Descartes (1596–1650) raised many if not most of the fundamental questions in the foundations of cognitive science. He contracted tuberculosis from his mother at birth (she died of it), was a sickly child and a relatively frail adult. He was schooled by Jesuits in mathematics and philosophy (and they allowed him to work in bed until noon, a practice he kept throughout his life). For a while he socialized in Paris, enlisted in the army, then at age 32 he moved to Holland where he wrote his most important works. He died of pneumonia at the age of 54 after catching a cold trudging through the snow at 5:00 a.m. tutoring Queen Christina of Sweden in philosophy.

Persons vs. animals

According to Descartes, animals have no minds, and their behavior can be explained solely in terms of mechanical principles, and in particular by reflexes. Persons, on the other hand, have mind and body. If the behavior is involuntary it too can be explained on purely mechanical principles, just as with animals, but if it is voluntary, then the mind must be invoked. This mechanical view of the body was part of Descartes's general deterministic mechanical (non-human) worldview, and seems to have been inspired by a visit to the French Royal Gardens at St Germain-en-Laye near Paris. There mechanical robots moved and even "talked" in a realistic way, controlled by the footsteps of visitors on pads connected to water pipes and valves. Descartes saw an analogy with the nervous system (as it was conceived in his day):

hydraulic tubes ∷ nerves,
water ∷ "animal spirits"[1]
springs and motors ∷ muscles.

On the biological side, he was perhaps the first to describe the *reflex arc*; external stimuli move the skin, which pulls on filaments within each nerve tube, which opens "valves" allowing the flow of animal spirits stored in the ventricles to trigger the muscles (he didn't say how). The flow of animal spirits also powered digestion as well as some psychological functions, such as sensory impressions, the passions (love, hate, desire, joy, sadness, wonder), and memory (repeated experience makes certain pores in the brain larger and easier for the animal spirits to flow through). Eventually, however, Descartes's anatomy gave way to Harvey's as his physics gave way to Newton's.

Mind and body

Voluntary actions were explained by acts of the will: "the will is free in its nature, that it can never be constrained. . . . And the whole action of the soul consists in this, that solely because it desires something, it causes a little gland to which it is closely united to move in a way requisite to produce the effect which relates to this desire" (*Passions of the Soul*). This is the pineal gland, which is suspended between the anterior ventricles so as to influence and be influenced by the animal spirits stored there. Thus, Descartes seems to have held at least a modified ventricular theory (see figure 3.1).

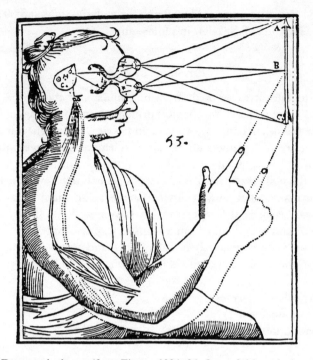

Figure 3.1 Descartes's theory (from Finger, 1994: 26, figure 2.16; reproduced by permission of Oxford University Press)

For Descartes, mind was a distinct substance from body and the principles covering the one do not extend to the other.[2] He had at least three arguments for this position. The most famous is his "cogito ergo sum" argument:

(1) I can't doubt that I exist as a thinking thing (*Cogito ergo sum*: I think, therefore I am).
(2) I can doubt that I exist as a body (I might be being fooled by an evil demon).
(3) Therefore, my mind is not the same as my body.

This argument has been subject to much justified criticism and it is generally considered to be defective; Bob Dylan might be the same person as Robert Zimmerman, yet one could doubt that the one is rich without doubting that the other is. Descartes also argued that mind and body were distinct on the basis of the fact that:

(4) Bodies are unthinking and essentially extended in space, minds are essentially thinking things and not extended in space.
(5) Bodies are divisible and have parts, minds are not divisible and have no parts.

(We leave evaluating these points as an exercise.) So *minds* are thinking, unextended, indivisible substance and their acts of will are free and undetermined. On the other hand *bodies* are unthinking, extended, divisible substance, and their behavior is mechanically determined. Descartes's discussion has three important corollaries for cognitive science, and for our subsequent discussion in later chapters. *First*, the contents of our mind are completely conscious and introspectable: "there can be nothing in the mind, in so far as it is a thinking thing, of which it is not aware . . . we cannot have any thought of which we are not aware at the very moment it is in us." *Second*, our introspective access to these contents is "authoritative" – no one else has as much authority as to what you are thinking as you do. *Third*, these contents are independent not only of the body, but of the rest of the world around it – they are internal to the mind.

Mind–body interaction

If body and mind are distinct substances, how are they related? We have just seen that according to Descartes, the mind can wiggle the pineal gland and so cause muscles to contract. Likewise, effects on the skin can cause the pineal gland to move and so affect the mind. In short, we have mind–body causal interaction (in chapter 8 we will survey problems with this theory).

Persons

Finally, Descartes at times identified the person with the just mind: "But what am I? A thing which thinks. What is a thing which thinks? It is a thing which doubts, understands, affirms, denies, wills, refuses, which also imagines and feels" (*Meditations*). "This I (that is to say, my soul by which I am what I am) is entirely and absolutely distinct from my body, and can exist without it" (*Meditations*). This of course runs against the grain of contemporary cognitive science where the methods of natural science, such as biology and neurophysiology, are being extended to cognition. On the other hand he sometimes says more contemporary things: "I am not only lodged in my body as a pilot is in a vessel, but that I am very closely united to it and so to speak intermingled with it that I seem to compose with it one whole" (*Meditations*). In his last work *Passions of the Soul* (1649) he divided activities into three spheres: (1) those that belong just to the mind (intellectual and volitional), (2) those that belong just to the body (physiology), and (3) those that belong to a "union" of the two (emotions and sensations).

3.3   Cortical Localization vs. Holism

Gall and Spurzheim

It was Franz Joseph Gall (1758–1828) more than anyone else who put the issue of cortical localization into play, though as we will see, the effect was decidedly mixed. Gall was German by birth and began lecturing on the subject in Vienna in 1796. He was joined by his pupil and future collaborator Spurzheim in 1800. In 1802 he was ordered by the government (at the insistence of the Church, which objected to the "materialism" of his doctrine) to cease lecturing. After a tour of Germany, they settled in Paris in 1807. Their first major treatise appeared between 1810 and 1819 in four volumes (Spurzheim collaborated on volumes 1 and 2) under a title which began: *Anatomy and Physiology of the Nervous System in General and the Brain in Particular.* . . . Gall later (1825) completed a six-volume study, *On the Functions of the Brain and the Functions of Each of its Parts*, which was translated into English ten years later. Although scorned by most scientists (one called it "that sinkhole of human folly"), phrenology won Gall wide popularity – and a handsome livelihood.

Before turning to Gall's "phrenology" (the physical localization of mental function by outward manifestations by bumps on the skull: "phrenology" was a term invented by a student and was not used by Gall), it is important to realize that at least part of his influence was based on his medical skills: "everyone agreed he was a brilliant brain anatomist," and he made fundamental contributions to neuroscience, including his comparative work on brain size which indicated that larger amounts of cortex are generally associated with more intelligent organisms. "No one before Gall had shown so clearly that brain size paralleled mental development" (Fancher, 1979: 45). These achievements have been obscured by Gall's dubious inference:

(1)   The mind can be analyzed into a number of *specific faculties* or capacities (Gall assumed these faculties were innate).
(2)   Mental capacities have *specific locations* in the brain.
(3)   Physical locations of specific mental capacities manifest themselves by a *greater mass of tissue*.

1		2		3		4
STRIKING	implies	FACULTY	implies	CORTICAL	implies	CRANIAL
BEHAVIOUR	⇌		⇌	ORGAN	⇀	PROMINENCE
	causes		causes		causes	
(talent,		(innate		(activity		(size varies
propensity,		instinct)		varies		with underlying
mania)				with size)		organ)

Figure 3.2   Gall's inference (from Young, 1970: 36)

(4)   This mass will *distend the skull* and enable those capacities to be read by those knowledgeable in craniology (the measurement of skulls).

One might diagram Gall's methodology as in figure 3.2. Gall observed 1 and 4, and went on to infer 2 and 3. Gall himself reported that he first came to the idea behind phrenology when at age 9 he observed that classmates with bulging eyes had good verbal memories. He hypothesized that a brain area responsible for verbal memory was abnormally enlarged and pushed out the eyes. Gall wrote: "I could not believe, that the union of the two circumstances which had struck me on these different occasions, was solely the result of accident. Having still more assured myself of this, I began to suspect that there must exist a connection between this conformation of the eyes, and the facility of learning by heart" (1835, vol. I: 57–8). Gall does not say how he "still more assured" himself of this correlation, perhaps by more anecdotal observations. In any case, his mature methodology was not much better. For instance, he concluded that *destructiveness* was located above the ear (for Gall the hemispheres were duplicates of each other) because: (1) it is the widest part of the skull in carnivores, (2) prominence here was found in a student "so fond of torturing animals that he became a surgeon," (3) this area was well developed in an apothecary who later became an executioner. In addition to his anecdotal style of testing his theory, Gall's position suffered from having no principled basis for selecting the mental faculties associated with various locations, and different practitioners came up with different sets. In the end Gall identified 27 faculties, 19 of which also occur in animals (Gall got his list mainly from the Scottish philosopher Thomas Reid, who proposed roughly 24 active powers of the mind, and about six intellectual powers). Here are Gall's faculties (Corsi, 1991: 155):

1   instinct of reproduction
2   love of one's offspring
3   attachment and friendship
4   defensive instinct of oneself and one's property

 5   instinct for cruelty, inclination to kill
 6   cleverness, sharpness, know–how
 7   feeling of possessiveness and inclination to steal
 8   pride, haughtiness, fierceness, love of authority
 9   vanity, ambition, love of glory
10   circumspection and foresight
11   memory of things and facts
12   sense of spatial relations
13   memory for people
14   sense of words, names, or verbal memory
15   sense of the spoken word, or philological gifts
16   sense of color or pictorial talent
17   sense of tonal relations or musical talent
18   sense of the relationships of numbers
19   sense of mechanics, construction, architecture
20   comparative wisdom
21   depth of thought and metaphysical spirit
22   sense of humor and sarcasm
23   poetic talent
24   goodness, benevolence, sweetness, compassion, sensitivity, moral sense, conscience, sense of justice
25   faculty of imitating, mimicry
26   God and religion
27   steadfastness, constancy, perseverance, tenacity

Gall's associate, Spurzheim (1776–1832), gave phrenology its modern character. He adopted the term "phrenology" and elaborated Gall's notions by distinguishing intellectual and emotional faculties, and increasing the number (see figures 3.3 and 3.4). Spurzheim and Gall separated in 1813 – Gall stayed in Paris and Spurzheim went on eventually to lecture in America (you can see his skull in the Warren Museum at the Harvard Medical School).

Flourens

Phrenology's most famous opponent was Marie-Jean-Pierre Flourens (1794–1867), a respected anatomist, physiologist, and prodigy, who received his medical degree and published his first scientific paper at age 19. Flourens believed in laboratory experimentation, and his method was to remove areas of the brain ("ablation") of small animals (birds, rabbits, dogs) which phrenologists associated with some specific behavioral trait, then nurse the animal back

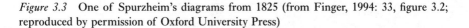

Figure 3.3 One of Spurzheim's diagrams from 1825 (from Finger, 1994: 33, figure 3.2; reproduced by permission of Oxford University Press)

to health and compare the behavior of the ablated animal with a non-ablated control. He regularly failed to confirm phrenological predictions. Given this failure he concluded that the cortex functioned holistically: "All sensations, all perception, all volition occupy concurrently the same seat in these organs. The faculty of sensation, perception, and volition is then essentially one faculty" (Finger, 1994: 36). But this inference was not fully warranted; by taking slices from these small brains he cut *across* anatomically and functionally distinct regions of the brain. Time would suggest that Flourens had the right kind of methodology, but the wrong theory, whereas Gall had the right kind of theory, but the wrong methodology.

Broca

The decisive step historically in the legitimization of the localization of func-tion was taken by the French physician and scientist Paul Broca (1824–80), mentioned earlier. Already before Broca's work the malady of *motor aphasia*

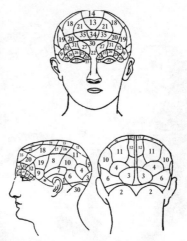

THE "POWERS AND ORGANS OF THE MIND," ACCORDING TO SPURZHEIM,
Phrenology, or the Doctrine of Mental Phenomena, 1834.

AFFECTIVE FACULTIES		INTELLECTUAL FACULTIES	
PROPENSITIES	SENTIMENTS	PERCEPTIVE	REFLECTIVE
? Desire to live	10 Cautiousness	22 Individuality	34 Comparison
* Alimentiveness	11 Approbativeness	23 Configuration	35 Causality
1 Destructiveness	12 Self-Esteem	24 Size	
2 Amativeness	13 Benevolence	25 Weight and	
3 Philoprogenitiveness	14 Reverence	Resistance	
4 Adhesiveness	15 Firmness	26 Coloring	
5 Inhabitiveness	16 Conscientiousness	27 Locality	
6 Combativeness	17 Hope	28 Order	
7 Secretiveness	18 Marvelousness	29 Calculation	
8 Acquisitiveness	19 Ideality	30 Eventuality	
9 Constructiveness	20 Mirthfulness	31 Time	
	21 Imitation	32 Tune	
		33 Language	

Figure 3.4 One of Spurzheim's diagrams from 1834 (from Boring, 1951: 55, figure 1;
reproduced by permission of Prentice-Hall, Inc.)

(inability to communicate with speech) was well known to follow certain kinds
of strokes (interruption of blood supply to the brain, often due to clotting).
Ironically, it was Gall's account of one such case that was "the first specifically
noted correlation of a speech deficit with injury to the left frontal lobe of the
cortex." Broca's diagnosis of Monsieur Leborgne ("Tan") in 1861 was the first
such localist account to be widely accepted. It is now regarded by many as "the
most important clinical paper in the history of cortical localization" (Finger,
1994: 38). The story of Tan is interesting. Aubertin (1825–93), a contemporary of Broca's, was attracted earlier than Broca to localist doctrines regarding
speech, and after studying a particular patient for a long time, he challenged
the skeptical Society of Anthropology in Paris to perform an autopsy on the

patient: "if at autopsy the anterior lobes are found intact, then I renounce the ideas which I have sustained." Before this could take place however, Broca got a 51-year-old patient who had become aphasic at age 30. All he was known to utter regularly was something like "tan," which became his nickname, and occasionally, though rarely (once in Broca's presence), he would say "Sacré Nom de Dieu!" Broca asked Aubertin to conduct an examination, after which Aubertin "unhesitatingly declared that [the patient] suffered from a lesion in the left frontal lobe of the cortex." Within a few days Tan died of gangrene, Broca performed an autopsy and brought the brain to the next meeting of the Society of Anthropology. It had an egg-sized lesion on the left side of the brain. The center of the lesion (the presumed point of origin) coincided with the lower part of the third convolution of the left frontal lobe.

In a few months, Broca had another case, an 84-year-old man with sudden loss of speech, who upon autopsy was discovered to have a small lesion in exactly the same spot as the center of Tan's lesion. Broca gathered a number of other cases as evidence to the same conclusion. In each case, Broca noted, the lesion was to *the same part* of the *left hemisphere* of the brain – right hemisphere damage of the same region was not implicated in the loss. In his honor this area is now called "Broca's area," and the syndrome is called "Broca's aphasia." Here is a sample (from Akmajian et al., 517):

Examiner: Tell me, what did you do before you retired?
Aphasic: Uh, uh, uh puh, par, partender, no.
Examiner: Carpenter?
Aphasic: (*shaking head yes*) Carpenter, tuh, tuh, tenty [20] year.
Examiner: Tell me about this picture.
Aphasic: Boy . . . cook . . . cookie . . . took . . . cookie.

Wernicke

In the 1870s, Carl Wernicke (1848–1905) went further, showing that damage in a portion of the temporal lobe led to a language disorder characterized by a loss of comprehension rather than speech. The conception of mental functioning of the brain in play at the time of Wernicke was one where sensory information of different kinds was projected onto the cortex at various points on the sensory strip, and stored in surrounding tissue in the form of "images." Specific motor acts were also stored near the motor strip as "images." The remaining brain tissue was thought to be *association areas* which linked the various sensory and motor centers. Wernicke was the first to propose explaining motor ("Broca's") aphasia by way of damage to the area storing "images" of articulatory movements for speech. But he is most famous for the discovery and explanation of the opposite syndrome (now called "Wernicke's aphasia") where the subject can speak perfectly fluently, though even familiar words may be mispronounced, but whose comprehension is impaired. The lesions causing this kind of aphasia are located in the temporal lobe near the auditory area. Such patients hear the words, know they are being addressed, and try to respond, but they just don't understand what is being said. Here's a sample:

Doctor: What brings you to the hospital?
Patient: Boy, I'm sweating, I'm awfully nervous, you know, once in a while I get caught up, I can't mention the tarripoi (*sic*), a month ago, quite a little, I've done a lot well, I impose a lot, while on the other hand, you know what I mean, I have to run around, look it over, trebbin (*sic*) and all that sort of stuff.   (Fancher, 1979: 69)

Localist conclusions based on trauma were soon reinforced by experimental work. In particular, Eduard Hitzig (1839–1907), a psychiatrist, and Gustav Fritsch (1838–1927), an anatomist, working on a dressing table in the bedroom of Hitzig's home in Berlin, identified in 1870 distinctive cortical sites for a variety of movements in a dog, by stimulating the exposed brain with mild electric current. David Ferrier (1843–1928) replicated Fritsch and Hitzig's work and evoked much more specific and intricate behavior in monkeys: the twitch of an eyelid, the movement of just one finger. Finally, anatomists were beginning to reveal the fine structure of the cortex. Korbinian Brodmann (1868–1918) in particular produced a map of the cortex with 52 distinct areas (see figure 3.5). However, since there were no consensual criteria for discriminating such areas, different researchers typically came up with different maps. It is clear that this view of neural organization (conjoined with the emergence of the synapse doctrine of neuronal function to follow), and the theory of reflex arcs, provided a sturdy foundation for the view that mental activity was subserved by associations among primitive ideas, as realized in specific connected pathways and centers in the brain.

3.4   Nerve Net Theory vs. the Neuron Doctrine

The microscope was introduced by Robert Hooke (London) in 1665. In 1718 Anton von Leeuwenhoek (Delft, Holland) published (at age 84!) views of the

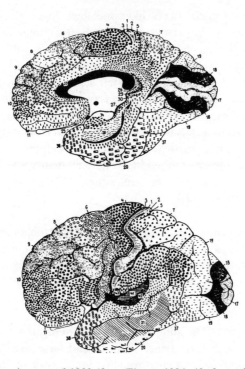

Figure 3.5 Brodmann's areas of 1909 (from Finger, 1994: 42, figure 3.15; reproduced by permission of Oxford University Press)

peripheral nerve of a cow which he claimed showed many individual hollow tubes of the sort Descartes (and others) had imagined carried "animal spirits" from the sensory organs to the brain (perception), and from the spinal cord to the muscles (behavior). The problem with early microscopes – their glass actually – was that they refracted light of different wavelengths by different amounts. This was called "chromatic aberration" and it was a serious problem given the extremely small scale of neural material. The development of relatively powerful and non-distortional "achromatic" microscopes in the early 1820s allowed "microscopists" to identify nerve cell bodies and some of their extensions. The first reasonably accurate microscopic views of nerve cells and fibers came from "the founder of histology" Jan Purkyne (1787–1869), a former philosophy student and discoverer of the "Purkyne shift." One of Purkyne's students, Gabriel Valentin (1810–83), published in 1836 a microscopic image of a nerve cell (a "kugeln" or globule). This is "the first of its kind in the biological literature." Valentin noted the sharp outline of the cell membrane and noted that the cell often gave rise to a tail-like appendage, but he thought the cell body and appendage were each surrounded by a sheath; "thus Valentin missed the critical point that the nerve fiber arises from the nerve cell." In 1837 Purkyne gave a talk in Prague where he described large ganglion cells in the cerebellar cortex, now called "Purkyne cells." Purkyne also noticed that a "tail-like ending faces the outside and, by means of *two processes* mostly disappears into the gray matter." These "processes" ultimately came to be called "dendrites." Still, crucially, he could not discern how these fibers were related to the cell bodies. In 1838 Theodor Schwann (1810–82) proposed the "cell theory": the entire body, inside and out, is made up of individual cells. Cell theory was accepted for every part of the organism *except* the nervous system. The reason for this exception was the existence of two difficulties:

1   Microscopes could not tell whether all nerve fibers arise directly from nerve cells or whether some of them could exist independently.
2   It couldn't be seen whether the long thin branching fibers have *definite terminations*, or whether they ran together with neighboring thin branches to form a *continuous network*.

The first view required the additional idea that neurons act at sites of contact and leads to the "neuron doctrine." The second view postulated that activity spreads in a continuous fashion through the network of branches. In 1833 Christian Ehrenberg compared nerve fibers to the capillary vascular system; the continuity of the arterial-venous system provided the model for the later "nerve net" theory.[3] At the same time researchers were trying to see if they could reduce the huge variety of branching patterns. In the end they settled on two, what we today call "axons" and "dendrites." (Cajal's "Law of Dynamic Polarization" stated that every neuron is a unit that receives input in its dendrites and sends output in its axon(s) – but that comes later.) Deiters, in 1865, and Koelliker, in 1867, proposed that axons were independent, though dendrites might form a net.

Based mostly on his illustrations of 1853, Koelliker seems to have been the first to actually establish that nerve fibers arise from nerve cells. Deiters, in 1865, made the first clear distinction between what we now call axons and dendrites: "It is ironic that by his clear observations on dendrites and on the single axon Deiters had placed himself on a direct path to the neuron doctrine and indeed to modern times, but by the introduction of his second set of fine fibers he at the same time contributed to the reticular [nerve net] theory" (Shepherd, 1991: 47). New and more powerful techniques were needed to settle this issue. The key advance was the introduction in 1870 of the Golgi stain.

Golgi

It was Camillio Golgi (1843–1926) who in 1873 reported on his important silver nitrate staining method, which he discovered in a kitchen at the hospital near Milan where he worked. This process is difficult to apply reliably, but when it worked it clearly stained cells black against a yellow background revealing all relevant morphological features.

It was Golgi's opinion, one that he thought was supported by the results of his staining technique, that the axons formed a dense, fused network, much as the circulatory system does ("anastomosis"): "In fact the method was inadequate for establishing this; thinning of the terminal branches was mostly due to failure of complete staining, and the branches were too thin in any case for the pur-ported anastomoses to be resolved clearly by the light microscope. This fateful misinterpretation was to become his reticular theory of nervous organization" (Shepherd, 1991: 91). Golgi also thought the role of dendrites was mainly nutri-tive. This network conception led him to oppose cerebral localization and to endorse holism of brain function. In 1883 he wrote a long review article in which he summarized his findings. Particularly relevant are these theses:

Eleventh: In all the strata of the gray substance of the central nervous organs, there exists a fine and complicated diffuse nervous network . . . decomposing into very slender filaments, and thus losing their proper individuality, pass on to be gradually confounded in the network. . . . The network here described is evidently destined to establish a bond of anatomical and functional union between the cellular elements of extensive zones of the gray substance of the centers.

Fifteenth: Another corollary from what precedes is that the concept of the so-called localization of the cerebral functions, taken in a rigorous sense, . . . cannot be said to be in any manner supported by the results of minute anatomi-cal researchers.   (Shepherd, 1991: 99–100)

Amazingly, Golgi carried on his distinguished research career while also rector of the University of Pavia, and a senator in Rome.

Cajal

Various anatomists of the time opposed this network theory, but it was Santi-ago Ramon y Cajal (1852–1934) who contributed most to its rejection. After seeing a sample of Golgi stains in Madrid in 1887, he set out to improve the method by cutting thicker sections and studying neurons prior to myelination. In his first paper of 1888 Cajal stated he could find no evidence for either axons or dendrites undergoing anastomosis, and so forming continuous nets. Subsequent studies confirmed this judgment and in a 1889 review of this work he argued that nerve cells were independent elements.

In 1889 Cajal traveled to Berlin to present his views at a conference. There he met, among others, Wilhelm von Waldeyer (1836–1921), who was influenced by Cajal's views, and who in 1891 wrote a favorable and influential theoretical review of the literature. In this review he claimed that the "neuron" (nerve cell) is the anatomical, physiological, metabolic, and genetic unit of the nervous system. The word "neuron" was introduced in this way, as was the *neuron doctrine*:

I   The axis cylinders [axons] of all nerve fibers . . . have been shown to originate directly from cells. There is no connection with a network of fibers or any origin from such a network.

II   All these nerve fibers terminate freely with "end arborizations" without a network or anastomotic formation.   (Shepherd, 1991: 181–2)

In 1894 Cajal was invited by the Royal Society of London to give the prestigious Croonian Lectures (entitled "La fine structure des centres nerveux") which became the basis for his later 1909 two-volume work on the neural structure of the nervous system. This was a landmark address and paper in the history of neuroscience, synthesizing his earlier experimental work, as well as the work of Golgi, Deiters, and Koelliker, and accompanied by slides of his amazing drawings: "These are the images that, more than any others, have implanted themselves in the minds of succeeding generations of scientists concerning structures of different nerve cell types and their interconnections in the nervous system" (ibid., 254). Cajal concluded that each nerve cell consists of three parts, each with a distinct function: the cell body and "protoplasmic prolongation" (now "dendrite") for reception of impulses, the "axis cylinder" (now "axon") for transmission, and the axis cylinder terminals for distribution. This is basically the modern view. Still, neuron doctrine followers could not explain how neurons communicate with one another if they did not fuse.

Charles Sherrington (1857–1952) speculated on the gaps between neurons, and between neurons and muscle cells, and in 1897 called them "synapses" (from the Greek for "to join"). In a famous passage in 1897 he wrote: "So far as our present knowledge goes, we are led to think that the tip of the twig of the arborescence is not continuous with, but merely in contact with, the substance of the dendrite or cell body on which it imposes. Such a special connection of one nerve cell with another might be called a synapse." Earlier, in the 1870s, Emil du Bois-Reymond (1818–98) had hypothesized that excitatory transmissions from nerves to effector cells could take place electrically or chemically – the details of which awaited the technology of the twentieth century.

As late as 1906 (when both Golgi and Cajal received the Nobel prize for their work) Golgi attacked three central theses of the neuron doctrine: (1) the neuron is an embryological unit, (2) the neuron is one cell, (3) the neuron is a physiological unit. Golgi still clung to his view of axons as a fused network and forming large, holistic networks. In his Nobel lecture he wrote: "When the neuron theory made, by almost unanimous approval, its triumphant entrance on the scientific scene, I found myself unable to follow the current of opinion, because I was confronted by one concrete anatomical fact; this was the existence of the formation which I have called the diffuse nerve network" (Shepherd, 1991: 261). "The conclusion of this account of the neuron question, which has had to be rather an assembly of facts, brings me back to my starting-point, namely that no arguments, on which Waldeyer supported the theory of the individuality and independence of the neuron, will stand examination" (ibid., 265). He was therefore opposed to doctrines of cortical localization as well.

3.5 The First Half of the Twentieth Century

Lashley

Holism (remember Flourens?) made something of a comeback with the work of Karl Lashley (1890–1958) and his associates, especially Shepherd Franz (1874–1933). In their initial studies (1917) Franz and Lashley found that brightness discrimination and simple maze learning can remain intact after varying degrees of damage to the cortex. Lashley concluded that decrements in intellectual capability were a function of lesion size, not lesion location (see figure 3.6). In 1929 Lashley summarized this work, enunciating his famous principles of equipotentiality and mass action:

Equipotentiality: "The term 'equipotentiality' I have used to designate the apparent capacity of any intact part of a functional area to carry out, with or without reduction in efficiency, the functions which are lost by destruction of the whole. This capacity varies from one area to another and with the

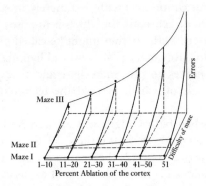

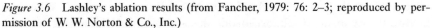

Figure 3.6 Lashley's ablation results (from Fancher, 1979: 76: 2–3; reproduced by permission of W. W. Norton & Co., Inc.)

character of the functions involved. It probably holds only for the association areas and for functions more complex than simple sensory or motor coordination."

Mass action: "I have already given evidence, which is augmented in the present study, that the equipotentiality is not absolute but is subject to a law of mass action whereby the efficiency of performance of an entire complex function may be reduced in proportion to the extent of brain injury within an area whose parts are not more specialized for one component of function than for another."

Note Lashley's qualification of these doctrines to exclude sensory and motor functions. As we will see, work on single-fiber (and single-cell) recording in the 1960s and 1970s by Lettvin et al., Hubel and Wiesel, etc., lead to some extremely localist conclusions regarding these systems.

Hebb

Finally, one can see Donald Hebb's (1949) work *The Organization of Behavior* as a sort of synthesis of localist and holist tendencies. Hebb started from where Lashley left off – attempting to find a way to account for what appeared to be both distribution and localization in the way in which the brain represented information. Hebb's solution was influenced strongly by the work of a neuroanatomist, Lorente de Nó, whose analysis of neural circuitry led him to the view that there were "re-entrant" neural loops within the brain. From these studies Hebb abstracted the notion that there could be circuits in the brain

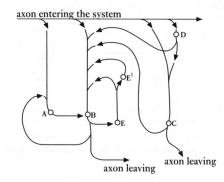

Figure 3.7 Hebb: neural loops (from Hebb, 1972: 70, figure 23; figures 3.7–3.10 reproduced by permission of W. B. Saunders Co.)

within which activity "reverberated," and that these circuits could therefore act as a simple closed loop (see figure 3.7).

On Hebb's view, behavioral patterns are built up over time via connections formed between particular cells (localist) into *cell assemblies*. But how did these circuits come into being? Hebb proposed that there is a neural mechanism by which this could happen – so-called "Hebb's Postulate": cells that fire together, wire together. This slogan (which was not Hebb's) covers two situations each of which can be found in Hebb's writings. First, there is the situation, as Hebb put it, "When an axon of cell A is near enough to excite a cell B and repeatedly or persistently takes part in fixing it, some growth process or metabolic change takes place in one or both cells such that A's efficiency as one of the cells firing B, is increased" (1972: 62). Second, there is the situation where there is simultaneous firing of cells A and B, as in Hebb's figure (see figure 3.8).

This kind of simultaneous "co-activation" provides a model for association at the neural level. Over time, cell assemblies could become locked in larger *phase sequences* which recruit many cell assemblies (holistic), and underlie more complex forms of behavior.

The neuron at mid-century

By the end of the first half of the twentieth century a certain picture of the neuron, the synapse, and neural firing had emerged in broad conformity with the neuron doctrine. Here are the basic elements of that picture (following Boring et al., 1939; Hebb, 1972).

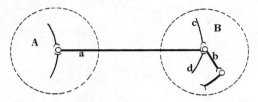

*A mechanism of establishing synaptic connections. A,a group of active neurons,
of which only one (a) is shown completely; B, a second group of neurons
active at the same time, of which only two are shown completely. Since a and
b are active together and an axon of a is close to b, a will become connected
with (better able to facilitate) b.*

Figure 3.8   Hebb's postulate (from Hebb, 1972: 64, figure 29)

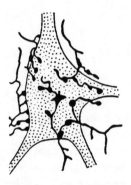

Synapses: synaptic knobs (black) making contact with a cell body
(stippled). Only a few knobs are shown; the cell body and its
dendrites may be completely covered by them. (From E. Gardner,
Fundamentals of Neurology, W. B. Saunders).

Figure 3.9   Synaptic knobs making contact with cell body (from Hebb, 1972: 68, figure 28)

There are a number of different types of neurons (we return to this in later
chapters). In each case the *dendrites* receive information, the *axon* sends out
information. There are generally many dendrites and one axon, though the
axon can branch at the end. The *cell body* can also receive information directly
(see figure 3.9).

The *synapse* is the point at which an axon makes contact with the dendrite
or cell body. The enlargement at the end of the axon is the *synaptic knob*. The
axon (and cell body) works in an *all-or-none* fashion. The axon is like "a trail
of gunpowder" – it uses up all its stored fuel at each point and so works without
decrement. The dendrite, on the other hand, works with decrement: "[it] is
more like a bow and arrow system in which a weak pull produces a weak effect."
Over much of its length, the dendrite acts in a *graded*, not in an all-or-none
fashion.

The *nerve impulse* is the fundamental process of information transfer in the
nervous system. It is characterized by the following features:

1   The impulse is an *electrical* and *chemical* change that moves across the neuron. The *rate varies* with the diameter of the fibre: from about 1 meter/second for small diameters to about 120 meters/second for large diameters.

2   This disturbance can set off a similar disturbance across the synapse in a second neuron, in a muscle (to contract) or in a gland (to secrete).

3   Neurons need a definite time to "recharge." This is the *absolute refractory period* lasting about 1 millisecond. Given the refractory period, a neuron can fire at a maximum rate of about *1,000 per second.*

4   Immediately after firing, nothing can make the neuron fire again. A little later it can be fired by a strong stimulation. This is the *relative refractory period* lasting for about a tenth of a second. Although a strong stimulation does not produce a bigger impulse, it can stimulate the neuron more *frequently*, by catching it earlier in the refractory period – intensity of stimulation is translated into frequency of firing. A cell fired at a rapid rate for a prolonged period begins to fatigue by building up sodium ions on the inside of the cell, and it can take an hour or so to recover from this.

5   The action potential is driven by *positive sodium ions* located on the outside of the semipermeable membrane moving through it to the inside and exchanging with *negative potassium ions*, which move out, creating a negative charge on the outside of the membrane. This destabilizes the adjacent region of the axon and the process takes place again, which again destabilizes an adjacent region, etc. In this way the negative charge moves down the axon. Immediately after destabilization the cell begins to re-establish the original balance by pumping out the sodium ions from the inside surface (see figure 3.10). This process takes about 1 millisecond (0.5 msec in large fibers, 2 msecs in small fibers).

6   Cells can be *inhibited* from firing. This is the *hyperpolarization* vs. the depolarization of cells. Polarization is when negative ions and positive ions are on different sides of the membrane.

7   Cells can *summate* inputs from different sources. Summation can occur on a sensory surface or at a synapse. Since the probability that a single impulse will fire a neuron is low, summation increases the probability of firing.

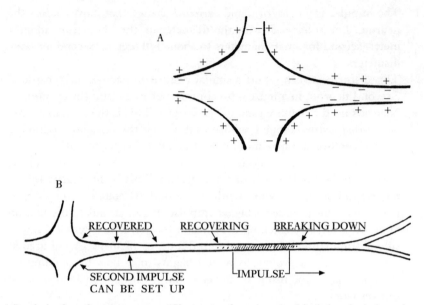

(*A*) polarization of resting neuron. (*B*) passage of one impulse (shaded region) along the axon: showing that two or more impulses can occur at the same time in the neuron, since a second one can be started in the "recovered" region as soon as the first has moved along the fiber and the cell body has recharged itself. The process is known to be far more complex than diagram *A* would suggest.

Figure 3.10   Polarization and passing of an impulse (from Hebb, 1972: 70, figure 29)

Study questions

What was Descartes's theory of mind and body?

What is "phrenology"?

What sort of methodology did Gall use for testing phrenological hypotheses?

How many faculties of mind did Gall settle on?

How many faculties of mind did Spurzheim settle on?

What are some typical examples of local mental faculties from Gall or Spurzheim?

What was the original evidence for the "localization" of brain function for language (Broca, Wernicke)?

What is "Broca's" aphasia?

What is "Wernicke's" aphasia?

What was the controversy between nerve-net theory (Golgi) and the neuron doctrine (Cajal)?

Why did it take so long to resolve?

What was Waldeyer's contribution?

What is the "neuron doctrine"?

In what four different senses was the neuron the basic unit of the nervous system?

What was the evidence for equipotentiality (Lashley)?

What is "Hebb's postulate"? Compare it to James's postulate (P1).

What is the basic structure of the neuron?

What is its basic cycle of operation?

What challenges have there been to the doctrine that the neuron is the anatomical unit of the nervous system?

What three features challenged the doctrine that the neuron is the physiological unit of the nervous system?

Notes

1 "Animal spirits" were taken to be a highly purified component of blood, which was filtered out before reaching the brain.
2 In the metaphysics of the time, which came basically from the Greeks, especially Aristotle, a substance is any kind of thing whose existence does not depend on the existence of another kind of thing.
3 In some ways, contemporary "connectionist" cognitive modeling (see Part III) can be seen as an intellectual descendant of this earlier nerve net theory, but at a functional, rather than a structural level.

Suggested reading

History

The best single source for the history of the study of the nervous system is Finger (1994). Corsi (1991) also contains good historical text and some of the best color plates available. The rise of the neuron doctrine is explored in fascinating detail in Shepherd (1991), which contains (pp. 239–53) the first half of Cajal's influential Croonian Lecture. This chapter relies heavily on these sources, though all detailed citations have been suppressed to make this chapter readable. For more on Descartes's psychology, see Hatfield (1992) and references therein, and for more on Descartes's internalism see McCulloch (1995), chapter 1.

The history of cerebral localization is surveyed in Young (1970), see especially chapter 1 on Gall and chapter 4 on Broca. Boring (1957), chapter 3, contains interesting biographical and bibliographical information on both Gall and Spurzheim. See Fodor (1983) for an interesting discussion of Gall's important non-phrenological contributions to the architecture of the mind. See also Corsi (1991), chapters 3 and 5.

Biology

For an authoritative introduction to the biology of the neuron and nervous system see Shepherd (1994), especially chapters 1–9, as well as Kandel et al. (1995). A well-illustrated introductory textbook covering many of the same topics is Beatty (1995). For an authoritative and detailed look at the state of knowledge of the neuron at mid-century see Brink (1951). A highly readable overview of the contribution of neuroscience to cognitive science can be found in Gardner (1985), chapter 9. Churchland (1986) briefly surveys the history of neuroscience, outlines the modern theory of neurons and functional neuroanatomy, then plunges into its philosophical implications. A good chapter-length survey of neuroscience can be found in Stillings et al. (1995), chapter 7.

4

Neuro-Logical Background

4.1 Introduction

The investigations we will survey in this chapter study the computational character and resources of the nervous system by studying formal analogs (or idealized versions) of neurons and neural networks. These formal analogs themselves are often called "neural nets." We first look at McCulloch and Pitts' (1943) ground-breaking work on the switching logic of the nervous system. This work was to lead in two different directions in the 1960s and 1970s. On the one hand it precisely conceptualized how a nervous system could be seen as doing binary computation by using neural switching circuits. It is the only paper cited by von Neumann in his 1945 EDVAC report, and contributed to the development of the digital computational theory of mind. Since McCulloch and Pitts networks do not learn, making them do so requires giving them modifiable thresholds and/or connection strengths, and this leads naturally to the perceptron research of Rosenblatt (1958), since a simple perceptron is a two-layer network of McCulloch and Pitts units with modifiable thresholds and/or connection strengths. This takes us finally to its critique by Minsky and Papert (1969). Perceptron work eventually evolved into contemporary connectionism. Hence the McCulloch and Pitts paper can be seen as a sort of branch point in the history of cognitive science, leading on the one hand to serial, digital theory and on the other hand to parallel, distributed theory. We then turn to Lettvin, Maturana, McCulloch, and Pitts' (1959) work on the semantics of the visual system of the frog, and what the frog's eye tells the frog's brain. This is the natural outgrowth of questions concerning the representational character of nervous activity – an issue raised in the original McCulloch and Pitts paper.

4.2   Neural Networks and the Logic of Propositions

We saw earlier than in 1890 William James had proposed that the activity of a given point in the brain, at a given time, is the sum of other points of activity inputting to that point, and the strength of each input is proportional to:

1   the number of times each input accompanied the activity of the given point;
2   the intensity of such activation;
3   the absence of another rival point where this activity could be diverted.

The idea behind (1) and (2) seems to be that the strength of the connections between points could be increased by the frequency and intensity of co-activation (recall James's associational principles of *frequency* and *intensity* in partial recall). So each input has a strength or "weight" (again, see the "James neuron" of chapter 1). Condition (3) seems redundant if the given point is doing summation of its input, since diverted activity simply will not be counted as input. However, we might play with the idea that "diversion" is a primitive form of "inhibition" – which has veto power over the summation process. So taken, we are on the road to our next type of unit, the so-called McCulloch and Pitts neuron.

McCulloch and Pitts

The first generally cited study of the formal, computational properties of the nervous system is the 1943 paper by McCulloch and Pitts (hereafter M&P). The paper is rather condensed and at times obscure, even by industry standards. We will rehearse their basic finding, sticking close to their own discussion. M&P begin by reviewing certain "cardinal assumptions" of the theoretical neurophysiology of their time. They summarize these for the purposes of formalization in their calculus as follows (1943: 22):[1]

1   the activity of the neuron is an "all-or-none" process;[2]
2   a certain fixed number of synapses must be excited within the period of latent addition in order to excite a neuron at any time,[3] and this number is independent of previous activity and position in the neuron;[4]
3   the only significant delay within the nervous system is synaptic delay;[5]
4   the activity of any inhibitory synapse absolutely prevents excitation of the neuron at that time;[6]
5   the structure of the net does not change with time.

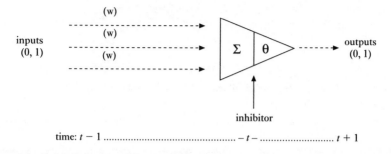

Figure 4.1   A McCulloch and Pitts neuron

Putting these features together, a M&P neuron could be diagrammed as shown in figure 4.1. The M&P neuron (Σ) sums its input during summation interval t. If it gets inhibition it is quiet. If it does not get inhibition it fires if and only if it equals or exceeds threshold (θ). The basic idea that connects neural networks with the formal systems is the principle that:

(P1)   The response of any neuron [is] factually equivalent to a proposition which proposed its adequate stimulus (1943: 21).

That is, each neuron can be assigned the proposition that conditions sufficient for its firing have been met:

(P1′)   Every neuron can be assigned a proposition of the form: the conditions for my activation are now met.

When the neuron fires, that proposition will be true; when it does not fire, that proposition will be false. Hence the "all-or-none" feature of neurons is mapped into the truth-values of a proposition. Furthermore:

(P2)   Psychological relations existing among nervous activities correspond . . . to relations among the propositions (1943: 21).

And so the "switching circuitry" of the nervous system gets mapped by the two-valued logic of propositions. M&P proceed to construct a formal system for modeling neural activity, and proving certain theorems about such models.[7] The system itself is quite opaque,[8] but their diagrammatic representation of neural nets was influential, and has been incorporated into the literature in one form or another.[9] For example, in figure 4.2, the firing of neuron 2 represents the fact that 1 has fired.[10] In figure 4.3, the fact that neuron 3 has fired represents the fact that neuron 1 or 2 has fired. In figure 4.4, the firing of neuron 3 represents that fact that neurons 1 and 2 both have fired.

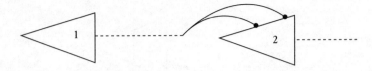

Figure 4.2   A delay net (from McCulloch and Pitts, 1943, figure 1a)

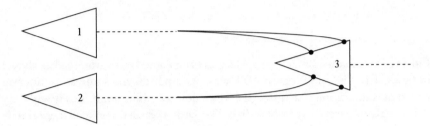

Figure 4.3   An OR net (from McCulloch and Pitts, 1943, figure 1b)

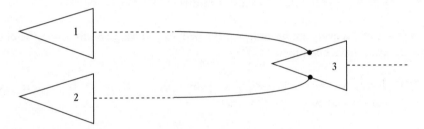

Figure 4.4   An AND net (from McCulloch and Pitts, 1943, figure 1c)

Unfortunately, these figures do not explicitly reflect either inhibition or thresholding. Subsequent diagrams of M&P neurons and networks have simplified these somewhat. Inhibition is represented as an open bulb, excitation as an arrow, and thresholds are included in the unit (see figure 4.5). The table at the foot of the figure gives the "laws of firing" for each unit. Note that nothing prevents a M&P neuron from having many inputs, and so nothing prevents them from being wired up in arbitrarily complex patterns. M&P argue that networks of such units (including loops), when provided with memory, are computationally quite powerful:

(P3)   Every net, if furnished with a tape, scanners connected to afferents [inputs], and suitable efferents [outputs] to perform the necessary

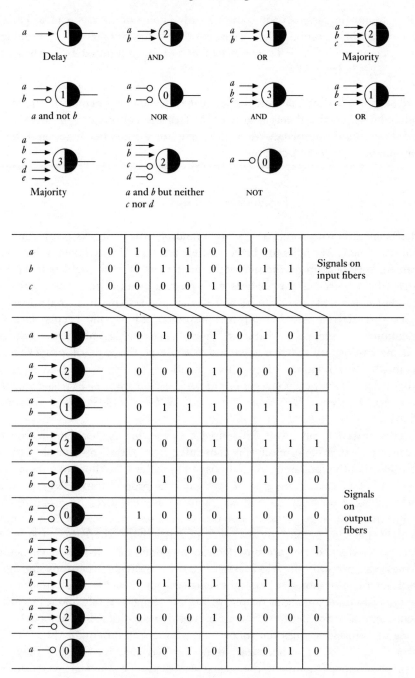

Figure 4.5 M&P neurons (from Minsky, 1967: 35, figure 3.1-1)

motor-operations, can compute only such numbers as can a Turing machine; second, that each of the latter numbers [viz numbers computable by a Turing machine] can be computed by such a net (1943: 35).

The part of a Turing machine not dedicated to the tape (memory) is its finite state control, so the theorem also establishes the equivalence of M&P nets and finite state automata. We will return to Turing machines and their computational power in chapter 6.

Psychological consequences

M&P conclude with some very general (and obscure) remarks on the epistemology of nets. At one point, however, they remark: "To psychology, however defined, specification of the net would contribute all that could be achieved in that field – even if the analysis were pushed to ultimate psychic units or 'psychons,' for a psychon can be no less than the activity of a single neuron. Since that activity is inherently propositional, all psychic events have an intentional, or 'semiotic,' character. The 'all-or-none' law of these activities, and the conformity of their relations to those of the logic of propositions, insure that the relations of psychons are those of the two-valued logic of propositions. *Thus in psychology, introspective, behavioristic or physiological, the fundamental relations are those of two-valued logic*" (1943: 37–8; emphasis added).

This proved to be a very influential doctrine, but is there any reason to accept it? *First*, it is not clear why they infer, from the all-or-none activity of neurons, that the fundamental relations in psychology are those of two-valued logic. It is true that neurons *can be* assigned the propositions M&P assign to them, and that the relations between them *can be* formalized by propositional connectives, but it is certainly not necessary. For instance, for all we know thoughts may correspond to patterns of neural activity, where the patterns are statistically defined and are not Boolean functions of constituent elements. *Second*, the propositions M&P associated with individual neurons and networks of them do not give the right semantics for thought. The propositions we typically think are about people, places and things – rarely about the sufficient conditions for neurons firing. So even if propositional logic models the firing or neurons, it does not follow that it models the thought those firings instantiate. *Third*, it is not clear from the text what relationship they see between thinking (thoughts), the formal nets, neural nets, and the propositions assigned to such nets. At times they write as if only neural activity instantiates thought. At other times they write neutrally about the psychology of "nets." What is at issue here is the question of "multiple realizability" or "multiple instantiation." That is, does thought reside just in the (logical) *organization* of the net, or does it matter what kind of *material* the net is constructed out of? If the latter, then thought may be realized only in nervous systems (or causally equivalent systems). If the former, then any matter could have thought provided it were organized in a causally sufficient way. In particular, a silicon-based machine could have thoughts if it could be designed to instantiate the appropriate net. This may be the beginning of the influential doctrine that the hardware does not, within limits, matter. (We return to this question shortly, after Turing machines.)

4.3   Perceptrons

The perceptron created a sensation when it was first described. It was the first precisely specified, computationally oriented neural network, and it made a major impact on a number of areas simultaneously.
(Anderson and Rosenfeld, 1988: 89)

The study of perceptrons marks a kind of double turning point in the history of connectionism, first in their relation to the "cybernetics" movement of the time, and second in relation to the just developing digital computational movement of the time. First, their introduction in the 1950s by Frank Rosenblatt added some much-needed discipline to the chaotic "cybernetics" movement. As Rosenblatt noted early on: "Those theorists . . . have generally been less exact in their formulations and far from rigorous in their analyses, so that it is frequently hard to assess whether or not the systems that they describe could actually work in a realistic nervous system . . . the lack of an analytic language comparable in proficiency to the Boolean algebra of the network analysts has been one of the main obstacles. The contributions of this group should perhaps be considered as suggestions of what to look for and investigate" (1958: 389). Second, as we will see, perceptrons were the subject of precise scrutiny and withering criticism by Minsky and Papert (1969), and this work helped to turn the tide against the "neuro-logical" approach of the 1950s and towards the digital computational approach of the 1960s and 1970s.

Rosenblatt

In what form is information stored or remembered? How does information contained in storage, or in memory influence recognition and behavior? . . . The theory to be presented here takes the empiricist or "connectionist" position with regard to these questions.

(Rosenblatt, 1958: 386–7)

About ten years after McCulloch and Pitts published the results of their studies, Frank Rosenblatt and his group began studying a device called the "perceptron," which has been described as "a McCulloch-Pitts network with modifiable connections."[11] Rosenblatt's original introduction of the perceptron (a "hypothetical nervous system or machine," 1958: 387) was in opposition to the "digital computer" view, according to which "storage of sensory information is in the form of coded representations" (1958: 386). Rosenblatt grants that "the hypothesis is appealing in its simplicity and ready intelligibility" (ibid.), but it has led to: "a profusion of brain models which amount simply to logical contrivances for performing particular algorithms" (ibid.).[12] Rosenblatt continues: "The models which have been produced all fail in some important respects (absence of equipotentiality, lack of neuroeconomy, excessive specificity of connections and synchronization requirements, unrealistic specificity of stimuli sufficient for cell firing, postulation of variables or functional features with no known neurological correlates, etc.) to correspond to a biological system" (1958: 388). This reads like a contemporary list of the "lures of connectionism," as we will see. According to Rosenblatt, no fine-tuning of the computer model will correct these problems: "a difference in principle is clearly indicated" (ibid.). What was needed was an alternative to the "network analysts," an alternative which would provide a language: "for the mathematical analysis of events in systems where only the gross organization can be characterized, and the precise structure is unknown" (1958: 387–8). To this end Rosenblatt lists the assumptions on which he modeled his perceptron:

1   The physical connections of the nervous system which are involved in learning and recognition are not identical from one organism to another.
2   The original system of connected cells is capable of certain amount of plasticity.
3   Through exposure to a large sample of stimuli, those which are most "similar" (in some sense which must be defined in terms of the particular physical system) will tend to form pathways to the same sets of

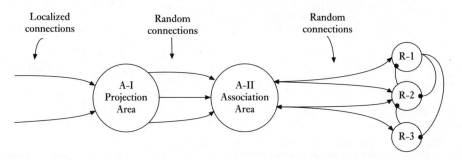

Figure 4.6 Organization of the original perceptron (from Rosenblatt, 1958: 389, figure 3)

responding cells. Those which are markedly "dissimilar" will tend to develop connections to different sets of responding cells.

4   The application of positive and/or negative reinforcement . . . may facilitate or hinder whatever formation of connections is currently in progress.

5   *Similarity* in such a system is represented at some level of the nervous system by a tendency of similar stimuli to activate the same sets of cells.

(1958: 388–9)

Most of these assumptions are present in current connectionist systems, though for connectionists talk of "plasticity" and "developing connections" is interpreted functionally, in terms of connection strength changes, not in terms of evolving hardware.

The organization of a perceptron

Rosenblatt (1958) outlines two main perceptron architectures: the first with three layers of connections and four layers of units, the other with two layers of connections and three layers of units. He concentrates his attention on the simpler one.[13] The four-layer (units) perceptron includes a Retina, an A-I Projection Area, an A-II Association Area, and a set of Responses. The first layer of connections is localized, the second and third are random (see figures 4.6 and 4.7).

There are five basic rules of organization of the perceptron (here somewhat simplified):

1   Stimuli impinge on the retina and it responds in an all–or–nothing fashion.

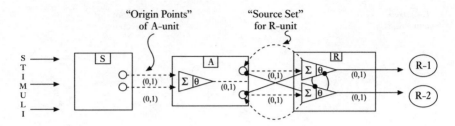

Figure 4.7   Organization of a three-layer (by units) perceptron

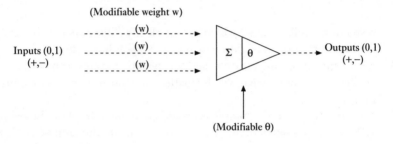

Figure 4.8   A Rosenblatt neuron

2 Impulses are transmitted to sets of cells (A-units) in A-I and A-II. (The A-I cells may be omitted.)
   The set of retinal points transmitting impulses to a particular A-unit will be called the *origin points* of that A-unit. These origin points may be either excitatory or inhibitory. If the sum of excitatory and inhibitory impulses is equal to or greater than threshold, then the A-unit fires on an all-or-nothing basis (see figure 4.8).[14]

3 Between the projection area and the association area connections are assumed to be random.

4 The responses are cells that respond in much the same fashion as A-units. The arrows indicate that up to A-II transmission is forward, but between A-II and the responses there is feedback. Freedback can in principle be either excitatory to its own source-set, or inhibitory to the complement of its own source-set. The models investigated typically used the second pattern. The responses of such a system are mutually exclusive in that if R-1 occurs it will inhibit R-2 and its source set, and vice versa.

5 For learning to take place it must be possible to modify the A-units or their connections in such a way that stimuli of one class will tend

to evoke a stronger impulse in the R-1 source set than in the R-2 source set.

The Mark I perceptron

As with other neuro-logical models, a perceptron could be studied by being simulated on a digital computer or by actually being built. The Mark I perceptron was an actual machine residing in the Cornell University Aeronautical Laboratory. Its retina was a grid of 20×20 photocells to which pictures were presented for classification. These were connected randomly (with up to a ratio of 1 photocell to 40 association units) to 512 association units, and these were connected to 8 binary response units which responded with +1 or −1. The Mark I learned a number of different categorizations, and was able to generalize in interesting ways (see Block, 1962, and references therein).

Training an elementary perceptron: the "perceptron convergence procedure"

Imagine we are training a perceptron to sort pictures of males (M) and pictures of females (F). If we give it an F and it responds with an F, then ignore the weights on the connected A-units and R-units. If we give it an M and it responds with an M, do the same. If we give it an F and it responds with an M, change the weights on the active connected A-units and R-units (lowered if the response should have been −1, raised if the response should have been +1). If we give it an M and it responds with an F, do the same (see Block, 1962: 144).

Perceptron convergence theorem (simplified): If F and M are linearly separable categories (see below), then there is an elementary perceptron that given enough training will learn to discriminate those categories (see Block, 1962: 145, theorem 9).

Evaluation and conclusions

Rosenblatt analyzed the behavior of a number of different perceptrons. The main conclusions of interest to us include:

1   In an *undifferentiated*, random environment, a perceptron can learn to associate specific responses to specific stimuli, but the probability of a

correct response diminishes as the number of learned stimuli increases, and generalization is impossible.

2   In a *differentiated* environment, where each response is associated with a distinct class of similar stimuli, the probability of a correct response increases with the number of association cells, and the probability that a previously unseen stimulus will be correctly categorized follows the same pattern.

3   The memory of the perceptron is *distributed*, in the sense that any association may make use of a large proportion of the cells in the system, and the removal of a portion of the association system would not have an appreciable effect on the performance of any one discrimination or association, but would begin to show up as a general deficit in *all* learned associations. (1962: 405)

Conclusion

We see in Rosenblatt's work some important themes that recur in contemporary connectionism:

1   a critique of digital computational approaches in terms of biological implausibility;
2   neurally inspired architecture;
3   emphasis on statistical vs. logical methods;
4   emphasis on pattern recognition and learning;
5   use of parallel processing and distributed representations.

In the early 1980s connectionists found ways around some of the limitations of simple perceptrons, and network studies now flourish – though Minsky and Papert suspect that their original doubts about the limitations of perceptrons carries over, with minor modifications, to current work (see the Epilogue: The New Connectionism, to the 1988 edition of their 1969 book). We will return to this question after an introduction to connectionist machines in chapter 11.

4.4   Linear Separability and XOR: McCulloch and Pitts Nets and Perceptrons

The connective XOR and its negation illustrate a simple but important lesson concerning the computational power of nets of neuron-like units organized as (elementary) perceptrons.

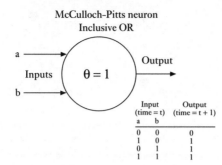

Figure 4.9 A simple M&P OR neuron (from Anderson, 1995: 49, figure 2.9; reproduced by permission of the MIT Press)

Linear separability

Imagine a unit with two inputs, P and Q, and a threshold such that if the sum of the inputs is over threshold, then the output is 1, otherwise it is 0 (as shown in figure 4.9). Suppose inputs are the output of some other units, so they too are either 1 or 0. Let's suppose that the threshold for the unit is such that it gives a 0 if both P and Q are 0, but it gives a 1 otherwise (this is the rule for OR):

P	OR	Q
1	1	1
0	1	1
1	1	1
0	0	0

We can let each input line be a "dimension" and since there are here two input lines we have two dimensions, and the possible inputs to our OR-unit can be diagrammed in a two-dimensional plane . On this we plot the conditions under which a certain truth function of x, y, is off (0) or on (1), where x = the first value and y = the second. We plot OR as in figure 4.10. In this graph we can draw a straight line separating the off states (0) from the on states (1) (figure 4.11). This shows that OR is linearly separable. It can be shown that 14 of the 16 elementary truth functions are also linearly separable – only XOR and its negation (see below) are not.

XOR

The two truth functions that are not linearly separable are exclusive "or" (XOR) and its negation (see figure 4.12). That XOR and its negation are not

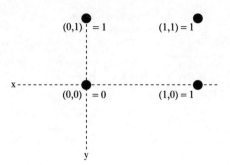

Figure 4.10   Cartesian coordinates for OR

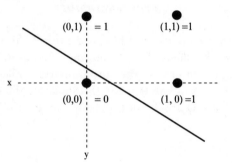

Figure 4.11   OR is linearly separable

P	Q	P XOR Q	NOT (P XOR Q)
1	1	0	1
1	0	1	0
0	1	1	0
0	0	0	1

Figure 4.12   Truth tables for XOR and its negation

linearly separable can be seen from its graph (figure 4.13). It takes two lines to separate the on states (1) from the off states (0). This shows that XOR is not linearly separable. The same is obviously true for the negation of XOR, since its values are represented simply by exchanging 0s for 1s in the graph.

This idea of linear separability can be generalized to more than two input units (more than two dimensions). For instance, we might have a unit con-

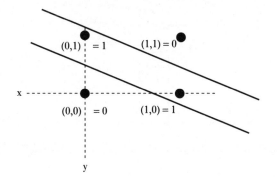

Figure 4.13 XOR is not linearly separable

nected to three input lines: P, Q, R. To diagram this we would need a three-dimensional space, such as a cube. But a line would not divide it into two regions, one on, one off. Rather, we need a plane to do this. With more than three input lines most people's spatial intuitions abandon them, but the idea is the same. The surface that separates such higher-dimensional spaces is called a "hyperplane." More exactly, the equation for this "hyperplane" just is: *the points in this space where the sum of the product of synaptic weights times inputs equals the threshold*. If a hyperplane exists for a space of inputs, then that category of inputs is linearly separable, and can in principle be learned.

McCulloch and Pitts nets and XOR

Single McCulloch and Pitts *units* can compute 14 of the 16 possible truth functions of two inputs. The two they cannot compute are exclusive "or" (XOR) and its negation. However, a McCulloch and Pitts *net* can compute XOR (and its negation) by simply conjoining an AND unit to two input units such that the AND unit turns the system off if and only if both of the input units are on.

Perceptrons and XOR

We noted earlier that perceptrons as Rosenblatt conceived them are specially structured M&P nets with one layer of modifiable connections, and that devices with this structure satisfied the perceptron convergence theorem (PCT). Since a M&P network can compute XOR, can't a perceptron compute

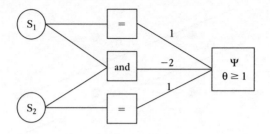

Figure 4.14   A "perceptron" that computes XOR (from Quinlan, 1991: 33, figure 1.11)

it? Certainly some networks that have been called "perceptrons" can, as in figure 4.14 (where the threshold on ψ is 1). Note the weights that the network uses: <1, 1, –2>. Could these be learned by the perceptron training procedure? And if they could, would XOR be an example of a linearly inseparable function learnable by the perceptron training procedure? (And if not, is XOR an example of a function a perceptron can compute, but not learn how to compute?)

The answer is that yes, this perceptron could learn <1, 1, –2>, and so it would be an example of a linearly inseparable function learnable by the perceptron training procedure. The trick is that we have made the first layer of connections unmodifiable *and we have tacitly set them uniformly by hand at 1 each*: <1, 1, 1, 1>. These values have not been learned by the perceptron training procedure, and when combined with the weights on the modifiable layer of connections, they cannot be guaranteed to be learned by that procedure. Recall that the perceptron convergence theorem states that if the function is linearly separable, then with enough training a perceptron is guaranteed to learn it. We now see that the converse has the form: if the data are *not* linearly separable, then there is *no guarantee* that enough training will eventuate in the perceptron learning them. The perceptron might hit on a solution, as with XOR above, but there is no guarantee that it will.

Furthermore, this perceptron, though it may learn XOR with the set of weights <1, 1, 1, 1> on the unmodifiable layer, will not be able to learn a function requiring the first layer *not* to be weighted <1, 1, 1, 1>. That is, a function requiring the first layer to take on some other values than uniform 1s will not be representable by this perceptron, and not learnable via the training procedure. If we were to go in and change these weights by hand so that the perceptron could learn the correct weights on the modifiable layer, then there would be some other function (perhaps XOR) that the perceptron could not learn.

4.5   Simple Detector Semantics

The idea behind "simple detector semantics," as we will call it, is that a neural process (or more generally any "network") is about what turns it on – the neural activity indicates the presence of or *detects* the features that the neurons are tuned to: the unit or set of units is *on*[15] when the assigned feature (an object, property, or state of affairs in the environment) is present, the unit is *off* otherwise. The slogan is:

(SDS)   Units or sets of units (neurons or sets of neurons) represent what turns them on.

This conception goes by many names including "indicator," "covariation," "causal," and "informational" theories of representation. It has been inspired in part by results in single-fiber and single-cell recordings of neurons. This idea was driven home forcefully for the first time by Lettvin et al. in their classic paper "What the frog's eye tells the frog's brain."

Lettvin, Maturana, McCulloch, and Pitts, *"What the frog's eye tells the frog's brain"*

To understand what the frog's eye tells the frog's brain it is important to understand some characteristics of the frog.

The frog

1   The frog hunts by vision.
2   Its eyes do not move, as ours do, to follow the prey, its body moves, so its eyes are actively stabilized, it has no fovea or region of greater acuity in vision.
3   It also has only a single visual system, retina to colliculus, not a double one such as ours.
4   It does not see, or is not concerned with, the detail of stationary parts of the world around it.
5   It will starve to death surrounded by food if it is not moving.
6   It will leap to capture any object the size of an insect or worm, provided it moves like one; hence it is easily fooled.
7   It escapes danger by means of the strategy of leaping to where it is darker.   (Lettvin et al., 1959: 231)

The detectors

The frog's eye-to-brain pathways contain four fiber groups which are concentric in their receptive fields. Moving from the center of the array outwards one encounters:

1   The *contrast detector* which tells, in the smallest area of all, of the presence of a sharp boundary, moving or still, with much or little contrast.

2   The *convexity detector* which tells, in a somewhat larger area, whether or not the object has a curved boundary, if it is darker than the background and moving on it; it remembers the object when it has stopped, providing the boundary lies totally with that area and is sharp; it shows most activity if the enclosed object moves intermittently with respect to a background. The memory of the object is abolished if a shadow obscures the object for a moment.

3   The *moving edge detector* which tells whether or not there is a moving boundary in a yet larger area within the field.

4   The *dimming detector* which tells how much dimming occurs in the largest area, weighted by distance from the center and by how fast it happens.

The "bug detector"

The convexity detector (fiber 2 above) turns out to have some useful features: "Such a fiber [fiber 2] responds best when a dark object, smaller than a receptive field, enters that field, stops, and moves about intermittently thereafter. The response is not affected if the lighting changes or if the background (say a picture of grass and flowers) is moving, and is not there if only the background, moving or still, is in the field. Could one better describe a system for *detecting an accessible bug*?" (1959: 253–4; emphasis added). Lettvin et al. give the semantics of this detector as follows: "What, then, does a particular fiber in the optic nerve measure? We have considered it to be how much *there is in a stimulus of that quality which excites the fiber maximally, naming that quality*" (1959: 253; emphasis added). This last passage tells us that the authors take the firing of the detector to "name" a particular stimulus quality; that is, *the firing of the detector represents the presence of that stimulus quality*. The first passage suggests that, in its natural environment at least, the stimulus quality detected is had mostly by accessible bugs. Likewise, we might discover that certain neurons in the cat's visual cortex are on when exposed to a bar of light forming a horizontal line, whereas other neurons are on when exposed to a bar of light forming a vertical line or specific angles in between. We might say the cat has oriented "edge detectors."[16] Various other detectors have been reported in the literature,[17] though contrary evidence has emerged as well.[18]

Problems with simple detector semantics

The firing of "fiber 2" is said to *signal the presence of bugs because bugs turn it on*. Such a simple idea is bound to have problems, and this one is no exception. Here we focus on problems arising specifically out of the underscored idea.

The right-cause or depth problem

In the course of causing fiber 2 to fire, photons have been emitted from the sun, bounced off particles in the atmosphere, bounced off grass and trees, bounced off a bug only to be absorbed in a frog's retina and transformed into electrical impulses which give rise to other electrical impulses which eventually cause fiber 2 to fire. Question: why say that it is (just) the bug that the firing of fiber 2 detects, when there are all of these *other causal* components? Why isn't fiber 2 detecting the retina, or the tree or the sun? What determines the correct *depth* of the causal chain?

The spread or qua problem

If we want to identify the relevant cause of the fiber's firing as a *bug*, what justifies favoring that categorization? After all, the piece of matter reflecting the light can also correctly be categorized in a whole variety (or "spread") of other ways: *winged thing, potential pest at picnics, potential victim of insect spray, small dark thing, erratically moving blob 93 million miles from the sun*, and so forth. Why say that the firing picks its target out qua (as a) bug, and not qua (as) any of these other candidates? These two problems can be illustrated as in figure 4.15.

The misrepresentation or disjunction problem

A third problem is the misrepresentation problem: how is misrepresentation possible? (This problem was made famous by Fodor under the label the "disjunction problem."[19]) Applied to (SDS) and the frog it goes like this: although the frog's fiber 2 fires in the presence of a (moving) bug, it also fires in the presence of a fly-sized magnet: "A delightful exhibit uses a large color photo-

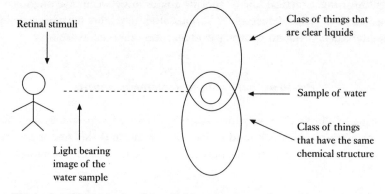

Retinal stimuli

Class of things that
are clear liquids

Sample of water

Class of things
that have the same
chemical structure

Light bearing
image of the
water sample

The depth problem: why does "water" pick out a property of something at a certain
point, at a certain "depth," in the causal chain that ends up with our using the word
"water"? The spread problem: why does "water" pick out from the very many
properties of water the property that it does?

Figure 4.15   The depth problem and the spread problem (from Braddon-Mitchell and
Jackson, 1996: 69, figure 3; reproduced by permission of the publisher)

graph of the natural habitat of a frog from a frog's-eye view, flowers and grass.
We can move this photograph through the receptive field of such a fiber, waving
it around at a 7-inch distance: there is no response. If we perch with a magnet
a fly-sized object 1 degree large on part of the picture seen by the receptive
field and move only the object, we get an excellent response. If the object is
fixed to the picture in about the same place and the whole moved about, then
there is none" (1959: 242–3). Notice what has happened. The frog story
originally had two components: first, there is our little semantic theory (SDS)
which says that the firing of fiber 2 represents what turns it on; second, there
is the description of that fiber as a "bug detector." But then we just saw that
fiber 2 also responds to an erratically moving magnet (MM). Here is the
problem. Fiber 2 is described as a "bug detector," but it also responds to MMs.
So by (SDS) it is *also* an MM detector. So what it detects is either a bug OR
a magnet – it is a bug-OR-magnet detector. However, if it is (really) a bug-OR-
magnet detector, then it *correctly* represents the MM as a bug-OR-MM. It does
not misrepresent the MM as a bug. This makes *misrepresentation impossible*.
However, misrepresentation *is* possible, so 1 or 2 must be false. In short, a
potential case of misrepresentation is converted by the theory (SDS) into the
correct representation of a disjunction, since the fiber fires when exposed to a
bug or a magnet. In fact, there is no reason *in the story so far* to call fiber 2 a
"bug detector" (that also misdetects magnets) rather than a "magnet detector"
(that also misdetects bugs).

What are we to do? We could (1) claim that Lettvin et al. misdescribed the semantics of fiber 2 in calling it a bug detector – rather it is a *small-dark-erratically moving-blob* detector – notice that the way it is first introduced is as a "convexity" detector (which isn't accurate either). In which case MMs are not misrepresented at all and there is no problem. Or we could (2) modify (SDS) by adding something about the "natural environment" of the frog:

(SDS-NE)   Units or sets of units (neurons or sets of neurons) represent what turns them on, in the natural environment of the system.

The idea is that fiber 2 evolved to help the frog survive by locating food in an environment replete with bugs (not MMs). In either case, however, we have to modify the original story.

Notes

1   One "cardinal assumption" of then current neuroscience not reflected in this list is that signal velocities can vary with diameter of the axon.
2   The "all-or-none" character of the action potential which dominated M&P's discussion has since (due to more sophisticated recording techniques) been seen to be accompanied by graded activity spread out over many milliseconds. These "cardinal assumptions" also did not include the role of neurotransmitters in this activity.
3   In effect each neuron has an associated threshold which must be met or exceeded in order to fire.
4   In effect, inputs all have the same strength or "weight."
5   In effect, there is a refractory period during which a neuron cannot fire.
6   Note that the unit does not sum excitatory and inhibitory inputs, as do later formal neurons in perceptrons and (most) connectionist networks.
7   The system was based on the work of Whitehead and Russell (1925) and Carnap (1937).
8   For instance, Minsky (1967: 36): "The original McCulloch-Pitts paper is recommended not so much for its notation as for its content, philosophical as well as technical."
9   For instance, McCulloch and Pitts' diagrams were used by von Neumann in his EDVAC report of 1945 – whereof more later.
10   In these diagrams two filled circles are required to excite a neuron; contrast AND with OR. In other words, the threshold is implicitly 2.
11   See Cowan and Sharp (1988).
12   Here Rosenblatt mentions Minsky – among others. Perhaps reading of one's work as a "logical contrivance" motivated some of Minsky's subsequent comments.
13   Here we are counting actual layers of connections, not just modifiable layers.

14 A Rosenblatt neuron first sums its weighted inputs, then, if that sum is equal to or above threshold, it outputs. If the sum does not equal or exceed threshold it is quiet.

15 Or it may simply be significantly more active. We will mean by "on": *on (vs. off) or significantly more active; mutatis mutandis* for "off."

16 See Hubel and Wiesel (1979).

17 See Gross et al. (1972) for "hand detectors" in macaques.

18 See Stone (1972).

19 See Fodor (1984, 1987). Cummins (1989, ch. 5) calls this the "misrepresentation problem." We follow Cummins here.

Study questions

McCulloch and Pitts (M&P)

What five assumptions about the nervous system did M&P make for their formalization?

How accurate were each of these assumptions relative to the neuron at mid-century?

What "character" of nervous activity allows propositional logic to apply to it?

What two basic principles connect neural networks with formal systems?

Draw a M&P unit for: delay, and, or.

What is the computational power of M&P networks, when supplemented with memory?

What is the historical importance of the M&P article?

What three potential problems for M&P's psychological conclusions were mentioned in the lecture?

Rosenblatt: perceptrons

What were Rosenblatt's five complaints against "computational" models?

What five assumptions about the nervous system were built into the perceptron?

Original perceptron

How was the original perceptron organized: what were its layers of units, what were the connections between layers of units?

Elementary (simple) perceptron

How was the elementary (simple) perceptron organized: what were its layers of units, what were the connections between layers of units?

How many layers of modifiable connections are there?

Are response units in perceptrons mutually inhibitory?

Between what layers is there just feedforward?

Between what layers is there feedback?

In what sense is a perceptron's memory "distributed"?

In what sense is a perceptron's processing "parallel"?

How, in general, does one train a perceptron?

What are three conclusions Rosenblatt draws from his experiments with perceptrons?

What five themes of contemporary connectionism can be found in Rosenblatt's discussion?

Linear separability and XOR: McCulloch and Pitts nets and perceptrons

What is a linearly separable function?

Show that XOR is not a linearly separable function.

Can a (simple) perceptron compute XOR?

Can a (simple) perceptron learn XOR?

Can a (simple) perceptron learn only functions that are linearly separable?

What does the perceptron convergence theorem say?

Can a (simple) perceptron compute and learn to compute a function that the perceptron convergence theorem does not guarantee it can learn?

Simple detector semantics (what the frog's eye tells the frog's brain)

What is "simple detector semantics"?

What four detectors were discovered in the frog; i.e. what did each do?

What is the structure of the receptive fields for the four detectors discovered in the frog?

Which was called a "bug" detector and why?

Why call it a "bug detector" if, as Lettvin et al. showed, a frog will attempt to eat an appropriately moving *magnet*?

What is the "misrepresentation (or 'disjunction') problem"?

How does it arise for frogs?

Suggested reading

General

The best collection of writings on this period is Anderson and Rosenfeld (1988), which contains a wealth of articles on related matters as well as helpful introductions. A useful overview discussion of McCulloch and Pitts networks, perceptrons, and XOR can be found in chapter 1 of Quinlan (1991). This chapter has the additional advantage of relating these topics to both associationism and connectionism. Another good short survey discussion is Cowan and Sharp (1988). A concise recent survey of this period can be found in McLeod et al. (1998). Anderson and Rosenfeld (1998) contains fascinating interviews with some of the pioneers of neural modeling.

McCulloch and Pitts

Minsky (1967), chapter 3, contains a clear formal discussion of McCulloch and Pitts networks, and most of the surveys listed above discuss M&P networks.

Perceptrons

In addition to the surveys listed above there are numerous short discussions of perceptrons in the literature. See, for instance, Wasserman (1989), chapter 2, and Caudill and Butler (1993), chapter 3. Unfortunately, they are marred as a group by different characterizations of the notion of a perceptron. It is useful to go back and look at Rosenblatt's own discussion (1962). Block (1962), sections 1–8, provides a lucid introduction to perceptrons as neurally inspired computational devices. A good general discussion of perceptron learning can be found in Nilsson (1965/90).

Part II

The Digital Computational Theory of Mind

Introduction

The principal subject of Part II is the *digital computational theory of mind* (DCTM). We view this theory as one of two special cases of the more generic *computational theory of mind* (CTM). (The other special case, the *connectionist* computational theory of mind (CCTM) will be investigated in Part III). The computational theory of mind also is itself profitably viewed as a special case of the older *representation theory of mind* (RTM):

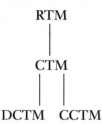

Our approach will be semi-historical. The RTM goes back at least to the British empiricists Locke and Hume (see chapter 1), but the CTM seems to have emerged only in the middle of this century with the invention of the modern digital computer, even though general purpose programmable "calculating machines" go back at least to Babbage in the middle of the nineteenth century. The idea that digital computers can be programmed to think or display some intelligence is usually credited to Alan Turing, though it is not as clear that he also championed the idea that human thinking or intelligence is a case of digital computation. The idea that human cognition might be a species of computation is natural if one simultaneously holds that (1) minds mentally manipulate mental representations, and (2) digital computers are algorithmic symbol manipulators.

Our strategy in Part II is to first introduce the reader to some elements of digital computation (which is relevant to cognitive science) without bringing in cognitive modeling. If computers algorithmically manipulate symbols, then we can ask after the *manipulation* aspect of computers, and the *symbol* aspect of computers. This is what we do. We first (chapter 5) illustrate digital modeling with the historically important demonstration project SHRDLU. We then (chapter 6) survey some digital architectures that were influential for different reasons: Turing machines, von Neumann machines, production systems, and Pandemonium. We taxonomize these architectures along dimensions of memory and control. Next (chapter 7) we survey the strengths and weaknesses of three popular symbol schemes: logic (predicate calculus), semantic networks, and frames/scripts. Then, with this digital computational material in place, we turn to formulating (chapter 8) and criticizing (chapter 9) the concept of mind inspired by this computational story.

Terminological note   We are using the word "digital" as a name for a certain style of theorizing about the mind, and we make no attempt to define it exactly (all of the many attempts have failed). Others prefer to call this style "symbolic," "classical," and even "rule-based." None of these is completely adequate. It is best not to fasten on the label, but to look at the important features of the machines so labeled. In this respect "digital" at least has the virtue that the kinds of machines that inspired these models during the period 1960–80 were routinely called "digital" computers.

5

A Sample Artificial Intelligence Model: SHRDLU

5.1 Introduction

Early natural language processing programs such as ELIZA (who dispenses therapy by way of a keyboard and monitor) gave the appearance of intelligence by exploiting a set of programming tricks that used key-words to trigger canned responses and turned "patient's" statements into questions. This could, on occasion, be very persuasive. For instance, there is one recorded conversation where an employee (VP) of a computer company got on line with ELIZA without knowing it (see Boden, 1977: 96):

VP: Do you think that I can use the computer this morning?
ELIZA: Why do you ask?
VP: I might be able to make some additional telcomp sales.
ELIZA: Why aren't you sure?
VP: My prospective customers have never seen a demonstration of the system.
ELIZA: Does this mean very much to you?
VP: Of course it does.
ELIZA: You seem very positive about that.
VP: This is ridiculous.
ELIZA: What do you mean this is ridiculous?
VP: Is there any reason why I can't use the computer now?
ELIZA: Tell me more about your prospective customers.
VP: Please dial me up on 491-1850.

When VP phoned a sleeping colleague, he got the following dialogue:

VP: Why are you being so snotty to me?
Colleague: What do you mean why am I being snotty to you?

Who says people don't talk like ELIZA? Still, despite ELIZA's seductive appeal (one secretary, who knew ELIZA was a computer program, still asked others

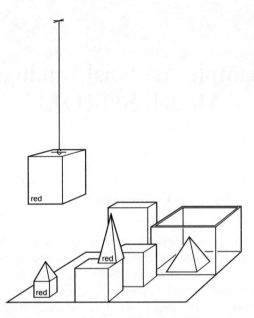

Figure 5.1 "Pick up a big red block" (from Winograd, 1972: 8, figure 2; reproduced by permission of Academic Press)

to leave the room while they chatted) there was nothing going on behind the scene: no reasoning, no planning, no semantic (meaning) analysis, no conversational strategies, no awareness of the environment, no knowledge, etc.

Terry Winograd's 1971 MIT doctoral dissertation appeared to substantially change all that. SHRDLU[1] was designed to "understand" (the scare-quotes are Winograd's) language in a limited domain: a micro-world of colored blocks, colored pyramids, and a box – all on a table top. SHRDLU provides a syntactic and semantic analysis of questions, statements, and commands; it reasons about this blocks world and it plans movements and responses in accordance with conversational strategies and motives.

5.2   SHRDLU Dialogue

As the following dialogue[2] between Winograd and SHRDLU illustrates, it seems to have been remarkably effective. Blocks world starts as in figure 5.1. The lines in lower case were typed in by Winograd, and the upper case lines are the computer's response. Other lines are comments describing some of the features being exhibited. The responses took about 10 seconds.

1   pick up a big red block.
    OK.

The system answers "OK" when it carries out a command. In order to pick up the red block, it had to clear it off by finding a space for the green one and moving the green one away.

2   grasp the pyramid.
    I DON'T UNDERSTAND WHICH PYRAMID YOU MEAN.

There are three pyramids in the scene, so the program does nothing.

3   find a block which is taller than the one you are holding and put it into the box.

The system has to figure out what is meant by "one" and "it," as well as using deduction to decide which block it is holding.

BY "IT," I ASSUME YOU MEAN THE BLOCK WHICH IS TALLER THAN THE ONE I AM HOLDING.

Printed out to keep us informed.

OK.

The hand has to set down the red block to pick up the taller blue one.

4   what does the box contain?
    THE BLUE PYRAMID AND THE BLUE BLOCK.
5   what is the pyramid supported by?

Earlier the system responded to "the pyramid" by saying "I don't understand which pyramid you mean." Now, it assumes that we mean the one just mentioned.

THE BOX.
6   how many blocks are not in the box?

Negatives such as "not" and "no" are handled whether they appear in clauses or noun groups (such as "no boxes").

FOUR OF THEM.
7   is at least one of them narrower than the one which I told you to pick up?

The phrase "at least one of them" must be analyzed to refer back to the previous question, and "the one which . . ." must also refer to blocks. Noun groups can have complicated numbers such as "at least one," "more than three," "exactly seven," etc. The memory of past events is used to deduce which block is "the one which I told you to pick up." Notice the complicated syntactic structure in which "the one" is actually the object of a clause embedded two levels deeper.

YES, THE RED CUBE.
8   is it supported?

Passives can be used without a "by . . ." phrase.

YES, BY THE TABLE.
9   can the table pick up blocks?
NO.

The semantic rules make this a nonsensical question which therefore must be false.

10   can a pyramid be supported by a block?
YES.

The deductive system finds an actual example, so it knows this is possible.

11   can a pyramid support a pyramid?
I DON'T KNOW.

The question makes sense, but there is no example in the scene, so there is no easy way to tell without being able to examine the robot's programs.

12   stack up two pyramids.
I CAN'T.

The robot tries and fails.

13   the blue pyramid is mine.
I UNDERSTAND.

This data is added to the database.

14   I own blocks which are not red, but I don't own anything which supports a pyramid.
I UNDERSTAND.

Two new theorems are created for proving things about "owning."

15   do I own the box?
NO.

The box supports whatever it contains, including a pyramid.

16   do I own anything in the box?
YES, TWO THINGS: THE BLUE BLOCK AND THE BLUE PYRAMID.
17   will you please stack up both of the red blocks and either a green cube or a pyramid?
OK.

Logical connectives such as "and," "or," "either," etc. are handled in both the grammar and semantics. A command is executed even if it looks like a question. The command is carried out by the following series of steps: it puts a green cube on the large red block (note that it chooses the green cube with nothing on it), then removes the small pyramid from the little red cube, so that it can use that cube to complete the stack as specified. . . .

18   which cube is sitting on the table?
THE LARGE GREEN ONE WHICH SUPPORTS THE RED PYRAMID.

Ordinarily the system would be satisfied with calling this "a big green cube," but since we asked "which cube" it has to be more specific in naming it. The use of substitute nouns (such as "one" and pronouns in answers makes the discourse more natural.

19   is there a large block behind a pyramid?
YES, THREE OF THEM: A LARGE RED ONE, A LARGE GREEN CUBE AND THE BLUE ONE.
20   put a small one on to the green cube which supports a pyramid.

"A small one" must contrast with the earlier phrase "a large block," so this means "a small block."

　　OK.
21　put the littlest pyramid on top of it.

Words like "littlest" are not in the dictionary but are interpreted from the root forms like "little."

　　OK.
22　how many things are on top of green cubes?
　　I'M NOT SURE WHAT YOU MEAN BY "ON TOP OF" IN THE
　　PHRASE "ON TOP OF GREEN CUBES."
　　DO YOU MEAN:
　　　1 – DIRECTLY ON THE SURFACE
　　　2 – ANYWHERE ON TOP OF?

When there are several interpretations and none is clearly better, the system has to ask the user for more information. The paraphrases were included with the dictionary definitions of "on," and the request for more information occurs automatically when the heuristics for resolving ambiguities aren't sufficient. A request like this can also occur when the meaning of a pronoun such as "it" or "they" is unclear.

{22a　I mean}2.
　　THREE OF THEM.
23　had you touched any pyramid before you put the green one on the
　　little cube?
　　YES, THE GREEN ONE.

The system deduces from its memory what event is being referred to, and can relate other events to it in time. The analysis includes complex tenses of verb groups, and there are special facilities for keeping track of the various forms of irregular verbs like "have."

24　when did you pick it up?
　　WHILE I WAS STACKING UP THE RED CUBE, A LARGE RED
　　BLOCK AND A LARGE GREEN CUBE.

A time is described by naming the main goal which was being worked on.

25   why?

The system remembers immediately previous sentences to understand questions like this and the following ones.

TO GET RID OF IT.

By keeping track of selected parts of the original subgoal tree, the system has some understanding of its own motives.

26   why did you do that?
     TO CLEAN OFF THE RED CUBE.

"That" refers to the action mentioned in the answer.

27   why did you clear off that cube?

Here, "that" means the one just referred to.

     TO PUT IT ON A LARGE GREEN CUBE.
28   why did you do that?
     TO STACK UP THE RED CUBE, A LARGE RED BLOCK, AND A LARGE GREEN CUBE.
29   why did you do that?
     BECAUSE YOU ASKED ME TO.

It remembers what it did, not how the request was worded.

30   how did you do it?

"It" refers to the action mentioned in the last question, rather than the answer.

     BY PUTTING A LARGE RED BLOCK ON THE TABLE; THEN LETTING GO OF IT; THEN PUTTING A LARGE GREEN CUBE ON IT; THEN LETTING GO OF THAT CUBE; THEN PUTTING THE RED CUBE ON THAT CUBE; THEN LETTING GO OF THAT CUBE.

This is a description of the top-level subgoals used to achieve the goal.

31   how many objects did you touch while you were doing it?

Time references can refer to a time span, using words like "while."

> FOUR OF THEM.

32   what did the red cube support before you started to clean it off?
     THE GREEN PYRAMID.

By remembering what has been moved, it is possible to deduce things about earlier states of the scene. We can use complex nestings of clauses like "before you started to clean it off."

33   there were five blocks to the left of the box them.

"Then" must refer to the time mentioned in the last sentence.

> NO, ONLY FOUR OF THEM: THE RED CUBE, TWO LARGE GREEN CUBES, AND A LARGE RED BLOCK.

Earlier in the dialogue, new information about "owning" was accepted at face value. But the system knows that it has complete information about the basic properties of objects, including location. It checks any statements about location or other such properties to see whether it agrees or disagrees.

34   put the blue pyramid on the block in the box.

This is syntactically ambiguous, but is understood without ambiguity since the parsing corresponding to "put the blue pyramid which is on the block in the box" does not make sense in the current scene, while "put the blue pyramid on the block which is in the box" does.

> OK.

35   is there anything which is bigger than every pyramid but is not as wide as the thing that supports it?

The system understands quantifiers such as "every," "any," "some," etc., and structures such as "bigger than," "as wide as," etc. Here "it" refers to a noun group within the same sentence but two levels up in the parsing tree.

> YES, THE BLUE BLOCK.

36   does a steeple {. . .}
     SORRY, I DON'T KNOW THE WORD "STEEPLE."

The system interrupts immediately when it sees a word it can't figure out.

37 a "steeple" is a stack which contains two green cubes and a pyramid.

The quote marks indicate that we are defining a new word.

I UNDERSTAND.

38 are there any steeples now?
NO.

The new definition is used as a description to recognize steeples.

39 build one.
OK.

The description given in the definition is enough to deduce a plan for building new objects as well as recognizing them. The word "one" means "a steeple," and the plan is carried out. First, one of the large green cubes is cleared off by removing the red cube and two pyramids. Then the two green cubes and the tall red pyramid are stacked up to fit the description.

40 call the biggest block "superblock."
OK.

We can also give objects names.

41 have you picked up superblock since we began?
YES.

42 why did you drop it?
BY "IT," I ASSUME YOU MEAN THE SUPERBLOCK. I CAN'T EXPLAIN A NONEXISTENT EVENT.

There is no record in memory of any block being dropped.

43 is there anything to the right of the red pyramid?
YES, FOUR THINGS: THE BOX, THE RED CUBE, THE BLUE PYRAMID, AND THE BLOCK NAMED SUPERBLOCK.

Once an object has a name, the name is used to help identify it in responses.

44 thank you.
YOU'RE WELCOME!

Idioms can be defined without modifying the grammar.

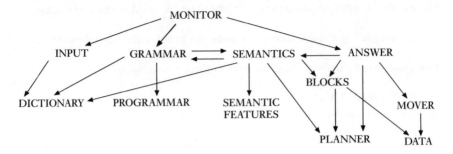

Figure 5.2   The organization of the system (from Winograd, 1972: 5, figure 1; reproduced by permission of Academic Press)

Note that SHRDLU: distinguishes statements, questions, and commands; uses knowledge of the table top; does syntactic and semantic analysis of the input; constructs and reports on its plans and uses conversational strategies (including using the presumed goals and intentions of the speaker); and uses general reasoning to respond appropriately.

5.3   The Program

SHRDLU consists of the twelve design components illustrated in figure 5.2. One of the major breakthroughs of Winograd's program was the way these components interacted. Each component can, with some restrictions, consult the others in an orderly way during the course of computation, and this in part accounts for the human-like way in which SHRDLU integrates goals and problem solving in obeying commands (see lines 1–3 of the dialogue above), integrating verbal information (see lines 13, 14 above), and answering questions (see lines 7–11, 15–29 above). SHRDLU responded within roughly 15–20 seconds (on 1972 hardware!) and the "robot" arm moved at about human speed. The important components for our purposes are: (1) the syntactic parser, (2) the set of semantic procedures, and (3) the cognitive-deductive system.

Syntax

Certain problems must be faced by syntax, such as assigning words to their proper parts of speech (noun, verb, adjective, etc.) and determining grammatical relations between words and phrases (subject, object, etc.). For instance, consider the different "him" in the sentences:

DEFINE program SENTENCE

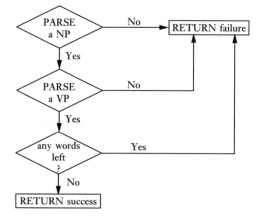

Figure 5.3   Sentence parser (from Winograd, 1972: 83, figure 23)

1   (a)   Arthur wants to see him ("him" does not = Arthur)
    (b)   Arthur wants someone to see him ("him" can = Arthur)

SHRDLU's syntax is an implementation of Halliday's (1970) "systemic grammar" in a special Lisp-based language called Programmar. A typical program for parsing a sentence might look like figure 5.3. Given a sentence such as:

2   The giraffe ate the apples and peaches

we would get an analysis like that in figure 5.4. The syntax does not operate automatically and completely; it can call a semantic routine during parsing, and either syntax or semantics can call on the cognitive-deductive system to help direct the parsing.

Semantics

One of the distinctive features of SHRDLU is its so-called "procedural semantics." The meaning of linguistic expression is represented by programs to do something, written in a micro-PLANNER version of PLANNER (see Hewitt, 1971): "One basic viewpoint underlying the model is that all language use can be thought of as a way of activating procedures within the hearer. We can think

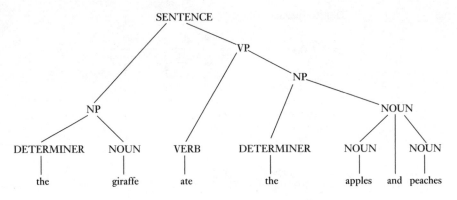

Figure 5.4 Parse of a sentence (from Winograd, 1972: 91, figure 27; figures 5.4–5.6 reproduced by permission of Academic Press)

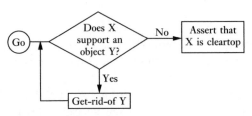

Figure 5.5 Procedural description for the concept CLEARTOP (from Winograd, 1973: 169, figure 4.5)

of any utterance as a program . . ." (Winograd, 1973: 170). For example, to "clear off" has as its semantics the program CLEARTOP (see figure 5.5). This idea was extended to whole sentences as well:

3 (a) Clear off the table (imperative)
  (b) Is the table cleared off (interrogative)
  (c) The table is cleared off (declarative)

Each sentence is converted into a set of PLANNER instructions: for direct physical action (command), for some information (question), for storage or modification of existing knowledge (statement). A phrase such as:

4 A red cube which supports a pyramid

would be represented in PLANNER as in figure 5.6.

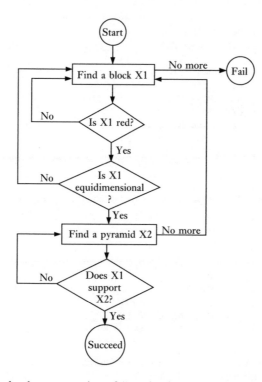

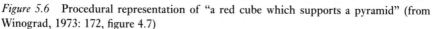

Figure 5.6 Procedural representation of "a red cube which supports a pyramid" (from Winograd, 1973: 172, figure 4.7)

Cognitive-deductive system

The database of SHRDLU consists of facts like those listed in figure 5.7. These sorts of facts, plus the procedures, are integrated with a general deductive system which tries to satisfy a given goal by setting up successive subgoals. The currently active goal stack looks like the one shown in figure 5.8.

5.4   Limitations

Winograd (1973) ends his discussion with some cautionary notes. He sees two basic ways in which SHRDLU might be inadequate as a model of human natural language processing. *First*, there is the way the process is directed: the syntax comes up with acceptable phrases and the semantics

```
(IS B1 BLOCK)
(IS B2 PYRAMID)
(AT B1 (LOCATION 100 100 0))
(SUPPORT B1 B2)
(CLEARTOP B2)
(MANIPULABLE B1)
(CONTAIN BOX1 B4)
(COLOR-OF B1 RED)
(SHAPE-OF B2 POINTED)
(IS BLUE COLOR)
(CAUSE EVENT27 EVENT29)
```

Figure 5.7   Typical data expressions (from Winograd, 1973: 168, box 4.1)

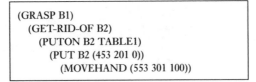

Figure 5.8   Currently active goal stack (from Winograd, 1973: 171, box 4.2; reproduced by permission of W. H. Freeman and Co.)

(or cognitive-deductive system) decides whether to continue along that line of parsing or not. But he thinks this is too hierarchical: "A language model able to implement the sort of 'heterachy' found in biological systems (like the coordination between different systems of an organism) will be much closer to a valid psychological theory" (1973: 184). *Second*, the model fails to deal with all the implications of viewing language "as a process of communication between two intelligent people" (1973: 184). For instance, certain interpretations of sentences will be favored because the hearer knows that the speaker shares general knowledge about the real world. Consider the reference of "it" in:

5 (a) I dropped a bottle of Coke on the table and *it* broke. (bottle or table)
   (b) Where's the broom: I dropped a bottle of Coke on the table and *it* broke. (preferred: bottle)
   (c) Where's the glue: I dropped a bottle of Coke on the table and *it* broke. (preferred: table)

If this capacity of humans is to be simulated in a program, lots of *commonsense knowledge* will have to be built into it.

Winograd later (1980: 215) noted that there were some "obvious problems" with the SHRDLU approach to natural language processing. For instance: *third*, the notion of word definition by program, even though it opened up possibilities beyond more traditional logical forms of definition, was still inadequate. Consider the geometrical forms that inhabit blocks world – a pyramid or a sphere is defined by its shape, not what one does with it. Also, a bachelor is defined in terms of his properties of being unmarried, adult, and male, not what one can do with him. In the face of these problems, Winograd himself turned to the more general and fundamental problem of devising a better system of knowledge representation (see Bobrow and Winograd, 1979).

The fields of artificial intelligence and cognitive science have also found SHRDLU inadequate in certain fundamental ways. For instance, *fourth*, SHRDLU doesn't really know very much about its own blocks world (color, ownership, etc.). And *fifth*, it is not clear at all how to "scale up" SHRDLU to include more knowledge, either of this micro-world, or of the world in general. *Sixth*, this is exacerbated by the fact that there was no learning aspect to SHRDLU, though later the STRIPS program (Fikes and Nilsson, 1971) explored this issue. And *seventh*, SHRDLU really did not know what it was talking about in the literal sense that its "world" was virtual. As Fodor (1980a) put it: "The device is precisely in the situation Descartes dreads: it is a mere computer which dreams it's a robot," and so the problem of dealing with and integrating information from the external world did not have to be faced. But to model us, that problem will have to be faced.

5.5   Historical Role of SHRDLU

In spite of all these limitations we should not lose sight of the fact that SHRDLU was a tour de force of programming showing how to integrate syntactic and semantic analysis with general knowledge. It showed that if the database was narrow enough the program could be made deep enough to display human-like interactions. This inspired expert systems research, such as MYCIN (Shortliff), that has produced serious contributions to the field of knowledge engineering.

Notes

1   According to a personal communication from Winograd to Boden (1977: 501), "One row of the keyboard of a standard linotype typesetting machine consists of

these letters, and typesetters often 'correct' a mistake by inserting them in a faulty line so that the proofreaders will easily spot that a mistake has been made. Bad proofreading may result in this deliberate gibberish being printed in the final text – a fact made much of in *MAD* magazine. Being an ex-devotee of *MAD*, Winograd picked this nonsense word as the name for his program." Hofstadter (1979: 628) repeats the same explanation. According to Waltz (1982: 120), "Winograd's program is called SHRDLU after the seventh through twelfth most frequent letters in English" – an opinion repeated by Gardner (1985: 158).

2   From Winograd (1972). It is slightly modified in Winograd (1973).

Study questions

How did ELIZA manage to give the appearance of intelligent conversation for short periods of time?

What are some examples of SHRDLU going beyond canned responses in dealing with language input?

What are some general features of SHRDLU's conversational abilities?

What five components does SHRDLU consist of? Say something about each.

What limitations did Winograd and the artificial intelligence (and cognitive-science) community decide SHRDLU had?

What was SHRDLU's historical role in artificial intelligence and cognitive science?

Suggested reading

SHRDLU

The basic work for understanding SHRDLU is Winograd (1972). A shorter version appears in Winograd (1973). Winograd (1977), lecture 2, places SHRDLU in perspective by looking at computer systems for knowledge representation and natural language understanding in general. Wilks (1977), lecture 3, does the same thing from a different point of view. Winograd (1980) contains a critical discussion of SHRDLU, and Winograd (1983) is an accessible and authoritative introduction to computer language processing. Barr, Cohen, and Feigenbaum (1981), chapter 4, survey natural language processing, as well as SHRDLU. Tennant (1981) surveys the field of natural language processing and chapter 5 discusses SHRDLU. A more recent semi-popular discussion of SHRDLU can be found in McTeal (1987). Kobes (1990) explores the implications of SHRDLU's virtual blocks world for central doctrines in current cognitive science.

General history of artificial intelligence

Augarten (1984) is a well-illustrated history of computation. For a readable chapter-length introductory survey of the history of artificial intelligence (AI) with special reference to cognitive science, see Gardner (1985), chapter 6. Minsky (1966) and Waltz (1982) are practitioners' surveys that are also accessible to the outsider (and interesting to compare for changes over 15 years). Barr, Cohen, and Feigenbaum (1981) surveys some major programs in AI up to about 1980. Boden (1977) takes a popular but philosophical approach, and McCorduck (1979) is a popular and enjoyable history, as is Crevier (1993). Dreyfus (1972/9) is AI's most (in)famous review and critique – the introduction to the revised edition brings us to about 1979. Copeland (1993b), chapters 1–5, reviews and critically assesses some major AI projects. Feigenbaum and Feldman (1963) is a historically important and influential anthology of early AI programs. The future history of AI (up to 2099!) is anticipated in Kurzweil (1999), which also contains many URLs for interesting and relevant webpages.

6

Architecture(s)

6.1 Introduction: Some Preliminary Concepts

This chapter introduces, illustrates, and taxonomizes typical digital machine organizations or "architectures." To say how a machine is organized is to say something about how information is stored and what determines how that information flows through the system. It is not to say either what the machine is made of (relays, vacuum tubes, transistors, etc.), nor is it to say what program the machine is running. It is rather like a design or blueprint for the machine that leaves these out, in the way that a blueprint for a building might leave out details of materials and occupants. But before turning to architectural matters there are two general important contrasts we must understand.

Algorithms/effective procedures vs. programs

To begin with, we will make a sharp distinction between an "algorithm" or "effective procedure," and a "program." The essence of an *algorithm* (or effective procedure) is that it is a series of steps for doing something that is guaranteed to get a result. More precisely, it is a finite sequence of well-defined steps, each of which takes only a finite amount of memory and time to complete, and which comes to an end on any finite input. A *program* is a finite list of instructions from some (programming) language. Programs usually are intended to encode an algorithm and we will henceforth assume that a program does that. Therefore, any device following a program will execute some finite number of instructions, each of which takes only finite memory and finite time, and it will eventually come to a halt (in practice, of course, it can, like your word processor, simply wait for further instructions). The relation of an algorithm to a program is similar to the relation between a number and a numeral: a single number can be designated by many numerals (e.g. arabic, roman, binary), just as a single algorithm can be coded into many programs from many languages (Basic, Pascal, Lisp, Prolog). Or better, the relation between a program and an algorithm is like the relation between a word (sound, shape) and its meaning – different words can have the same meaning (*cat*, *Katz*, *chat*) in different languages. Showing that a certain program is defective does not show that the encoded algorithm is defective, since the problem might be with the language being used to encode it.

Weak vs. strong equivalence

We will also distinguish between two ways in which algorithms (or machines running programs) can be said to be "equivalent." The "weak equivalence" of two algorithms is when they give the same output for each input. For instance, suppose two multiplying algorithms are each given the numbers 32 and 17 as input, and they both return 544 as output. If they returned the same output of all inputs the algorithms would be said to be *weakly equivalent*. But these two multiplying algorithms may have gone about their tasks in very different ways. The first algorithm may have multiplied 32 and 17 by ADDING 32 to itself 17 times – it could have been built out of just an adder and a counter. This is called multiplication by *successive addition*. The second algorithm, on the other hand, might have multiplied 32 and 17 more like we do:

```
  32
  17
 224
  32
 544
```

First take 2 and multiply it by 7, then carry the 1 over to the 3, then multiply the 3 by 7 and add the 1, giving 224. Then do the same with 32 and 1, giving 32. Then add 224 and 32 as above giving the result 544. Notice that on this method one multiplies 32 first by a part of 17, viz. 1, then one multiplies 32 by another part of 17, viz. 1, then one adds the two partial products together giving the whole product. Appropriately enough, this is called the *partial products* method. This method will given the same output as the successive addition method – they will be *weakly equivalent*, but they get their answers in different ways, and so they are not strongly equivalent. Two (or more) algorithms are *strongly equivalent* if they not only produce the same outputs for the same inputs (i.e. they are weakly equivalent), but they also do it in the same *way*; that is, they go through the same intermediate steps. So, of course, (1) if we could show that one machine goes through steps that another machine does not go through, that would be fairly direct evidence against their strong equivalence. More indirectly, (2) one might show that the "complexity profiles" for the two machines are different. For instance, suppose we give the two machines a wide range of numbers to multiply. As the numbers get bigger, one machine takes proportionally longer time to multiply them, but the other machine bakes a disproportionately longer time to process them. Or we might compare memory used or the errors made, and find them different in the two machines (see Pylyshyn, 1979). We will see that the distinction between weak and strong equivalence is important in assessing the psychological plausibility of a computational model of a cognitive capacity. We want the model not to just do what the cognitive capacity does, but to do it the *way* the cognitive capacity does it. Typically, a psychological experiment is a test of strong equivalence of some cognitive capacity and a model of it, using such measures as reaction times and error rates.

6.2   Turing Machines

Biographical note   Alan Turing was born in London on June 23, 1912. He was educated at Sherborne School and Kings' College, Cambridge (Math). In April 1935 von Neumann visited Cambridge from Princeton to teach a course for about a month: "Alan certainly met him this term and most likely through attending this course . . . it might well have been a result of a meeting of minds when on May 24 Alan wrote home 'I have applied for a visiting fellowship for next year at Princeton'" (Hodges, 1983: 95). Turing did go to Princeton (PhD Math 1938) where he studied with Alonzo Church. As he wrote his mother one week after his arrival: "The mathematics department here comes fully up to expectations. There is a great number of the most distinguished mathematicians here – von Neumann, Hardy, Weyl, Courant and Einstein." While at Princeton he published his most famous technical paper in 1936/7 "On Computable Numbers, with an Application to the *Entscheidungsproblem*."[1] In this paper Turing first defined precisely what he called "(automatic) computing machines," which we now call "Turing" machines in his honor. Upon his return to England and for the next six years he worked for the Foreign Office – actually for the British Code and Cypher School at Bletchley Park, a highly secret operation in a country house about 50 miles north of London. Here his "Colossus" computer helped break the German "Enigma" codes. It has been estimated that this work shortened the war in

Europe by two years. After resigning from the Foreign Office in 1945 he joined the National Physical Laboratory in London, and was leader in designing the ACE (Automatic Computing Engine) project. In 1949 he accepted the position of Assistant Director of "Madam," the Manchester Automatic Digital Machine, at Manchester University. In 1950 he published his most famous non-technical paper "Computing Machinery and Intelligence." In that article he proposed what he called the "imitation game" – what is now known as the "Turing test" for intelligence. In 1952 he was convicted of homosexuality. He apparently committed suicide (he was conducting experiments with potassium cyanide, so it could have been an accident) on June 7, 1954.

Turing machines (TMs) have a relatively simple structure and mode of operation. This makes them easy to prove things about, but entirely impractical to use for computation, which explains why nobody has bothered to actually build one. We first look at the structure and operation of a Turing machine, then we turn to some general properties of Turing machines.

Structure and operation

Intuitively, TMs are abstract computing devices with two principal parts: a tape and a read-write head (with a machine table and a scanner), as shown in figure 6.1. This figure incorporates the following four central structural notions concerning Turing machines: tapes, head, scanner, and machine table.

Structure

Tape: The tape can be supplemented indefinitely in both directions, it is divided into squares, and each square contains either a single symbol from a predetermined vocabulary or it is blank.

Head with scanner: The head moves back and forth relative to the tape, reading or writing a symbol on the tape.

Machine table (program): This is a finite list of instructions each of which specifies five pieces of information: (1) the current state, (2) the input (read) symbol, (3) the output (write) symbol, (4) a head movement to the left or right, (5) the next state.

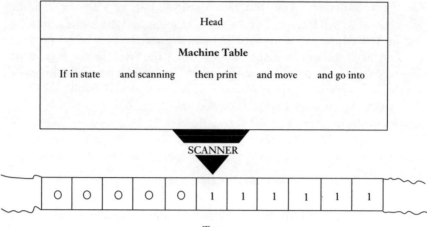

Figure 6.1   Turing machine architecture

These structural components are put into operation during a computation as follows:

Operation

Control: The movement of the head is determined by the machine table which is sensitive to two things: the current internal state of the machine, and the symbol it is presently scanning. The head then (1) writes a specific symbol on the current square, and (2) moves left one square, right one square or remains where it is. The machine then goes into its next state mentioned in its machine table.

Programming a TM: This consists of specifying its machine table and initial tape configuration in such a way that it will start on this initial symbol and halt on the halt symbol. The final tape configuration constitutes the output one wants.

Computation: A *computation* consists of executing the instructions, starting with the initial tape configuration, an initial internal state, and ending with the halt symbol. The final configuration of the tape is the output/result of the computation.

Input: This takes the form of the initial tape configuration.

Output: This is the final tape configuration.

Head				
Machine Table				
if in state	and scanning	then print	and move	and go into
1	None	0	R	2
2	None		R	3
3	None	1	R	4
4	None		R	1

SCANNER

Figure 6.2　Turing's first machine (adapted from Turing, 1936/7: 119)

As an example, figure 6.2 shows Turing's (1936/7) first illustrative machine, which prints alternate 0s and 1s with spaces in between. The tape is blank to begin with (hence the "None" in column 2) and the machine can print either "0" or "1." "R" means the machine is to move one square to the right of the current square, "P" means it is to print. We start the machine on a blank square in state 1, then:

State Operation
1　It prints a "0," then moves one square to the right, and goes into state 2.
2　It moves to the right one square and goes into state 3.
3　It prints a "1," then moves one square to the right and goes into state 4.
4　It moves one square to the right and goes into state 1 (etc.).

Turing machine cycle:　We will summarize Turing machine operation by saying the machines have a cycle of: read, write, move, go into next state.

Many theorems have been proven about TMs, but one of the most interesting is Turing's original (1936) theorem:

Turing's theorem:　There exist "universal TMs" (UTMs) that can mimic the moves of any other TM.

Figure 6.3   Operation of Turing's first machine

	1	2	3	4	5	6	7
Y	__L1	__L1	YL3	YL4	YR5	YR6	__R7
_	__L1	YR2	HALT	YR5	YL3	AL3	YR6
1	1L2	AR2	AL3	1L7	AR5	AR6	1R7
A	1L1	YR6	1L4	1L4	1R5	1R6	__R2

Figure 6.4   Minsky's universal Turing machine (from Haugeland, 1985: 139, box 3; reproduced by permission of the MIT Press)

For the record, the smallest known universal Turing machine is Minsky's (see figure 6.4). If we think of a specific TM as codifying or formalizing a procedure for doing something that can be represented on its tape, then the idea that a universal TM can mimic the behavior of any specific TM suggests that a universal TM can codify any procedure that can be written on a TM tape. And since TMs are automatic step-by-step procedures, maybe a UTM explicitly codes the notion of an effective procedure, and algorithm. This has led to the so-called "Church-Turing" thesis (put in our terms):

Church-Turing thesis: For any effective procedure for calculating a function there exists a TM that computes the function calculated by that procedure (i.e. which does what that procedure does).

The notion of an "effective procedure" is an intuitive, not a formal, notion, so no theorems can be proven about it. However, every time the notion *has* been made precise, the new notion has been proven to be equivalent to a Turing machine.

Technical Digression   In 1931 Kurt Gödel introduced the important class of *recursive functions*, functions that can be specified in a step-by-step manner from very basic numerical operations. In 1936 Church wrote that "the purpose of the present paper is to propose a definition of effective calculability" (see Davis, 1965: 90). He went on to do this in terms of "Lambda-definability" and he demonstrated that definability in his "Lambda-calculus" was equivalent to recursiveness. He concluded: "The fact, however, that two such widely different and (in the opinion of the author) equally natural definitions of effective calculability turn out to be equivalent adds to the strength of the reasons adduced below for believing that they constitute as general a characterization of this notion as is consistent with the usual intuitive understanding of it" (ibid.). Shortly thereafter, in his (1936/7) paper, Turing showed that every Turing machine computable function is recursive and every recursive function is Turing machine computable. So effective calculability can be defined as Lambda-definability, which is equivalent to recursiveness (Church) and recursiveness is equivalent to TM computability (Turing), so effectiveness is TM computability (Church–Turing):

Church (1936)
Thesis: effective procedure (intuitive) = Lambda-definability
Theorem: Lambda-definability = recursiveness

Turing (1936/7)
Theorem: TM computable = recursive

Church–Turing
Theorem: Lambda-definability = recursiveness = TM computable
Thesis: effective procedure = TM computable

Later researchers showed that a whole variety of systems formulated to capture the notion of effective calculability (Normal systems, Post systems, Thue systems, Semi-Thue systems, Markoff algorithms) were equivalent to Turing machines. It was shown by Wang in 1957 that every recursive function is flowchart computable (computable by machine specified by a standard flowchart) and more recently that the Fortran Pascal and Lisp programming languages are equivalent to Turing machines.

Thus, there is some inductive support for the idea that being computable by a Turing machine is weakly equivalent to being an effective procedure. The upshot of this thesis is that a universal TM can do what any effective procedure can do. Insofar as our cognitive capacities can be seen as effective procedures, a UTM can model the input–output pairings of such a capacity, and so be weakly equivalent to it. This gave legitimacy, in the minds of some at the time, to the notion that one could build a thinking computer by programming it properly, and that one could understand human cognitive capacities in terms of effective procedures implemented in the brain.

6.3   von Neumann Machines

Biographical note   John von Neumann was born in Budapest on December 28, 1903, with the name Neumann Janos (John) Lajos (in the Hungarian fashion, last names are given first). His father was given the honorary title "Margittai" ("from Margitta"), so von Neumann's full name was actually "Margittai Neumann Janos Lajos". A German publisher converted "Margittai" to the German "von," hence "John von Neumann" – thought you'd want to know. Until 1913 he was educated at home by governesses selected in part for their language abilities. By age 10 he knew French, German, Latin, and classical Greek. As a child his favorite subject was history, and he read through his parents' 44-volume set on general history. In 1913, at ten years old, he was enrolled for eight years at a well-respected high school in Budapest. In 1921 he entered the University of Budapest to study mathematics. He had a habit of showing up only for exams, and he spent much of his time in Berlin attending the lectures of Haber (chemistry) and Einstein (statistical mechanics). In 1923, under pressure from his father to get a "practical education," he enrolled in Zurich's ETH (Eidgenossische Technische Hochschule) to study chemical engineering. His interest in pure mathematics was sustained by regular contact with the mathematicians Weyl (whose course von Neumann took over for a period while Weyl was away) and Polya, who were in Zurich at the time. In 1926 he took his PhD in mathematics from the University of Budapest (his dissertation was published in 1928). In 1927 he was appointed Privatdozent at the University of Berlin at 24 – the youngest in the history of the university. In 1930 he was appointed to the mathematics faculty at the Institute for Advanced Studies (IAS), Princeton. In 1943 he visited England: "I have developed an obscene interest in computational techniques." Because of his knowledge of hydrodynamics, he was invited by Robert Oppenheimer to the Manhattan project at Los Alamos as a mathematical consultant to study the properties of implosion. He noted that the computational problems for simulating implosion took much too long. In 1944 he spent two weeks at punch-card machine operation, wiring the tabulator plugboards: "He found wiring the tabulator plugboards particularly frustrating; the tabulator could perform parallel operations on separate counters, and wiring the tabulator plugboard to carry out parallel computation involved taking into account the relative timing of the parallel operations. He later told us *this experience led him to reject parallel computations in electronic computers and in his* *design of the single-address instruction code where parallel handling of operands was guaranteed not to occur* [emphasis added]." On September 7, 1944, von Neumann visited the Moore School of Electrical Engineering (University of Pennsylvania) to discuss the design of the EDVAC (electronic discrete variable arithmetic computer), the successor of ENIAC. In the spring of 1945 while at Los Alamos he wrote the "First Draft of a Report on the EDVAC." In June of 1945 he mailed a preliminary draft of the report, with blanks to be filled in, names to be added, to the Moore School where covers were put on it and it was distributed without being completed by von Neumann. "The document is powerful; a mere 100 pages of mimeographed text gives the fundamentals of the stored-program computer . . . it soon found its way into the hands of many different groups in the United States and England interested in building high-speed computing devices. In effect it served as the logical schematic for many of the early stored-program computers." In 1955 von Neumann contracted bone cancer. In 1956 he wrote the Stillman lectures (Yale) "The Computer and the Brain," and on February 8, 1957, he died.

So called "von Neumann" machines (vNMs) or "register architecture" machines are designed, in part, to overcome the liabilities of Turing machines.[2] The prototypical von Neumann machine is the one specified in von Neumann's original study (1945), which formed the basis for the Burks, Goldstine, and von Neumann (1946) memo for Princeton's Institute for Advanced Studies (IAS) Computer (see 1946: 98–9):

1.1 [Fully automatic] Inasmuch as the completed device will be a general-purpose computing machine it should contain certain organs relating to arithmetic, memory-storage, control and connection with the human operator. It is intended that the machine be fully automatic in character, i.e., independent of the human operator after the computation starts. . . .

1.2 [Memory] It is evident that the machine must be capable of storing in some manner not only the digital information needed in a given computation . . . , but also the instructions which govern the actual routine to be performed on the numerical data. . . . Hence there must be some organ capable of storing these program orders. There must, moreover, be a unit which can understand these instructions and order their execution.

1.3 [Stored Program] Conceptually we have discussed above two different forms of memory: storage of numbers and storage of orders. If, however, the orders to the machine are reduced to a numerical code and if the machine can in some fashion distinguish a number from an order, the memory organ can be used to store both numbers and orders. . . .

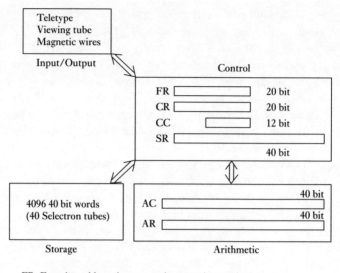

FR: Function table register–stored current instruction
CR: Control register–stored next instruction
CC: Control counter–stored address of next instruction
SR: Selection register–stored word just fetched from storage
                              or word just sent to storage
AC: Accumulator–used for arithmetic operations
AR: Arithmetic register–used in conjunction with AC

Figure 6.5 von Neumann machine architecture (from Pohl and Shaw, 1981: 141, figure 5.1; reproduced by permission of W. H. Freeman and Co.)

1.4 [Control]   If the memory for orders is merely a storage organ there must exist an organ which can automatically execute the orders stored in the memory. We shall call this organ the *Control.*

1.5 [Arithmetic]   Inasmuch as the device is to be a computing machine there must be an arithmetic organ in it which can perform certain of the elementary arithmetic operations. . . .

The operations that the machine will view as elementary are clearly those which are wired into the machine. . . .

1.6 [Input-Output]   Lastly there must exist devices, the input and output organ, whereby the human operator and the machine can communicate with each other. . . .

These components can be diagrammed as shown in figure 6.5. Pylyshyn (1984) usefully generalizes von Neumann's original specification as follows: "Virtually every architecture that is widely available is of the type that many people refer to as von Neumann (though this name is sometimes used rather loosely to mean 'conventional'). This architecture – which has been universal practically since the design of the Princeton I.A.S. computer – is a register machine in which symbols are stored and retrieved by their numerical 'addresses', control is transferred sequentially through a program (except for 'branching' instructions), and operations on symbols are accomplished by retrieving them from memory and placing them in a designated register, applying a primitive command to them, then storing the resulting symbol back in memory. Although there are variants on this pattern, *the main idea of a sequential process proceeding through a series of 'fetch', 'operate', and 'store' operations has been dominant since digital computation began"* (1984: 96–7; emphasis added).

von Neumann machine cycle: we will summarize the von Neumann machine cycle of operations as: fetch, operate, store. The fact that only one instruction is executed at a time causes a restriction in the flow of information through the machine. This restriction is sometimes called the "von Neumann bottleneck."

Programming a von Neumann machine: syntax in the physics

We have seen that the basic cycle of operations in a von Neumann machine is: fetch an instruction, operate on (execute) it, and store the result, and a program is a set of instructions in some programming language for carrying out some algorithm. We want now to see how, at least in broad outline, programming a von Neumann machine works – how do we get a physical machine to do what we tell it? Or, to put it more dramatically, if a program is the "mind" of a computer, and flip-flops, registers, and gates are its "body," then how do we solve the mind-body problem for computers?[3]

We begin with a simple assembly language program to compare the contents of two memory locations (register 1 and register 2) and say "OK" if they are the same, "NO" if they are different. Here is the program (from Copeland 1993b, chapter 4). Descriptions of what each instruction does are in curly braces.

The "Compare and print" program
1   Compare: register 1 register 2
{compare the contents of register 1 and 2 and put a 0 in a match register if they are different and a 1 in the match register if they are the same}

2   Branch-on-0 6
{Check the match register and if it is 0, jump to line 6 of the program}
3   Output-as-character 1001111
{This is the ASCII code for the letter O}
4   Output-as-character 1001011
{This is the ASCII code for the letter K}
5   Branch 8
{Jump to line 8}
6   Output-as-character 1001110
{This is the ASCII code for N}
7   Output-as-character 1001111
{This is the ASCII code for O}
8   Halt

Program description

Starting at line 1, the program checks the contents of register 1 and 2, compares them, and stores a 1 if they are the same, a 0 if they are different. At line
2 the program jumps to line 6 if the contents don't match and prints first an
N, then an O, i.e. NO, then halts at line 8. If at line 2 the registers match, then
it goes on to print an O and a K, i.e. OK, then jumps at line 5 to line 8 and
halts. So the computer answers No if the numbers don't match, OK if they
do, and halts after either answer.

Compiling the program

Since our computer is a binary digital machine all these instructions will have
to be converted into binary code. This is done by the *compiler*, which trans-
lates the instructions into binary code, including the references to registers and
program line numbers. A sample table of bit code for the commands in our
program might be:

Operation	Bit-code
Compare	00000011
Branch-on-0	00000100
Brach	00000110
Output-as-character	00000101
Halt	00000001

The registers referred to in the instructions must also be given binary code in
order for the computer to find them.

Registers	Bit-code
1	01
2	10
21	10101
25	110111

The compiled program

The result of compiling the assembly language program would be:

Instruction		*Register(s)/Characters*
1	**Compare** 00000011	1 10 (**Registers**: 1, 2)
2	**Branch-on-0** 00000100	10101 (**Register** 6)
3	**Output-as-character** 00000101	1001111 (O)
4	**Output-as-character** 00000101	1001011 (K)
5	**Branch** 00000110	1100111 (**Register** 25)
6	**Output-as-character** 00000101	1001110 (N)
7	**Output-as-character** 00000101	1001111 (O)
8	**Halt** 00000001	

The compiler assigns these instructions and registers to addresses in memory: the operation gets one address register (e.g. 10 below), the register names get others (e.g., 11, 12 below).

The compiled program in memory

The result of a compiled program in memory would be:[4]

Line 1 {compare registers 01, 10}
10   00000011
11   1
12   10
Line 2 {Jump on 0 to register 10101 = 21}
13   00000100
14   10101
Line 3 {Output–as–character 1001111 = O}
15   00000101
16   1001111
Line 4 {Output–as–character 1001011 = K}
17   00000101
18   1001011

Line 5 {Jump to register 1101 = 25}
19   00000101
20   11001
Line 6 {Output-as-character 1001110 = N}
21   00000101
22   1001110
Line 7 {Output-as-character 1001111 = O}
23   00000101
24   1001111
Line 8 {Halt}
25   00000001

Each register is just a row of flip-flops, each of which can be in one of two states: on or off. So ultimately the programmed computer is just a specific configuration of flip-flops – some on, some off. To run the program one pushes a button or the equivalent that starts the physical process going of copying the first instruction into the instruction register. The machine is so designed ("hard-wired") that when the flip-flops in the instruction register are set, for example, to 00000011, it executes a comparison and the contents of registers 1 and 2 are compared, yielding a 1 or a 0 in the match register. The next instruction specified in the program is then copied into the instruction register and the machine continues this fetch–operate–store cycle until it halts – all in accordance with the laws of physics–cum–electrical engineering. There is no ghost in the machine. The syntax of the program's instructions are compiled into distinct physical arrays of flip-flops. That's how we can make the machine do what we tell it.

von Neumann machines vs. Turing machines

This architecture is not subject to complaints against TMs: (1) vNMs allow both direct (absolute, random) access and indirect (or relative) access in memory, whereas a TM allows only indirect (relative) access; (2) the program can be stored as data in memory; and (3) it has specialized computational organs such as an arithmetic unit (TMs have no special-purpose circuits). Some call the first two ideas "the primary architectural advance of the von Neumann design" (Haugeland, 1985: 143). The von Neumann architecture allows one to exploit "subroutines" to their fullest; that is, they can be called at any point in a computation, and after they are executed the computation can proceed where it left off as if the subroutine had been simply the prior instruction in the program. The use of subroutines induces "modularity" on a computational system, in the sense that once a subroutine works correctly, it can be inserted into a program where needed and it will do its computation. It only need be represented once in memory no matter how often it is called. If a program can be assembled from numerous previously debugged subroutines, then it has a better chance of functioning correctly. And if something goes wrong, subroutines allow one to isolate the problem quicker: first find the defective subroutine, then go in and fix it. Finally there is the issue of *how* the machine computes the functions it computes. Different architectures have different "complexity profiles" – the number of steps, time, or memory required to run different algorithms differs; in the limiting case, different architectures cannot execute identical algorithms directly: "For example, the number of basic steps required to look up a string of symbols in a Turing machine increases as *the square of the number of strings stored.* On the other hand, in what is called a 'register architecture' (an architecture possessing what is usually called random access memory . . .) [a von Neumann machine], the time complexity can, under certain conditions, be made *independent of the number of strings stored* . . . something that is impossible in a Turing machine, despite the fact that the Turing machine can be made weakly equivalent to this algorithm. . . . A register machine . . . makes various additional algorithms possible, including binary search, in which the set of remaining options is reduced by a fraction with each comparison, as in the game 'Twenty Questions' . . . These algorithms *cannot be executed directly* on a Turing machine architecture" (Pylyshyn, 1984: 97–9; emphasis added).

6.4 Production Systems

Production systems (PSs) of Newell and Simon (1972) and Newell (1973) descend from the systems of the same name by E. Post (1943). Production systems have been popular in *psychology* for modeling a variety of cognitive capacities, and they have been popular in *artificial intelligence* in the construction of expert systems.

Newell and Simon (1972) explicitly recommend PSs for modeling cognitive phenomena left out of behaviorism's focus on stimuli and responses (see chapter 2), and neuroscientists' focus, at that time, on neural hardware (see chapter 3): "the information processing theories discussed in this book represent a specific layer of explanation lying between behavior, on the one side, and neurology on the other . . ." (1972: 876). Newell characterized PSs as follows: "A production system is a scheme for specifying an information processing system. It consists of a set of productions, each production consisting of a condition and an action. It has also a collection of data structures: expressions

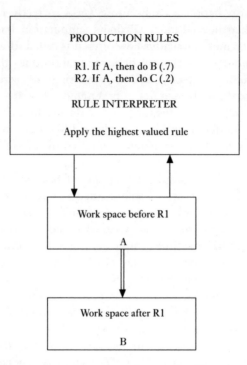

Figure 6.6   Production system components and operation (1)

that encode the information upon which the production system works – on which the actions operate and on which the conditions can be determined to be true or false. A production system, starting with an initially given set of data structures, operates as follows. That production whose condition is true of the current data (assume there is only one) is executed, that is, the action is taken. The result is to modify the current data structures. This leads in the next instant to another (possibly the same) production being executed, leading to still further modification. So it goes, action after action being taken to carry out an entire program of processing, each evoked by its condition becoming true of the momentary current collection of data structures. The entire process halts either when no condition is true (hence nothing is evoked) or when an action containing a stop operation occurs" (1973: 463). Newell diagrams overall production system architecture as shown in figure 6.6.

PSs have three major components: a set of *production rules*, of the form: if A (the condition), then do B (the action); a *memory work space* (sometimes called the "context"); and a *rule interpreter* which applies the relevant rule to the results in the work space. A typical *cycle of operation* for a PS involves:

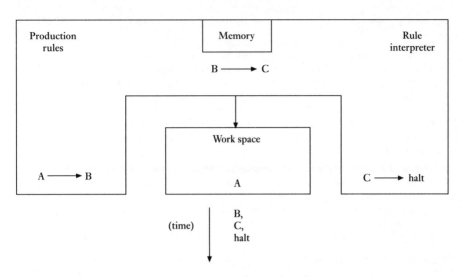

Figure 6.7   Production system components and operation (2)

1   matching the condition, A, of some production to the results of the work space;
2   resolving conflicts between productions for the right to write on the work space;
3   acting on the work space by doing B.

Production system cycle

We will summarize a production system (PS) cycle of operations as: match, resolve, act.

A production system halts when no more productions apply to the work space (or a special halt symbol is encountered). It may not be obvious from figure 6.6 that productions can compete in parallel for access to the work space, but they can – it is only the firing of productions that is serial. We can illustrate this better in figure 6.7.

One *programs* a production system by writing a set of production rules which, when given the input data in the work space, halts with the desired output having been produced in the work space. We get a variety of specific production systems by varying such things as the work space and timing (see Newell, 1973: 516). For example, consider the simple system shown in figure 6.8.

PRODUCTIONS:

P1. IF On-CL *green* THEN Put-On-CL *produce*
P2. IF On-CL *packed in small container* THEN Put-On-CL *delicacy*
P3. IF On-CL *refrigerated* OR On-CL *produce* THEN Put-On-CL *perishable*
P4. IF On-CL *weights 15 lbs* AND On-CL *inexpensive* AND NOT On-CL *perishable* THEN Put-On-CL *staple*
P5. IF On-CL *perishable* AND On-CL *weighs 15 lbs* THEN Pub-On-CL *turkey*
P6. IF On-CL *weighs 15 lbs* AND On-CL *produce* THEN Put-On-CL *watermelon*

INTERPRETER:

1. Find all productions whose condition parts are TRUE and make them applicable.
2. If more than one production is applicable, then deactivate any production whose action adds a duplicate symbol to the CL.
3. Execute the action of the lowest numbered (or only) applicable production. If no productions are applicable, then quit.
4. Reset the applicability of all productions and return to S1.

Figure 6.8   A sample production system (from Barr, Cohen, and Feigenbaum, 1981: 191)

Applying the productions to what is in the work space (here called "On-CL") we get the following computation:

1   On-CL = green, weighs 15 lbs
{i.e. put the data: green, weighs 15 lbs, in the work space}
P1 fires
2   On-CL = *produce*, green, weighs 15 lbs
{P1 has added "produce" to the work space}
P3 fires
3   On-CL = *perishable*, produce, green, weighs 15 lbs
{P1 has added "perishable" to the work space}
P5 fires
4   On-CL = *turkey*, perishable, produce, green, weighs 15 lbs
{P5 has added "turkey" to the work space. It is not clear why P5 was not written to forbid this – say by adding "not-produce" to its condition}
P6 fires
5   On-CL = *watermelon*, turkey, perishable, produce, green, weighs 15 lbs
{P6 has added "watermelon" to the work space. It is not clear what being a watermelon and a turkey amounts to}
6   HALT

This example illustrates some of the programming difficulties one can get into with PSs. In this example, as the annotations suggest, the productions must be written carefully so as to apply correctly. Note that if the order of P5 and P6 had been reversed, then "watermelon" would have been the final addition and there would have been no problem.

There are a number of different methods for resolving conflicts between productions in the work space, should they arise. For instance, one could add a measure on the matching process to determine which fit best. Or there might be a history of activation associated with each production and the most active (or frequent or recent) production fires (see Anderson, 1983, for discussion and testing).

Production systems vs. von Neumann machines

Production system architecture differs from vNMs in interesting ways that are sometimes thought to be *advantages*. *First*, in contrast with TMs and von Neumann machines, there is no separate, external control structure beyond the rule interpreter. Conflict resolution aside, a production fires if and only if its condition matches the contents of the work space. This introduces a certain desirable *parallelism* into the system, but as we just saw, it also makes it diffi-cult for PSs to respond with a specific sequence of actions: the intended algo-rithmic structure of the machine's rules may be difficult to enforce (we will see analogs of this problem in many connectionist architectures). *Second*, infor-mation is operated on in terms of its description in the work space, not in terms of its absolute or relative address – it is "content" addressable rather than "location" addressable. Think of the police going to an address (an anonymous tip) and arresting whoever is there (location addressing), vs. having a finger-print of somebody and finding the person who matches it. It is true that content addressing can be simulated on a von Neumann Machine by "hash coding," where the location of the content, and so the content itself, is some logical-arithmetic function of the entry argument or probe.[5] However, these techniques are available for only highly restricted forms of information. And even for the information they work on, these methods require elaborate control through use of "collision functions" to keep the hash code from yielding mul-tiple, or the wrong, addresses. This makes them quite brittle and graceless in their degradation. PSs, on the other hand, can degrade more gracefully by using the measurements in their match-subcycle. *Third*, some have claimed that PSs have an advantage over vNMs in being *highly modular*: "Since pro-duction systems are highly modular, there is a uniform way of extending them, without making distributed alterations to the existing system" (Pylyshyn, 1979: 82). And Haugeland (1985: 162) goes even further, saying: "Production systems promote a degree of 'modularity' unrivaled by other architectures. A *module* is an independent subsystem that performs a well-defined task and interacts with the rest of the system only in narrowly defined ways ... A production ... will activate itself when and where conditions are right, regardless of what any other production knows or decides." The idea is that a production in a PS is like an instruction in a vNM, and productions may be added and subtracted more freely (i.e. with fewer required additional changes elsewhere in the program) than von Neumann instructions – keeping conflict resolution in mind. But as we saw, this modularity comes at a price.

Among the *disadvantages* of PSs are (1) their *inefficiency* (since they must perform every action whose condition is satisfied, it is difficult to make them go through predetermined sequences of steps); and (2) their *opacity* (it is hard to express or to see algorithmic structure in them). Both of these problems are in large part due to the modularity and uniformity of productions – they cannot hierarchically call other productions the way subroutines in a von Neumann program can.

6.5   Intermezzo: Pandemonium

The final machine is not so much a general computational architecture as it is a model for pattern recognition and learning. And although the model was proposed many years before connectionism bloomed, it contains many general ideas found in contemporary connectionism and was driven by some of the same considerations. Hence, it is a kind of intermediary between digital and connectionist models. According to Selfridge (1959): "The basic motif behind our model is the notion of parallel processing. This is suggested on two grounds: first it is often easier to handle data in a parallel manner, and, indeed, it is usually the more 'natural' manner to handle it in; and secondly, it is easier to modify an assembly of quasi-independent modules than a machine all of whose parts interact immediately and in a complex why" (1959: 513). Because of this, "Pandemonium does not ... seem on paper to have the kinds of inherent restrictions or inflexibilities that many previous proposals have" (1959: 513).

Architecture

In its simplest form, Pandemonium consists of a decision "demon" (remember, it's PanDEMONium) who listens to lots of cognitive "demons," and each cognitive demon is looking at the incoming data, trying to identify its proprietary feature or property. The closer the data are to the target, the louder that

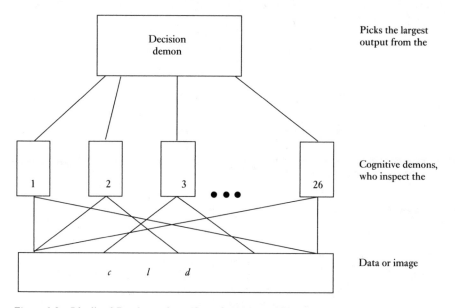

Figure 6.9 Idealized Pandemonium (from Selfridge, 1959: 515, figure 1)

demon shouts, and the decision demon chooses the one who shouts the loudest. This is schematized in figure 6.9.

For instance, the data might consist of letters of the alphabet, and cognitive demons 1–26 might each be experts at a single letter. Then, even though an incoming *d* resembles a *c* and an *l*, it resembles a *d* more, so the *d*-demon will shout the loudest: "in many instances a pattern is nearly equivalent to some logical function of a set of features, each of which is individually common to perhaps several patterns and whose absence is also common to several other patterns" (Selfridge, 1959: 516). So Selfridge amends the idealized Pandemonium to contain a layer of computational demons (see figure 6.10). The cognitive demons now add weighted sums of the computational demons. The layer of computational demons is independent of the task and must be reasonably selected (by evolution or the experimenter) in order for learning to take place.

Learning

And it is learning that Pandemonium is designed for. Selfridge describes two kinds of learning procedure for Pandemonium. The first is learning through

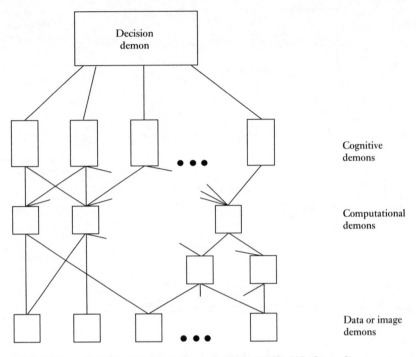

Figure 6.10   Amended Pandemonium (from Selfridge, 1959: 517, figure 3)

"feature weighting": "feature weighting consists in altering the weights assigned to the subdemons by the cognitive demons so as to maximize the score of the entire . . . Pandemonium" (1959: 518). Selfridge then discusses a variety of methods available for feature-weight changing rules. The second kind of learning procedure is "subdemon selection": "The first adaptive change, feature weighting, optimized these weights, but we have no assurance at all that the particular subdemons we selected are good ones. Subdemon selection generates new subdemons for trial and eliminates inefficient ones, that is, ones that do not much help improve the score" (1959: 521). Selfridge envisages that control is also to be subject to demonic change: "In principle, we propose that the control operations should themselves be handled by demons subject to changes like feature weighting and subdemon selection" (1959: 523). Finally, Selfridge noted that so far his description of Pandemonium "has been on the basis of constant monitoring by a person who is telling the machine when it makes an error" (1959: 523). But we might also wonder if the machine can improve its performance (learn) on its own: "I suggest that it can in the following way: one criterion of correct decisions will be that they are fairly unequivocal, that is that there is one and only one cognitive demon whose output far outshines the rest" (1959: 523). Selfridge concludes briefly by sketching a Pandemonium model for Morse code, or more precisely "to distinguish dots and dashes in manually keyed Morse code" (1959: 524), but he does not report any results.

Selfridge and Neisser (1960) report preliminary results of CENSUS, a machine with Pandemonium architecture for recognizing 10 hand-printed letters of the alphabet: A, E, I, L, M, N, O, R, S, T. The inputs were projected on an "image" (or input store) of 32 × 32 (1,024) pixels. CENSUS computed the probability of a letter given the image using 28 features. According to Selfridge and Neisser, CENSUS made only about 10 percent fewer correct identifications than human subjects. However, there are least three major problems in scaling up the machine: *first*, segmenting the letters from cursive script; *second*, using learning to modify the probabilities; and *third*, using learning to generate its own features, which presently are restricted to those the programmer can think up. As they comment, in closing: "We can barely guess how this restriction might be overcome. Until it is, 'Artificial Intelligence' will remain tainted with artifice" (1960: 68). Until the arrival of connectionism in the early 1980s almost 20 years later, nothing arrived to remove the taint.

Pandemonium, perceptrons, and connectionism

It is easy to see why Pandemonium played a role in the development of connectionism. Here, as with perceptrons, we find the idea of pattern recognition by means of the parallel activity of many highly interconnected units, each of which handles minimal information, but who conspire via local interactions to produce globally appropriate decisions. Furthermore, as with perceptrons, the system learns by weight changes using a variety of learning methods. Perhaps distinctive to Pandemonium is the postulation of control demons and their selection. It is not clear what analog these notions have in perceptrons or contemporary connectionist theorizing.

6.6 Taxonomizing Architectures (I)

One way of constructing a taxonomy is to decide, on the basis of some general principles, what categories will be used, then look at individuals to see which category they fit into. This method risks not categorizing its domain along dimensions that are intrinsic to the things being categorized. Another way of

	TM	VNM	PS	Pandemonium
Control	localized	localized	partially distributed	distributed?
Memory	indirect	direct location-addressable	direct content-addressable	direct content-addressable

Figure 6.11   A taxonomy of architectures

constructing a taxonomy is to look at examples (from different categories) and try to generalize on the dimensions of categorization. This method risks proliferating mutually incommensurate extrapolations from the data. We have looked at some typical standard architectures; is there any natural way of taxonomizing them? One thing that has emerged is that there are always at least three important aspects of a (digital) computational device, that is, representations, memory, and control: any (digital) computational device must be able to store *representations* in *memory*, and every such device must be able to change states in a specifiable way – *control*. So perhaps these three dimensions could form the basis of a taxonomy. We have not yet surveyed representation schemes, so we will restrict ourselves to the last two (see figure 6.11).

Control is *local* if there is a single source for all control in the machine, otherwise it is *distributed*. Memory is *indirect* if it is organized so that the machine must pass through one address to get to others. It is *direct* (or *random*) otherwise. Memory is *location addressable* if data is stored and accessed at a place located by address only, and it is *content addressable* if it is stored and accessed by content.

These architectural features impose certain restrictions on basic computations with these machines. Importantly. TMs and vNMs are importantly serial in their computation, whereas PSs are partially parallel and Pandemonium is almost fully parallel in its computation.

Notes

1 "Decision-problem," i.e. is there a general procedure for deciding whether an arbitrary formula from some system is a theorem of the system or not.
2 We call these "von Neumann" machines because they came down to us from von Neumann's EDVAC report of 1945. However, it seems that Turing (1946) also deserves credit for some central ideas. But we can't have two Turing machines, can we?
3 The mind–body problem, as we will see later, is the problem of how mental phenomena relate to physical phenomena.

4 The numbers in the left column are register numbers (i.e., addresses in the computer) in decimal for ease of reading.

5 For instance, the middle two bits of the entry argument might represent the address of its content, or one might do an exclusive-or on the two halves of the string, or one might break the input string up into equal length strings, then sum them arithmetically.

Study questions

Introduction

What is an algorithm/effective procedure vs. a program?

What is computer "architecture"?

What is strong vs. weak equivalence of two machines?

Turing machines (TMs)

What are the main elements of a TM?

How are they organized?

How does a TM function?

How does one program a TM?

Describe the input, output, and computation of a TM?

What is the TM cycle?

What is Turing's theorem?

What is the Church–Turing thesis?

Why is it a thesis and not a theorem?

What implication is there for cognitive science of putting the theorem and the thesis together?

von Neumann machines (vNMs)

What are the main elements of a vNM?

How are they organized?

What is the vNM cycle?

How does one program a vNM?

What advantages does a vNM have over a TM as a model of human cognitive organization?

What is the "von Neumann bottleneck"?

Why is it thought to be a problem?

Production systems (PSs)

What are the main elements of a PS?

How are they organized?

What is the PS cycle?

How does one program a PS?

Rewrite the sample productions to avoid the problems mentioned in the text.

In what ways are PSs parallel and in what ways are they serial?

How do PSs differ from both TMs and vNMs?

What are the pros and cons of PSs?

Pandemonium

What is the "basic motif" of Pandemonium?

What is the general structure of Pandemonium?

What two types of learning procedures did it use?

What similarities are there between Pandemonium and connectionist systems?

Taxonomizing architecture(s) (I)

What is the difference between local and distributed control?

What is the difference between indirect (relative) and direct (random) memory access?

What is the difference between location addressable and content addressable memory?

Which machine(s) compute serially?

Which machine(s) compute partially serially and partially in parallel?

Which machine(s) compute mostly in parallel?

Suggested reading

General

Accessible chapter-length introductions to computation for non-specialists can be found in Glymour (1992), chapter 12, and White (2000). A clear book-length introduction that relates computation to logic is Boolos and Jeffrey (1989). The most readable non-technical general introduction to machine architectures is Haugeland (1985), chapter 4.

Turing machines

See Hodges (1983) for more on Turing's life and career. A lengthy, thorough, and surprisingly accessible discussion of TMs can be found in Penrose (1989), chapter 2. Barwise and Etchemendy (1999) is an introduction to TMs with software to build and test them. One of the first comprehensive studies of Turing machines is Davis (1958), and his anthology (1965) contains the classics of the field of computability and decidability. A classic introduction to Turing machines is Minsky (1967), especially chapters 6 and 7. An older survey of equivalences between Turing machines and other systems can be found in Gross and Lentin (1970). A more recent survey can be found in Odifreddi (1989), part I. Dawson (1998), chapter 2, is a good introduction to TMs and their relevance to cognitive science.

Church–Turing thesis

See Copeland (1996b) for a brief but informative survey article. The 1987 issue of *Notre Dame Journal of Formal Logic* 28(4) is devoted to the Church–Turing thesis. Copeland (1997) discusses the question whether the class of functions computable by a machine is identical to that computable by TMs (he argues they are not), and relates that issue to common (mis)formulations of the Church–Turing thesis and more relevantly the application of these misformulations to cognitive science. See Gandy (1988) for a detailed, and fascinating, history of the origins of the Church–Turing thesis.

von Neumann machines

Von Neumann machine history has been explored in many places. Augarten (1984), chapter 4, is a useful non-technical history of the stored program computer from ENIAC to UNIVAC, and has a useful chronology of the landmarks of computation. Slightly more technical discussions of specific machines such as ENIAC and the IAS machine can be found in Metropolis et al. (1980), especially part IV. See Heims (1980), chapters 2 and 14, and Aspray (1990), especially chapters 1 and 2, for more on the life and career of von Neumann. Some general theory of register (von Neumann) machines can be found in Minsky (1967), chapter 11, and in Clark and Cowell (1976), chapters 1–3. For more on hash coding see Pohl and Shaw (1981: 239ff).

Production systems

A good introduction to Post's systems can be found in Minsky (1967), chapter 13. Newell and Simon (1972, "Historical Addendum") contains a brief history of PSs. Barr, Cohen, and Feigenbaum (1981, III. C4) cover PSs. PS architectures have been used in many expert systems (see Kurzweil, 1990), as well as to model specific psychological capacities (see chapter 8).

Pandemonium

Besides the works mentioned in the text one can find scattered descriptions and uses of Pandemonium in Dennett (1991).

7

Representation(s)

7.1 Introduction

To adequately account for human cognitive capacities we will have to see cognition as involving the "manipulation" (creation, transformation, and deletion) of *representations*, and as a consequence, models of cognitive capacities will have to simulate these processes. This raises two questions:

(Q1) What sorts of representations do computational models "manipulate" (create, transform, delete)?

(Q2) How do these representations represent what they do – what determines just what they represent?

The first question (Q1) is called *the problem of representations* [with an "s"], and the second question (Q2) is called *the problem of representation* [without as "s"]. An answer to (Q1) would reveal the (i) structure and (ii) important features of the major schemes of computer representation. An answer to (Q2) would have to tell us (i) under what conditions something is a representation, that is represents something, and (ii) what determines exactly what it represents.

Terminological digression   Talk of representation(s) is often related to talk of "symbols," "semantics," "meaning," "reference," "intentionality," "content," "aboutness," etc. Each of these words has its advantages and its disadvantages. For instance, if "symbol" is taken broadly to mean anything that represents, then it is harmless to speak of representations as symbols – and we will sometimes use it this way for stylistic variation. But in ordinary use "symbol" has a much more restricted application, as when one

Continued

says: this sentence/rock has a strange symbol in/on it I don't understand. "Semantics," "meaning," and "reference" give the idea of standing for something else, but they naturally apply mainly to items in a linguistic system. So we settle on "representation" in part by default – it applies quite broadly to all sorts of relevant things, but it carries few irrelevant connotations. Finally, the morphology of the word "representation" suggests they involve *re-presentations*, and there may be a grain of truth in this: we generally gloss representation in terms of one thing X standing for another thing Y, re-presenting it, as it were.

Before turning to these two questions we will survey a few preliminary issues. *First*, although we will be interested primarily in "mental" representation, it behooves us not to lose sight of the fact that many different sorts of things represent, and their modes of representation are correspondingly diverse: percepts, memories, images, expressions from natural and artificial languages (such as numerals, arithmetic and logical symbols, Cartesian coordinates), expressions from special notational systems (such as music and dance), wiring diagrams, blueprints, maps, drawings, photographs, holograms, statues, meters, and gauges. There are even occasional ad hoc representations, such as a chipped tree or small stack of rocks to mark a trail. *Second*, discussion is complicated by an unstable terminology. We adopt the following terminological conventions (though we will have to be lax, especially when reporting the views of others, since not everyone speaks this way):

Atomic representations: they have no internal representational structure: no part of them represents anything.

Complex representations: they are built up from atomic representations: parts of them represent.

Compositional representations: what the whole represents is a function of (can be figured out from) what the parts represent, as well as their structural relations.

For example, in English (which is after all a representational system) the word "Venus" refers to a particular planet, but no part of it refers to or means anything (so it is atomic). But we can also refer to the planet Venus with the phrase: "the morning star" (or "the last star seen in the morning"). Here the component expressions do have a meaning, and the meaning of the whole is a function of the meaning of these parts and their grammatical arrangement (so it is complex and compositional). But now consider the idiomatic expression "kick the bucket" (= die). Here the parts have a meaning, but the meaning of the whole is not determined by these parts plus their grammatical organization (so it is complex but not compositional). To know this meaning you just have to memorize it. Closer to home, suppose the register of a computer has the following information in it:

```
----------------------------------
1 | 0 | 0 | 1 | 0 | 1 | 1
----------------------------------
```

Construed as ASCII code for the letter "k" it is non-compositional, since one cannot determine what it means without looking up the ASCII code from a table. But construed as a binary coded digital number (75), it is compositional, since that can be figured out via the place-value system of binary numbers.

7.2 The Variety of Representations: Some Standard High-level Formats

There are a variety of proposals in the computational and cognitive science literature as to the nature of representations (with an "s"). In digital computational models of cognition, data structures play the primary role of representation. Just as some programming languages are "high-level" – they are easy for programmers to use, and they get translated (compiled, interpreted) into lower-level code the machine can use more directly – so some knowledge representation systems are "high-level" because they are easy for modelers to use, and they also get translated into primitives the machine can use more directly, such as strings, arrays, trees, etc. Typical formats for high-level representation include the logic (the predicate calculus), semantic networks, and frames.

Logic: predicate calculus (PC)

The predicate calculus (PC), also called "quantification theory," has the virtue of a long and distinguished history in logic, where its syntax, semantics, and deductive power have been more thoroughly studied than any competing notation. The sample PC presented here consists of seven types of expressions:

predicates, names, connectives, variables, open sentences, quantifiers, and sentences, each with associated syntactic rules for well-formedness, and semantic rules for reference and truth.

Predicates

It is customary to capitalize the first letter of a predicate:

F( ): ( ) is female
T(,): ( ) is taller than ( )

Names

It is customary to decapitalize the first letter of a name:

a: Agnes
b: Betty

Syntactic rule
A predicate plus the required number of names is a sentence:

F(a): Agnes is female
T(a,b): Agnes is taller than Betty

Semantic rule
A sentence of the form:

predicate + name(s)

is true if and only if the thing(s) named has the property or relation predicated of it. For example:

"F(a)" is true if and only if a has the property F i.e. if and only if Agnes has the property of being female

"T(a,b)" is true if and only if a bears the relation T to b i.e. if and only if Agnes bears the relation of being taller than to Betty

Connectives

Here the blanks are to be filled by sentences.

__&__: __and__
__v__: __or__
__→__: if__then__
−__: not__

Syntactic rule
A connective plus the required number of sentences is a sentence:

F(a) & T(a,b): Agnes is female and Agnes is taller than Betty
F(a) v T(a,b): Agnes is female or Agnes is taller than Betty
F(a) → T(a,b): If Agnes is female then Agnes is taller than Betty
−F(a): Agnes is not female
−T(a,b): Agnes is not taller than Betty

Semantic rules
A sentence of the form:

Sentence + & + Sentence

is true if and only if the first sentence is true and the second sentence is true (analogously for "v" and "→").

A sentence of the form:

−Sentence

is true if and only if the sentence S is not true.

Technical Digression: Variables and Quantifiers In 1879 The German mathematician and philosopher Gottlob Frege published his book *Begriffsschrift* (Conceptscript) which was to revolutionize logic with its first-ever analysis of sentences using variables and quantifiers. Surprisingly, this began one of the intellectual adventures of the twentieth century – the "logicist" attempt to show that mathematics is a branch of logic and its consequences. In 1902 Bertrand Russell discovered a contradiction in Frege's (mature) system and Whitehead and Russell tried to overcome this in their monumental work *Principia Mathematica* (1910–13). In 1931 a young Austrian logician Kurt Gödel showed that any attempt to formalize

Continued

mathematics in a logical system like Russell and Whitehead's must end in failure. In 1936 Alan Turing used Gödel's results and techniques to prove a basic theorem in computer science: the unsolvability of the halting problem – a TM cannot be programmed so as to tell whether any other TM will halt or not on an arbitrary input. Frege's logic, though not his unusual two-dimensional notation system, is now standard. Here we enrich our elementary logic with these two devices, quantifiers and variables.

Variables

x, y

Syntactic rules: open sentences

1   A predicate with at least one variable is an *open sentence*:

F(x): x is female
T(x,y): x is taller than y
T(x,b): x is taller than Betty

2   A connective plus the required number of open sentences is an *open sentence*:

F(x) & T(xy): x is female and x is taller than y
T(x,b) → F(x): if x is taller than Betty then x is female

Quantifiers

Here the ellipses are to be filled in by anything that is well formed according to the syntactic rules.

(Ex) [. . . x . . .]: there exists an x such that . . . x . . .
(Ey) [. . . y . . .]: there exists a y such that . . . y . . .
(Ax) [. . . x . . .]: for every/all x, . . . x . . .
(Ay) [. . . y . . .]: for every/all y, . . . y . . .

Syntactic rule: sentences
The result of prefixing the appropriate number of quantifiers (with the appropriate variables) to an open sentence is a sentence:

(Ex) (Ey) [Fx & Txy]: there exists an x and there exists a y such that x is
   female and x taller than y
(Ax) [Txb → Fx]: for every x, if x is taller than Betty, then x is female

Semantic rules: sentences
A sentence of the form:

Existential quantifier + open sentence

is true if and only if there is something that has the property or relation
predicated by the open sentence:

"(Ex) Fx" is true if and only if there is something, x, that is F i.e. has the
   property of being female

A sentence of the form:

Universal quantifier + open sentence

is true if and only if for each object, that object has the property or bears
the relation being predicated by the open sentence:

"(Ax) Fx" is true if and only if for each object, x, it is F, i.e. it has the
   property of being female
"(Ax) [Fx → Txb]" is true if and only if for every object, it has the
   property that if it is female, then it is taller than Betty

Inference rules
&-simplification: from a sentence of the form "X & Y" infer: X, or infer
   Y (i.e., one can infer each).
Modus ponens: from sentences of the form "X → Y" and X infer a sentence of the form Y.

These structural rules specify the form of representations, and the rules of
inference allow the system to make deductions. For instance, suppose the
system needs to get the representation:

(C)   TALLER(AGNES, BETTY), i.e. Agnes is taller than Betty

and it is given the premises:

(P1)   FEMALE(AGNES) & NOT TALLER(BETTY, AGNES), i.e. Agnes is female & Betty is not taller than Agnes

(P2)   FEMALE(AGNES) → TALLER(AGNES, BETTY), i.e. Agnes is female and Agnes is taller than Betty

The system can use P1 and **&-simplification** to get:

(1)   FEMALE(AGNES), i.e. Agnes is female

Then the system can use (1), P2, and **modus ponens** to get the target:

(C)   TALLER(AGNES, BETTY), i.e. Agnes is taller than Betty

This is typical of how a system using a PC representational system would draw inferences.

Strengths and weaknesses of PC

Strengths
The main strengths of PC are that (1) it has an explicit semantics, and (2) its formal mathematical properties are very well understood. Furthermore, (3) it is a natural way of expressing some ideas, and (4) it is highly "modular" in the sense that one can enter and delete particular statements independently of others.

Weaknesses
One major weakness of PC representations for computer models of cognition comes from the fact that pieces of information that typically go together "in the world" are not stored together as any kind of unit. This makes it difficult to retrieve relevant information quickly and efficiently when it is needed. Some researchers therefore propose representational schemes that collect relevant information together in various ways for efficient use. Two such schemes are especially popular: semantic networks, and frames/scripts.

Semantic networks (SNs)

Semantic networks (SNs) were originally introduced as a formalism for modeling human associative memory for word meaning (hence "semantic": see

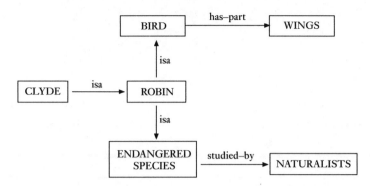

Figure 7.1 The robin network (from Barr, Cohen, and Feigenbaum, 1981: 184)

Quinlan, 1966, 1968). They are in effect a kind of graph structure, consisting of *nodes* (circles, boxes, dots) connected by *links* (arcs, arrows, lines). Some nodes represent objects (so-called "individual nodes") and some nodes represent properties (so-called "generic nodes"). The links typically represent relations between these items. Fragments of a semantic network represent situations. Each of these have analogs in the PC:

Individual nodes :: PC names
Generic nodes :: PC one-place predicates
Links :: PC relational predicates
Network fragments :: PC statements

Figure 7.1 shows a sample network we will comment on – take a moment to study it. We see nodes and links combined to make fragments of networks, which then combine to make the whole network.

Inference
Inference is captured not by deducing sentences from other sentences using inference rules, but by "spreading activation" in the network, for instance, as activation spreads out along the lines radiating from "robin," the system reflects such elementary inferences as: "A robin is a bird" or "A bird has wings." The existence of "isa" links allow nodes to inherit properties from distant parts of the network. For instance, any network containing the fragment animal network illustrated in figure 7.2 will allow the lower-level nodes to inherit the features of higher-level nodes and so to infer, for example, that

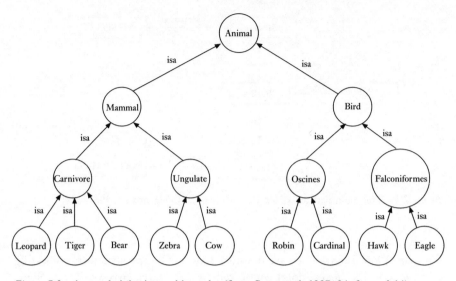

Figure 7.2   A sample inheritance hierarchy (from Staugaard, 1987: 94, figure 3.14)

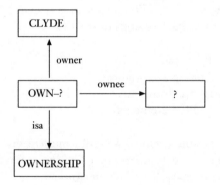

Figure 7.3   Question network (from Barr, Cohen, and Feigenbaum, 1981: 187)

a lion is an animal. These structures are appropriately called "inheritance hierarchies."

Questions

Questions can be asked of a SN by giving it a fragment of a network with a piece missing, then if the network can match the question fragment against the network it will return the missing piece as the *answer*. The question "What does Clyde own?" can be represented as in figure 7.3. The SN will match a

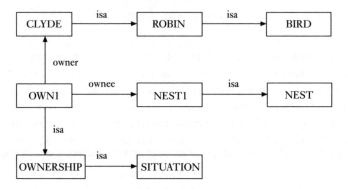

Figure 7.4 Answer network (from Barr, Cohen, and Feigenbaum, 1981: 187)

portion of the network in figure 7.4, and return the answer "a nest." So SNs can process information by spreading activation and matching.

Strengths and weaknesses of SNs

Strengths
The main strength of SNs can be seen in figure 7.1. In SN notation (vs. PC notation) the symbols "robin" and "bird" occur only once, and all the relevant information about robins or birds is connected to that node by links. This allows the system to collect together information about robins, birds, etc., together.

Weaknesses
The main weaknesses of SNs are *first*, they have a problem naturally representing such concepts as typicality/normalcy, disjunction, and negation. How would a network represent the fact that all robins are birds, but that just typical birds can fly, and just normal birds have wings? Something could be a bird and not fly and not have wings. How would a SN represent that fact that Clyde is a robin or a sparrow (and not both)? Or that Clyde is not a tiger? *Second*, unless controlled, activation can spread too far, as in:

Clyde is studied by naturalists (unlikely)

Some way of isolating the appropriate inferential material is still required. *Third*, SNs have no explicit, precise semantics the way PC does. *Fourth*, we do not have results regarding their formal properties, as we do with PC.

Frames and scripts

One of the most popular and flexible types of chunked data structure is Minsky's "frames." We quote Minsky's introduction of the notion at length because it contains many ideas, some not usually included in accounts of this notion: "Here is the essence of the theory: When one encounters a new situation (or makes a substantial change in one's view of the present problem), one selects from memory a structure called a *frame*. This is a remembered framework to be adapted to fit reality by changing details as necessary. A *frame* is a data-structure for representing a stereotyped situation, like being in a certain kind of living room, or going to a child's birthday party. Some of this information is about how to use the frame. Some is about what one can expect to happen next. Some is about what to do if these expectations are not confirmed. We can think of a frame as a network of nodes and relations. The top levels of a frame are fixed, and represent things that are always true about the supposed situation. The lower levels have many *terminals* – slots that must be filled by specific instances or data. Each terminal can specify conditions its assignments must meet. (The assignments themselves are usually smaller subframes.) Simple conditions are specified by *markers* that might require a terminal assignment to be a person, an object of sufficient value, or a pointer to a subframe of a certain type. More complex conditions can specify relations among the things assigned to several terminals. Collections of related frames are linked together into *frame systems*. The effects of important actions are mirrored by *transformations* between the frames of a system. . . . *Different frames of a system share the same terminals*; this is the critical point that makes it possible to coordinate information gathered from different viewpoints. Much of the phenomenological power of the theory hinges on the inclusion of expectations and other kinds of presumptions. *A frame's terminals are normally already filled with 'default' assignments*. Thus a frame may contain a great many details whose supposition is not specifically warranted by the situation. The frame systems are linked, in turn, by an *information retrieval network*. When a proposed frame cannot be made to fit reality – when we cannot find terminal assignments that suitably match its terminal marker conditions – this network provides a replacement frame. . . . Once a frame is proposed to represent a situation, a *matching* process tries to assign values to each frame's terminals, consistent with the markers at each place. The matching process is partly controlled by information associated with the frame (which includes information about how to deal with surprises) and partly by knowledge about the system's current goals" (see Haugeland, 1997: 111–37).

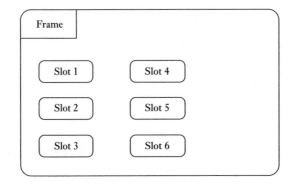

Figure 7.5 A generic frame (from Staugaard, 1987: 97, figure 3.16)

Let's unpack some of the main ideas in this long quotation. A frame represents *stereotypical* information about a (kind of) object, property, or situation. (Although Minsky extends the notion of frames to sequences of events, it is common practice to give them the special name of "scripts" and we will follow this practice.) A frame collects together information that "goes together" in the world in the form of *slots* in the frame (see figure 7.5).

Slots are either filled by *experience*, by *default values*, or by *pointers* to other frames (and scripts). We will illustrate these ideas, and more, with some concrete examples.

Room frames

For example, consider what we know about rooms. *First*, we know that a room has a typical structure. In frame theory this means that a room frame will have slots with pointers to various typical constituents (see figure 7.6). *Second*, we know that there are different typical kinds of rooms, so another set of pointers will direct the system to these (see figure 7.7).

Restaurant frames

Or consider what we know about typical restaurants. First we have the information that a restaurant is a specific kind of eating establishment. Then we have as slots, places where specific information fits into the frame. In the generic restaurant frame, for instance (see figure 7.8), the type needs to be fixed, the location, etc., and these slots can be filled by other frames. The more complete the filling in, the more complete the machine's "understanding."

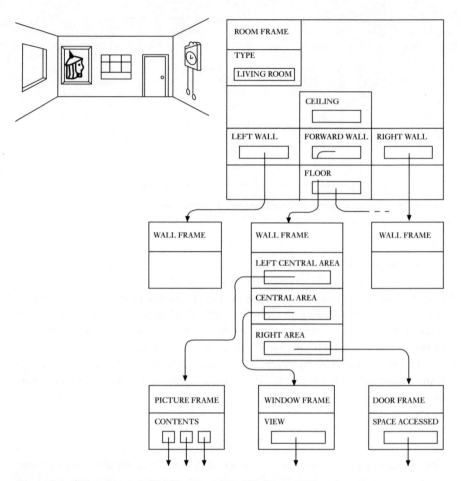

Figure 7.6   Room frame (from Winston, 1977: 186, figure 7.5)

Scripts/action frames

Scripts (also called "action frames") are stereotyped sequences of events which either record stereotypical *expectations* regarding these events, or form the basis of *plans* for directing actions. They can be called by frames, or they can be initiated to solve some problem or satisfy some goal. We will illustrate two uses of scripts: scripts called by frames to form the basis of an expectation regarding some event sequence, and those used to form the basis of a plan of action to solve some problem or achieve some goal.

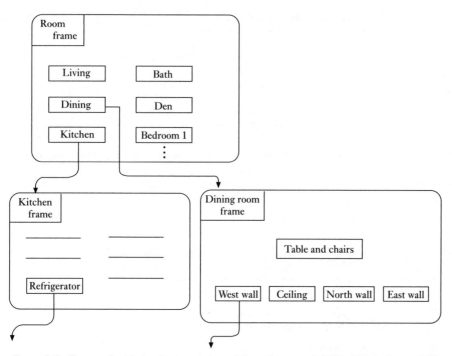

Figure 7.7 Frames for kinds of rooms (adapted from Staugaard, 1987: 100–1, figures 3.19, 3.21)

Eating–at–a–restaurant script
For the first use of a script, let's return to the restaurant frame just discussed. Notice that the "event-sequence" slot in the restaurant frame calls the "eating-at-a-restaurant" script. What does that look like? A sample is shown in figure 7.9.

Two broad kinds of information are contained in this script. First, there are the "ingredients" of the script: the props, roles, point of view, and so forth. These specify the participants or "actors" in the script and the situation in which they perform. Second, there is the stereotypical temporal sequence of events. In the script in the figure it would record, for instance, one's expectation to pay for one's food after getting/eating it at a sit-down restaurant, but one's expectation to pay for it before getting/eating it at a fast food restaurant.

Move–disk script
The second use of scripts is to solve a problem or satisfy some goal. Such a script (or action frame) might have the simplified form seen in figure 7.10.

Generic RESTAURANT Frame
Specialization-of: Business-establishment
Types:
    range: (Cafeteria, Seat-yourself, Wait-to-be-seated)
    default: Wait-to-be-seated
    if-needed: IF plastic-orange-counter THEN Fast-food,
               IF stack-of-trays THEN Cafeteria,
               IF wait-for-waitress-sign or reservations-made
                    THEN Wait-to-be-seated,
               OTHERWISE Seat-yourself.

Location:
    range: an ADDRESS
    if-needed: (Look at the MENU)

Name:
    if-needed: (Look at the MENU)

Food-style:
    range: (Burgers, Chinese, American, Seafood, French)
    default: American
    if-added: (Update alternatives of restaurant)

Times-of-operation:
    range: a Time-of-day
    default: open evenings except Mondays

Payment-form:
    range: (Cash, Credit card, Check, Washing-dishes-script)

Event-sequence:
    default: Eat-at-restaurant script

Alternatives:
    range: all restaurants with same Foodstyle
    if-needed: (Find all Restaurants with the same Foodstyle)

Figure 7.8   Restaurant frame (from Barr, Cohen, and Feigenbaum, 1981: 217–18)

Here we imagine an *actor* doing something to an *object* and this will involve certain *tasks* which move the object from the *source* to a *destination*. For instance, imagine the problem of getting a robot to move three disks from one peg to another peg, stacked in the same order (see figure 7.11). The robot might be instructed to begin by placing the top disk, A, on to the middle peg. The script/action frame for this might look as in figure 7.12.

Further scripts/action frames would specify the further actions necessary to solve the problem and achieve the goal, that is, continue moving the rest of the disks (from top to bottom) to the middle peg, resulting in the stack C, B, A. Then move the disks (from top to bottom) from the second peg to the third peg, resulting in the stack A, B, C, thus solving the problem. Although this

EAT-AT-RESTAURANT Script

Props:	(Restaurant, Money, Food, Menu, Tables, Chairs)
Roles:	(Hungry-persons, Wait-persons, Chef-persons)
Point-of-view:	Hungry-persons
Time-of-occurrence:	(Times-of-operation of restaurant)
Place-of-occurrence:	(Location of restaurant)

Event-sequence:

first:	Enter-restaurant script
then:	if (Wait-to-be-seated-sign or Reservations) then Get-maitre-d's-attention script
then:	Please-be-seated script
then:	Order-food script
then:	Eat-food script unless (Long-wait) when Exit-restaurant-angry Script
then:	if (Food-quality was better than palatable) then Compliments-to-the-chef script
then:	Pay-for-it Script
finally:	Leave-restaurant script

Figure 7.9 Eating-at-a-restaurant script (from Barr, Cohen, and Feigenbaum, 1981: 218–19)

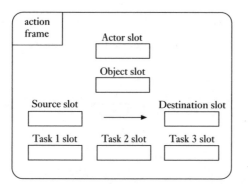

Figure 7.10 Generic script/action frame (adapted from Staugaard, 1987: 103, figure 3.23)

example is artificially simple, it gives the idea of how scripts might be used to direct event sequences, and not just record event sequence expectations.

Strengths and weaknesses of frames/scripts

Strengths

The main strength of frames/scripts is their ability to group relevant information together for easy access, and so frames, scripts, schemata, etc., have

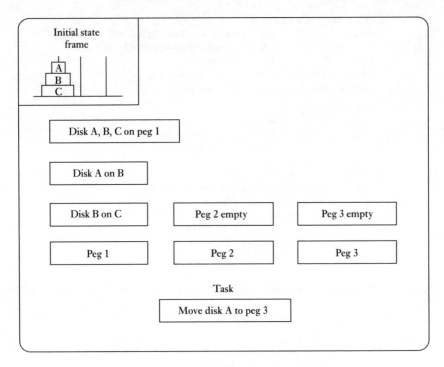

Figure 7.11   Initial disk state (from Staugaard, 1987: 105, figure 3.25)

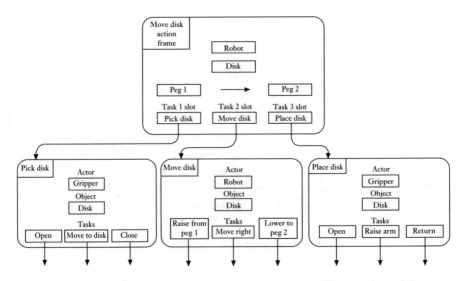

Figure 7.12   Move disk script/action frame (from Staugaard, 1987: 104, figure 3.24)

	PC	SN	F/S
Explicit semantics	Yes	No	No
General theory	Yes	No	No
Organizes information usefully	No	Yes	Yes

Figure 7.13 Some virtues and vices of high-level representations

played a significant role in artificial intelligence and even a role in cognitive psychology.

Weaknesses
The main weaknesses of frames/scripts is that (1) they (like semantic networks) have no explicit semantics, (2) nor (as with semantic networks) is there any general theory of their scope and limitations. Finally (3), there is the problem of information that does not belong in any particular frame or script, but is a part of our general commonsense understanding, e.g. the idea of paying for goods or services, or the idea that unsupported disks fall when released.

High-level formats: general assessment

All three representation schemes, then, have certain general virtues and vices, which we can tabulate as in figure 7.13. We would like to have a representation system with all the virtues and none of the vices of the above.

7.3 The Nature of Digital Computational Representation

The second question we raised at the outset concerns the nature of representation. On the digital computational theory, *how do representations represent?* Or, *in virtue of what do representations represent what they do?* With regard to the three formalisms just surveyed, we can ask: how does "T(a,b)" (= Taller

(Agnes, Betty)) represent the fact that Agnes is taller than Betty? How does the left portion of the semantic network represent the fact that Clyde is a robin? How does the room frame represent a room (and not a car)? How does the restaurant script represent the typical order of events in eating at a restaurant? (and not visiting a dentist?) Well? The silence is deafening. It is a striking fact about these latter notational systems that their representations are not explicitly compositional, or as we will say, they have no *explicit* compositional semantics. And for all systems we have surveyed, it is not a part of the computational story to say what these representations are *about*. We know what they are *intended* by their programmers to be about because of the English-like words that appear in them. These words may help *us*, but interpreting these words is not a part of the *computer* program. We might put it like this: what do these representations represent to or for the *computer* rather than *us*?

Interpretational semantics (IS)

One possible story (Cummins, 1989, chapters 8 and 10) is that digital computational representations represent by *being isomorphic to what they are about*. According to Cummins's way of developing this account, the kind of representation to be found in computers is distinctive enough to warrant a special label "simulation representation" ("s-representation").

An example

Suppose we want to explain how a pocket calculator adds. To add is to be correctly described by the plus (+) function; how does a pocket calculator do that? By manipulating *numerals* that represent numbers. How do we add on a calculator? We follow the push-the-button sequence: clear, first addend, plus, second addend, equals. The answer appears on the display. To get a machine to add one has to design it so that when one gets it to represent the addition operation and two numbers:

1 we can interpret button pressings as numbers,
2 we can interpret displays as numbers,
3 the device causally associates sequences of button pressings with displays,
4 if a token of the button pressing events interpreted as n and m were to occur, then a token display event interpreted as $n + m$ would normally occur as a consequence.   (Cummins, 1989: 90)

Representation

But where did the connection between button pressings, displays, and numbers come from, if not the human interpreter? According to Cummins, the fact that the above sequence of operations is *isomorphic* to plus (+) makes these representations of numbers. If the buttons were mislabeled and/or the display wires crossed, we would have to discover what symbolized what, but we would do that by finding which symbol–number correlation satisfied the plus operation. As Cummins says at one point: "there is a . . . sense in which it [an adding machine] represents numbers because it adds: we can speak of it as representing numbers only because it simulates + under some interpretation" (1989: 93). And in this sense a graph or equation represents sets of data, or a parabola represents the trajectory of a projectile.

Problem
One question this proposal will have to face is how to get the representation to be about the *right things*, since all sorts of objects can be made isomorphic with representations. If a machine can be interpreted as multiplying, it can be interpreted as adding. Indeed, there are an unlimited number of things that it can be interpreted as representing, if isomorphism were sufficient. One proposal for dealing with this problem is what might be called the "selection-by-purpose" approach. This is a two-step procedure whereby we first get all the isomorphic interpretations, then we select the "right" one on the grounds that it has something special to do with the purpose of the computation. But of course this second step is not computational, and so takes us outside the domain of computation. Thus, we are again in the situation that the computational answer to question (Q2) – what is the nature of representation: how do representations represent what they do? – is incomplete.

The problem of logical relations

We earlier (chapter 4) posed three problems for the simple detector semantics of the frog: the right cause (or depth) problem, the spread (or qua) problem, and the misrepresentation (or disjunction) problem. Now that we have surveyed some standard high-level computer representation systems, we can raise a fourth problem – *the problem of accounting for logical relations between representations*. (We could have raised this problem for the frog, but it seems pointless to speculate on logical relations between frog representations.) With the DCTM we are on much stronger ground since logical relations are among the most thoroughly studied and completely implemented relations in computer science – and here is where the predicate calculus (PC) shines as a knowledge representation scheme.

But there is an important wrinkle. As we saw in our exposition of PC, the system is determined by two sorts of rules: syntactic rules for building and inferring sentences, and semantic rules for assigning references and truth values. Some logical relations, such as the notion of inference and proof, are "syntactic." Others, such as the notions of truth and entailment (P entails Q if the truth of P guarantees the truth of Q), are "semantic." And we have seen that truth in PC depends on the notion of reference, and that is a notion that links representations to the world, and hence is outside the official limits of computational explanations. However, it has been known since the early 1930s that for many systems of representation, if one representation P from that system entails another representation Q from that system, then there is a proof (an inference according to the rules) in that system from P to Q. That is, the system has a kind of "completeness." And when a system has this kind of completeness, then the theory of proof ("proof theory") can stand in for the theory of truth relations ("model theory") – internal proof relations *mimic* external truth relations. Now, one thing digital computers are good at is tracking inference relations between representations, and this has given some hope that computational representations can be said to have not only "syntactic" logical relations, but "semantic" logical relations as well. We will see in the next chapter that the ability of computers to use internal inference relations to track external truth relations is seen by some as a powerful incentive for giving computer representations some sort of semantic content.

Study questions

Introduction

What two questions characterize the general issues surrounding representation?

What are atomic, complex, and compositional representations? Give an example of each.

Logic: predicate calculus (PC)

Represent the following statements in the PC.

Betty is female
Betty is taller than Agnes
Something is female
Everything is taller than Agnes or Agnes is not female

What is one major problem that a PC representation system has?

Semantic network (SN)

How do SNs overcome the major problem with predicate logic?

Represent the following sentence in a SN:

   Agnes is taller than Betty and Betty is female

By what mechanism do SNs make inferences?

By what mechanism do SNs answer questions?

What are some problems SNs have?

Frames (and scripts)

What is a frame?

What is a script?

What two main uses do scripts have?

Give a sample frame for "car."

Give a sample script for "visiting a doctor's office."

What strength(s) do frames and scripts have?

What weakness(es) do frames and scripts have?

The nature of representation

What problem is there for all three representation systems regarding how they represent what they do?

Suggested reading

Introduction

For a good introductory discussion of the problems of representation see Cummins (1989), chapter 1. Cummins (1986) discusses ways in which information may be "in" the system, but not "explicitly represented." For an introduction to data structures see e.g. Tremblay and Sorensen (1984).

The variety of digital computational representations

Barr, Cohen, and Feigenbaum (1981) offer a survey of the representation schemes discussed here, as well as some not discussed. Rich (1984, chapter 7) discusses semantic networks, frames, and scripts. Cherniak and McDermott (1985), chapter 1, also survey representations and their role in AI. Staugaard (1987), chapter 3, contains a very good survey of all the representation systems discussed here from a robotics/AI point of view. Partridge (1996) surveys the representational schemes covered here, as well as general issues of knowledge representation in AI. Thagard (1996), chapter 1, related representations to computation, then (chapters 2 and 4) discusses predicate logic and frames from a cognitive science point of view.

Logic: predicate calculus

Jeffrey (1991) is a clear introduction to logic. Rich (1983) devotes chapter 5 to predicate calculus representation. Mylopoulos and Levesque (1984) contains material especially relevant to PC. McDermott (1986) and Hewitt (1990) critically assess the role of logic in AI.

Semantic networks

One of the first works to explore the psychological use of SNs in modeling memory was Quinlan (1966), parts of which appeared as Quinlan (1968). The theoretical adequacy of semantic networks is explored in detail in Woods (1975). Knowledge level issues are explored in Brachman (1979), which also contains useful history and suggestion for overcoming inadequacies. Psychological applications can be found in Norman and Rumelhart (1975).

Frames/scripts

The classic study of frames remains Minsky (1975), and it is still recommended reading. Winograd (1975) discusses frames in relation to general issues of machine representation, as does Hayes (1980). For a more psychological approach to frames and scripts see Schank and Abelson (1977), or the survey in Eysenck and Keane (1990).

The nature of digital computational representation

McDermott (1976) and Hayes (1979) highlight the problem of the labels in representation doing too much work. An attempt to characterize computation as embedded in the world can be found in McClamrock (1995).

Interpretational semantics

Interpretational semantics is introduced in Haugeland (1985), chapter 3, elaborated in Cummins (1989), and modified in Cummins (1996). It is critically discussed in Horgan (1994).

The problem of logical relations

A readable and authoritative introductory discussion of how external truth relations can outrun internal proof relations can be found in Tarski (1969). Rey (1997), chapter 8.2, briefly discusses deductive relations in computation, from a cognitive science perspective. Any good text in symbolic logic will discuss the completeness of some systems of logic and the incompleteness of others, but a particularly intuitive discussion can be found in Jeffrey (1991).

8

The Digital Computational
Theory of Mind

8.1 Introduction

The driving idea behind the computational model of cognition is the idea that *cognition centrally involves the notions of mentally manipulating (creating, transforming, and deleting) mental representations of the world around us*, and that *computers are automatic symbol manipulators par excellence*. We went on to identify two major aspects of digital computers – architecture and representation. We divided architecture into its two main components, memory and control, and taxonomized some famous architectures on the basis of these notions. We also surveyed some influential representation schemes in digital artificial intelligence. We turn back now to the cognitive side. Are there any more specific reasons for taking the computer "analogy" seriously, that is, for thinking it is literally true – that *cognition really is a species of (digital) computation*? What is the nature of *mental* representation? How does computation relate to consciousness? What kinds of *cognitive* architectures are there?

These are some of the questions we must at least face, if not answer. Much of current cognitive psychology and cognitive neuroscience is devoted to investigating these questions. We will not go into the details here. What we are interested in is the general computational framework within which so much of "information processing" psychology is carried out. Since there are a variety of possible computer architectures, it would be a mistake to suppose that the computer model requires any particular cognitive organization. In the next few sections we will ignore the organizational details of different kinds of computers and focus on the fact that they all automatically manipulate representations according to general principles. We will then return to the question of cognitive organization at the end.

8.2 From the Representational Theory of Mind to the Computational Theory of Mind

The DCTM did not emerge *ex nihilo*; it can instructively be viewed as a special case of a more general theory, the so-called Representational Theory of Mind (RTM).

The representational theory of mind

We first formulate the representational theory of mind in its basic form as follows:

(RTM)
1 Cognitive states are relations to (mental) representations which have content,
2 Cognitive processes are (mental) operations on these representations.

On this account, believing would be one relation to a representation, intending another, and desiring yet another, and different representations would constitute different things believed, intended, and desired. Two influential philosophical traditions come together in the RTM – one descending from Hume, the other from Frege and Russell. Each of these traditions has its strengths and weaknesses.

Hume

For Hume, mental representations are "ideas" and we "entertain" them when we are in mental states such as believing, desiring, and intending. Mental processes for Hume are sequences of associated ideas, and we explain behavior by citing current relevant ideas. However, this does not tell us what their "semantics" is – what they are "about" and how they are "about" what they are about. In other words, Hume's account of ideas and mental processes does not tell us how, for example, a belief can have a truth value, and ideas in a belief can determine a reference and be about something. Hume seems to have held that ideas are like *images* and are about what they *resemble* or resemble most. But resemblance has all sorts of problems as a theory of representation. *First*, it is both not general enough and too general; *second*, it does not really account for mental reference; and *third* it does not accommodate truth and falsity. It is instructive to look at each of these in more detail. To see the *first*, notice that many of our ideas are not *images* that can resemble something (thing of abstract notions like "justice"), they are more like *concepts*. And even when they are images (thinking of the Eiffel Tower as having an image of the Eiffel Tower), they are sometimes too specific to be correct. One's image of the Eiffel Tower probably also represents it as having a certain general shape, orientation, relative size, viewing perspective (from the side, not from the top), etc. Yet none of these features is essential to thinking about the Eiffel Tower. On the other hand, some images are excessively indeterminate (some people say "ambiguous"). Wittgenstein's influential example of this was a stick figure with one leg in front of the other, drawn on a slope – is the figure walking up, or sliding down? Both are captured exactly by the sketch. To see the *second*, notice that in general, resemblance is not sufficient for representation. Your left hand resembles itself (and your right hand), but it does not represent them. A political cartoon might resemble an R. Nixon imitator more than the actual R. Nixon, but we don't want to say the cartoon is therefore about the imitator rather than Nixon. Finally, to see the *third*, images themselves are not true or false – what is true or false is something more "sentential" or "propositional" rather than something "nominal." We don't say, for example, "the Eiffel Tower" is true/false; we say, for example, "The Eiffel Tower was built by Gustav Eiffel" is true/false.

Frege and Russell

The Frege–Russell theory attempts to take steps to overcome at least the second and third of these objections to Hume. Russell (1918) introduced the term "propositional attitude" into the theory of mind for any mental state that involves having an "attitude" to a proposition (P). Typical examples include believing that P, desiring that P, intending that P. Frege (1892, 1918) held that, say, believing that P consists of two components. *First*, there is the proposition P believed, which gives the *content* of the thought – what the thought is *about*. This proposition can be true or false, so the content of the belief can be true or false, and thus the belief can be true or false. *Second*, there is the relation between the person and the proposition which he called "grasping." Different ways of "grasping a proposition" yield the different attitudes. For instance, suppose that P = Mars has life on it. One can believe that P (Mars has life on it), hope that P, fear that P, desire that P, etc. Frege never said what "grasping" a proposition amounts to, and although he analogized grasping a proposition to perceiving a scene, he ultimately declared that it was a "mystery" – a mystery made all the more pressing given his conception of propositions as abstract entities. Just how can a spatio-temporal entity such as a person "grasp" an abstract entity? But even if we had an account of grasping propositions, how would the fact that we grasped one proposition rather than another help to explain our behavior? If I am thirsty and believe that there is a beer in my refrigerator, that belief can play a causal role in *producing* my behavior, and citing that belief can play a causal-explanatory role in *accounting* for my behavior. How would grasping an abstract entity play such a role? What we need here is not a mental relation to an abstract content, but *a relation to something mental that has content* and can play a role in psychological explanation.

Propositional attitudes

Later in this chapter and the next we will see how important the class of "propositional attitudes" is to the DCTM. For now we will just take a brief look at them. The propositional attitudes (beliefs, desires, intentions, etc.) have both common and distinctive characteristics and it will be useful to organize our discussion in this way.

Common characteristic

(1)   As we have just seen from Frege and Russell, these states are called "propositional attitudes" in part because they can all be factored into two parts: the propositional content, and a part that constitutes the "attitude proper" towards that propositional content (what Searle, 1979, 1983, calls the "psychological mode"). Likewise, attributions of propositional attitudes typically have the form: "xAp," where "x" represents a person, "A" represents an attitude (believes, desires, intends), and "p" represents a content. We normally report a propositional attitude with an attitude *verb* plus a propositional-expressing *sentence*:

Verb	+	*Sentence*
believe		(that) there is life on Mars

Sometimes the language requires us to bend a little to accommodate certain verbs:

Verb	+	*Sentence*
desire		(that) there be life on Mars
want		there to be life on Mars
intend		that I go to Mars

But we can still see an attitude to a proposition in each of these cases.

Direction of fit:	mind-to-world	world-to-mind
Propositional attitude:	$\times \begin{Bmatrix} \text{believes} \\ \text{knows} \end{Bmatrix}$ that p	$\times \begin{Bmatrix} \text{desires} \\ \text{intends} \end{Bmatrix}$ that p

Figure 8.1 Propositional attitudes and direction of fit

Distinctive characteristics

(2)   One important difference among the attitudes has to do with what is called the "onus of match" (Austin) and "direction of fit" (Anscombe, Searle). Although propositional attitudes share the feature that they fit the world when they are satisfied, the way they do that can be different for different attitudes. For instance, *beliefs* represent an antecedently given world, and if the world fits them they are true, but if it fails to fit them, the belief is false. We will say that beliefs (and some other attitudes) have a *mind-to-world direction of fit*. *Desires* and *intentions*, on the other hand, are like blueprints for the way the world is to become – the world is to fit them, and when the world becomes the way they represent it, they are satisfied. We say that desires and intentions have a *world-to-mind direction of fit*. Notice that the attitude and the direction of fit always go together in that it is not the case that some beliefs have one direction of fit, other beliefs have the other. This is because *the attitude determines the direction of fit*. And since the elements of the proposition, P, determine the way the world is represented to be or become, *the proposition determines the conditions of fit* (no matter what the direction of fit may be) (see figure 8.1).

(3)   Another potential difference among the attitudes has to do with the experiential character of the attitude, or the lack of such experiential character. For example, if you *fear* that there is an intruder in the house you probably have a fairly specific feeling, one that you will not confuse with *desiring* that there be an intruder in the house. But if you *believe* that there is life on Mars (or an intruder in the house, for that matter), is there a specific "belief feeling" that accompanies it in the way fearing and desiring seem to be accompanied? Furthermore, there is the question whether these "feelings" are essential to holding the attitude or *only* an accompaniment. These are current topics of debate in cognitive science, and we will return to some of them later.

The score
Hume's theory (association of ideas + resemblance) has the advantage of an account that accommodates psychological explanations, but it has no workable account of representational content – images are (1) too special and restricted

a class of mental representations to serve as the model for all mental reference, and (2) they give us no account of how propositional attitudes can be true or false, fulfilled or unfulfilled, etc. Frege and Russell's theory accommodates the notion of representational content in general that can be true or false, etc., but it gives no account of psychological explanation. We would like a theory that both accounted for psychological explanation and representational content.

The basic digital computational theory of mind

Before we elaborate and justify the full digital computational theory of mind (DCTM), we will first sketch a bit of history and motivation for the computational approach, then present the DCTM in its basic form.

A bit of history

In 1947, Alan Turing gave a lecture entitled "Intelligent Machinery" where he proposed "to investigate the question as to whether it is possible for machinery to show intelligent behavior." He then imagines various ways of "building an 'intelligent machine'" (scare quotes in the original). In particular, he investigates ways of training the machine, since, as he jokes, "It would be quite unfair to expect a machine straight from the factory to compete on equal terms with a university graduate."

The "Turing test"
In his famous 1950 paper "Computing machinery and intelligence" he introduces what he called the "imitation game," which in a simplified form came to be known as the "Turing test" for machine intelligence. Here is how Turing (1950) himself motivates, sets up, and then pronounces on the test:

> *Motivation*   I propose to consider the question "Can machines think?" . . . I shall replace the question by another, which is closely related to it and is expressed in relatively unambiguous words.

> *The imitation game*   The new form of the problem can be described in terms of a game which we call the "imitation game." It is played with three people, a man (A), a woman (B), and an interrogator (C) who may be of either sex. The interrogator stays in a room apart from the other two. The object of the game for the interrogator is to determine which of the other two is the man and which is the woman. He knows them by labels X and Y, and at the end of the game he says either "X is A and Y is B" or "X is B and Y is A." . . . The ideal arrangement is to have a teleprinter communicating between the two rooms. . . . We now ask

the question, "What will happen when a machine takes the part of A in the game?" Will the interrogator decide wrongly as often when the game is played like this as he does when the game is played between a man and a woman? These questions replace our original "Can machines think?"

The new problem has the advantage of drawing a fairly sharp line between the physical and the intellectual capacities of a man.

Winning the game   I believe that in about fifty years' time it will be possible to program computers, with a storage capacity of about 10^9, to make them play the imitation game so well that an average interrogator will not have more than 70 percent chance of making the right identification after five minutes of questioning. The original question, "Can machines think?" I believe to be too meaningless to deserve discussion. Nevertheless I believe that at the end of the century the use of words and general educated opinion will have altered so much that one will be able to speak of machines thinking without expecting to be contradicted.

Note that although Turing discusses the conditions under which one might conclude that a *digital computer* can think, this is not by itself a claim that *human thinking* is computation. That is, some digital computation might be "thinking" (Turing often used scare quotes here), and human cognition might be thinking, but human cognition might not be digital computation. It is hard to find Turing actually *claiming* that human thinking is a species of digital computation. In his 1947 lecture (mentioned above), Turing makes the provocative remark: "All of this suggests that the cortex of the infant is an unorganized machine, which can be organized by suitable interfering training. The organizing might result in the modification of the machine into a universal machine or something like it" (1947: 120). The idea seems to be that the cortex starts out as a kind of jumble of connected neurons (a connectionist machine?) and by means of training/education it becomes organized into something approximating a universal Turing machine. If we add the idea that it is in virtue of the computational states of the cortex that the brain has the cognitive states that it has, we would have an early version of the computational theory of mind.

The field of artificial intelligence, and to some extent cognitive science, has seen the "Turing test" as a test for thinking (intelligence, cognition, mentality, etc., these different terms are used indiscriminately). If passing the test (winning the game) is sufficient for "thinking" and a computer can be programmed to pass the test, then the essence of thinking must be computation. And if thinking is just running mental algorithms (what else could it be?), then the Church-Turing thesis tells us that these can be carried out by Turing machines. And Turing's theorem tells us that each of these machines can be mimicked by a universal Turing machine. So, the reasoning went, thinking is a species of computation on something equivalent to a universal Turing machine, say a von Neumann machine or a production system. Thus, the job of artificial intelligence, cognitive psychology, and neuroscience, is to discover the actual algorithms of the mind. (We will say more about this line of reasoning in the next chapter.)

Putnam and Turing machine functionalism
In 1960 Hillary Putnam published "Minds and machines," where he investigates the *analogy* between minds and Turing machines with respect to the mind–body problem. But again, it is not clear that a computational theory of mind is being contemplated. For instance, he comments at one point that "I do not claim that this question [whether or not it is ever possible to identify mental events and physical events] arises for Turing machines." Why not, one might ask, if mental events are computational processes? Later Putnam comments: "I may be accused of advocating a 'mechanistic' world-view in pressing the present analogy [between minds and Turing machines]. If this means that I am supposed to hold that machines think, on the one hand, or that human beings are machines, on the other, the charge is false." This does not sound like a computational theory of mind – a theory that mental states are computational states. Putnam, in the same article, points out explicitly that Turing machines are multiply realizable in the sense that "a given 'Turing machine' is an *abstract* machine which may be physically realized in an almost infinite number of different ways". But importantly *he does not run the same argument for mental states*. That point is made explicitly in his 1967 article "The nature of mental states" (original title "Psychological predicates"), which may well be the paper that inspired the computational theory of mind. The crucial steps in Putnam's (1967) discussion are *first*, the identification of psychological states with functional states: "I shall, in short, argue that *pain* is not a brain state, in the sense of a physical-chemical state of the brain (or even the whole nervous system) but *a functional state* of the whole organism" (emphasis added). Then *second*, he urges the multiple realizability of psychological states: "a mammalian brain, a reptilian brain, a mollusc's brain . . . any extraterrestrial life that may be found that will be capable of feeling pain. . . ." Now we have it that (1) Turing machines are multiply realizable, (2) psychological states are multiply realizable, and (3) psychological states are functionally specified. Putnam can now argue that the *best explanation* of the joint multiple realizability of Turing machine states and psychological states is that Turing machine states specify the relevant functional states, and so specify psychological states. Of course one might (uncharitably) complain that Putnam does not say anything about

cognition, only pain. Yet there are reasons for supposing that Putnam had simply picked pain as a popular *example* mental state, and that the argument could be generalized to *mental states in general*. For instance, when arguing against the "brain state identity theory" he comments: "the brain state theorist is not just saying that *pain* is a brain state; he is saying that *every* psychological state is a brain state." Clearly Turing machine functionalism would *also* have to be a theory of all psychological states, if it is to compete against the brain state theory of all psychological states (note the generality): "if the program . . . ever succeeds, then it will bring in its wake a . . . precise definition of the notion 'psychological state.'" And recall, the paper is not entitled "The nature of *pain* states" (nor was it originally titled "*Pain* predicates"), but "The nature of *mental* states" – the generality is important. So it was more likely Putnam, rather than Turing, who made the crucial move from the "intelligence of computation" to the "computational theory of intelligence."

Block and Fodor
Block and Fodor (1972) finally completed the process of formulating a computational conception of mind by extending Putnam's proposal from Turing machines (or probabilistic automata) to computational systems in general (Fodor, of course, has extended and refined the CTM to include such doctrines and topics as: the language of thought (1975), modularity (1983), folk psychology and the analysis of propositional attitudes (1987), narrow content and intentional generalizations (1994).

Newell and Simon
So far we have been recounting the history of the CTM exclusively from within philosophy, but in cognitive science more generally there were influences from other sources, in particular from artificial intelligence (AI). One of the most influential papers in this regard was the one by Newell and Simon (1976), which introduced:

> *The Physical Symbol System Hypothesis.* A physical symbol system has the necessary and sufficient means for general intelligent action.

Note that this proposal endows a system with the capacity for "intelligent action," not cognition or mind directly, and one might argue that we are more willing to call the behavior of mechanical systems "intelligent" than we are to say they have minds – nobody seems inclined to say "smart bombs" have minds. But undoubtedly it is tempting to suppose that a precondition for intelligence is cognition or mind, and that seems to be the way the field has treated the proposal. But what is a "physical symbol system"? It is a set of physical symbols (e.g. symbols realized in silicon or neurons) and operations, housed in a machine: "A physical symbol system consists of a set of entities, called symbols, which are physical patterns that can occur as components of another type of entity called an expression (or symbol structure) . . . Besides these structures the system also contains a collection of processes that operate on expressions to produce other expressions. . . . A *physical symbol system is a machine that produced through time an evolving collection of symbol structures*" (1976; emphasis added). Since the "machine" mentioned here is equivalent to a universal Turing machine (UTM), the above hypothesis makes having the capacity for intelligent action equivalent to realizing a UTM.

The computational theory of mind

With those historical remarks in place, let's turn to the generic computational theory of mind (CTM) as currently formulated (the formulation of the CTM we use here is adopted from Fodor, 1987). The CTM account of cognition in general, and mental states such as the propositional attitudes in particular, can now be seen as a special case of RTM. It is an attempt to specify in more detail the nature of the relations, operations, and representations involved:

1   the *relations* in RTM are computational,
2   the *operations* in RTM are computational,
3   the *representations* in RTM are computational.

We will take up the first two points now, the third in the next section.

The formality constraint

Regarding computational relations and operations, Fodor (1981b) argues that computational theories of mind must obey what he calls the "formality constraint": "I take it that computational processes are . . . symbolic because they are defined over representations, and they are formal because they apply to representations in virtue of (roughly) the *syntax* of the representations. . . . Formal operations are the ones that are specified without reference to such semantic properties of representations as, for example, truth, reference and meaning . . . formal operations apply in terms of the, as it were, shapes of the objects in their domains . . . the computational theory of mind requires that two thoughts can be distinguished in content only if they can be identified with relations to formally distinct representations" (1981: 227). The formality constraint seems natural enough when one thinks about what programming a digital computer amounted to. We write programs (TM tables, vNM instructions, PS productions) that would operate directly on the form or shape of the data structure, not on what it was about.

Terminological note   Fodor, in stating the formality constraint, often uses "formal" and "syntactic" interchangeably. Devitt (1989, 1991), for one, has complained vigorously that "formal" has to do with the intrinsic shape (form) of something, whereas "syntactic" has to do with the extrinsic relations it bears to other representations. While we can agree with the importance and relevance of this distinction, it does not seem that the field respects it in these terms. (Frege and Russell spoke of "logical form," and Carnap spoke of "logical syntax.") We will take "syntactic" as a stylistic variant of "formal."

Attitudes

The formality constraint tells us when we have two representations, but when do we have two attitudes? What, for instance, distinguishes a belief from a desire from an intention? Consider Mr. Bubblehead (see figure 8.2). Here we see a collection of representations stored under the headings "beliefs," and "desires." What makes a representation a part of a belief, rather than a desire, is the way it interacts with other representations – the way it is utilized and operated on in theoretical and practical reasoning. If you *want* a drink and *believe* there is a coke in the fridge, then other things being equal you will *intend* to go to the fridge, get the coke, and drink it. It is customary to refer to the set of interactions between representations that constitute belief as the "belief box," the set of interactions between representations that constitute desires the "desire box," and so on for the other propositional attitudes (see Mr. Bubblehead again). These "boxes" are simply convenient ways of visualizing complicated computational relations. These computational relations and operations are typically given to the machine by programming it, though they are sometimes hardwired (we return to this distinction in the Coda). For now we retain the neutral terminology.

Representations also have meaning, or as we will say, they have "mental content" in that they express some proposition and so are about something. We can formulate the generic CTM as follows:

(CTM)
1   Cognitive states are *computational relations* to *computational mental representations* which have content.
2   Cognitive processes (changes in cognitive states) are *computational operations* on *computational mental representations* which have content.

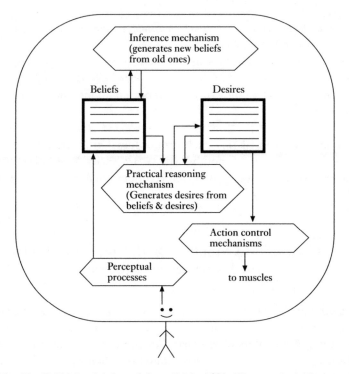

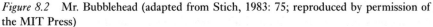

Figure 8.2 Mr. Bubblehead (adapted from Stich, 1983: 75; reproduced by permission of the MIT Press)

So far we have a generic computational theory of mind. How do we get to a specifically *digital* theory? This is currently a matter of some dispute (which we will return to later). For now we will simply note two reasonable conditions:

Architecture   One constraint we might put on making a computational theory of mind digital is by saying that *the computational architecture (memory and control) must be digital.*

Representations   Another constraint we might put on making a computational theory of mind digital is by saying that what makes it digital is that *the representations must be digital.*

In light of these, we can formulate the basic DCTM as the following digital specification of the CTM:

(B-DCTM)

1   Cognitive states are *computational relations* to *computational mental representations* which have content.
2   Cognitive processes (changes in cognitive states) are *computational operations* on *computational mental representations* which have content.
3   The computational architecture and representations (mentioned in 1 and 2) are *digital*.

Finally, it should be noted that each propositional attitude, such as "belief," is actually a rich cluster of notions (there are many kinds of beliefs) and consequently there will be a variety of computational relations in the belief family.

8.3   The Digital Computational Theory of Mind and the Language of Thought

Notice again that (CTM) analyzes cognitive states and processes into *two parts*: a computational relation or operation, and a mental representation. It is a general feature of digital machines that they compute in some kind of code. If computation is a species of digital computation, then the mind manipulates (creates, transforms, and deletes) mental representations, and these mental representations form, at bottom, a kind of machine code for the brain. The code structure of this system has suggested to some that mental representations form a language-like system. This has become known as *the language of thought (LOT) hypothesis* (see Fodor, 1975). Incorporating this idea into (CTM) gives us our first official version of the digital computational theory of mind:

(DCTM)

1   Cognitive states are *computational relations* to *computational mental representations* (in the language of thought) which have content.
2   Cognitive processes (changes in cognitive states) are *computational operations* on *computational mental representations* (in the language of thought) which have content.
3   The computational architecture and representations (mentioned in 1 and 2) are *digital*.

To the extent that there is evidence for a language of thought, there will be support for one aspect of DCTM. What is the LOT and what reasons are there to accept it?

The language of thought

The basic idea behind the language of thought (LOT) hypothesis is that cognition involves a *language-like* representation system. Clearly, spoken natural languages have some properties irrelevant to cognition, such as being spoken, being used to communicate, being acquired, etc., so the language of thought will not be like (spoken) natural language in these respects. But in what respects? Typically these:

(LOT)
1　The system has a basic "vocabulary" for representation, which can include concepts, percepts, images etc.
2　The vocabulary items are combinable in accordance with general principles – i.e. the system has a "syntax."
3　The vocabulary items and structured combinations of them are *about* something – they have a compositional "semantics."

On Fodor's original conception, such a system is analogous to the "machine language" of a computer, and as such it is a part of its design – it does not need learn it. So by analogy, LOT would be a part of our genetic endowment and should be viewed as the system we think in before we learn our first language. Of course, it is possible that this system takes time to mature and so is not (like our second set of teeth or gray hair) complete at birth. This "nativistic" component to the LOT hypothesis is extremely controversial and we will not assume it in what follows. How will the existence and nature of such a system help the DCTM? The motivation for the DCTM from the language of thought is roughly this: humans have a mental system which they use to represent the world around them in their planning and reasoning, and so do computers. Furthermore, our system of mental representation is productive and systematic, and so is the computer's. So this further analogy between us and computers supports the view that aspects of our mental life can be viewed as computation. Let's look at these two motivations in more detail.

Motivations for the LOT: modes of presentation (ways of representing)

A (very) short story: Alice and Betty are leafing through their 1959 high school yearbook from Hibbing, Minnesota. Getting to the end, Alice comments:

"Zimmerman, remember him, Robert Zimmerman? Skinny guy with a lot of hair. Left town right after high school. Heard he tried U. Minn., but didn't graduate. Left town. Wonder what ever happened to him?" Their reminiscing is cut short by a glance at the clock. It's 6:30. Time to get ready. Have had tickets to a Bob Dylan concert for three months and it starts at 8:00. End of story. Is this situation possible? It would seem so. But how so, if Bob Dylan *is* (that) Robert Zimmerman, then how can they wonder what ever happened to him and at the same time know who they are going to hear in concert? One wants to say: ah, yes, but they don't *realize* that the Bob Dylan they read about all the time and are going to hear, is the same person as their anti-social classmate in high school. How to explain this possibility?

According to LOT, this kind of story gives us some reason to think that Alice, Betty, and people in general, deploy representations of the world, in thinking about the world, that depict things as being a certain way – we "picture" them or "describe" them to ourselves – and a symptom of this fact is that we may fail to recognize the same thing depicted in two different ways. That said, we still don't have an argument that these representations are anything like a "linguistic" system, in being syntactically structured and semantically compositional. Let's look briefly at reasons for thinking this.

Motivations for the LOT: productivity

This motivation for the LOT derives from the fact that human thought seems to be productive, in the sense that we can think an indefinitely large series of distinct and novel thoughts, for example, 1 is a number, 2 is a number, and so on. This ability seems to be limited not by anything intrinsic to the thinking, but by extrinsic factors such as motivation and attention, longevity, etc. Yet we are finite creatures with finite memory and operations, so how can we explain this capacity to produce a potential infinity of distinct thoughts? The LOT says: we have a finite representational system with a compositional structure, and the LOT allows old pieces to be put together in new combinations.

Motivations for the LOT: systematicity

This motivation for the LOT hypothesis has the form: human (and some animal) cognition has certain systematic properties that the LOT hypothesis would explain, and other theories cannot. So by inference to the best explanation, we should conclude that the LOT hypothesis is true.

Thought

Fodor (1987) originally put the argument for the LOT based on the *systematicity of thought* like this: "LOT says that having a thought is being related to a structured array of representations; and, presumably, to have the thought that John loves Mary is ipso facto to have access to the same representations, and the same representational structures, that you need to have the thought that Mary loves John. So *of course* anybody who is in a position to have one of these thoughts is ipso facto in a position to have the other. LOT explains the systematicity of thought" (1987: 151).

Inference

Fodor and Pylyshyn (1988) propose a second, though related, consideration in favor of the LOT based on the *systematicity of inference* like this: "theories [embracing LOT] are committed to the following striking prediction: inferences that are of similar logical type ought, pretty generally, to elicit correspondingly similar cognitive capacities. You shouldn't, for example, find a kind of mental life in which you get inferences from P & Q & R to P, but you don't get inferences from P & Q to P" (1988: 46–7).

As these authors note, there are few, if any, examples of minds capable of one sort of thought or inference, but not capable of other related thoughts or inferences – there are no "punctate minds" capable of, say, 73 unrelated thoughts. In each case the argument for the LOT goes like this: thought and reasoning are in fact systematic, the LOT hypothesis says thought and inference are carried out in a language-like system of representation. If the LOT hypothesis were true, then the systematicity of thought and inference could be explained. There is presently no better explanation for the systematicity of thought and inference. So probably the LOT hypothesis is true.

These considerations in favor of LOT (modes of presentation, productivity, and systematicity) are only as good as the empirical evidence in favor of systematicity, and some connectionists argue that these claims need serious qualifications.

8.4 DCTM and the Mind–Body Problem

The DCTM can be elaborated in such a way that it (1) offers the best available solution to a traditional philosophical puzzle, the so-called "mind–body problem," and (2) provides a fruitful framework for empirical investigations into cognition. This is something few if any other theories of mind can boast and as such it deserves careful scrutiny.

The mind–body problem

The mind–body problem can be put thus: what is the relationship between mental phenomena (states, events, and processes) and physical phenomena (states, events, and processes)? One of the advantages of DCTM is that it provides a framework for constructing successful theories in cognition, and it does this, in part, because (1) it offers a solution to the mind–body problem that is free from the objections of other theories, and (2) it makes *psychological explanation* of behavior an acceptable kind of *causal explanation*. We will work our way up to this by first examining the competing views and exposing their weaknesses.

The competition

Dualistic interactionism

This is the view, made famous by Descartes (see chapter 3), that the world has *two different substances*, the mental and the physical. Mental substance is conscious and temporal but not spatial (and so not divisible and not subject to the laws of physics) whereas physical substance is both temporal and spatial (and so divisible) and subject to the laws of physics. These substances *interact causally* – mental events can cause physical events, and physical events can cause mental events.

Pro
The *interactive* part goes well with our commonsense intuitions that physical causes (drinking a lot) can have mental effects (drunkenness), and that mental causes (deciding to wave goodbye) can have physical effects (waving goodbye).

Con
1   The *dualistic* part is incompatible with experimental psychology, which includes many of the same methods as the physical sciences, and which would not seem applicable to mental substance (see above).
2   The *causal* part is a mystery – how can something non-spatial and non-material cause something spatial and material to happen without violating principles of conservation of energy, etc.?

Epiphenomenalism

This is the view that although physical phenomena can cause mental phenomena, mental phenomena cannot cause physical phenomena. On this view, just as the blinking lights on (or heat from) a computer are a by-product of its operation and do not contribute to its processing, so mental phenomena such as thought are just a by-product of the working of the brain, and do not contribute to the course of action.

Pro

1   This avoids the second objection to dualism – there are, for instance, no violations of conservation of energy and momentum.

Con

1   It does not avoid the first objection to dualism.
2   It makes human thought, decisions, etc., irrelevant to the course of human history, and this is a bit hard to accept.

Radical behaviorism

The view that mental phenomena *just are* certain kinds of behavioral dispositions – dispositions to react to certain stimuli with certain responses.

Pro

It "solves" the mind–body problem by *dissolving* it – there is no relationship between the mental and the physical because there is no mental.

Con

1   Without overwhelming evidence it is too hard to believe that there are no mental phenomena and no "interaction" between mind and body at all.
2   Psychology has not turned out this way at all. Current cognitive psychology posits elaborately structured mental causes for behavior.

Logical (analytical) behaviorism

This is the semantic view that every statement ascribing mental phenomena is *equivalent to* some behavioral hypothetical (if such-and-such were to happen, then so-and-so would result) statement, in much the same way as statements ascribing fragility to a glass are analyzed in terms of its breaking if dropped, etc.

Pro
1   It accounts for mental causation as the instantiation of a behavioral hypothetical (so-and-so happened because: if such-and-such were to happen, then so-and-so would result, and such-and-such DID happen).

Con
1   There is no reason to suppose that such behavioral hypotheticals can be given for all mental phenomena – no one has ever given even *one* adequate analysis.
2   It does not account for (mental) event causation: coming to feel thirsty and noticing that there is a glass of water on the table caused her to reach out for the glass. This is the fundamental sort of causation.

Physicalism

(This is also called the *identity theory* because it postulates a mental-physical identity.) There is a weaker version of the identity theory and a stronger version.

Token physicalism
This is the view that each *token (particular) mental phenomenon* is identical with some *token (particular) physical phenomenon*, but that mental and physical types may not correspond. Suppose that for humans every actual pain is a C-fiber stimulation, and that C-fibers are made ultimately of hydrocarbons. Suppose that Martians are made of silicon and when they feel pain S-fibers are stimulated. These S-fiber stimulations would be different types of physical phenomena, and so different types of mental phenomena.

Type physicalism
This is the view that each *type of mental phenomenon* is identical to some *type of physical phenomenon*. So, two systems can exhibit the same type of mental phenomenon (e.g., pain) only if they exhibit the same type of physical phenomenon (e.g., C-fiber stimulation). Thus, since silicon is distinct from hydrocarbon, a silicon-based Martian and a hydrocarbon-based human could not both be in pain, if pain is C-fiber stimulation and C-fibers are hydrocarbon. Type physicalists are also token physicalists (how could one claim that all types of mental phenomena are identical to types of physical phenomena, but particular tokens of mental phenomena are not tokens of physical phenomena?). Type physicalism is a highly reductive theory – it *reduces* mental phenomena to physical phenomena, though unlike "eliminativism," it does not deny that

there are mental phenomena. (Note: saying that Bob Dylan is Robert Zimmerman does not *eliminate* Bob Dylan – there still is Bob Dylan.)

Pro token physicalism
1   It provides an account of mental event causation, because each particular mental event IS (identical with) some physical event, so "mental" causation is a species of physical causation.

Pro type physicalism
1   Besides inheriting the above virtue of token physicalism, it provides a reference for our mental notions, e.g., pain is C-fiber firing – it answers the question: what state does a system have to be in to feel, e.g., pain?

Con token physicalism
1   It does not provide a reference for our mental notions, e.g., *pain*; it does not answer the question: what state does a system have to be in to feel, e.g., pain?

Con type physicalism
1   It identifies the type of psychological phenomenon with a type of physical phenomenon, yet it seems that psychological phenomena depend more on "software" than on "hardware." It is possible that silicon-based Martians can be in pain, or believe that the Earth is round, provided that they are running the right software.
2   The natural domain for mental (or at least cognitive, we will return to this) phenomena seems to be systems that *process information*, not systems made out of such-and-such stuff.

The score so far
Token physicalism is too weak to be satisfactory and type physicalism is too strong. Can we have the virtues of the identity theory without its vices?

Supervenience

One popular way of getting these benefits is called "supervenience," and when combined with functionalism (see below) it is one of the most popular pictures of the mind–body relationship at present – so we will take a bit of time developing this idea. What does this mean? First some examples outside the mind–body problem. All sorts of states supervene on other states. G. E. Moore seems to have introduced the notion with an example from art. Consider a painting, say the Mona Lisa. Now consider a molecule-for-molecule duplicate of the Mona Lisa – twin Mona Lisa. Could the first be a beautiful painting, but not the second? They are identical down to their paint molecules; so anything beautiful about the one would seem to be exactly as beautiful about the other. So it looks like the answer is "no," and we say that the beauty of the painting *supervenes* on its physical properties (paint molecules). Or consider baldness – could one person who is molecule-for-molecule (and so, hair-for-hair) identical to his twin be bald without the twin being bald? Again, the answer seems to be "no." Molecular twins have identical hair distribution, they are identically bald and we say that baldness *supervenes* on physical properties (hair distribution). In general, then, we say:

Generic supervenience (*GS*):   A-facts (beauty, baldness) *supervene* on B-facts (paint, hairs) if no two possible situations are identical with respect to their B-facts (paint, hairs), but differ with respect to their A-facts. Or put the other way around: if two situations are the same with respect to their B-facts (paint, hair), then it is necessary for them to be the same with respect to their A-facts (beauty, baldness).

Now let's return to the more controversial domain of the mind–body problem.

Generic mind–body supervenience (*GMBS*):   Mental facts (states and processes) *supervene* on physical facts (states and processes) if no two possible situations are identical with respect to their B-facts (physical), but differ with respect to their A-facts (mental).

There are three ideas embedded in these examples and characterizations of supervenience. *First*, a "higher-level" property (beauty, baldness, being mental) *covaries* with a "lower-level" physical property – look at the "sharings" and "differings." *Second*, the higher-level property is somehow *dependent* on the lower-level physical property; in this way the physical facts fix or determine the higher-level fact – settle the physical facts and you settle all the other facts. And *third*, still, the higher-level property is *not reducible* to the lower-level physical property – unlike type physicalism, it's a different property. This kind of a position is sometimes called *property dualism*. So we get some of the virtues of type physicalism without its suspicious reductionism. Spelling out these ideas more precisely gives us different conceptions of supervenience. There are two places where differences traditionally arise in (GS) and (GMBS): (1) saying what kind of possibility or necessity is involved, and (2) saying what kind of situations are at issue.

Possibility necessity: We might mean to say that B-facts determine A-facts by logical necessity ("logical supervenience") or by natural law (natural supervenience). These are different; it is a law of nature that nothing travels faster than light (186,000 miles/sec.), but there is nothing logically contradictory about saying something traveled at one more mile per second than that – perhaps the universe could have had different physical laws.

Situations: We might want to say that the situations in which we test for same-ness and difference of A- and B-facts are "local," are restricted to the indi-viduals involved – think again of the Mona Lisa and the bald man. In this case, A-facts "supervene locally" on B-facts if any individual who duplicates the B-facts, will duplicate the A-facts. Or we might want to include the whole context in which the individual is embedded – the whole world it is a member of. In this case, A-facts "supervene globally" on B-facts if any world that duplicates the B-facts will thereby duplicate the A-facts. The difference becomes impor-tant if the A-facts involve relations to the world the system finds itself in (unlike our original examples of beauty and baldness). For instance, two organ-isms that are physically identical might have different survival or "fitness" values because of differences in the environments they find themselves in, so the Darwinian biological property of fitness would not supervene locally on physical make-up. But it would supervene globally, because then we would have to keep the whole world the same, including the environment the organism finds itself in.

Opinions differ as to the proper supervenience relation between mind and body: is it logical or natural, local or global? (see Suggested reading). But no matter which we pick, something seems to be missing; we don't have an answer to the question: "what *are* mental phenomena?" in the way that theo-ries we have looked at so far have answered that question. Supervenience gives us a (complicated) relation between mind and body (in that sense it answers the question: what *is* the relation?), but it does not give us real insight into the mental – after all, beauty supervenes on paint and baldness supervenes on hair. Our next and final theory attempts to have the best of supervenience, and close that gap.

Functionalism

Functionalist theories in general identify things by their functions, by what they do. A mousetrap, for instance, is something that traps mice. A carburetor is something that mixes gas and air in a combustible ratio, then introduces this mixture into the cylinders. Neither a mousetrap nor a carburetor are defined in terms of what they are *made of*. Indeed, each of these kinds of things can be made of anything with enough structure to carry out the function – wood, plastic, brass, steel, etc. So if there were a "type physicalism" of mousetraps and carburetors, it would definitely be wrong. Being a mousetrap and being a carburetor are "multiply realizable" – each of them can be realized in a wide variety of stuff. In the same spirit, functionalist theories of mind claim that mental phenomena should be identified via their functions. But what are the functions of mental phenomena? What do they do?

Here functionalist theories of mind depart slightly from general usage (where "function" means what the system does, e.g., catching mice). Functionalism does not say that, for example, a belief is something that has a particular function, like a mousetrap does. Rather, functionalism treats the notion of mental "function" as the notion of *a representation playing some sort of role in the cognitive system*. Recall Mr Bubblehead. His beliefs and desires were pictured as boxes containing representations of the content of those beliefs and desires (*what* he believed and *what* he desired). But the box-pictures (and box-talk) were convenient shorthand fictions for complicated *roles* that the representational contents played in the system – for the complicated *relationships* that those representations have with other representations and to the system itself. The relationships (roles) that functionalists allow are *input* relations, *output* relations, and relations to other *internal* states and processes.

Functionalism and the mind–body problem

Functionalism agrees with token physicalism in distinguishing state, event, process *tokens or instances* from state, event, process *types* or kinds. *Pure functionalism* answers the mind–body question by saying that every mental state, event, process *type* is identical to some functional state, event, process *type* of the system. Pure functionalism leaves it open what the system is made of. *Physicalistic functionalism* says that every mental state, event, process *token* is *identical* to a physical state, envnet, process *token*. Thus, according to physicalistic functionalism (as with token physicalism) there are no free-floating mental phenomena – all mental phenomena are at bottom identical with physical phenomena.

Terminological note All contemporary functionalists are in fact physical functionalists, so we will use "functionalism" to mean "physical functionalism" unless a contrast is explicitly mentioned.

Pro functionalism

Functionalism has the advantages of dualism, behaviorism, and physicalism without their disadvantages. *First*, like *dualism* and unlike *behaviorism*, functionalism treats mental causation as a species of genuine causation because it treats "mental" particulars as physical particulars – there are particular mental events which cause particular physical (and other mental) events – whereas *dualism* must treat it as a special mysterious relation.[1] *Second*, also like *behaviorism*, functionalism defines mental phenomena relationally, but unlike behaviorism, functionalism allows relations between *internal* states as well as relations between input and output states, to define these phenomena. *Third*, unlike *type physicalism*, which identifies mental types with physical types, and so seems to preclude *multiple realizations* of cognition in matter, functionalism allows this possibility. That is, if psychological state types are physical state types, then there would have to be some physical property shared by all systems capable of any mental phenomena, and many people hold that there is no reason to suppose cognitive systems might not be constructed out of matter as diverse as neural tissue and silicon. Finally, *fourth*, unlike *token physicalism*, functionalism has a characterization of mental phenomena types – it has something to say concerning the question: what must systems share to exhibit the same mental phenomena?

Machine functionalism and the DCTM

Since there are many potential roles/relationships in a complex system that could be used to define mental states, we need to constrain the possible choices – how might we do that?

(Generic) machine functionalism

Machine functionalism is not tied to any particular computational architecture. As a matter of historical fact, though, machine functionalism takes its inspiration from Turing machines (though von Neumann machines would perhaps serve better). Any "machine" with input, internal, and output relations will serve because machine functionalism allows only three types of role/relationship to be functional states, and so to be used to characterize mental phenomena: *input* roles/relations, *internal* roles/relations, *output* roles/relations. According to machine functionalism, *each type of mental state (process, etc.) is identical to some type of functional state (process, etc.) of the machine*, and each type of functional state (process, etc.) is defined in terms of input, internal, and output roles/relations in the system.

The DCTM

We get the digital computational theory of mind (DCTM) from machine functionalism if we make the *functional relations* mentioned in machine functionalism be the *computational relations* mentioned in DCTM (and of course we keep the representations in the LOT). In this way we can see that the DCTM is a special case of machine functionalism and machine functionalism is a special case of functionalism. And since functionalist answers are supposed to be the best answers to the mind–body problem, the DCTM gets the benefits of being a functionalist answer to the mind–body problem. This, then, is the final motivation for the DCTM.

Functionalism, supervenience, and physicalism

If mental state (let's include processes) types are functional state types, and mental state tokens are physical state tokens, then what is the relation between the functional and the physical? One standard answer is that functional states "supervene" on physical states; that is, if two systems share all physical properties (states) they must share functional properties (states). And this can be made plausible if one thinks of functional states in terms of what the system *can do*, i.e. what the system can cause to happen. Surely physically identical systems will have the same causal powers, one can do just what the other can do, so physically identical systems ought to have the same functional states. Think of a mousetrap. Now think of a molecule-for-molecule twin mousetrap. Surely, any mouse the first can trap, the second can trap too.

Let's return to the mental. If mental phenomena just are functional phenomena and functional phenomena supervene on physical phenomena, then mental phenomena supervene on physical phenomena. And that means that physical twins will have the same mental states (and your twin will think just like you). That's provocative enough to return to, and we will (see chapter 9).

8.5 DCTM and Representational Content

We can see that DCTM accommodates a causal account of psychological explanation, and therefore gives us part of what we want from a theory of mind. How does it do with the problem of content? In earlier chapters we noted strengths and weaknesses of the "semantics" of two systems capable of some sort of representation: the frog and the digital computer.

Bug detector meets data structure

Frog

Regarding the frog, on the positive side, its visual system can represent (detect and track) particular objects and situations in its environment, limited though its range may be. In chapter 4 we formulated a theory of content (semantics, aboutness) for this system called "simple detector semantics" (SDS). On the negative side, it was hard to see how, on SDS, a frog could *misrepresent* those objects and situations, or even represent *just* those objects and situations. And since it left completely open the question of logical relations between representations, it was hard to see how SDS could be the whole representational story.

Digital computer

The digital computer, on the other hand, could naturally accommodate logical relations between representations, but how could it naturally detect or track particular objects and situations in its environment? Recall (see chapter 7) that the only proposal we had as to how digital representations represent what they do – what connects the representation to what they represent – was interpretational semantics (IS) whereby isomorphism between representation and represented underwrote the representation relation. But we saw that thinking about interpretation as isomorphism is too liberal. Rather, it looks as though what the machine is "thinking about" is determined by the programmer (broadly construed to include the community which interprets the input and output of the machine). For instance, if the programmer loads a program telling the machine to move a bishop to such-and-such a position we might take the machine to be solving a chess problem. If the programmer loads a program telling the machine to move a tank battalion to such-and-such a position we might take the machine to be planning desert warfare. Conceivably, these could be isomorphic, formally identical programs – only annotations to the program (which are intended for *us, not the machine*) would be different. We have no computational answer to the question: what makes the computer, then, "think about" chess vs. war? We need some connection to the environment.

The official view: functional role

As we noted earlier, functionalism analyzes cognitive phenomena in terms of three kinds of relations: input, internal, and output. For example, consider the belief: *that man is tall*. What are the relations that might fix the content of this representation? One author (see Fodor, 1981a) suggests the following:

Input	noticing the man's height
Internal	inferring from it the belief: *someone is tall*
Output	saying "That man is tall"

On this view, the content of the belief is fixed or determined by all the relevant relations it participates in, its *functional role*. One of the strengths of this sort of theory is that it attempts to combine the virtues of the frog (connection with the environment) and the data structure (logical relations). To see this let's return to our original example of thinking: *that man* is tall:

1   The *input* component relates the occurrence of the representation to a particular man, much as the frog's fiber-2 firing was related to a neighborhood bug. Furthermore, the *output* component relates the representation to the utterance of a sentence in much the way that the frog's fiber-2 firing is related to zapping the bug.
2   The *internal* relationship of inference to *someone is tall* in this example is like our earlier discussion (see chapter 7) of entailments between digital representations.

So according to this view, mental representational content has *two factors* (or aspects) – an internal factor (internal functional or "conceptual" role) that relates a representation to other representations, and an external factor (external functional role) that relates a representation to objects and situations in the world, and so forms the basis of mental reference and the truth or falsity of various psychological states. Block (1986) has called these two versions "short-armed" and "long-armed" conceptual or functional roles. However, we will reserve the term "conceptual role" for the short-armed, internal factor, whatever that might be exactly: *conceptual role* = internal functional role = "short-armed" conceptual role; *external functional role* = "long-armed" conceptual role.

DCTM and functional role

What is *computational* about "long-armed" functional roles – the external input and output relations of functionalism? When discussing functionalist analysis of mind, such external functional relations are often illustrated with phenomena such as perception (input) and action (output). However, when discussing, say, Turing machine functionalism, input and output relations are reading and writing on the tape. But the tape is the machine's *memory*, not the environment; it is not "outside" the machine. Thus, paradigm cases of (machine) functionalism restrict content to internal conceptual roles. So, should we formulate DCTM as a version of functionalism in terms of external, long-armed functional roles, such as perception and action? Or should we formulate DCTM merely in terms of internal conceptual role?

It would seem that if we are going to respect the *formality constraint*, then once information is represented in the computer, it can only be acted upon in virtue of its form, and this suggests strongly that content is determined by just internal, conceptual role. If this is right, then DCTM is a narrower theory than functionalism in the sense that functionalism allows that external functional role can play a role in determining the content of a thought. On the other hand, DCTM agrees that mental states and processes are computational relations and operations over mental representations which have content. But it is not an official part of DCTM how that external dimension of content is fixed, only how the internal conceptual role is determined. Again, DCTM claims that cognitive states and processes are computational relations to and operations on representations (data structures). These structures *have* content – they represent something. But (1) what they represent plays no direct role in these computations, only the "form," "syntax," "structure" of the representations does and (2) what they represent is not (always) explicable in computational terms. In a sense, then, DCTM assumes or presupposes a (partially) non-computational account of content. Well, so be it. Let's turn to the computational part: what is conceptual role and what determines it?

Conceptual role

The general idea behind conceptual role (CR) theory – let's call it "generic" CR theory – is this:

(G-CR)
   The content of a representation is determined by the role the representation plays in the conceptual system of which it is a part.

One gets different CR theories by spelling out the nature of the representations involved, the nature of the roles they play, and the nature of the conceptual system they are a part of. For instance, one early influential proposal connected CR with conditional probability (see Field, 1977: 390):

(CP-CR)
   Two representations have the same conceptual content if the conditional probability of one representation, relative to additional pieces of information, is the same as the conditional probability of the other, relative to those same pieces of information.

This suggestion has a number of limitations as a psychological theory, not the least of which is that *any* difference in beliefs can make concepts differ in their content, yet we seem to be able to change our beliefs about something without changing the concept itself. Furthermore, such a definition of (sameness of) content means that content cannot be compared between people, since it is relative to the system that contains it. Finally, there is the problem of calculating these probabilities, which grow exponentially.

There are three options here: (1) *concepts* and *thoughts* could be given conceptual roles simultaneously and independently; or (2) conceptual roles of *concepts* are basic, thoughts are made out of concepts and so inherit their conceptual roles from their constituent concepts; or (3) the conceptual role of *thoughts* is basic, and the conceptual role of concepts is whatever they contribute to the conceptual role of all of the thoughts they are constituents of. Different theorists choose different options.

DCTM

Applying this idea to DCTM, recall that according to the LOT hypothesis, representations are either simple vocabulary items in the LOT, or they are complex representations constructed out of vocabulary items in the LOT. So the LOT version of option (1), where concepts and thoughts are equally basic, would be:

(LOT-TC)

The content of an item ("words" or "sentences") in the LOT of a system is determined (at least in part) by its relations to other items ("words" or "sentences") in the LOT of that system. [Thoughts and concepts are equally basic.]

The LOT version of option (2), where concepts are basic, would be:

(LOT-C)

The content of *sentences* in the LOT (thoughts) is determined by the CR of their constituent "words" (concepts) plus their internal structural relations, the content of *words* in the LOT (concepts) is determined by their relations to other words (concepts) in the LOT of the system. [Concepts are basic.]

What sort of relations participate in conceptual role and so fix content? Conceptual role theorists rarely are specific, and when they are, they rarely say the same thing. One popular proposal connects CR with "inference" relations. Since customarily inferential relations involve the notion of truth, they are defined primarily over sentences (thoughts), and the conceptual role of words (concepts) is derivative. In its generic form, the LOT version of option (3), where thoughts are basic, would be:

(LOT-T)

The content of "words" in the LOT (concepts) is determined by their contribution to the "sentences" of the LOT (thoughts) they occur in. The content of "sentences" in the LOT (thoughts) is determined by their inferential role in the system. [Thoughts are basic.]

What sorts of "inferences"? Again, theorists differ (is this getting boring?). Inferences might include: (a) only (valid) deductive inferences,[2] (b) (valid) deductive inferences and (cogent) inductive inferences, and (c) the above two plus the "decisions" one makes.

An example of proposal (b) is due to Block (1986): "A crucial component of a sentence's conceptual role is a matter or how it participates in *inductive* and *deductive* inferences" (1986: 628; emphasis added). An example of proposal (c) is also due to Block: "Conceptual role abstracts away from all causal relations except the ones that mediate inferences, *inductive* or *deductive*, *decision making*, and the like" (1986). However, if we follow the lead of digital representations surveyed earlier (see chapter 7) it will be *valid deductive inferences* that point the way to an inferential theory of content, because it is valid deductive inferences that reveal information that is a part of the concepts involved, rather than merely collateral, incidental information about whatever falls under the concept. Valid deductive inferences alone reveal what must be true if the world is the way "R" represents it to be. We will now incorporate the ideas that: representations are in the LOT, thoughts are basic, and valid deductive inferences characterize conceptual roles, by formulating the DCTM conceptual role theory of content as follows:

(DCTM-CR)

1   If "R" is a sentential representation (thought) in the LOT, then its content is determined by the fact that "R" participates in the (valid) inferential relations:

(P)   From "R" one may infer . . . ["R" serves as a premise]

(C)   From . . . one may infer "R" ["R" serves as a conclusion]

2   The specific inference relations associated with "R" give the specific content of R.

3   If "R" is a subsentential representation (concept) in the LOT, then its content is the contribution it makes to the content (inferences) of all the thoughts it occurs in.

The specific inference relations (P), (C) give the specific content of R. The proposal made by defenders of the DCTM is that at least some aspect of the representational content, the computationally relevant aspect, is captured by its inferential role. The usual examples of this approach come from the

connectives of the predicate calculus (see chapter 7). Consider "&" (= and).
Given "P & Q" one can infer "P" and one can infer "Q." And given "P" and
given "Q" one can infer "P & Q." Now, says the CR theorist, these inference
rules give the conceptual role of "&" ("and"):

(DCTM-CR:&)
   The conceptual role of a representation "P & Q" is determined by the following (valid) deductive inferences:
      From "P & Q" infer "P"
      From "P & Q" infer "Q"
      From "P" and from "Q" infer "P & Q:

And if content is given by conceptual role, we can conclude that the *content* of
"&" ("and") is determined by the inference relations it participates in, then
the content of "&" ("and") is determined by (DCTM-CR:&). Conceptual role
theorists, of course, must generalize this project to *all representations with
content*. That is, CR theorists must fill out schema (DCTM-CR) for every
representation in the system with content. Unfortunately, conceptual role
theorists have mostly remained content to repeat (DCTM-CR:&) ad nauseam,
and we should be suspicious of their reluctance (or inability) to provide a
representative range of sample analyses.

8.6   DCTM and Consciousness (I)

We have already, from time to time, invoked the notion of "consciousness" and
it is time to foreground this concept and try to assess its relation to the DCTM.
To begin with, though, the word "conscious(ness)" has a number of related
uses, some of which are not relevant to our present purposes:

1   *Consciousness-of* something in the environment (also "awareness of" and
    "attending to"). For instance, "She was conscious of a humming noise
    coming from the CD player."
2   *Meta-consciousness* (also "higher-order awareness," "meta-awareness,"
    "internal access," and "attending to") as thinking about one's own
    mental states. For instance, "She became conscious/aware of her strong
    desire for sushi."
3   *Phenomenal consciousness* (also "experiential" and "qualitative" con-
    sciousness) as being what it is like to have a certain experience: the taste
    of pineapple vs. chocolate or the smell of a rose vs. a goat.

4 *Conscious-awakeness* as in "She lost consciousness at noon then regained it after an hour."

5 *Self-consciousness* (also "self-awareness") as being consciousness of oneself as the subject of consciousness. (To be distinguished from another use of "self-conscious" as in "Teenagers are too self-conscious to be spontaneous.")

And there may be more. In this chapter we will be concerned primarily with meta–consciousness, and in the next chapter with consciousness-of and phenomenal consciousness.

Consciousness as meta-cognition

One idea is that consciousness involves *having thoughts about one's mental states.* Typically, we are in such meta-states when we can report our lower-level states. It is cases where this is absent that highlight the phenomena. In everyday life we may lack this kind of consciousness when we go on "automatic pilot" while performing routine tasks, such as driving the same route to work. We do not realize at the time we are performing the task – we suddenly realize we are at work but can't remember how we got there. There are also analogous examples from science.

Split brain

Interesting scientific examples of this come from so-called "split brain" patients – patients whose cerebral hemispheres have been surgically separated (see Gazzaniga and LeDoux, 1978). A normal visual system has information passed from eye to brain in accordance with figure 8.3.

To get visual information to just one hemisphere, an image needs to be projected onto just the right portion of each retina. This was accomplished by having the subject fixate on a point, then projecting different information onto each region of the retina (see figure 8.4).

Since language is mainly a left hemisphere phenomenou (for right-handers), subjects could see things they couldn't report: "One of the immediate and compelling consequences of brain bisection was that the interhemispheric exchange of information was totally disrupted, so that visual, tactual, pro-prioceptive, auditory, and olfactory information presented to one hemisphere could be processed and dealt with in that half-brain, but these activities would go on outside the ream of awareness of the other half-cerebrum . . . only pro-cessing going on in the left hemisphere could be verbally described by patients,

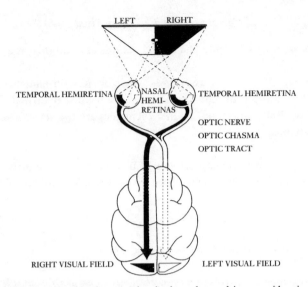

The anatomical relationship that must be clearly understood in a consideration of visual studies on the bisected brain are shown here. Because of the distribution of fibers in the optic system, information presented to each eye is projected almost equally to both hemispheres. In order to assure that information is presented to only one hemisphere, the subject must fixate a point. As a consequence of the anatomical arrangement shown here, information projected to the right visual field goes only to the left hemisphere, and vice-versa.

Figure 8.3 Visual lateralization (from Gazzaniga and LeDoux, 1978: 4, figure 2; figures 8.3–8.5 reproduced by permission of Kluwer Academic Plenum Publishers)

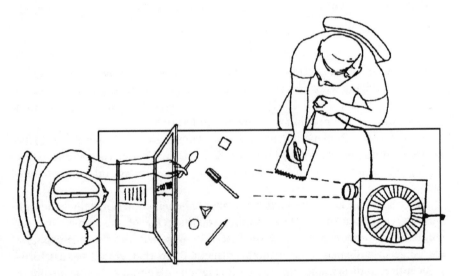

The basic testing arrangement used for the examination of lateralized visual and stereognostic functions.

Figure 8.4 The basic testing arrangement (from Gazzaniga and LeDoux, 1978: 5, figure 3)

since it is the left hemisphere that normally possesses natural language and speech mechanisms. Thus, for example, if a word (such as 'spoon') was flashed in the left visual field, which is exclusively projected to the right hemisphere . . . the subject, when asked, would say, 'I did not see anything,' but then subsequently would be able, with the left hand, to retrieve the correct object from a series of objects placed out of view . . . Furthermore, if the experimenter asked, 'What do you have in your hand?', the subject would typically say 'I don't know.' Here again, the talking hemisphere did not know. It did not see the picture, nor did it have access to the . . . touch information from the left hand, which is also exclusively projected to the right hemisphere. Yet clearly, the right half-brain knew the answer, because it reacted appropriately to the correct stimulus" (Gazzaniga and LeDoux, 1978: 3–5). In a famous case subjects shown sexually explicit pictures to their right hemispheres and nothing to their left hemisphere, when asked what they saw said "nothing," but they blushed and giggled. And there are interesting examples of complicated confabulations. The situation is portrayed in figure 8.5.

Here is the report: "When a snow scene was presented to the right hemisphere and a chicken claw was presented to the left, P. S. [the patient] quickly and dutifully responded correctly by choosing a picture of a chicken from a series of four cards with his right hand and a picture of a shovel from a series of four cards with his left hand. The subject was then asked, 'What did you see?', 'I saw a claw and I picked the chicken, and you have to clean out the chicken shed with a shovel.' In trial after trial, we saw this kind of response. The left hemisphere could easily and accurately identify why it had picked the answer, and then subsequently, and without batting an eye, it would incorporate the right hemisphere's response into the framework. While we knew exactly why the right hemisphere has made its choice, the left hemisphere could merely guess. Yet, the left did not offer its suggestion in a guessing vein but rather as a statement of fact as to why that card had been picked" (Gazzaniga and LeDoux, 1978: 148–9). It would seem that the left hemisphere has meta-consciousness, whereas the right hemisphere has just, on these occasions at least, consciousness-of.

Dichotic listening

There are also many psychological experiments where normal subjects perform interesting apparently *cognitive* tasks, but report being completely unaware of it. Consider the often reported results of Lackner and Garrett (1972). Subjects, who were wearing earphones, heard an ambiguous sentence in one ear and a disambiguating contextual sentence at much lower volume in the other ear:

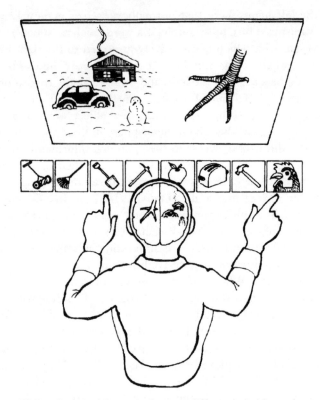

The method used in presenting two different cognitive tasks
simultaneously, one to each hemisphere. The left hemisphere was
required to process the answer to the chicken claw, while the right
dealt with the implications of being presented with a snow scene.
After each hemisphere responded, the left hemisphere was asked to
explain its choices.

Figure 8.5   The chicken-snow experiment (from Gazzaniga and LeDoux, 1978: 149,
figure 42)

> *Right ear*   Visiting relatives can be a bore (ambiguous)
> *Left ear*   I hate relatives who visit often vs. I hate traveling to visit rela-
>   tives (context)

Subjects were asked to paraphrase the right ear sentences and any subject who
reported hearing anything intelligible in the left ear had their data thrown out.
The remaining subjects showed a definite preference to paraphrase the ambiguous sentence in the direction of the appropriate context sentence. This is best

explained in terms of the subject receiving and processing these sentences without being aware of them.

Consciousness and computers (I)

Clearly we could build a machine so that it scans those representations, much in the way a laptop computer with energy management scans itself to find out if the screen, hard drive, etc., are on. In that sense such a machine might be "aware that it is aware" of something, and so in this fairly minimal sense, the machine might be "conscious." However, as we will see later, there may well be more to consciousness than this.

8.7   Modular (Cognitive) Architectures

Earlier we looked at the organization of various machines in terms of memory and control. We called such organization (machine) architecture. In the theory of mind it is useful to have a broader notion of organization, one that can include machine architecture as a special case, but which allows other things to determine organization as well. This might be called "cognitive architecture" and it has to do with the cognitive organization of the system.

Background: unitary architectures

We will call a cognitive architecture *unitary* if it treats all cognition (as opposed to sensory input and behavioral output) as homogeneous, as based on a single set of principles. Typically, unitary models of cognition represent minds as constructed out of two kinds of components. At the edges there are input (sensory) data and output (motor) responses. Most importantly, at the center is the central processing unit, and "all higher level cognitive functions can be explained by one set of principles" (Anderson, 1983: 2). This is shown diagrammatically in figure 8.6.

When the "cognitive" perspective replaced behaviorism in psychology and the cognitive sciences during the 1960s, it brought with it a conception of mental functioning as mental computation. The most pervasive example of computational devices at the time was the standard stored program register architecture von Neumann machine. Inadvertently, a particular computational architecture became identified, in many minds, with the cognitive architecture

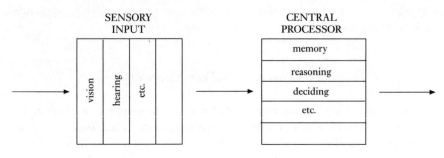

Figure 8.6   Unitary architecture

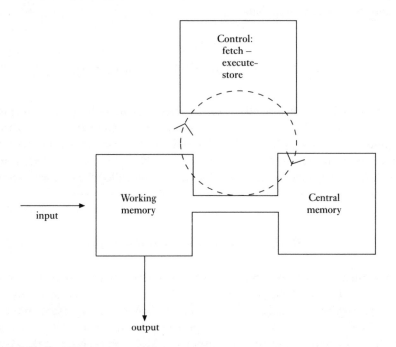

Figure 8.7   Generic computer architecture

in a computational approach to psychology. This kind of model of cognition as computation identifies major components of a mind with the major components of a von Neumann computer (see figure 8.7).

The memory of the vNM is analogized to the long-term memory of the organism, the control mechanism tells the system what to do next according to the stored program, and the input devices are like perception, the output devices are like behavior.

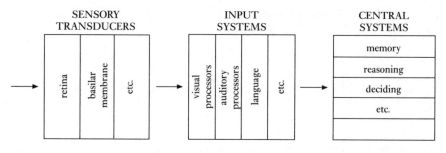

Figure 8.8 Modular architecture

Modular (cognitive) architectures

Recently another cognitive architecture has been proposed to account for the relationship between incoming stimuli and the central cognitive systems, a theory which by the 1990s had become virtual orthodoxy: "modularity" theory (see figure 8.8).

In traditional unitary architectures sensory inputs contrast only with a central processor, but in modular architectures there are "input systems" (ISs) which contrast with two other types of components: sensory transducers[3] and central systems (CSs).

Input systems as modules

According to Fodor (1983), normal human beings develop special kinds of mental capacities he calls "input systems" (ISs). These capacities form a psychological "natural kind," and so have many scientifically interesting properties in common over and above the properties which pick out that class. The "defining" property of ISs is functional – it is a characterization of what the system *does*. And what ISs do is track the environment – *they represent the character and arrangement of things in the world* on the basis of law-like information provided by transducing proximal stimuli. For instance, the intensity and distribution of light (photons) on the retina becomes patterns of electrical signals sent up the optic nerve. This results in a certain percept which represents the character and arrangement of the things in the world that caused it (see figure 8.9).

In addition to the above functional property, ISs have nine scientifically investigatable nonfunctional characteristics. These are the features of a *module*,

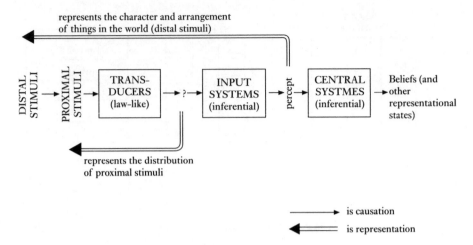

Figure 8.9 Levels of representation: what an IS does

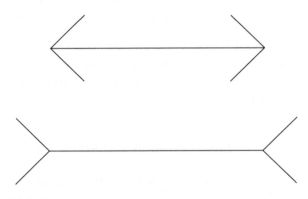

Figure 8.10 Müller-Lyer figure

and cognitive capacities can be *modular* to various degrees. Typically, ISs respond to a *specific* (distal) stimulus *domain*; they are *mandatory* in that if they can operate on the input, they will; they are *limited as to central access* in that the processes are extremely difficult if not impossible to consciously introspect; they are *fast* in that they operate in tenths of seconds; they are *informationally encapsulated* in that they do not have access to information represented elsewhere in the system which may be pertinent to its current processing. Illusions such as the Müller-Lyer provide a good illustration. Knowing that the line segments are equal in length seems not to affect one's perception of their relative length (see figure 8.10). Furthermore they have *shallow output*, in the sense that they quickly deliver an introspectable "level of representation"; they are associated with *specific neural structures*, and in part because of this they have *characteristic breakdown patterns* and *characteristic pace and sequencing of development*.

Central systems, on the other hand, have a very different function – *their job is to make considered judgments*, either about what is the case (the structure of space-time) or what the system is to do (where to go to graduate school). Central systems do not exhibit the nine features of ISs mentioned above, or at least not to the extent ISs do. Associated with the different function of CSs are two very different nonfunctional features. First, CSs are what Fodor calls "isotropic" in that facts relevant to the confirmation of a hypothesis can be drawn from *anywhere* in the system. There is no reason why, for instance, the luminosity of fireflies might not be relevant to the question of the chemical basis of anesthesia. Second, CSs are what Fodor calls "Quinean" in that the degree of confirmation given to any particular hypothesis is sensitive to such properties of the *whole system* as systematicity, plausibility, and conservatism. Both of these features are *holistic*, and are contrary to the function and functioning of ISs.

Types of modularity

Fodor's modularity is but one of a number of possibilities. Let's distinguish the following.

Internal vs. external

A system, S, is *externally* modular (or modular with respect to other systems) when its internal workings are independent of those other systems (it may, of course, depend on the output of some systems for its own *input*). A system, S, is *internally* modular when it itself is analyzable into distinct subsystems which themselves are externally modular with respect to the whole system. The opposite of external and internal modularity is homogeneity or high interactivity. Many combinations are possible, and some are associated with well-known research programs. For instance, a system can be internally and externally modular, or a system can be internally and externally interactive (connectionism?), or a system can be externally modular but internally interactive (Fodor), or a system can be internally modular but externally interactive.

Hard vs. soft

Modularity (whichever of the above we pick and whatever it amounts to exactly) can be *hard* if it is due to "hardwired" features of the system, for example dedicated circuits. Modularity is *soft* when it is due to "software" considerations, e.g. incompatible representation schemes, unreadable data structures, conflicting control structures, or memory management.

One could be a soft modularity theorist without being a hard modularity theorist – that is, think the circuitry is fairly homogeneous or at least not dedicated, but "programming" (by experience or evolution) imposes modularity on it.

Appendix
Modularity: Gall vs. Fodor

We have briefly reviewed two "modular" views of the mind – Gall's in chapter 3, and Fodor's in this one. How do they compare?

1   Gall's and Fodor's lists of candidate modules (or "faculties" in Gall's terminology) are remarkably different. We saw Gall's list in chapter 3. Fodor is more tentative: "Candidates might include, in the case of vision, mechanisms for color perception, for the analysis of shape, and for the analysis of three-dimensional spatial relations. They might also include quite narrowly task-specific 'higher-level' systems concerned with the visual guidance of bodily motions or with the recognition of faces of conspecifics. Candidates in audition might include computational systems that assign grammatical descriptions to token utterances; or ones that detect melodic or rhythmic structure of acoustic arrays; or, for that matter, ones that mediate the recognition of the *voices* of conspecifics" (1983: 47). Three differences are striking: (1) there is almost no overlap; (2) Fodor's modules are much narrower than Gall's – they are rarely commonsense units and they rarely have an easy label in the language; (3) Fodor's modules are (so far) restricted to perceptual systems, whereas Gall's modules are more like personality traits, propensities, and talents.

2   Gall partitions the mind into modules (what Fodor calls "vertical" faculties) whereas Fodor allows for "horizontal" faculties as well. Here is Fodor's characterization of this distinction: "a horizontal faculty is a functionally distinguishable cognitive system whose operations cross content domains" (1983: 13). So typical examples of a horizontal faculty might be memory, reasoning, attention, and (in the olden days) judgment, since one can remember, attend to, etc., an indefinite variety of kinds of things: "vertical faculties are *domain specific*, they are *genetically determined*, they are associated with *distinct neural structures*, and . . . they are *computationally autonomous*" (1983: 21).

3   Both Gall's and Fodor's modules are hardwired, but Gall also thought that (1) the wiring was mostly in the same place for everybody, and (2) com-

petence in that faculty was proportional to brain mass dedicated to it. Given that the skull fits the brain "'as a glove fits a hand' Phrenology followed as the night follows the day" (Fodor, 1983: 23).

4   Because of the last point, Gall's method was to find correlations between psychological traits and tissue mass (via bumps on the skull) across people, and for each faculty there is one location in the brain where it is located for everybody. Fodor's methodology, on the other hand, is general science (we see to what degree features 1–9 are present for a given cognitive capacity), and there is no presumption that the hardware is located in the same place for all people. We can summarize some of the important differences as follows:

	Gall	*vs.*	*Fodor*
Personality trait	Y		N
Commonsense	Y		N
Tissue mass	Y		N
Same location	Y		N

Notes

1   This is not to claim that physical causation is free from mystery, only that DCTM allows us to have one mystery rather than two.
2   Recall that valid deductive inferences from, e.g., P to Q have the property that if P is true, Q must be true too – i.e. validity preserves truth.
3   These serve to convert outside energy into a format usable by the mind/brain, and we will ignore them in what follows.

Study questions

From the RTM to the DCTM

What are the two main theses of the representational theory of mind?

What was Hume's conception of thought and mental representation?

What were its strengths and weaknesses?

What was the Frege/Russell conception of thought and mental representation?

What were its strengths and weaknesses?

What are "propositional attitudes"? Give examples.

What is "direction of fit" as a means of categorizing propositional attitudes?

What is experiential character as a means of categorizing propositional attitudes?

How is the CTM related to the RTM (i.e. how do we get the CTM from the RTM)?

What is the "formality constraint"?

How does Mr Bubblehead illustrate the CTM theory of propositional attitudes?

What are the two main theses of the CTM?

What are the three main theses of the B–DCTM?

The DCTM and the LOT

What are three main theses of DCTM?

What are the three basic features of the language of thought (LOT)?

What is the argument from "ways of representing" for the LOT?

What is the productivity of thought?

What is the argument for the LOT from productivity?

What is the systematicity of thought?

What is the argument from the systematicity of thought for the LOT?

What is the systematicity of inference?

What is the argument from the systematicity of inference for the LOT?

The DCTM and the mind–body problem (M–BP)

What is the M–BP?

State and assess dualistic interactionism as an answer to the M–BP.

State and assess epiphenomenalism as an answer to the M–BP.

State and assess behaviorism as an answer to the M–BP.

State and assess the identity theory (physicalism, central state materialism) as an answer to the M–BP (**hint**: there are two versions of this, type and token).

State and assess functionalism as an answer to the M–BP.

What advantages does functionalism have over type physicalism as an answer to the M–BP? (**hint**: multiple realizability).

What is (Turing) machine functionalism and what advantages does it have over (plain) functionalism?

DCTM and representational content

What is the "official view" on mental content?

How would it apply to thinking *that man is tall*?

What is external ("long-armed") vs. internal ("short-armed") functional role ("conceptual role")?

Which role does the "formality constraint" dictate and why?

What two ways are there of taking conceptual role and which way does the DCTM favor?

What would be the conceptual role of, e.g., "and" vs. "or"?

DCTM and consciousness

What is meta-consciousness?

What is one everyday example of the apparent absence of meta-consciousness?

What is one laboratory example of the absence of meta-consciousness?

Could an artifact (machine) be meta-conscious?

Unitary cognitive architectures

What are the two major components of unitary theories of cognition?

What are the three unitary cognitive architectures based on the three machine architectures?

What are their strengths and weaknesses?

Modular cognitive architectures

What are the three major components of a modular cognitive architecture?

What is the function of sensory transducers?

What is the function of input systems (ISs) – what do they do?

What is it for an IS to be domain-specific?

What is it for an IS to be information-encapsulated?

What is the function of central systems (CSs) – what do they do?

What are the two main features of central systems (CSs)?

What two different types of modularity are there?

Where would Fodor fit into this classification?

Suggested reading

General

There are a number of recent survey books, articles, and chapters on the DCTM. Block (1990) is perhaps the most authoritative article-length presentation; see also Block and Segal (1998). Pylyshyn (1984) is much more for specialists and Pylyshyn (1989) summarizes some of this book. Crane (1995) is a very readable general discussion. Glymour (1992), chapter 13, von Eckardt (1993), chapter 3, Kim (1996), chapter 4, Jacob (1997) chapter 5, Rey (1997), chapter 8, Cooney (2000), part V, all introduce and discuss some version of the DCTM under a variety of different labels.

From the RTM to the DCTM

The representational theory of mind was labeled by Fodor in a number of publications, but (1981b), Introduction: something of the state of the art, and chapter 9: Methodological solipsism as a research strategy in cognitive science, are good introductions. McCulloch (1995), chapters 2 and 3, discusses the empiricist theory (in the personage of Locke, rather than Hume), and the Frege-Russell theory of thought. See Churchland (1988), chapter 3.4, for an attempt to make sense of the notion of "grasping" an abstract proposition. For more on propositional attitudes and direction of fit see Searle (1979, 1983: ch. 1).

The DCTM and the LOT

Fodor (1975) initially formulated the LOT hypothesis and surveyed much of its empirical support and many of its consequences for cognitive science. Fodor (1987) and Fodor and Pylyshyn (1988) discuss productivity and systematicity arguments for LOT. A highly readable survey of issues surrounding LOT can be found in Maloney (1989).

The DCTM and the M–BP

The Fodor (1981a) article is a readable introduction to the mind–body problem in the context of cognitive science. There are numerous good recent textbook discussions of the mind–body problem and the major theories of mind that attempt to answer it. See, for instance, Churchland (1988), chapters 2–5, Kim (1996), chapters 1–5, Braddon-Mitchell and Jackson (1996), Rey (1997), Goldberg and Pessin (1997), chapter 2, and Armstrong (1999). For more on supervenience see the authoritative short article by Kim (1994), then look at Chalmers (1996b), chapter 2, and Kim (1993). Kim (1996), chapter 4, is a good introduction to (Turing) machine functionalism.

The DCTM and representational content

Introductory surveys of conceptual (functional) role semantics, with further references, can be found in Cummins (1989), chapter 9, and Lepore (1994). Field (1977) introduced the idea of relating conceptual role to subjective probability. Harman (1982, 1987) offers an explication and defense of "long-armed" conceptual role semantics. A more advanced, spirited discussion and defense of conceptual role semantics can be found in Block (1986).

The DCTM and consciousness

A more complete list of reading follows the next part of our discussion of consciousness in chapter 9. However, an excellent general survey of topics in consciousness can be found in Güzeldere (1997). Dennett (1991), chapter 3, and Chalmers (1995b), (1996b), chapter 1, are excellent introductions to the philosophical challenges of consciousness. Meta-consciousness, under the title of "higher-order" and "internal monitoring" theories of consciousness, is developed in some detail by Rosenthal (1986, 1997) and Lycan (1990). It is critically discussed by Dretske (1993, 1995: ch. 4). Block (1995) elaborates the distinction between "access" consciousness and "phenomenal" consciousness.

Unitary and modular cognitive architecture

Unitary
Block and Fodor (1972), especially sections II and III, argue against Turing machine architectures for cognition, and for a more general computational conception. Newell and Simon (1972) – see also Newell 1973 – is the classic study of production system architectures for cognition. See Marr (1977) for critical aspects of production systems. More recent cognitive studies based on production systems can be found in Anderson's ACT system (1983), elaborated in (1993), and Klahr et al. (1987). See Laird et al. (1987) for an early exposition of the PS-inspired Soar architecture, and Newell (1990) for a book-length development. Newell et al. (1989) compare Anderson's ACT and

Soar architectures. See Lehman et al. (1998) for an introduction to Soar as a cognitive architecture.

Modular

Fodor (1983) sets out and defends a modular architecture; Fodor (1985) is a summary of that work (with commentary and replies by Fodor); and Fodor (1986, 1989) further elaborates on the modularity theme. Harnish and Farmer (1984), Bever (1992), and Segal (1996) distinguish various forms of modularity. Bever (1992), Harnish (1995), and Atlas (1997) are critical of various aspects of Fodor's modularity doctrine. Garfield (1987) contains a collection of articles for and against modularity and Hirschfeld and Gelman (1994) explore the idea that central systems exhibit domain specificity, an important feature of input systems, as does Karmiloff-Smith (1992) – see Fodor (1998) for discussion.

9

Criticisms of the Digital Computational Theory of Mind

9.1 Introduction: The Turing Test (Again)

We have seen that the DCTM can be stated fairly precisely, it constitutes a coherent answer to the venerable mind–body problem, and it has been an influential and fruitful framework for empirical investigation into cognitive capacities. What more could one want? Well, for starters, is it true? A popular conception of whether or not a system "can think" is the famous "Turing test." Reread the passage from chapter 8. These passages have some notable features. *First*, although the word "intelligence" occurs in the title of his paper, Turing carries on the discussion in terms of "thinking," and this raises questions concerning the relationship between such notions as: intelligence, thinking, cognition, mental, etc., which Turing does not explore. Notice that we are inclined to say that a machine literally adds or plays chess (maybe even intelligently?), but we are not so happy with saying that such a machine therefore thinks, cogitates, or has a mental life. *Second*, notice how complicated the imitation game is, with different genders and assistants trying to help or fool the interrogator (we left this part out of the quotation). Why not just put a variety of people in front of a "teleprinter," and give them some reasonable amount of time to decide which of two communicators is a computer? (Although Turing appears to sanction a simplified version of the game in section 6, reply 4, where the interrogator is supposed to decide if a sonnet comes from a person or a machine.) Since this more simplified set-up has come down to us as the "Turing test" we will use Turing's label "imitation game" for his more complicated set-up. *Third*, notice how the interrogator's questions are directed at discerning which is the man and which the woman, not which is the computer and which the human. *Fourth*, notice that Turing does not explicitly say what the interrogator is entitled to conclude when the computer wins the imitation game: It thinks? It's good at imitating thinking? Or something else? What *can* be concluded? *Fifth,* notice that Turing himself introduces the test as a replacement for the question: "Can a machine think?" It is legitimate to ask what the replacement is for. He says at one point in the passage that the question is "meaningless," but it is not clear what he means by that, since it has enough meaning for Turing to write about it for pages and to suggest a very specific replacement for it. Perhaps Turing was being a bit of a "verificationist" here, and he wanted to replace a (scientifically) unverifiable and so (scientifically) "meaningless" question with a (scientifically) verifiable and so (scientifically) meaningful one. *Finally,* notice that intelligence, thinking in general, is characterized in terms of being indistinguishable from human performance, and this suggests a strong anthropocentric (and perhaps cultural) bias in Turing's test. Is it a bias in the general concept of thinking as well – is the standard for thinking in general set by its similarity to human thinking?

How good is the Turing test? Assuming that it is proposed, as Turing seems to have proposed it, as a condition that is sufficient, but not necessary, for thinking, could something pass the Turing test and not be said to think? Probably the most dramatic counterexample is Block's (1990) "conversation jukebox." This is a machine (programmed by aliens? a cosmic accident? It doesn't matter) with every plausible conversation up to some specific limit on length of sentence (say 100 words), or length of conversation (Turing's original 5 minutes?). Since there are these limits, the program will be a finite list – huge, but finite. The interrogator asks question Q1, then the conversation jukebox selects an appropriate answer, say A1. The interrogator then asks another question Q2, and the jukebox responds with an appropriate answer A2, and so forth. By design, it will be impossible to tell the conversation jukebox from a human communicant and so it will pass the Turing test. Since we are reluctant to say that this machine thinks or has intelligence, it would seem that the conversation jukebox is a counterexample to the Turing test – passing the test is not sufficient for intelligence.

One moral seems to be that appropriate verbal behavior is not sufficient for thinking. Perhaps some more global behavior would be sufficient. Maybe, as various authors have suggested, thinking is related to being "massively adaptable," that is, being able to fulfill goals by planning, reasoning, and deciding over a wide variety of environmental conditions. But even this may not do, since an enlarged "behavioral jukebox" could be just as successful in its environment as the conversation jukebox was in its environment, but intuitively be no more intelligent. We may have to conclude that the concept of thinking is related to the causes of the behavior, not to the pattern of behavior itself. We turn now to arguments directed at this second conclusion.

9.2 Against Strong AI: Searle and the Chinese Room

Searle's "Chinese room" argument is probably the most widely discussed objection to the DCTM. Commentators do not agree, either as to what the central argument is, or what is wrong with it (should this make us suspicious?). The way Searle (1980: 417) first formulates his position is as follows:

The Position
1   Intentionality in human beings (and animals) is a product of causal features of the brain . . . certain brain processes are sufficient for intentionality.
2   The main argument of this paper is directed at establishing the following claim: *Instantiating a computer program is never by itself a sufficient condition of intentionality.*

Notice that "intentionality" is a technical term; do not confuse it with "intentional" meaning "on purpose." (Searle doesn't say what intentionality is, other than the general "aboutness" of many mental states. We will return to this issue.)

These two propositions have the following consequences:

3   The explanation of how the brain produces intentionality cannot be that it does it by instantiating a computer program. This is a strict logical consequence of (1) and (2).
4   Any mechanism capable of producing intentionality must have causal powers equal to those of the brain.
5   Any attempt literally to create intentionality artificially (strong AI) could not succeed just by designing programs but would have to duplicate the causal powers of the human brain.

In the body of the paper, however, the target Searle sets up is "strong AI" vs. "weak AI":

Weak artificial intelligence (AI):   the view that "the principal value of the computer in the study of the mind is that it gives us a very powerful tool" (1980: 417).

Strong artificial intelligence (AI):   "the claim that the appropriately programmed computer literally has cognitive states and that the programs thereby explain human cognition" (1980: 417).

Note that here we have "cognitive state," not "intentionality." And when Searle constructs his example, it is actually a counterexample to a fairly specific proposal; the claim that a machine that runs Schank's story comprehension program: "1. can literally be said to *understand* the story and provide the answers to questions, and 2. that what the machine and its program do *explains* the human ability to understand the story and answer questions about it" (1980: 417). The central theses of this part of the paper are:

(T1) Computational states are *not sufficient* for story understanding or cognitive states or intentionality, and

(T2) Computational processes *will not explain* story understanding or cognitive processes or intentionality.

Before looking at the counterexample to Schank we need to ask ourselves how we are supposed to generalize from story understanding to cognitive states in general. Searle comments that: "the same arguments would apply to Winograd's SHRDLU . . . Weisenbaum's ELIZA . . . , and indeed any Turing machine simulation of human mental phenomena" (1980: 417). We assume Searle means that his argument is to apply to any "computational" simulation. We have here, then, three potential targets for the argument. The first and most restricted target is just Schank's original story "understanding" program – does this program allow the machine to understand stories? A second and less restricted target is the idea that there are programs for giving a machine intentional states in general (mental states, including understanding, that are *about* something). The third and least restrictive target is the idea that there are programs for giving a machine "mental states" in general (intentional or not). Searle seems to be assuming that, first, the kind of argument used against Schank's program for story understanding can be constructed against any computer simulation or explanation. And, second, that the argument can be extended to intentional states in general and perhaps to all cognition or all mental phenomena.

A methodological principle

Before constructing his counterexample, Searle formulates a principle that he will use:

(P of I)   One way to test a theory of mind is to ask oneself what it would be like if my mind actually worked on the principles that the theory says all minds work on.   (1980: 417)

Apparently the idea is that if somebody proposes a theory of a cognitive capacity, then that theory can be tested by asking oneself: what would it be like if the theory was true? Let's call this the "principle of introspection" (P of I). How are we to interpret it? Consider the process of sentence understanding. A theory of sentence understanding might propose processes of speech recognition involving measurement of voice onset time (see Lisker and Abramson, 1964), or a process of accessing a mental lexicon (see Forster, 1978), and activating even contextually irrelevant meanings all in the course of understanding a sentence. Are these theories false because (1) introspection does not reveal them, or (2) when imagining that our mind works that way, it did not seem plausible? Notice that we would not accept (P of I) with "brain" substituted for "mind." Why should we accept it here, unless we are to assume that all cognition is in principle introspectively available? (We will return to this issue shortly.)

The counterexample

Searle imagines himself locked in a room and given batches of Chinese writing. Since Searle knows no Chinese he does not know that there are really four different groups of sentences here. One is the *story*, the second is a *script* for interpreting the story, third are some *questions* about the story, and the fourth is a group of *answers* to the questions. Finally, Searle is given a set of rules in English, the "program," for correlating the answers with the questions. It is unclear if (or how) the inhabitant of the room is to apply the script to the stories in answering the questions. If not, the Chinese room does not parallel Schank's program. So we will assume it does. By comparison, Searle is given the same things in English, and from the outside there is no significant difference in his performance; his answers in Chinese are as reliable as his answers in English, as judged by native speakers. Searle goes on to conclude: "In the Chinese case unlike the English case, I produce the answers by manipulating uninterpreted formal symbols. As far as the Chinese is concerned, I simply behave like a computer; I perform computational operations on formally specified elements. For the purposes of the Chinese, I am simply an instantiation of the computer program. Now the claims made by strong AI are that the programmed computer understands the stories and that the program in some sense explains human understanding" (1980: 418).

What the example shows: Searle

The conclusion Searle draws from this is that:

1   As regards the first claim, it seems to me quite obvious in the example that
    I do not understand a word of the Chinese stories. . . .
2   As regards the second claim, that the program explains human understand-
    ing, we can see that the computer and its program do not provide sufficient
    conditions of understanding since the computer and the program are
    functioning, and there is no understanding. But does it even provide a
    necessary condition or a significant contribution to understanding? . . . not
    the slightest reason has been given to suppose that they are necessary condi-
    tions or even that they make a significant contribution to understanding.
                                                                (1980: 418)

Intentionality and causal properties of the brain:
simulation vs. duplication

What would it take to give a machine those properties that make us capable of
having intentional states? At one point Searle answers: "Only something that
has the same causal powers as brains could have intentionality" (1980: 423).
According to Searle, no purely formal model will ever be sufficient for intentionality because the formal properties themselves have no causal power except
when instantiated in a machine to produce the next stage of the program. The
causal powers Searle thinks are required for intentional phenomena go far
beyond just moving the machine into its next state. But Searle is careful to
acknowledge that some other physical or chemical process could produce these
intentional effects – it's an empirical question. So really, contrary to the above
quote, Searle is only requiring that to duplicate the intentional capacities of
the brain (perception, action, understanding, learning, etc.), one need only
duplicate *causally relevant powers sufficient for those effects*: "If you can exactly
duplicate the causes you could duplicate the effects" (1980: 422). Since brains
have all sorts of causal powers not directly relevant to intentional phenomena,
such as life-sustaining activity (which can be replaced if damaged by life-
support machinery), one need not duplicate the whole causal potential of a
human brain to duplicate human intentionality. The empirical question is:
exactly what powers of the brain are causally relevant to intentionality? Searle
does not know; nobody at present knows.

Searle ends his article with a discussion of the question: why have
researchers thought that when it comes to cognition, but not, say, meteorol-
ogy, *simulation is duplication*? – a computer simulation of digestion will not
make a pizza disappear. His answer is that *first*, they have taken too seriously
the analogy: the mind is to the brain as a program is to hardware (1980: 423).
The analogy breaks down at the two points we have already rehearsed: it leaves
out the *causal powers* of the brain sufficient for intentional states and processes

(and not just sufficient for state transition); and it leaves out the *intentional content* of mental phenomena. *Second*, researchers have been seduced by the notion of "information processing." Defenders of strong AI argue that since a computer does information processing and humans do information processing, humans and computers share an information-processing level of description – the algorithmic level. But, says Searle, "In the sense in which people 'process information' . . . the programmed computer does not do 'information processing.' Rather, what it does is manipulate formal symbols . . . its . . . symbols don't have any meaning as far as the computer is concerned" (1980: 423). *Third*, the widespread acceptance of the Turing test has left a residual *behaviorism* in strong AI, i.e. that passing the Turing test is sufficient in order to have a machine that thinks. But the Chinese room purports to be a counterexample to that. *Fourth*, there is a residual *dualism* in strong AI in that: "The project is to reproduce and explain the mental by designing programs, but unless the mind is not only conceptually but empirically independent of the brain you couldn't carry out the project. . . . This form of dualism . . . insists . . . that what is specifically mental about the mind has no intrinsic connection with actual properties of the brain" (1980: 423–4).

9.3   The Digital Computational Mind in the Chinese Room

We now want to see how the Chinese room argument holds up against the DCTM as we have formulated it. We will organize our evaluation along the two main dimensions of the DCTM: the computational relation that indicates the type of cognitive *state* or *process* (e.g. belief, reasoning) and the *representational content* of that state or process.

Systems reply

Taken as a counterexample to the claim that computational states and processes are not sufficient for being in a cognitive state, such as believing, desiring, intending, etc. (or process), the argument has serious problems. It is true that the occupant of the room (the "control organ" as von Neumann would say) does not by himself know Chinese. It is, at a minimum, the *system as a whole* that knows Chinese (your left hemisphere doesn't know English, but you do).

Searle objects that he can "internalize" the program by memorizing it, and still he does not understand Chinese: "All the same, he understands nothing of

Chinese, and a fortiori neither does the system, because there isn't anything in the system which isn't in him. *If he doesn't understand, then there is no way the system could understand because the system is just a part of him*" (1980; emphasis added).

But there are problems with this reply. *First*, it does not follow that because Searle does not understand Chinese no part of him does. Maybe he is in the awkward position of split-brain patients in having a "part of" them able to do things, and actually do things, that they, the patients, are unaware of doing except by observing their own behavior. Such patients even typically deny being able to perceive and understand things that their disassociated hemisphere can perceive and understand. This illustrates that general principles of inference from whole to part, or from part two whole, are fallacious: water molecules are not wet and are not a liquid, but the whole (glass of water) of which they are a part is. A crowd can be numerous, but none of the persons in it are. If Searle does not think the "system" understands Chinese, it has to be for some other reason than this. *Second*, Searle remarks how different the Chinese "subsystem" is from the English "subsystem," saying: "The English subsystem knows that 'hamburgers' refers to hamburgers, the Chinese subsystem knows only that 'squiggle-squiggle' is followed by 'squoggle-squoggle'" (1980). But, we may ask, how can he help himself to this knowledge without the assumption that what the subsystem knows must be accessible to him introspectively, rather than behaviorally? Is Searle assuming here, as the earlier (P of I) suggests, that mental states must in principle be available to consciousness? *Third*, since Searle's Chinese room occupant is a person, and this person has all the above information represented in him and still "neither the biology nor the program, alone or together, are sufficient" (Rey, 1986: 173), it would seem that the only thing left that could have gone wrong is the way the information is "programmed." Perhaps *memorizing* the program is not necessarily "appropriately programming" the machine. It is more or less true that von Neumann machines are programmed by putting instructions and data structures in memory (and so "memorizing" them), but as Searle characterizes strong AI, it is not required that the program be running on a von Neumann machine – though undoubtedly these were the types of machines practitioners of strong AI in fact had in mind. We will see later that what counts as programming a "connectionist" machine is quite different.

Robot reply

Searle may have shown that algorithmic relations are not sufficient to induce understanding or intentionality – in the sense of being about actual things in the world. As Searle says: "Intentionality is by definition that feature of certain mental states by which they are directed at or about objects and states of affairs *in the world*" (1980: 424; emphasis added). But DCTM requires a semantic level as well as a syntactic level. According to DCTM, understanding is a *computational relation to a representation* and that representation is a (possibly complex) symbol which has *representational content* – it is about something. So the reply is: let's supplement the Chinese room with "robot" sensors such as a TV camera.

Searle seems to conclude that understanding is not computational because its representational content is not algorithmic. But although this might be correct against "strong AI," it would be a mistake regarding DCTM, since DCTM requires *symbols*, or *representations*. Searle objects (1980: 420) that incorporating causal relations into strong AI constitutes abandoning that position – it does not constitute programming. This may be right against strong AI (see below), but not against DCTM. Part of the problem here might be terminological. As we noted earlier, the notion of a "program" has a narrow, formal, syntactical construal as well as a broader syntactic-plus-semantic construal. On the broader, semantic construal, two formally identical (isomorphic) lists of instructions would be different programs if they were about different things – say chess pieces vs. tanks and troops. Strong AI could be construed narrowly to mean: the claim that "appropriate programming" is sufficient for intentionality (etc.) means that appropriate *algorithmic relations* are sufficient for intentionality (etc.). The Chinese room certainly casts that into doubt, but that is not the position of the DCTM, which takes programs and programming broadly.

Finally, Searle sometimes writes as if the robot input is just more Chinese characters: "Suppose, unknown to me, some of the Chinese symbols that come to me come from a television camera" (1980: 420). But this mischaracterizes the input. The system is now receiving *sensory information* in a very special way – some would say that in the case of vision the information is "quasi-pictorial" (Kosslyn, 1980). Furthermore, the system is causally connected with its environment. Fodor, in fact, objects along just these lines: "It is entirely reasonable (indeed it must be true) that the right kind of causal relation is the kind that holds between our brains and our transducer mechanisms (on the one hand) and between our brains and distal objections (on the other)" (1980b: 431). Searle's answer is that causal relations alone are not sufficient to give the system intentionality – for that, the system "would have to have, for example, some *awareness* of the causal relation between the symbol and the referent; but now . . . we have abandoned both strong AI and the Robot reply" (1980: 454). In response we might wonder: (1) why there has to be awareness *of the causal relation* between the symbol and the referent and not just awareness of the referent? (2) What awareness amounts to – is it consciousness? If so, is Searle assuming (there is no argument yet) that intentional states must be conscious or potentially conscious (see the "connection principle" below)? (3) And if he is, why does he assume (there is no argument yet) that consciousness cannot be explained computationally? We return to issues of consciousness shortly.

The Chinese room vs. the luminous room

More recently Searle (1991) has restated his Chinese room argument explicitly in the following form:

Axiom 1   Computer programs are formal (syntactic).
Axiom 2   Human minds have mental contents (semantics).
Axiom 3   Syntax by itself is neither constitutive of nor sufficient for semantics.
Conclusion 1   Programs are neither constitutive of nor sufficient for minds.

He then extends this argument with the following "axiom" and draws three more "conclusions" from them:

Axiom 4   Brains cause minds.
Conclusion 2   Any other system capable of causing minds would have to have causal powers (at least) equivalent to those [relevant powers] of brains.
Conclusion 3   Any artifact that produced mental phenomena, any artificial brain, would have to be able to duplicate the specific causal powers of brains, and it could not do that just by running a formal program. [from conclusion 1 and 2?]
Conclusion 4   The way that human brains actually produce mental phenomena cannot be solely by virtue of running a computer program. [conclusion 1 and axiom 4?]

The Churchlands (1991) reply with their "luminous room" analogy: suppose that someone tries to test the hypothesis that light is electromagnetic radiation by shaking a magnet in a dark room (shaking a magnet to make light is like running a program to understand Chinese). This person does not see any light, so they conclude that the hypothesis is false:

Axiom 1   Electricity and magnetism are forces.
Axiom 2   The essential property of light is luminance.

Axiom 3   Forces by themselves are neither constitutive of nor sufficient for luminance.

Conclusion 1   Electricity and magnetism are neither constitutive of nor sufficient for light.

Just as this would be bad physics, so following Searle's advice on the Chinese room would be bad artificial intelligence. According to the Churchlands, axiom 3 begs the question; it doesn't show anything about the nature of light – we need a research program for light to do that. This carries over to Searle's Chinese room argument: the luminous room argument has the same form as the Chinese room argument, the luminous room argument begs the question at axiom 3, so the Chinese room argument begs the question at axiom 3.

Searle replies to the Churchlands' "luminous room" objection like this: the analogy breaks down: light is caused by electromagnetic radiation, but symbols themselves have no relevant causal properties. And they have no intrinsic semantics – they can be interpreted as Chinese, chess, the stock market, etc. He poses this as a dilemma for the Churchlands: either syntax is formal (i.e. has to do with form, shape, or structure) or it is not formal. If it is just formal, then it has no causal powers and the analogy breaks down. If it is not just formal then something else must be doing the causal work, i.e. the hardware – the physics does the work, not the program.

But strong AI claims that the program is sufficient for a mind, so this is *not* strong AI. It is easy to see that the strength of Searle's reply depends on the strength of the disanalogy, and that in turn depends on the strength of Searle's reasons for thinking the "syntax" has no causal powers. Chalmers (1996a: 327) parodies this aspect of the argument:

1   Recipes are syntactic.
2   Syntax is not sufficient for crumbliness.
3   Cakes are crumbly.
4   Therefore, implementing a recipe is insufficient for a cake.

We turn to this issue shortly, and leave the argument here officially as a standoff.

The score

The systems reply raises the question of the role of conscious experience in cognition and thought, and the robot reply raises the question of the semantics (intentionality) of cognition. We need to explore both of these issues further, first consciousness, then content.

9.4   The DCTM and Consciousness (II)

Consciousness appears to be the last bastion of occult properties, epiphenom-
ena, and immeasurable subjective states – in short, the one area of mind best
left to the philosophers, who are welcome to it. Let them make fools of them-
selves trying to corral the quicksilver of "phenomenology" into a respectable
theory.

(Dennett, 1978b)

In the previous chapter we discussed meta-consciousness and how it might be
handled by the DCTM. Clearly we could organize a machine in such a way that
it scans its own internal representations and outputs appropriately. In that sense
it might be "conscious" of its own internal states. But there are two aspects of
our ordinary notion of consiousness left untouched by this idea of internal
higher-order states. The first is what we called (see chapter 8) "consciousness-
of," and the second is often called "phenomenal" consciousness.

Consciousness-of

We sometimes say that a system is *conscious of* something in the environment
if it *aware of* that thing; that is, the system is picking up information about
the environment and perhaps using that information to act on the environment. In this sense a TV camera or an industrial robot is conscious. But
consciousness-of seems too weak to be very interesting. And even when combined with consciousness as meta-cognition the result still seems pretty thin
as a "conscious" state. Think of Penrose's (1989: 410) example of a camcorder
recording itself in a mirror. In what interesting sense is it conscious? But when
consciousness-of is coupled to the next aspect of consciousness, they form an
important type of everyday consciousness.

Phenomenal consciousness

One idea is that what we left out of our earlier discussion of consciousness,
and what is crucial to interesting consciousness, is the look, feel, taste, smell,
sound, etc., of things, or as we will say, the *phenomenology*, *qualitative charac-*
ter, or *experiential aspects* of these states, the *what it is like* to be in those states.
Some authors emphasize this notion: "we can say that a mental state is con-

scious if it has a *qualitative feel* – an associated quality of experience" (Chalmers, 1996b: 4). Consider staring at a red circle on a white screen. Then remove the red circle and you will see a green circle of about the same size. Where in the world is this new "greenness"? It is not on the screen: that's white. It is not in your brain: that's gray. Some would say that your consciousness has the qualitative character of experiencing green. There are more labels for this feature including the 'phenomenological feel,' and the 'subjective aspect' of consciousness. One way of getting at what these phenomenological, experiential, or qualitative characteristics (often called "qualia") are supposed to be – what experiential aspects of consciousness are supposed to be – is by looking at situations where the qualia are either very *different* from ours or *missing altogether*.

Different

Nagel (1974) reminds us how different the sensory system of some other species, a bat for example, is from ours. The bat has specialized circuits in its brain for sending out high-pitched shrieks and then echolocating objects that reflect those waves. Using this technology, the bat is able to make a whole variety of precise discriminations regarding, say, size, texture, and motion – crucial for hunting. It is not too misleading to say the bat "sees" with its ears. Nagel then invites us to ask ourselves: what would it be like to be a bat and detect (see? hear?) a mouse via echolocation? It is very difficult – it is probably a totally different and perhaps unimaginable experience for us. Like us, the bat picks up information about mice (and perhaps is even aware of its awareness). What is so different (or what we cannot imagine) is the experiential character that goes with being a bat – bat qualia.

Missing: color

> *You might have a hypothetical person who could not see red, but who understood the physical theory of color and could apprehend the proposition "This has the color with the greatest wave-length," but who would not be able to understand the proposition "This is red" as understood by the normal uneducated person.*
>
> (Russell, 1918: 55)

Or consider Jackson's (1986) case of Mary, the color vision expert, who knows all there is to know scientifically about color vision, but is herself color blind (or raised in a black and white environment). She then undergoes an operation that allows her to see color (or she's removed from the black and white environment). Jackson contends that she *now* knows something about color, that she didn't know before – its qualitative character. Or, put more metaphysically and not epistemologically, there are now instances of something that were missing before – experiences by Mary of color. Something has been added to the world.

Missing: blindsight

One particularly interesting type of case where qualia is absent is so-called "blindsight." Blindsight subjects (with damaged visual systems) are able to correctly answer "forced choice" questions (they must give one answer or the other) about the scene their eyes are directed at, even though they have no visual experience, and may even think the question is a bit pointless: "The subject must be persuaded to play a kind of game, like 'if the grating (that you cannot see) is vertical, say "vertical", and if it is horizontal say "horizonal". Even if you have to guess.' Using forced choice methods, evidence has been produced that patients can detect visual events in their 'blind' fields, can locate them in space by pointing or by moving their eyes . . . can make discriminations between gratings [series of parallel lines] of different orientations with quite good (if not quite normal) accuracy, and can carry out some types of simple shape discriminations. . . . Despite the demonstration of visual discriminative capacity, the subject characteristically will say that he does not 'see'" (Weiskrantz, 1988: 188).

These results have been extended to another sensory modality: "Interestingly, a closely similar phenomenon has been reported in the somasensory mode for localization of touch on the hand of a patient. . . . It has been called 'blind-touch' . . . the patient could locate touch stimuli to her skin, but had no awareness of actually being touched" (ibid.).

DCTM and full-blown consciousness

Full-blown consciousness

Let's call our ordinary, interesting, notion of consciousness "full-blown" consciousness. There seem to be two typical kinds of case of ordinary full-blown consciousness.

In one typical kind of case, full-blown consciousness will involve all three of our previous notions: it will involve (1) *being aware of something in the environment*, (2) that awareness will usually have a *sensory qualitative character*, and

(3) that awareness (with that sensory qualitative character) will itself be the object of awareness – it will be *aware of its awareness*. This meta-awareness can then be the basis of reporting one's conscious states and controlling behavior in general.

In another typical kind of case, however, one is in a non-sensory mental state – such as solving a mathematical problem or deciding where to go to graduate school. Still, in these cases too there seems to be something distinctive that it is like to be in these states – there is a cognitive kind of qualitative character: *cognitive qualia*. So here are two typical consciousness scenarios:

1   environmental – information → sensory qualia ← aware of
2   cognitive state ← aware of

Recall (see chapter 8) that propositional attitudes were divided into a representational content (proposition) and an attitude. Some have suggested that the contents of cognitive states are always in a natural language, or pictorial image code. If this is right, then thinking these contents would be like having a memory of a sensory qualia. And on the side of the attitude, there does seem to be *something it is like* to reason, decide, desire, and even to believe.

In sum, we can say that full-blown consciousness involves being in a mental state with either sensory or cognitive qualia (what it is like to have that experience) and one is aware of being in a state with that qualitative character.

Consciousness and computers (II)

Can a computer have full-blown consciousness? *First*, we saw earlier that to get *awareness of something* in the environment the system needs to be linked to the world in such a way as to pick up information about the objects it is thinking about. We know from our discussion of machine representation (see chapter 7) that this is a serious problem for digital representation – it has no computational story to tell about information pick-up from the environment. We also saw that this was a part of the functionalist program, broadly, externally construed (remember "long-armed" conceptual role from chapter 8). In the DCTM this idea takes the form that computational operations operate on symbols. What makes a structure a *symbol* is that it *stands for* something – and what it stands for can involve linking it to the environment. So DCTM is conflicted over the question of information pick-up from the environment. On the one hand it does not seem to be a part of the computational story; on the other hand DCTM requires representations with content and that content may be environmentally determined. DCTM has not yet resolved this tension.

Second, to get the computer to be aware of its own internal states it seems that we need only program it appropriately. It is qualitative (sensory and cognitive) consciousness that is the problem. The conclusion that philosophers such as Nagel and Jackson drew from their thought experiments on bats and color-blind vision specialists is that experiential consciousness, the qualitative, phenomenal character, is not a physical feature of the world, and therefore that physicalism (materialism) is incomplete. We have left that metaphysical question open. What these considerations do point to for cognitive science, however, is what Levine (1983) calls "the explanatory gap," and what Chalmers (1996b) calls "the hard problem."

The explanatory gap

The idea here is that there is an explanatory gap between what we can say about the nervous system in physiological (physical) terms, and how we can explain conscious phenomena. It would seem that all the nerve firings and hormone secretions in the world will not add up to the visual experience of red, the taste of pineapple, or the smell of a rose. There is a gap in our ability to connect specific brain activity with specific conscious experiences, and unless we can bridge this gap, we cannot explain the experiences using just physiological notions.

The hard problem

The easy (relatively) problem in cognitive neuroscience is to explain which brain activity supports or correlates with which cognitive functions. There are certain areas and functions of the brain that are already understood to some extent as involved in various cognitive capacities (see Churchland and Sejnowski, 1992, for examples). But the hard problem is saying how and why just *these* brain events are connected with just *these* conscious phenomena. With respect to the hard problem, we have made no progress at all.

Some researchers think we will need new concepts, concepts that we presently lack, to understand how consciousness can arise from matter. They think that old materialistic concepts are fundamentally inadequate. McGinn (1991) believes we will never have these concepts because of biological limitations on our own conceptual powers. Others believe we will have to rethink the basic building blocks of our conception of the natural world to accommodate consciousness. Nagel (1993) put it nicely: "The central question is whether it makes sense to look for a method of conceiving and describing the features of consciousness that both fits into a common theoretical structure with neurophysiological concepts and is true to their nature. . . . Can we discover or create a common vantage point from which it would be possible to see how subjective experience and neurophysiology are internally connected? . . . We should have in mind the ideal of an explanation of consciousness that shows it to be a necessary feature of certain biological systems – an explanation that allows us to see that such a system could not fail to be conscious" (1993: 5–6).

Searle (1992) considers consciousness also as a natural phenomenon, one that is caused by (and realized in) the brain: "Mental phenomena are caused by neurophysiological processes in the brain and are themselves features of the brain. To distinguish this from the many others in the field, I call it 'biological naturalism.' Mental events and processes are as much part of our biological natural history as digestion, mitosis, miosis, or enzyme secretion" (1992: 1).

Chalmers (1996b), though he views consciousness as a *natural* phenomenon, does not view it as just a *physical* phenomenon: "Conscious experience arises from the physical according to some laws of nature, but it is not itself physical" (1996b: 161) "A theory of consciousness must invoke bridging principles to connect the physical and the phenomenal domains, principles . . . that are not themselves entailed by physical laws" (1996b: 164). "There is a system of laws that guarantees that a given physical configuration will be accompanied by a given experience" (1996b: 170). Chalmers calls his position "naturalistic dualism." It is up to future theory construction to close the explanatory gap and answer the hard problem to the extent that this can be done. Remember, we can't explain *everything*. Even physics "the science of everything" has basic principles it must just accept as the way the world is. It is presently unclear where explanation of consciousness will end. We will follow the lead of Nagel, Searle, and Chalmers (without settling their differences) and imagine that once the relevant *natural* facts have been fixed, consciousness will follow.

So *third*, what are the consequences for the issue of computers and qualitative consciousness? To get *qualitative consciousness* it may be necessary to build the machine out of the right kind of stuff. On Searle's way of putting it, if consciousness is a part of the natural world, then it is caused by something happening in our nervous system, and if we can duplicate the causes, we can duplicate the effects. That does not mean, as Searle stresses, that we have to build nervous systems like ours – that is an open empirical question. We may only have to duplicate some features of our nervous system, the others may be irrelevant to consciousness. Or in Chalmers's way of putting it, if we were to build a machine with an organization that satisfied psychophysical laws for consciousness, then consciousness would be present in that machine.

Summary

Three things are present in complete, full-blown consciousness (including consciousness-of): *first*, appropriate links to the world; *second*, appropriate programming; and *third*, appropriate hardware (Searle) or organization (Chalmers). It may be possible in principle to build a machine with full-blown consciousness, but we may not be able to explain why it is conscious other than to note that it is a fact of nature that systems with such and such physical constitution and organization do exhibit consciousness.

Cognition and consciousness: the "connection principle"

Suppose that "full-blown consciousness" is as characterized above. How do full-blown conscious states relate to cognition? There are at least three options in the air:

1   There is a *necessary* connection: if a state is cognitive, it must be conscious.
2   There is *no* connection: a cognitive state can be conscious or unconscious.
3   A cognitive state must be *accessible in principle* to consciousness (Searle: the "connection principle").

The *first* position seems too strong. Consider so-called "dispositional beliefs," beliefs one has in the sense of being disposed to accept or express them upon having them come to mind. For instance, consider the belief that zebras do not wear rain coats in the wild (Dennett). Didn't you believe this even before reading this sentence called it to consciousness? Or consider "standing beliefs"; we don't quit believing what we believe when we are asleep (think of your beliefs about yourself such as your name, phone number, etc.), yet we are not then conscious of them. If so, again, these cognitive states need not be conscious to exist. And, as we have already seen, the phenomena of "automatic pilot," blindsight, split brain, and dichotic listening suggest cognition without consciousness.

   The *second* position is the official position in much of AI, cognitive science, and perhaps cognitive psychology. It has been challenged recently by Searle (1990b, 1992: ch. 7). He calls (3) "the connection principle," and he reasons for it like this:

The setup

1   All intentional (mental representational) states, such as believing or desiring, whether conscious or unconscious, always have "aspectual shapes" –

a *way* they represent the world as being (see chapter 8 again). A person may believe that the star in the sky over there is Venus without believing it is the Morning Star, or without believing that it is the Evening Star, even though these are the same star. A person may want to drink some water without wanting to drink some H_2O, even though the water is H_2O.

2 There are only two ways in which these aspects can be characterized if they are not characterized in terms of introspectively available conscious aspectual shapes (ways of representing): behavior and neurophysiology.

3 These "aspectual features" cannot be exhaustively or completely characterized solely in terms of behavioral, or neurophysiological notions. None of these types of notion is sufficient to give an exhaustive account of aspectual shape – of what makes something *water* vs. H_2O, or what makes something *the Morning Star* vs. the Evening star (here Searle refers approvingly to the Nagel (1974), and Jackson (1986) articles discussed earlier).

The argument

4 Suppose there were "deep" unconscious intentional (mental, representation) states – e.g. "deep" unconscious beliefs.

5 Then these deep unconscious intentional states would have an aspectual shape – a way they represent the world as being. [from 1 above]

6 There would be nothing else to these deep unconscious intentional states, if they were to exist, than their neurophysiology and/or their effects on behavior. [from 2 above]

7 But neurophysiology and behavior do not determine aspectual shape. [from 3 above]

8 So deep unconscious intentional states have no aspectual shape.

9 All intentional states must have aspectual shape. [from 1 above]

10 So, deep unconscious intentional states do not exist. QED

We can pose two questions at this point concerning the argument. *First*, at step 2 Searle seems to have left out of consideration the option we played up in chapter 7, the data structures used in computer representations of the world. They are neither just "physiological" nor are they behavioral, and they are, on Searle's own grounds, not experiential – so how can the argument ignore them? *Second*, and relatedly, at step 3 Searle uses the "qualia" results of Nagel and Jackson to argue against the possibility of neurological or behavioral analyses of aspectual shapes – the way the world is represented to be. But many theoreticians believe that not all "aspectual shapes" or ways of representing something, have a distinctive qualitative character. They contend that believing that something is H_2O may have no distinctive qualitative aspect or that believing that Venus is the Morning Star may have no distinctive qualitative aspect. One could associate each of these with the taste of eggplant and it would not matter one whit as to what they represent. This issue is related to the first in that according to the DCTM, the missing data structures are just what would be used to represent non-qualitative aspects of thought. So Searle owes us an argument against this possibility. He may think he has one and we will return to this issue.

9.5 The DCTM and Mental Content

Conceptual role and the DCTM

We saw in the previous chapter that the "official" position of the DCTM regarding content is some sort of "conceptual role" (CR) theory. Generic conceptual role theory, as we saw, says that:

(G-CR)
> The content of a representation is determined by the role the representation plays in the conceptual system of which it is a part.

One gets different CR theories by spelling out the nature of the representations involved, the nature of the roles they play, and the nature of the conceptual system they are a part of. The version we settled on earlier identified CR with the deductive inferential role, which was then combined with the language of thought (LOT) hypothesis. And the fact that inferences are defined first and basically over thoughts ("sentences" in the LOT) means that the CR of concepts ("words" and "phrases" in the LOT) is given in terms of their contribution to the CR of the thoughts they occur in. Our resulting theory of content for the DCTM was:

(DCTM-CR)
1 If "R" is a sentential representation (thought) in the LOT, then its content is determined by the fact that "R" participates in the (valid) inferential relations:
   (P)   From "R" one may infer . . . ["R" serves as a premise]
   (C)   From . . . one may infer "R" ["R" serves as a conclusion]
2 The specific inference relation (P), (C) associated with "R" give the specific content of R.
3 If "R" is a subsentential representation (concept) in the LOT, then its content is the contribution it makes to the content (inferences) of all the sentences it occurs in.

We now want to pose some challenges for this theory.

(1) *Analyticity* What exactly is the scope of principles schematized as (P) and (C)? To adapt an example from Block (1986: 628), consider the following candidate inferences:

(CA)   Felix is a *cat* → Felix is an *animal*
(CM)   Felix is a *cat* → Felix *chases mice*

These are both quite different from our sample inference: from "P and Q" infer "P," in that "animal" is not a constituent of "cat" in the way "P" is a constituent of "P and Q." Furthermore, the truth-rule for "and" guarantees the validity (truth preservingness) of the inference from "and." What guarantees the inference (CA)? Is it just a fact about the concept *cat*, or is it (merely) a truth about cats? Contrast (CA) with (CM): the problem is justifying letting (CA) contribute to determining the content of "cat," but not letting (CM) so contribute. Or put it this way, idealist philosophers think that there is no physical matter and that everything is mental; panpsychists think that there are physical things, but that everything has a mind (and solipsists think they themselves are the only "things" that exist!). When one of these theoreticians thinks: *there goes a cat* or *there is a good Merlot*, do their thoughts have the same content as ours (supposing we are not idealists, panpsychists or solipsists)? The panpsychists seem to *make* inferences we would *not* make (*that's a good merlot → There is a mind*), and the idealist does *not* make inferences we *would* make (*there goes a cat → There goes a physical object*). Do these differences in inference constitute a difference in content or not? This is called the problem of "analyticity" – the problem of justifying the inclusion of a particular inference in the "analysis" of the content.

(2) *Relativism* If (DCTM-CR) is right, then content is relative to the system of representation (LOT). This raises the question how we can compare contents across people. How could different people agree or disagree about a given thought? Wouldn't they have to have the same inferential relations, and how would that be possible? Well, if the LOT was the same for all people, then it might be possible. But how could this be if people develop their psychologies from such different experiences? One answer (see Fodor, 1975) is that the LOT is innate, and so shared by all people. That helps to get us out of the present problem, but it does put a heavy burden on genetics.

(3) *Holism* What is to keep the inferences from spreading to the whole system, so that the content of two people's thoughts would be the same only if *they shared every other thought*? This would be so unlikely that we might not have any psychological principles to state at the level of content.

(4) *Compositionality* As characterized so far, the constituents of thoughts get their content from the role they play in thoughts. But the idea behind compositionality seemed to be that the content of a complex representation is determined by the *independent* content of its constituent representations, plus their structural relationships. The idea was that meaningful wholes are made up of independently meaningful constituents. Isn't there tension between these two ideas?

(5) *Truth* First, it is really not just the inference *pattern* that gives these symbols the semantics they have, because we have to suppose that the inferences are valid and so preserve *truth*. And this means that "P and Q" must be associated with a truth rule, such as the one given earlier (chapter 7) in the predicate calculus. But that truth rule is not itself an inferential procedure nor is it stated in the vocabulary of computation. The computational theory of content presupposes that another non-computational theory (truth theory or more generally "model" theory) has done important relevant work.

Conceptual role and wide content

The issue of truth raises the issue of reference, of aboutness, because a thought is true only if the relevant parts of the world actually are the way that thought represents them to be. And it is the aboutness or reference relations that determine these relevant parts. Are these relations to things in the world essential to thought contents, or are they outside thought contents?

Adapting Putnam's (1975b) terminology we will call a thought *narrow* if it does not presuppose the existence of anything outside the thought itself, and we will call a thought *wide* if it does. To take an uncontroversial example, at the level of the attitudes proper, *believing* that bachelors are unhappy is narrow because nothing is presupposed about the truth or reference of: bachelors are unhappy. One can believe it whether or not it is true. But one cannot *know* (or realize, recognize, etc.) that bachelors are unhappy unless it is true that they are unhappy – these attitudes are wide.

DCTM

We can see that DCTM (remember the "formality constraint") is a theory of narrow thoughts in that the issue of whether or not the machine believes that bachelors are unhappy is a question of whether the representation for "bachelors are unhappy" is stored in the belief box (e.g. long-term memory) or not. There is nothing in DCTM, as we have just seen, which allows the machine to distinguish believing that bachelors are unhappy from knowing that bachelors are unhappy, because truth is not a DCTM notion.

How about thought contents? Is there any reason for going "outside the head" for such contents – is there any reason to suppose that thought contents can be wide, or as we will also say, is there any reason to suppose that thought contents can be *external* to the system itself? Putnam (1975b, 1981) offers a series of interesting examples which are supposed to convince us that this is true, that *at least some contents are wide and external.*

Case 1 [Churchill ant trace]
"An ant is crawling on a patch of sand. As it crawls it traces a line in the sand. By pure chance the line that it traces curves and recrosses itself in such a way that it ends up looking like a recognizable caricature of Winston Churchill. Has the ant traced a picture of Winston Churchill, a picture that *depicts* Churchill? Most people would say that it has not. The ant, after all, has never seen Churchill, or even a picture of Churchill, and it had no intention of depicting Churchill. It simply traced a line (and even *that* was unintentional), a line that *we* can 'see as' a picture of Churchill . . . the line is not 'in itself' a representation of anything rather than anything else" (1981: 1).

Case 2 [tree picture]
"Suppose there is a planet somewhere on which human beings have evolved. . . . Suppose they have never imagined trees (perhaps vegetable life exists on their planet only in the form of molds). Suppose one day a picture of a tree is accidentally dropped on their planet by a spaceship which passes on without having other contact with them. [or "suppose the 'picture of a tree' that the spaceship dropped was not really a picture of a tree, but the accidental result of some spilled paints"] Imagine them puzzling over the picture. What in the world is this? All sorts of speculation occur to them: a building, a canopy, even an animal of some kind. But suppose they never come close to the truth. For *us* the picture is a representation of a tree. For these humans the picture only represents a strange object, nature and function unknown. Suppose one of them has a mental image which is exactly like one of my images of a tree as a result of having seen the picture. His mental image is not a *representation of a tree*. It is only a representation of the strange object (whatever it is) that the mysterious picture represents" (1981: 3–4).

Case 3 [Twin Earth]
"Suppose that somewhere in the galaxy there is a planet we shall call Twin Earth. Twin Earth is very much like Earth; in fact, people on Twin Earth even speak *English*. In fact, apart from the differences we shall specify in our science-fiction examples, the reader may suppose that Twin Earth is *exactly* like Earth. He may even suppose that he has a *Doppelganger* – an identical copy

– on Twin Earth. . . . One of the peculiarities of Twin Earth is that the liquid called 'water' is not H_2O but a different liquid whose chemical formula is very long and complicated. I shall abbreviate this chemical formula simply as XYZ. I shall suppose that XYZ is indistinguishable from water at normal temperatures and pressures . . . on Twin Earth the word 'water' means XYZ . . . on Earth the world 'water' means H_2O . . . in the sense in which it is used on Twin Earth . . . what we call 'water' simply isn't water; while . . . what the Twin Earthians call 'water' simply isn't water" (1975b: 228–9).

Although Putnam here conducts his thought experiment with the word(s) "water," the point extends to thoughts: you on Earth can and do think often of water (H_2O), whereas twin-you does not, twin-you thinks often of XYZ (and even calls it "water"). But as *we* use the word "water" (and we are using *our* word) the twin is not thinking of water (H_2O).

Conclusion

"Even a large and complex system of representations, both verbal and visual, still does not have an *intrinsic*, built-in, magical connection with what it represents – a connection independent of how it was caused and what dispositions of the speaker or thinker are" (ibid., 5). "One cannot refer to certain kinds of things, e.g. *trees*, if one has no causal interaction at all with them, or with things in terms of which they can be described" (1981: 17).

Insofar as our judgments comport with Putnam's, the contents of such representations must be, at least in part, wide or external. And notice that natural kind concepts, such as water, are particularly resistant to conceptual role analysis, because such inferences have little to do with the central aspect of their "meaning" – their *reference*. As Putnam (1988) notes, the Greeks had a very different conception of water, yet "water" is a perfectly good translation of *hydor* because both "water" and *hydor* refer to the same stuff. And until Dalton (and modern atomic chemistry) in the Renaissance, it was believed that the property of liquidity was due to the presence of water – thus alcohol and mercury flowed because of the presence of water. Clearly the concept of water played a very different role, yet what we think about when we think "water" thoughts is the same. And that is because conceptual role plays virtually no role in determining aboutness.

Content and computation: a problem

Suppose these conclusions regarding content are correct – suppose that conceptual role does not exhaust mental representational content, and that the content of at least some thoughts involves being related to things (objects, properties, situations) in the world (see chapter 8). We said earlier in chapter 8 that DCTM respects Fodor's "formality constraint," that is, computations are defined over formal, structural, syntactic properties of the representations they manipulate, not semantic properties such as reference and truth. So the following aspects of mental representations are in play (see Devitt, 1989, 1991, 1996):

mental syntax: satisfies the "formality constraint" and does not involve semantic properties.
narrow content: semantic properties that are "in the head."
wide content: semantic properties that involve relations to the world (truth conditions).

If we go on to assume the following principle:

(A)   The laws of the mind that cognitive science endorses just are the computational principles used by computational mechanisms that apply to these representations,

then we get three styles of cognitive theory, only the first two of which potentially satisfy the formality constraint on computation:

syntactic cognitive theory: the laws of the mind are sensitive only to non-semantic (formal, syntactic) properties of representations.
narrow cognitive theory: the laws of the mind are sensitive to narrow ("in the head") semantic properties of representations.
wide cognitive theory: the laws of the mind are sensitive to wide semantic properties of representations.

Anyone who accepts the CTM (with its "formality constraint") must subscribe to one of the first two approaches if they also subscribe to assumption [A]. This means that according to (DCTM), mental states and processes are not sensitive to wide content – wide content is divorced from computation, and this can lead to potential problems.

1   For example, as noted in chapter 7, we want DCTM to track logical relations between representations such as entailment. But entailment is a wide semantic property – it essentially uses the notion of truth. So how does the computational process keep track of the logical relations – how does proof respect truth?

2   Or to take a very different example, we want DCTM to explain behavior when that behavior has an appropriately "cognitive" explanation. For instance, if (a) you go to the refrigerator to get a drink because (b) you want to drink something and (c) you believe there is something to drink in the refrigerator, then we want DCTM to reconstruct this explanation in terms of principles of computational psychology – principles involving computational relations to, and operation on, computational representations. But how can we do this if referring to *your refrigerator* cannot be a part of the content of any representation?

Two-factor theories: a solution?

Recall that in chapter 8, when we introduced functionalism, we noted that it accommodated two functionalist factors: (i) so-called "short-armed" functionalism (also called "conceptual role" theory), which uses only relations internal to the head, and (ii) so-called "long-armed" functionalism, which (also) uses relations external to the head. Since the formality constraint dictates that only internal role has a formal, computational aspect, we ignored the external functional role.

One proposal is to revive that idea and identify the content of narrow psychological states, that is, "narrow content" with internal functional role (conceptual role), and to identify the content of wide psychological states, that is, "wide content" with an external functional role that determines a truth condition (for mind-to-world direction of fit). On this "two-factor" theory of content, mental states can have both narrow and wide content, or better, narrow and wide aspects of content, and each aspect has its job to do. The narrow aspect of content is internal and describable in computational terms, the wide aspect of content is external and describable in non-computational relational terms. On this view, a correct theory of mental content will have to get both factors right, but computation will only be a part of the story.

9.6   Against Cognitivism

A "machine" cannot usefully be defined as "a member of [a certain class of physical objects]" for the decision as to whether something is a machine depends on what that thing is actually used *for, and not just on its composition or structure.*

(Minsky, 1967: 3)

At the very end of his Chinese room paper, Searle comments: "Of course the brain is a digital computer. Since everything is a digital computer, brains are too" (1980: 424). This begins the second stage of the attack on the DCTM in general (cognition is a kind of computation), and "cognitivism" in particular – the view that in some non-trivial sense, the brain is a digital computer. These are distinct theses, since the brain might be a digital computer, but thinking might not be computation (Searle's view). Searle (1992: ch. 9) begins by posing "such absolutely fundamental questions as, what exactly is a digital computer? What exactly is a symbol? What exactly is an algorithm? What exactly is a computational process? Under what physical conditions exactly are two systems implementing the same program?" (1992: 205). Since "there is no universal agreement on the fundamental questions" (1992: 205), Searle goes back to Turing and gives a brief informal description of a Turing machine. He then adds "that is the standard definition of computation" (1992: 206). However, there *is* no "standard definition of a computer" – which is why Searle was unable to report one. There are standard definitions of a Turing machine, a Turing machine computation, and Turing machine computable functions. There are also many specific definitions relating Turing machines and other types of computers, definitions of what it is for each of these to perform a computation, and proofs regarding their computational powers (see Suggested reading for chapter 6). For instance, a machine with an architecture different from a Turing machine might still be shown to be *weakly equivalent* to a Turing machine in the sense that it will compute every function a Turing machine will compute. But there is no generally accepted definition of a "computer" or of a "computation" that can be used in cognitive science.

It is not clear how or why Searle thinks the class of computers is defined syntactically in terms of the assignment of 0s and 1s (one of Babbage's machines computed in decimal, as did the original ENIAC in decimal). Since 0s and 1s are simply a convenient coding device for a wide variety of symbols (letters, numerals, graphics) we should modify Searle's point to the assignment of *symbols*: the class of computers is defined syntactically in terms of the assignment of symbols. Still, a computer requires more than symbols – it requires at least memory, control, and certain capacities to process – a computer, after all, computes. It is not just an algorithm – a computer will *run* a program which *expresses* an algorithm. So, following our earlier discussion, we will assume these are all included in Searle's notion of an actual computer: a computer is at least a device which has a memory, control, and manipulates symbols.

Searle turns next to the issue of what one will find if one opens up a particular physical computer: "If you open up your home computer, you are most unlikely to find any 0s and 1s or even a tape" (1992: 206). Furthermore, there is a variety of stuff the computer might be made of: cogs and levers, hydraulics, silicon, neurons, cats and mice and cheese, pigeons, etc. In sum, according to cognitivism: "We could make a system that does just what the brain does out of pretty much anything" (1992: 207). This is so-called "multiple realizability," and according to cognitivism, just as a carburetor could be made out of brass or steel, a given program can be run on a wide variety of such hardware. Searle demurs: "But there is a difference: The class of carburetors and thermostats are defined in terms of the production of certain *physical effects*. That is why, for instance, nobody says you can make carburetors out of pigeons. But the class of computers is defined syntactically in terms of the *assignment* of 0s and 1s. The multiple realizability is a consequence not of the fact that the same physical effect can be achieved in different physical substances, but that the relevant properties are purely syntactical. The physics is irrelevant except in so far as it admits of the assignment of 0s and 1s [i.e. symbols] and of state transitions between them" (1992: 207).

Presumably the "relevant properties" referred to in this passage are those properties for being a (digital) computer. So it will be crucial that Searle be able to maintain this asymmetry between carburetors and computers – that multiple realizability for computers is not, as it is for carburetors, just a consequence of the principle that if you can duplicate the relevant causes, you can duplicate the relevant effects. We will maintain that, properly understood, computers are just like carburetors in this respect.

Before going on we must distinguish the computer qua *design* from the computer qua *physical object* that conforms to the design – the computer *type* from the computer *token*. Given a computer design (type), something, X, will be a token of it if and only if X instantiates that design. It will be a part of the design, however, that its physics moves it from (symbolic) state to (symbolic) state. The "syntax" is just a place holder at the design level for physical properties and relations at the instantiation level. For convenience let's call Searle's conception of computers and computation quoted above the "syntactic definition" of computers and computation. So far it is central to this conception that "the class of computers is defined syntactically in terms of the assignment of 0s and 1s."

The "syntax is not intrinsic to the physics" arguments

Searle draws out two further consequences of the syntactic definition of computers and computation:

(1) *Universal realizability* The same principle that implies *multiple realizability* would seem to imply *universal realizability* – everything would be a digital computer because any object whatever could have syntactical ascriptions made of it. You could describe anything in terms of 0s and 1s (1992: 207–8). More specifically (i) for any *object* there is some description of that object such that under that description *the object is a digital computer* (1992: 208) (everything is a computer). (ii) For any *object* there is some *program* such that the object *is implementing the program* – the wall behind my back is now implementing WordStar because there is some pattern of molecule movements isomorphic with the formal structure of WordStar (1992: 208–9) (every object has some program running on it).

(2)   *Syntax is observer-relative*   The ascription of syntactical properties is always relative to an agent or observer who treats certain physical phenomena as syntactical.   (1992: 208)

According to Searle these point have some serious consequences for cognitivism: "This could be disastrous because we wanted to know if there was not some sense in which brains were *intrinsically digital computers*; is there a fact of the matter about brains that would make them digital computers? It does not answer that question to be told, yes, brains are digital computers because everything is a digital computer" (1992: 208). "Proponents do not see universal realizability as a problem because they do not see it as a consequence of the deeper point that *"syntax" is not the name of a physical feature, like mass or gravity.* Syntax is essentially an observer relative notion" (1990b: 27; 1992: 209; emphasis added). "The same point can be stated without the notion of "syntax." A physical state of a system is a computational state relative to the *assignment* to that state of some computational role, function, or interpretation. The same problem arises without 0s and 1s because notions such as computation, algorithm, and program do not name intrinsic physical features of systems. Computational state are *not discovered within* the physics, they are *assigned to* the physics (1990b: 27; 1992: 201; emphasis added). Clearly Searle views these observations as counting against cognitivism, but it is not clear exactly what the argument is supposed to be. We will try to state the argument(s) more precisely.

Argument 1

1   The class of computers in *defined syntactically* in terms of the *assignment* of 0s and 1s.
2   If something is assigned it is *observer-relative*. [definition]
3   So, the fact that a (particular) object is a computer is observer-relative.
4   So, the fact that a brain is a computer, if it is, is observer-relative.
5   Something is observer relative if and only if it is not intrinsic. [definition]

6
  (a)   So brains are not *intrinsically* digital computers.
  (b)   So brains are not digital computers.

Notice the difference between the two versions of the conclusion. By this argument, a brain is not *intrinsically* a computer because being a computer is observer-relative. But of course then neither is my/your PC *intrinsically* a computer. Since my/your PC *is* a computer, we want to know: (Q1) *why* is being *intrinsically* a computer so important – why isn't it enough for a brain just to *be* a computer? (Q2) *What* exactly is it to be *intrinsically* a computer?

Q1: Why isn't it enough for a brain just to be a computer?

Searle: Because of *universal realizability* – everything is a digital computer, so it is trivial and uninteresting to be told that a brain is a computer.
Reply: What reason is there for believing that everything is a computer?
Searle: See universal realizability (i) again: you could describe anything in terms of 0s and 1s.
Reply: When arguing for universal realizability, Searle tends to give as examples of *computers*, physical realizations of *running programs* (the wall is running WordStar). But when theorists speculate that the brain is a (digital) computer they mean that it is capable of computing – a computer is a device that can compute, though it need not be computing at any given time.

Searle seems to assume:

A1   If something *can be described* as running (a segment of) a particular program over a stretch of time, it *is* running that program (over that stretch of time).
A2   Anything that is running a program (over a stretch of time) is computing.
A3   Anything that computes is a computer.

He then seems to argue:

1   The wall can be described as running a segment of WordStar, over a stretch of time.
2   So the wall is running WordStar (over that stretch of time). [A1]
3   So, the wall is computing. [A2]
4   So, the wall is a computer. [A3]
5   If the wall is a computer, then anything is a computer.

The conclusion only needs to be made explicit to realize that something has gone wrong – what? Here are some possibilities.

(1) (A1)   Searle may have overestimated the ease with which a physical object can be described as running (a segment of) a program (steps 1 and 2). Just because the object can be put in a 1–1 correspondence with a time slice of a program run, doesn't entail that it is running that program. Running a program requires that numerous counterfactuals be true, counterfactuals of the form: if the program had been given such-and-such, it would have computed so-and-so; that is, if it had been given a 2 and a 4 it would have printed "No" or if it had been given "Control F6" it would have printed in boldface.

(2) (A2, A3)   Searle may have also overestimated the closeness of the connection between computing and computers. One might give Searle his rather liberal notion of computation, but claim that to be a computer requires more. As we said earlier, it may require an architecture, memory, and control. It may be a part of our conception of a computer that it be capable of computing, not that it be computing.

(3) It is open to the DCTM to claim that the mind/brain is a particular kind of computer, not just "a computer." Consider the claim that the mind/brain is a von Neumann machine. Showing that one can map a segment of a WordStar run onto a time slice of the molecular movements of the wall is not sufficient to show that the wall is a von Neumann machine.

(4) Searle's position is that there is no fact of the matter that a PC is a von Neumann machine. Why? Because it *can be* described as another kind of machine. So what – a computer could be described as a door stop, a knife as a paper weight. The *challenge* (not the refutation) Searle offers DCTM is making sense of the idea that some descriptions, in particular, some computational descriptions, of systems are better than others. What could "better" amount to? Among other things these descriptions would be more accurate, allow better explanations and predictions of the machine's behavior. Intuitively, describing a PC as a von Neumann machine running WordStar, to continue Searle's example, is more accurate and allows for better explanations and predications of its behavior than describing a wall as running WordStar. The challenge is to say exactly why.

(5) Semantics: remember, there is at least one serious difference between the DCTM and strong AI – the DCTM gave cognitive states *semantics*, *representational powers*. Strong AI is a thesis about mentality and programs. On Searle's view, a program is formal, syntactic, non-semantic, non-representational. So even if Searle could show that anything could be viewed

as running a program formally defined, it would not follow that it could be viewed as running a program semantically defined as well. In this regard it is interesting that Searle's example of a wall running WordStar is one where no obvious (real world) semantics is at issue.

Q2: What exactly is it to intrinsically be a digital computer?

Seale: To be observer relative (syntax) is sufficient for being non-intrinsic. Properties such as mass and gravity are not observer-relative, so they are intrinsic.

Reply: It is not an observer-relative fact that a particular computer is running a particular program. It is an intrinsic physical fact about the computer that it is programmed in the way it is (remember the compiler story), just as it is an intrinsic physical fact about the computer that it has the weight it does. Of course, just as the computer could have had a different weight, it could have been running a different program. "Intrinsic" here just means "not observer-relative."

We have challenged both conclusions of the first argument. There is no reason to suppose that the brain is not a computer – intrinsic or otherwise. Nor is there any reason to suppose that the truth of the claim that the brain is a (digital) computer is trivial.

Argument 2

Another argument against cognitivism is suggested by some comments of Searle regarding the ambitions of cognitivism as a "natural science":

1   The class of computers is *defined syntactically* in terms of the *assignment* of 0s and 1s.
2   So, the syntax of a (particular) computer is observer-relative.
3   So, there is no fact of the matter about brains that would make them digital computers.
4   In natural sciences we discover, not assign, the properties things have.
5   So, "cognitivism" could not be natural science.
6   Cognitivism is supposed to be, and is understood to be, a natural science.
7   So, cognitivism as it is understood to be can't exist.

Is the claim that the brain is a digital computer a piece of "natural science"? Well, it is certainly supposed to be an empirical factual claim, but not all empirical factual claims are part of natural science. However, it is not clear that

Searle needs this extra step, since presumable if the syntax is not "intrinsic" (it is assigned, observer-relative, etc.) then it is not an empirical factual claim, but rather a decision.

The "syntax has no causal powers" arguments

Searle's second group of arguments against cognitivism surround the issue of causal powers: "According to cognitivism, the mechanisms by which brain processes produce cognition are supposed to be computational, and by specifying the programs we will have specified the causes of cognition" (1990b: 30; 1993: 215). "But the difficulty is that the 0s and 1s as such have no causal power at all because they do not exist except in the eyes of the beholder. The implemented program has no causal powers other than those of the implementing medium because the program has no real existence, no ontology, beyond that of the implementing medium. Physically speaking, there is no such thing as a separate 'program level'" (1990b: 30; 1992: 215). As before, these remarks are suggestive, but it is not clear exactly what the argument is. We begin, then, by trying to state the argument(s) more precisely.

Argument 1

1 An implemented program has no causal powers beyond the implementing medium.[2]
2 So, the "program level," the "syntax" itself has no causal powers.
3 So, in a programmed computer, the program has no power to cause program states – it is *realized in*, but not *caused by* the physics.
4 In a brain, intentional states are the effects of physical (biological) processes – intentional states are *realized in* and *caused by* the physics.
5 So, brains are not computers, and cognitivism is false.

The problem is the inference from the second to the third step. It is not a question of whether the *program itself* has causal powers, but whether the *programmed computer* has causal powers. We saw from the compiler story given earlier in chapter 6 that the programmed computer does have distinctive causal powers. Because of this, Searle's argument breaks down at step 3. Searle needs the conclusion that a computer's program state are realized in but not caused by the programming. But this is not true. And if step 3 is not true, then there is no asymmetry between programmed computers and brains.

Argument 2

Searle might object that no program states of a computer can be intrinsically intentional, so there is still a difference between programmed computers and brains:

1   The class of computers is *defined syntactically* in terms of the *assignment* of 0s and 1s.
2   So, the syntax of a (particular) computer is observer-relative.
3   So, there is no fact of the matter about brains that would make them digital computers.
4   So digital computers do not have symbols intrinsically.
5   So digital computers do not have intrinsic intentionality.
6   But brains have intrinsic intentionality.
7   So brains are not intrinsically digital computers, and cognitivism is false.[3]

We were given no argument for the claim that brains have intrinsic intentionality in the Chinese room discussion, nor in this one. But our discussion of wide content makes it clear that some argument is called for – recall Putnam's earlier discussion of "magical" theories of reference.

The syntax IS in the physics and DOES have causal powers

The machine – not just the hardware, but the programmed living machine – is the organism we study.

(Newell and Simon, 1976)

Recall that by implementing a program, the implementing medium becomes configured in such a way that given the laws governing the material, the state transitions follow one another in the proper, natural way – proper for executing the intended algorithm via the laws of electrical engineering (and ultimately physics). Searle fails to realize that programming an implementing medium changes that medium – it gives the medium new and specific structure, and so specific causal powers and effects. This is where thinking of computers as Turning machine designs (there being no such physical objects) and thinking of computation in general as being capable of description in terms of Turing machine computation – operating on a tape assigned 0s and 1s – is so misleading. The 0s and 1s on a Turing machine tape are (typically) binary representations of numerals, letters, etc. But the 0s and 1s that result from compiling a program into bit code in a von Neumann machine represent the configuration of flip-flops in the system, and since this is typically a difference in voltage, they represent a specific, physical fact about the programmed machine. And since this "syntax" is *physical structure* with *causal consequences*, we do not just "assign" it – physical structure is not "observer-relative." It is, in a perfectly normal sense, as *intrinsic* to the programmed machine as any structure is intrinsic to matter. (Since Searle gives mass and gravitation as examples of "intrinsic" physical properties both of which are *relational* in contemporary physics, he must mean by "intrinsic" *not observer-relative or dependent.*)

9.7   DCTM Hardware and the Brain

It was a part of the doctrine of "strong AI" that programming is sufficient for cognition, mentality, intelligence, etc., and that the only thing that mattered about the hardware was that it had enough causal structure to implement the program. Furthermore, it was characteristic of this work that it was done on computers with von Neumann architecture – stored-program, register machines. It might be argued that this is not essential, and that the style of programming required for mind could require a radically different kind of architecture.

But one can take a slightly different approach to this. One can argue that so far the only minds we have are biologically based, and in fact are rather similar in that biological basis. So if one is interested in how we work, how *our* minds/brains work, and not just in how some possible mind might work, one might feel it appropriate to evaluate DCTM as a model of *us* on hardware grounds as well.

DCTM hardware: essentially reduces to *flip-flops*, *registers* of flip-flops, *logic gates* constructed out of flip-flops, and *circuits* constructed out of the foregoing.

Brains: essentially reduce to analogues of those: *neurons*, *connected neurons*, and *"circuits"* of connected neurons.

DCTM hardware and the brain: similarities

Not very much that is informative can be said in favor of DCTM hardware as a model of the brain. For instance:

1   both have lots of basic elements,
2   both perform broadly "computational" functions,
3   both operate on electrical signals.

But the same could be said for a microwave oven or an airbag. If all that can be said is that there is a level of generality at which DCTM hardware and brains fall together, but this level of generality also captures microwave ovens and airbags, we have not said anything interesting.

DCTM hardware and the brain: differences

Here the analogy ends:

Components

1   There is just one relevant type of flip–flop in any DCTM machine, but there are a variety of different kinds of neurons in the brain (see figure 9.1).
2   Flip–flops are basically on or off, but neurons also exhibit functionally significant firing frequencies (remember what the frog's eye told the frog's brain in chapter 4), as well as analogue-to-digital conversion. On one proposal, it takes about a dozen electronic components to model gross neuron features (see Kent, 1981: 9, figure 1.2).
3   Neurons (vs. flip–flops) summate impulses from different axons (spatial summation) and from sequences of pulses from a single axon (temporal summation) simultaneously, and each can be a separate channel of information.
4   Neurons typically use a variety of neurotransmitters (see chapter 3), unlike DCTM hardware.
5   Neurons typically work at speeds in the milliseconds, current computer chips work in nanoseconds.
6   Various features of neuron fibers (such as diameter, etc.) can affect speed of transmission – which is useful when impulses must arrive from different distances at the same time. DCTM lines all carry information at the same rate.
7   There are an estimated 10^{12} neurons in the brain, so if each neuron averages 10^3 connections, that means there are about 10^{15} connections in the brain – more than DCTM hardware by orders of magnitude.

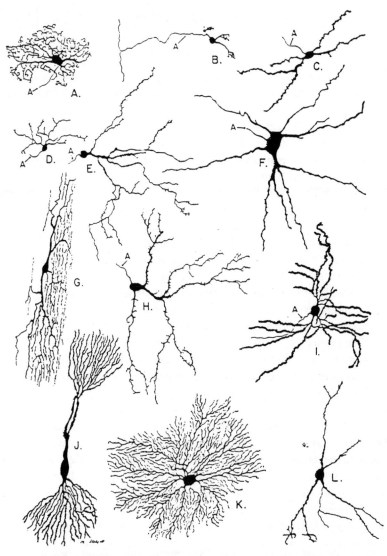

Dendritic tress of several real neurons. Savor the majestic ring of the anatomical designations of neural structures. Scaled drawings of some characteristic neurons whose axons (A) and dendrites remain within the central nervous system. A, Neuron of inferior olivary nucleus; B, granule cell of cerebellar cortex; C, small cell of reticular formation; D, small gelatinosa cell of spinal trigeminal nucleus; E, ovoid cell, nucleus of tractus solitarius; F, large cell of reticular formation; G, spindle-shaped cell, substantia gelatinosa of spinal cord; H, large cell of spinal trigeminal nucleus; I, neuron, putamen of lenticular nucleus; J, double pyramidal cell, Ammon's horn of hippocampal cortex; K, cell from thalamic nucleus; L, cell from globus pallidus of lenticular nucleus. Golgi preparations, monkey. (Courtesy of Dr Clement Fox, Marquette University.)

Figure 9.1   Some different types of neurons (from Anderson, 1995: 9, figure 1.2; reproduced by permission of the MIT Press)

Organization and functioning

8   Logic gates made of flip-flops average about 1 to 4 in connectivity, whereas brains average about 1 to 1,000, and can go as high as 1 to 100,000.

9   Logic gates have a fixed geometry of inputs and outputs, but neurons can grow and lose synaptic connections.

10   Logic gates output a certain metronomic frequency whereas neurons vary in output from 0 to 10^2 hz.

11   There is little correlated neural firing in the brain cortex, certainly no repeating time-cycle such as DCTM hardware employs.

12   Brains use attention mechanisms to select from the input array what is to be stored long-term, DCTM hardware does not.

13   There is no (anatomical) area of the brain that corresponds to permanent memory for all remembered items: "the evidence suggests that the brain's memory is incorporated into its structure at whatever point the stored information is to act. Its memory may be thought of as distributed throughout its structure" (Kent, 1981: 21).

14   The control structure of the brain seems to be organized more globally and from top to bottom (see Kent, 1981: 13, figure 1.5) in a way that reflects the evolutionary layering of later more advanced structures on earlier more primitive structures.

As far as the functioning of these structures goes there is an interesting symbiotic relationship: ". . . at each level, are a number of relatively independent processing elements pursuing their own jobs in parallel, while trading information with echelons above and below, and laterally with one another. It follows that it doesn't make sense to ask where in the brain any large-scale function is processed. Different aspects of it will be handled in different portions of functional subsystems which are represented at all major levels of the physical system. . . . The simplest early brains obviously had to be capable, in their own inelegant way, of surviving. During the course of evolution, complex structures capable of more sophisticated handling of the same basic functions became available. Rather than eliminating the older structures and duplicating their functions, the newer structures simply took control of the older ones and used them as subprocessors . . . not by turning them on when needed, but by inhibiting their actions except as desired. The beauty of this system is that if a higher center is suddenly damaged, the older, more primitive units, which are normally inhibited, are released to function on their own. . . . In the case of damage to lower centers, the multitude of processing elements available allows some of the higher levels to be reprogrammed to take over the functions of the lower level systems by simulating their operation" (Kent, 1981: 14–17).

The list given above is just a sampler, of course, but it conveys the idea that brain hardware and DCTM hardware are quite distinct. These similarities and differences are of course no accident; brains and computers evolved differently. All mammalian brains have basically the same neural components and gross organization (Kent, 1981: 15, figure 1.5). Rats and humans are more similar in this respect than either is to an ordinary digital computer. All digital computers have basically the same flip-flop components and gross organization (see von Neumann figure [6.5] again). IBM and Apple computers are more similar in this respect than either is to a human. Natural selection built brains out of available components (neurons) by using *lots of them* ("You want million-bit bytes, and ten thousand legged gates? Sure, how many trillion?") to solve immediate problems of *perception and action*. Commercial (unnatural?) selection built computers out of available components (vacuum tubes, semiconductors) by using few of them (too expensive), but by making them *very fast*, originally to solve problems of *mathematics and logic*. So it is not surprising that brains and computers are so different in how they are made and what they are good at.

9.8   The Domain and Scope of the DCTM

We have seen that the adequacy of the DCTM has been challenged on a number of fronts, most seriously perhaps is its silence on issues of phenomenal consciousness and wide content. In light of this we now have to face the question: what exactly does the DCTM apply to?

Mental phenomena, cognition, and propositional attitudes

Here is a list of candidates that gradually decreases in comprehensiveness. First, the DCTM (remember that M = Mind) could, as its name suggests, be a general theory of all *mental* phenomena (states and processes). Second, and more conservatively, it could be a theory just of *cognitive* phenomena – phenomena that are intuitively cognitive and involving the manipulation of mental representations. Finally, there is the most restricted conception of the domain of the DCTM to the *propositional attitudes* – states such as believing, intending, desiring, and so forth. It is of course controversial if and where to draw this last distinction. Perhaps, say, object perception is cognitive, but not a propositional attitude. Is there any reason for choosing a more restrictive domain over the more inclusive? Some authors think there is.

Mental or cognitive phenomena, but not digital computational

Some states and processes we intuitively think of as "mental" are not naturally thought of as digital computational. Here is an initial, and provisional, survey:

1 *Moods and Emotions*: according to Pylyshyn, these are "almost certain to involve a noncognitive component" (1984: 269), and we might add, a non-digital computational component.
2 *Sleep and dreaming* may not be covered by a digital computational theory.
3 *Creativity* may not be a digital computational process.
4 *Association* may not be a digital computational process.
5 *Non-cogntivie changes in cognition*: Pylyshyn (1984: 266ff) suggests that there are ways of producing changes in an organism's cognition that are not digital computational. These involve "variations in nourishment, growth and maturation of glands and organs (including the brain), injury and/or trauma." And Fodor (1975: 200) suggests the same for "the consequences of brute incursions from the physiological level." For instance: nausea, or the impact of sensory material on cognition. These types of changes are like hardware changes and interrupts in a digital machine. They are not a part of the purely computational algorithmic and representational explanation of the machine's behavior (though they are a part of the general machine explanation). Should we allow these to be part of the "computational" story? Fodor and Pylyshyn think not.

If these considerations are correct, then there are intuitively "mental" phenomena that are not (digital) computational and we will need to restrict the domain of application of the DCTM to only a portion of our mental life. We can organize many of the items on this list by noting that mental phenomena in general can be divided into states and processes and further can be divided into subcategories depending first on the *nature* of the phenomena, and second on its *history*, as Fodor and Pylyshyn noted above. *First*, mental states and processes can themselves be divided into two subcategories: experiential phenomena, and non-experiential phenomena. Experiential phenomena are characterized by their conscious, introspectively accessible experiential qualities, and being in one of these states or processes entails having certain sorts of sensory experiences. Non-experiential phenomena, on the other hand, have no essential qualitative character. Of course, it could be that many mental states

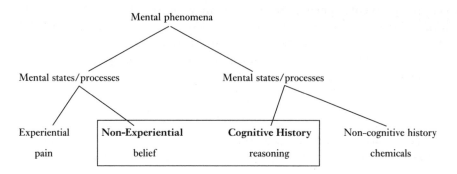

Figure 9.2 The domain and scope of the DCTM

and processes are a mixture of experiential and non-experiential aspects, perhaps even a spectrum from, say, pain to belief. The hope of the DCTM is that the functional component of these states and processes has an informative computational story. *Second*, mental states and processes can have a history that is either cognitive, such as reasoning, deciding, etc., or they can have a history due to non-cognitive events, something affecting the physical stuff on which cognition depends. We can diagram these options as in figure 9.2.

If this is roughly right, the DCTM will not be a general theory of mental phenomena, but a theory of the occurrence of certain cognitive phenomena under certain conditions. As such it could more accurately be described as the digital computational theory of cognition or propositional attitudes which arise from cognition. Notice that this also means the DCTM is not a solution to the "mind–body" problem, but only to the "cognition–body" problem. It should not be a surprise that scientific analysis cuts up a domain slightly differently than pre-science. As Fodor noted in a related context: "molecular physics vindicates the intuitive taxonomy of middle sized objects into liquids and solids. But the nearest kind to the liquids that molecular physics acknowledges includes some of what commonsense would not; glass, for example. So what?" (1987: 26). The inclination to promote a special theory of cognition to a general theory of the mind probably stems from the centrality of these states and processes in thinking about our own mentality and our identity as human beings. We are more willing to consider an organism that doesn't dream, sleep, etc. as lacking a mental life than one which has no cognitive states or propositional attitudes. So it is no accident that ancient definitions of "human" included "rational animal" and not "animal capable of dreaming" or "animal capable of emotions," and so forth. The propositional attitudes (belief, intention, desire, etc.) traditionally constitute the focus of our concept of mental phenomena because they are so close to human self-identity, and other phenomena, such as dreams, sleep, emotions, moods, and obsessions are deemed peripheral. None of this is necessarily good science, of course, it's just the way we have tended to think about ourselves and what we have collectively elevated to importance.

Notes

1   The text suggests a related "multiple realizability argument for no syntax intrinsic to the physics":

   (1)   Computation is symbol manipulation – operations on symbols,
   (2)   Symbols, identity, and difference of symbols, etc., are not defined physically,
      a.   computational states are multiply realizable,
      b.   so determining the physics does not determine the computational state,
   (3)   So the syntax of symbols is not intrinsic to the physics.

   But it doesn't *follow* that because a computational state is multiply realizable, fixing the physics doesn't fix the computational state. Consider the analogy: mothers can have many children (determining the mother does not determine a particular child), so determining a particular child does not determine a mother (wrong).

2   In the sense in which this is true of computers it is also true of brains ("duplicate the relevant causes and you will duplicate the relevant effects").

3   Or maybe there is the argument: intentionality is either intrinsic or due to the program; it's not due to the program (Chinese room argument), so it's intrinsic.

Study questions

The Turing test

Describe Turing's "imitation game."

Describe the Turing test.

What did Turing think one could conclude if a machine wins the imitation game?

What is the main objection to the Turing test? What do you think about it?

Against strong AI: the Chinese room and the luminous room

What is "strong" vs. "weak" AI?

What does Searle intend to show with his Chinese room argument?

Describe the Chinese room *situation*.

What is Searle's Chinese room *argument*?

What is the "brain simulator reply"?

What might be Searle's response?

What is the "luminous room" objection to the Chinese room argument?

What is Searle's reply?

Who do you think is right and why?

DCTM *and the Chinese room*

What is the "systems" reply?

What is Searle's response?

What is the "robot" reply?

What might be Searle's response?

What is the difference between "simulation" and "duplication"? Illustrate.

What, according to Searle, must we give a machine to make it understand, have intentionality, cognitive states, mentality, etc.?

Why, according to Searle, have researchers thought that strong AI is plausible?

Consciousness

What is consciousness-of?

Could an artifact (machine) be conscious-of?

What is phenomenal (qualitative) consciousness?

What is full-blown consciousness?

What are the two typical cases of full-blown consciousness?

What is the "explanatory gap"?

What is the "hard" problem (vs. the easy problem)?

Could an artifact (machine) have qualitative consciousness?

What are the three possible relations of cognition to consciousness?

What reasons are there for thinking that consciousness is not necessary for cognition?

What are "aspectual shapes"?

How are they related to neurophysiology and behavior?

What is Searle's "connection principle"?

Do you agree with the connection principle argument? Why/why not?

Content

What (again) is generic conceptual role (CR) theory of representational content?

What is the DCTM version of inferential role theory of content?

What is the analyticity objection to CR theory?

What is the relativism objection to CR theory?

What is the holism objection to CR theory?

What is the compositionality objection to CR theory?

What is the truth objection to CR theory?

What are narrow vs. wide psychological states?

What is the Churchill ant trace example for wide content? Discuss.

What is the tree picture example for wide content? Discuss.

What is the twin earth example for wide content? Discuss.

What is the problem with the DCTM if content is at least partially wide? Discuss.

What is a two-factor theory of mental content?

How might it get the DCTM out of the problem of wide content?

Against cognitivism

What are "strong AI," "weak AI," and "cognitivism"?

What is the "Church–Turing thesis"?

What is "Turing's theorem"?

What does Searle give as the "standard conception of a computer"?

What is "multiple realizability"?

What is multiple realizability a consequence of?

What are the two types of "universal realizability"?

What is universal realizability a consequence of?

What is it to be a computer "intrinsically"?

What is Searle's argument that the brain is not (intrinsically) a digital computer?

What kind of explanation of cognition does cognitivism promise?

What is the difficulty with this (computational) explanation of cognition?

What is the cognitivist scientific research program?

What two things should worry us about it?

How does Searle illustrate these worries (hint: the frog's eye, a word processor)?

What is Searle's argument that the brain is not a digital computer?

DCTM hardware and the brain

What are some similarities between digital hardware and neural hardware (aka the brain)?

What are some differences between digital hardware and neural hardware (aka the brain) *structurally*?

What are some differences between digital hardware and neural hardware (aka the brain) *functionally*: organization and processing?

The domain and scope of the DCTM

Give three examples of states or processes that we may call "mental," but which may not fall under the DCTM.

What feature of mental states did we conclude might make them candidates for inclusion in the domain of the DCTM?

What feature of mental processes did we conclude might make them candidates for inclusion in the domain of the DCTM?

Suggested reading

Turing test

The Turing test is discussed in Hofstadter (1981), and in some detail in Dennett (1985), Block (1990), French (1990), and Copeland (1993b), chapter 3. Feigenbaum and Feldman (1963) is the classic original collection of readings relevant to the topic of computers and intelligence, and Luger (1995) is a recent collection. On "massive adaptability" as an indication of intelligence see Copeland (1993b), chapter 4.6.

Chinese room and luminous room

Searle's Chinese room argument has been extensively discussed. A good place to start is with the commentaries on the original article in Searle (1980) and Searle's replies. A discussion that relates the Chinese room to cognitive architecture is Chalmers (1992). Both the Chinese room and the luminous room are discussed in Copeland (1993b), chapters 6 and 10.7, and in Rey (1997), chapter 10.2. Chalmers (1996b), chapter 9.3, argues for a version of strong AI, and chapter 9.4 discusses the Chinese room.

The DCTM and (phenomenal) consciousness

The number of works on consciousness has mushroomed in the last 15 years. There are now many books and articles on the subject, as well as chapters of texts and monographs (see chapter 8 again). For a concise, authoritative overview of issues surrounding the nature of consciousness and its major theories see Block (1994). For a substantial overview see Güzeldere (1997). Goldman (1993b) relates consciousness to broader issues in cognitive science, and Dennett (1991), chapter 12, generally disparages qualia, and the thought experiments that motivate it; Lormand (1994) replies.

For *books* (*anthologies*) from a scientific perspective see Marcel and Bisiach (1988), Hameroff et al. (1996), and Cohen and Schooler (1996). For a philosophical perspective see Block et al. (1997) and Shear (1997).

For *books* (*monographs*) from a philosophical perspective one might begin with Searle (1992), Flanagan (1992), Chalmers (1996b), and Seager (1999). For a more scientific perspective one could start with Edelman (1989) or Crick (1994), then at Searle (1997) for discussion.

Some *chapters* of current texts and monographs include Maloney (1989), chapter 7, Kim (1996), chapter 7, Braddon-Mitchell and Jackson (1996), chapter 8, and Rey (1997), chapter 11.

The *explanatory gap* is introduced in Levine (1983) and the *hard problem* is introduced in Chalmers (1996b), and both are further discussed in selections in Block et al. (1997).

Searle's *connection principle* was first introduced in Searle (1990b). It is repeated and set in a more general context in Searle (1992), chapter 7. Discussions of it can be found in the commentaries to the (1990) article, in Davies (1995) and Rey (1997), chapter 9.6.

Goldman (1993a) discusses the important and neglected issue of the qualitative feel (what we called "cognitive qualia") of propositional attitudes.

Mental content and DCTM

Good introductory surveys of problems with *conceptual role* theory can be found in Cummins (1989), chapter 9, Lepore (1994) and Cummins (1996), chapter 4. A more specific and advanced discussion can be found in Fodor and Lepore (1991 and 1992). *Wide* psychological states were introduced in Putnam (1975b) and have been extensively discussed in the philosophy of language – see Pessin and Goldberg (1996). The issue of *computation and wide content* was first raised in Stich (1978) and Fodor (1980a), and discussed at length in Stich (1983, 1991), Baker (1987), chapter 3, Devitt (1989, 1991, 1996: ch. 5), Fodor (1991), and Fodor (1994). *Two-factor theories* (as well as wide and narrow content) are discussed in various texts, see especially Kim (1996), chapter 8, Braddon-Mitchell and Jackson (1996), chapter 12, and Rey (1997), chapter 9. More advanced articles pro and con two-factor theories can be found in McGinn (1982), Block (1986), and Lepore and Loewer (1986). Horst (1996) is a general critique of CTM which focuses on the conventionality of symbols.

Cognitivism

Searle (1992), chapter 9, is essentially the same as Searle (1990b). The arguments are discussed in Chalmers (1995a) and (1996b: ch. 9), Copeland (1996a), and Harnish (1996).

Hardware and the brain

For some discussion of this issue see Crick and Asanuma (1986), Graubard (1988), especially essays by Cowan and Sharp, Schwartz, and by Reeke and Edelman. Wasserman (1989), appendix A, contains some brief remarks. See Kent (1981) for more on the "co-evolution" of brain and digital hardware, as well as comparison of the two.

The domain of DCTM

See Chalmers (1996b), chapter 1, for a discussion of the difference between what he calls "phenomenal" states, and "psychological" states, which is similar to our "experiential" and "cognitive."

Part III

The Connectionist Computational Theory of Mind

Introduction

The principal subject of Part III is the *connectionist computational theory of mind* (CCTM). We view this theory as one of two special cases of the more generic *computational theory of mind* (CTM). (The other special case, the *digital* computational theory of mind (DCTM) was investigated in Part II.) And, as we noted earlier, the computational theory of mind is itself profitably viewed as a special case of the older *representational theory of mind* (RTM):

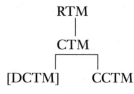

Our strategy in Part III is to first introduce the reader to some elements of connectionist computation by way of two historically important demonstration projects: Jets and Sharks, and NETtalk (chapter 10). If computers algorithmically manipulate symbols, then we can ask after the *manipulation* aspect of computers, and the *symbol* aspect of computers. These networks illustrate two different styles of connectionist modeling: the first uses an interactive activation and competition architecture (manipulation), and local representations (symbols). The second uses a three-layer feed-forward architecture (manipulation), and distributed representations (symbols). We then (chapter 11) look more closely at the theory behind connectionist models by looking at their basic building blocks (nodes and connections), how they are programmed, how they compute, and how they learn. Next we formulate a generic version of connectionism that spans various architectures and representational schemes. Finally, we taxonomize these architectures along dimensions of memory, control, and representation. Then, with this connectionist computational material in place, we turn to formulating (chapter 12), and criticizing (chapter 13) the concept of mind inspired by this connectionist computational story.

10

Sample Connectionist Networks

10.1 Introduction

Here we look briefly at two very different connectionist networks. The first, Jets and Sharks, is a simple and intuitive example of *localist* representations in an *interactive activation and competition* network. The second, NETtalk, a *three-layer feed-forward* network, is more complex and has gained some notoriety. It illustrates *distributed representations*, performs a human task, and uses the back propagation learning algorithm.

10.2 Jets and Sharks

McClelland introduces the "Jets and Sharks" network to account for the possibility of representing and storing general information in a system without general rules. The system stores specific information in terms of "exemplars" of objects and properties, and computes with activation that can spread between exemplars and representations of their properties in a way reminiscent of semantic networks discussed earlier (see chapter 7). These properties can reinforce each other when supported by a large number of instances, or they can compete, as when they are mutually exclusive. The purpose of the illustrative model is to show, among other things, that the activation and competition mechanism can: (1) retrieve the specific characteristics of particular exemplars, (2) extract central tendencies of classes of objects from stored knowledge of particular exemplars, (3) fill in plausible default values. Let's look first at the structure and operation of the network, then at some of these performance features.

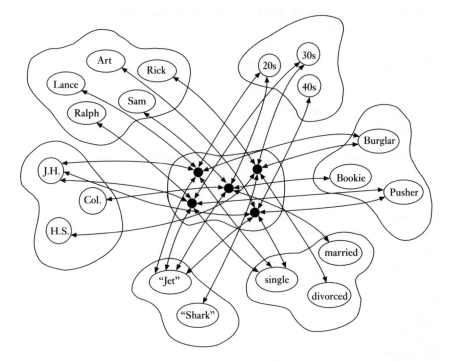

Figure 10.1 Jets and Sharks (from McClelland, 1981, reproduced in Rumelhart and McClelland, 1986b, vol. 1: 28; reproduced by permission of the MIT Press)

The network

Consider the network in figure 10.1. It contains 24 units in 7 groups.[1] Each unit: (1) has a resting level of activation less than 0, which it decays back to, and (2) it follows the activation passing rule: *sum up excitatory and inhibitory activation continuously, then pass on the result continuously.*[2] One group, the "instance" or "exemplar" group (filled units) represents individual gang members, and each instance unit is connected to a unit in each of the other "property" groups by mutually excitatory connections, indicated by the arrows. These connections represent the knowledge the network has of the properties of a given individual, such as his name, education, occupation, marital status, etc. Units within a group are related by mutually inhibitory connections, which implements the idea that individuals cannot have more that one property from each group (e.g. one individual cannot be both single and married). Before a probe is presented each node is at a resting level of activation. To give the network *input* one selects a node and clamps on the activation. The network *computes* by having the activation spread through-out the system, activating some units and inhibiting others. The network eventually settles down into equilibrium and that is the end of one computational cycle. The active nodes are the system's *output*. Now let's look at a pair of tasks that the network performs and which resemble aspects of human performance.

Typicality

For example, one could ask the network for information regarding Jets. In this case the network was probed with "Jet," activation was clamped onto the Jet node, and after 200 cycles of operation, the property nodes stabilized at the following values:

Probe   Jet
Age
—1920s: 0.663
Education
—Junior High: 0.663
Marital status
—Single: 0.663
Occupation
—Pusher: 0.334
—Burglar: 0.334
—Bookie: 0.334

These are the age, education, marital status, and occupations typical of a Jet, though no Jet has all of these properties. We might say that the network extracted the prototypical Jet.[3]

Default values

The network can also fill in default values for missing information. The network was lesioned between the "Lance" node and the "burglar" node, and then given the "Lance" probe. When activation spread after about 400 cycles the network stabilized with the following values, indicating that it filled in "burglar":

Name
—Lance   0.799
Gang
—Jets: 0.710
Age
—1920s: 0.667
Education
—Junior High: 0.704
Marital status
—Married: 0.552
—Divorced: 0.347
Occupation
—Burglar: 0.641

In this case the network used the occupation of those similar to Lance to guess his occupation. However, by increasing the instance-node to instance-node inhibition (from 0.03 to 0.05), the activation of nodes representing other individuals is suppressed and so their properties are not activated and the system will not return default occupation information on Lance. This mechanism of changing inhibition might correspond to asking oneself: "What exactly do I know about Lance?" versus the question "What is most likely true of Lance?"

Summary

This network and its performance illustrate a number of important features which we can organize as follows. *First*, it has a certain *architecture* – it has a certain number of units and certain connections between them. *Second*, it contains certain kinds of *representations* – its units each represent an individual or property; they are "local" (or "punctate"). *Third*, the network has a certain method of *computation* – it computes by passing on activation or inhibition, and by competition. *Fourth*, the network is *programmed* by specifying the activation passing rules associated with each unit. *Fifth*, the network does not *learn*, it is not *trained*. We will want to keep an eye on these general features of this network when comparing it to other networks.

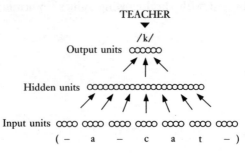

Schematic drawing of the NETtalk network architecture.
A window of letters in an English text is fed to an array
of 203 input units. Information from these units is
transformed by an intermediate layer of 80 "hidden"
units to produce patterns of activity in 26 output units.
The connections in the network are specified by a total
of 18,629 weight parameters (including a variable
threshold for each unit).

Figure 10.2 NETtalk network architecture (from Sejnowski and Rosenberg, 1987: 147, figure 1; figures 10.2–10.7 reproduced by permission of Complex Systems Publications)

10.3   NETtalk

NETtalk is a network developed by Sejnowski and Rosenberg to learn to pronounce written English text. It was trained by being given both continuous text and dictionary words along with correct pronunciations, and gradually adjusting its pronunciations to conform to the teaching standard. We now outline the main ingredients of NETtalk in terms of a general recipe for specifying connectionist machines: architecture, representation, computation, programming, and learning-training. We will also want to assess the model with respect to human performance.

Static features

Architecture

Units
    1   309
    2   3 layers:
        Input layer: 203 units, 7 groups of 29 units each

Output layer: 26 units
Hidden layer: 80 units

Connections
1   Each layer is connected just to the next layer.
2   Feed-forward: activation (and inhibition) begins at the input units and flows forward to the hidden units and on to the output units.

Representation

Input units
Each group of 29 units has:
1   one unit for each letter of the alphabet (26 units)
2   units for punctuation and word boundary (3 units)

Output units
Each of the 26 units encodes one of:
1   21 articulatory features
2   5 stress and syllable boundary markers

Hidden units
These need to be analyzed – we will return to them in the last section of this chapter.

We see that input and output representations can be viewed in one way as local, in another way as distributed. The input level is *local* in that each unit is local – each input unit represents a letter of the alphabet or an item of punctuation. The output level is *local* in that each unit is local – each unit represents an articulatory feature, syllable boundary, or level of stress. On the other hand, the input level is *distributed* with respect to the representation of words – since it takes more than one unit to represent words of more than one letter. Likewise, the output level is *distributed* with respect to speech sounds or "phonemes" – since it generally takes three articulatory features to make up one speech sound (phoneme). Thus the description of a representation as "local" or "distributed" is relative to what is being represented. It is customary to say a network has "distributed" representations if at least some of its representations are distributed. It is customary to say that a network is "local" if all of its representations are local.

(a)

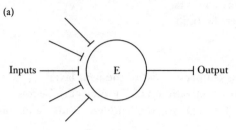

Processing unit

(b)

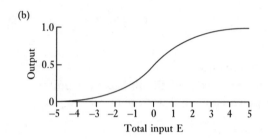

Figure 10.3   Output function (from Sejnowski and Rosenberg, 1987: 148, figure 2)

Dynamic features

Computation

1   Activations of input units ("input vectors") are multiplied by connection strengths to the hidden units to yield activations of hidden units ("hidden vectors").
2   Activations of hidden units are multiplied by connection strengths to output units to yield activations of output units ("output vectors").

Programming

Units
1   The system was programmed with a sigmoid activation rule, which has a gross profile similar to a neuron (see figure 10.3).
2   Thresholds were variable (we ignore thresholds in what follows).

Connections
1   Connections were assigned random initial weights between −0.5 and +0.5.

Learning/training procedures

1 The system used "back propagation" after each presentation of a word. In rough outline the procedure is as follows:
   (i) Compute the output of the network for a given input (word).
   (ii) Find its error, compared to the desired output (the difference).
   (iii) Propagate that error back through the network first to the hidden units, then to the input units.
   (iv) Modify the weights by some determined amount (the learning rate) to reduce the error (difference).
   (v) Repeat steps (i)–(iv) until the difference between the desired and the actual output is acceptable.
2 Two types of material were presented:
   (i) 1,024 words from a phonetic transcription of informal continuous speech by a first-grade child.
   (ii) 1,000 most common words from *Merriam Webster's Pocket Dictionary* presented in random order.
3 The material (text and words) were moved, in order, through a "window" of seven letters. Continuous text was stepped through letter by letter, whereas dictionary words were moved through the window individually. The middle, fourth, letter is the target, the remaining six are context – which supply needed information.

Results and analyses

Informal continuous text results

1 *Stress*:   99 percent after 5 passes.
  Phonemes: 95 percent after 50 passes.

The distinction between vowels and consonants was made early. Then came word boundaries, and after 10 passes through the corpus the speech was intelligible.

2 *Generalization/Transfer*:   439 word continuation was 78 percent correct.
3 *Damage*:   random variation in weights leads to gradual ("graceful") degradation of performance.
4 *Relearning*:   much faster than original learning (see figure 10.5).

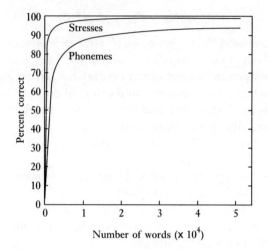

Figure 10.4 Learning curves for stress and phonemes (from Sejnowski and Rosenberg, 1987: 153, figure 4)

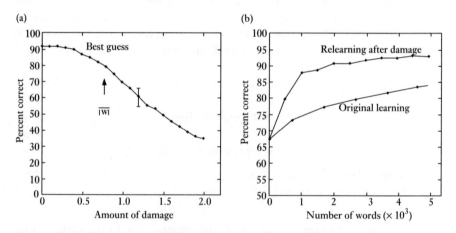

Figure 10.5 Performance (a) degradation and (b) relearning (from Sejnowski and Rosenberg, 1987: 154, figure 5)

Dictionary words results

1 Performance changes with changes in number of hidden units: 0, 15, 30, 60, 120 hidden units (see figure 10.6). For instance, with 0 hidden units it reached 82 percent, and with 120 hidden units it reached 98 percent.

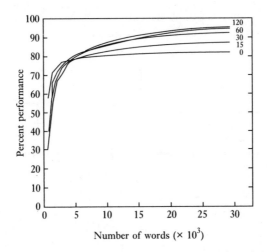

Figure 10.6 Consequences of changing hidden units (from Sejnowski and Rosenberg, 1987: 155, figure 6)

2 Generalization/transfer:
  (i) Start the network of 120 hidden units on 1,000 words at 98 percent, and give it 20,012 words:
    77 percent correct average first pass,
    85 percent correct end of first pass,
    90 percent correct after 5 passes.
  (ii) Try two hidden layers of 80 units each:
    87 percent correct on average for first pass,
    97 percent correct after 55 passes.
    The overall performance of the 120-unit single-layer network, and the 80-unit double-layer network was comparable.
3 Hidden unit analysis: levels of activation in the hidden layer were examined for each letter of each word after the 80-unit machine reached 95 percent on the dictionary task:
  (i) An average of 20 percent of the units (16 units) active per input, so it is neither a purely "local" nor a "holographic" system.
  (ii) Hierarchical cluster analysis (HCA: which items are similar, which groups of items are similar, which groups of groups are similar, etc.) reveals a complete separation of vowels and consonants, and further subdivisions as well (see figure 10.7). This same procedure of HCA was used for three networks starting with different

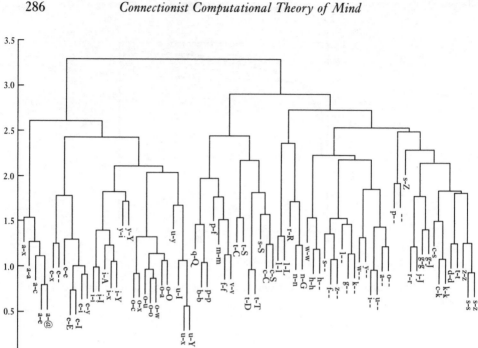

Figure 10.7   Hierarchical clustering of hidden units (from Sejnowski and Rosenberg, 1987: 158, figure 8)

random states. The pattern of weights was completely different, but the same hierarchies were revealed. This suggested to the authors (1987: 159) that "functional groupings of cells" is the level of invariant properties of networks.

It is tempting to say that these hidden units learned to detect vowels and consonants (as well as some finer categories). Some (Clark, 1993, chapter 4) have argued that because NETtalk cannot use this representation to, for example, categorize sounds as consonants vs. vowels, it should not be thought of as having the *concept* of consonants and vowels. One of the virtues of hidden units is that the representational repertoire of the machine is not limited to the categories the programmer thinks are in the stimuli, and it is free to extract whatever regularities it can find. This means that some hidden units may have an obvious interpretation in "our" categorization scheme, but others may not.

Notes

1   This is only a fragment of the total network of 68 units and it is not completely accurate (see below).
2   Though the simulation of the network on a digital computer is discrete, the slices are small enough to approximate continuity for the purposes of modeling.
3   The figure misrepresents Lance as single, hence Lance would be a "typical" Jet, but in the full network Lance is married.

Study questions

Jets and Sharks (JS)

What is the architecture of JS called?

What is the JS kind of representation scheme called and why?

What are three performance features that JS illustrates?

What is the activation passing rule for JS (in ordinary language)?

What do the arrows in JS represent?

How are units which are contained in the same group or "cloud" related to one another?

What is the input to JS?

What is the output of JS?

How does JS compute output from input?

NETtalk (NT)

What is the architecture of NT called?

What do the input nodes represent?

What do some collections of input nodes represent?

What do the output nodes represent?

What do some collections of output nodes represent?

In what respects are input and output levels of NT "local" and "distributed"?

What was discovered about representation in NT's hidden layer – what was coded there?

How does NT compute?

How does one program NT (ignoring thresholds)?

Outline the basic idea for training NT.

What are some features of the performance of NT that resemble human performance?

Suggested reading

Jets and Sharks can be explored on a home computer with the help of McClelland and Rumelhart (1988). It is covered in some detail in Bechtel and Abrahamsen (1991), chapter 2, and Clark (1989), chapter 5.3. *NETtalk* is discussed briefly in many cognitive science texts and in Clark (1993). A longer discussion of its interpretation can be found in Verschure (1992).

11

Connectionism: Basic Notions and Variations

11.1 Introduction

We turn now to a more systematic review of the basic notions used in connectionist machines. We will survey some of the variety of different machines that can be constructed using these notions, as well as some of what they have in common. It is possible to see such models as the most recent development in a line of thinking dating back many centuries. We already have introduced: classical associationism (chapter 1), Pavlov and conditioned reflexes (chapter 2), Lashley and Hebb (chapter 3), perceptrons (chapter 4), and Pandemonium (chapter 6). Some even see the move to connectionism as a kind of Kuhnian paradigm shift out of the digital, serial, symbolic, and into the analog, parallel, subsymbolic (see Schneider, 1987).

11.2 Basic Notions and Terminology

Ideally, these concepts should all be presented simultaneously, since they ultimately depend on each other for a complete understanding. This is impossible, so we will develop these topics in a particular order, but keep in mind that only after a full network has been presented and trained will it be clear how everything fits together.

Connections and weights

We begin with the connections between units, which may be compared to idealized axons, dendrites, and synapses. These are represented by a line or "edge." Each connection has a direction, and carries excitation (represented

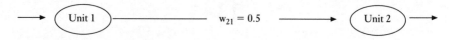

Figure 11.1   A simple connection

by an arrow or a positive number) or inhibition (represented by a small filled circle or a negative number). Finally, and most importantly, each connection has a "weight" or "strength." This is represented by a number which indicates how much activation (excitation if the number is positive, inhibition if the number is negative) the connection transmits. Counterintuitively, the notation for weights usually represents the weight on the connection from unit 1 to unit 2 as: w_{21}. That is, one reads the notation from right to left. A simple connection might look like the one shown in figure 11.1. In this case one half (0.5) of the activation sent out from unit 1 affects unit 2. A positive sign on the weight indicates *activation*, a negative sign on the weight indicates *inhibition*.

Units and activation

Units either get their activation from the environment ("input units"), and pass it on to other units, or they get their activation from other units and pass it on to the environment ("output units"), or they get it from other units and pass it on to other units ("hidden units"). "Units" or "nodes" may be compared to cell bodies of idealized neurons. Units will be represented by circles, with a line leading into them (their inputs), or a line leading out of them (their outputs), or both.

Each unit is in a certain state of activation, which can be positive, zero, or negative. Each unit also collects activation from those units that connect into it (the "fan in"), and a unit can pass on activation to each unit that connects out of it (the "fan out"). The collected input is called the "*net*" input activation, and the simplest method of calculating net input is just to sum the separate inputs of the fan in units. This net activation can then be combined with the previous activation level of the unit to give the (new) *current* activation level of the unit. In the simplest case we just let the new activation level be the net activation level. The unit can then pass on activation to the units in its fan out. This is the *output* activation. So there are three processes that can take place in a unit: net activation, current activation, and output activation (see figures 11.2 and 11.3).

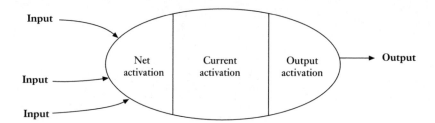

Figure 11.2 A unit and its components

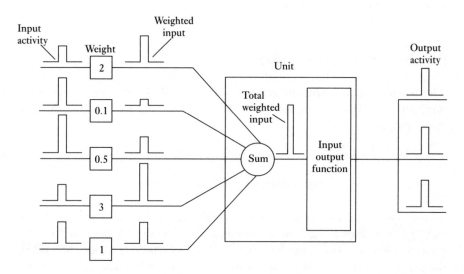

Figure 11.3 Connections and unit (from Hinton, 1992: 146, figure 10.2; reproduced by permission)

The activation passed by units to other units can be seen as setting a constraint on them. When the network runs, each unit tries to satisfy the often competing constraints set by the units it is connected to. The network reaches a stable state when the number of constraints that are satisfied cannot be increased.

There are various rules for calculating net, current, and output activation, some of which we will mention later. For now we will use just the simplest principle that current and output activation equals net activation and the net activation equals the sum of all inputs in the fan in, where each input has been multiplied by its weight:

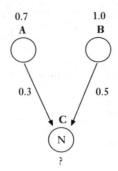

Figure 11.4   An example network

(N)   Net = Sum(input × weight)

The whole process, then, involves receiving weighted input along a connection, summing those weighted inputs to form Net, and passing Net through to the output.

Programming and computation

To *program* a network is to state its *activation rules*, its *thresholds* (if it has them), and to give *weights* to each of its connections. This can be done by the programmer, or the network can be trained to have a certain set of weights. When the machine is configured in the second way we say it has learned its weights rather than having been programmed with those weights. But once learned, a set of weights can thereafter be used to program another network. We return to learning shortly.

Example

Unit C get inputs from two units: unit A passes activation 0.7 along a connection with strength 0.3. Unit B passes activation 1.0 along a connection with strength 0.5 (see figure 11.4). What is the net input to unit C? Using formula (N) we notice that first we must multiply the output of each unit (A, B) times the weight of its connection to C. For A this is $0.7 \times 0.3 = 0.21$. For B this is $1 \times 0.5 = 0.5$. Finally, we sum these: $0.21 + 0.5 = 0.71$. This is the net activation of unit C.

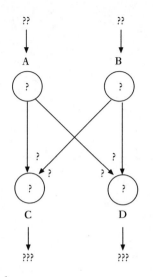

Figure 11.5 Simple network 1

Simple network

Consider the simple network in figure 11.5. This network has four units (A, B, C, D); each input unit is connected by excitation to each output unit. But to make it compute we need to program it by giving it activation passing rule(s) and weights (?), give it some input (??) and calculate the output (???). We now program this network by (1) assigning weights to each connection, and (2) specifying principles for computing the activation that each unit receives and passes on to the next step.

Connection weights

A–C = 0.1, A–D = 0.3, B–C = 0.2, B–D = 0.4

Activation

We let the net activation be the sum of the weighted inputs, as given by (N), we let the current activation equal the net activation, and we let the output equal the current activation. So in this simple system, the net activation as given by (N) is just passed through each unit. (This is not always so – remember NETtalk.) So the programmed network looks like figure 11.6.

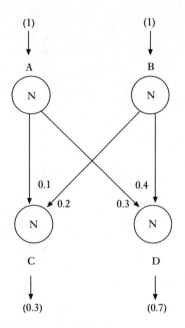

Figure 11.6 Programmed simple network 1

Computation

We now give the network some input and calculate the output. Input: let both input units receive an activation of 1 – as indicated in the figure in parentheses. *Unit A* receives activation of just 1, its net activation is therefore just 1 (see (N) again) and so it passes on activation of just 1. The same for *unit B. Unit C* receives activation from both A and B, so the net activation C will, according to (N), be the sum of: the activation of each unit feeding into it times the weight of each connection. From unit A, that will be $1 \times 0.1 = 0.1$, from B, that will be $1 \times 0.2 = 0.2$. So, by (N) we sum these two products and the result for unit C is $0.1 + 0.2 = 0.3$. That is:

 From A: $1 \times 0.1 = 0.1$
 From B: $1 \times 0.2 = 0.2$
   Sum $= 0.3$

So the net activation level of unit C is 0.3. Since it outputs its net activation level, its output is 0.3. *Unit D* also receives activation from both units A and B, so its output is calculated in exactly the same way:

 From A: $1 \times 0.3 = 0.3$
 From B: $1 \times 0.4 = 0.4$
   Sum $= 0.7$

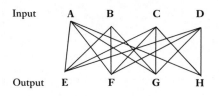

Figure 11.7 Simple associative network

So the net activation level of unit D is 0.7. Since it outputs its net activation level, its output is 0.7. Thus, the simple network 1, as programmed, outputs the values in parentheses at units C and D, given the input in parentheses at units A and B.

Pattern associator

We have just illustrated computation on a simple network. The next network, sometimes called a "pattern associator," will also be used to illustrate computation, but we will use it to illustrate additional features of networks as well: excitation and inhibition, pattern association, faulty input, and superimposed input patterns.

Structure

Consider the simple network of eight units shown in figure 11.7 (four input and four output), arranged in two layers with each unit in each layer connected to each unit in the other layer (Rumelhart and McClelland 1986a: 33–40).

Programming

As before, we let each unit pass on as output its net input (N). Each connection will be given a weight, some will be excitatory (+) and some sill be inhibitory (−). These assignments are hard to represent when networks get complicated, so we will now introduce the more perspicuous matrix style. These two diagramming techniques are equivalent and you can in principle go back and forth from one to the other (see figure 11.8).

Each question mark represents a weight, and we get a different network for every distinct assignment we make. To start with, we will work with the network shown in figure 11.9, with the following weights, which we will

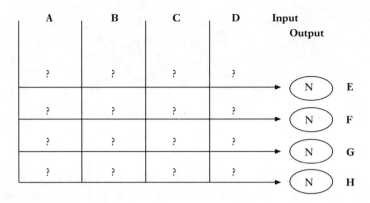

A	B	C	D	Input
				Output
?	?	?	?	N E
?	?	?	?	N F
?	?	?	?	N G
?	?	?	?	N H

Figure 11.8   Simple associative matrix network

A	B	C	D	Input: rose appearance
				Output: rose smell
−0.25	0.25	0.25	−0.25	N E ?
−0.25	0.25	0.25	−0.25	N F ?
0.25	−0.25	−0.25	0.25	N G ?
0.25	−0.25	−0.25	0.25	N H ?

Figure 11.9   Rose network

imagine associates rose appearances (activation on the input units) with rose smells (activation on the output units).

We will imagine that a flower's appearance can be broken down into four *general* components, say: A, the shape of each petal, B, the overall configuration of petals, C, the color of the petals, and D, the stem. We will imagine the same thing is true of its smell (though here the story will have to be given by science or the perfume industry). With this scheme in place we can let a specific activation value on a node represent a *specific* component. For instance, activating the A node with "1" might indicate a rose petal shape, and "−1" on node B might indicate a rose configuration of petals, and "−1" on node C might indicate a rose color, and so forth for the rest of the input and output nodes.

Computation

Given an activation value for each input unit we can compute the activation value for each output unit. For instance, we can give the input nodes (A, B, C, D) the following series of values (called an "input vector") written $\langle 1, -1, -1, 1 \rangle$:

A: 1
B: −1
C: −1
D: 1

The activation value of each output unit would, by (N) given before, be the sum of each of its four weighted inputs. For instance, output unit E:

Connection	Weight
A–E:	$1 \times -0.25 = -0.25$
B–E:	$-1 \times 0.25 = -0.25$
C–E:	$-1 \times 0.25 = -0.25$
D–E:	$1 \times -0.25 = -0.25$
	$Sum = -1.00$

So the net activation of unit E is −1, and since its output is the same as its net activation, its output is also −1 (as indicated in the rose network in parentheses). We can now say that the rose network yields as output for unit E, with input vector $\langle 1, -1, -1, 1 \rangle$, the output value −1. Similar calculations for output units F, G, H yield the values:

E: −1
F: −1
G: 1
H: 1

The output vector for the rose network is: $\langle -1, -1, 1, 1 \rangle$.

Exercise 1 Verify these values for F, G, H using (N) as we just did for E.

The rose network computes the output vector $\langle -1, -1, 1, 1 \rangle$ from the input vector $\langle 1, -1, -1, 1 \rangle$ by transforming an input vector into the output vector, and this transformation amounts to multiplying the input vector by the weights on the connections (by the weight matrix illustrated in the rose network). This is the basic computational method of these networks. Or, in other (older) words, it *associates* the output vector with the input vector. If the input vector represents, say, the visual appearance of a rose, and the output vector represents, say, the smell of a rose, then the rose network can be seen as associating the smell of a rose with its appearance – a rose appearance can bring back a rose smell.

Defective input

Interestingly, if the network is given faulty or defective ("degraded") input it can still perform useful computations – the network doesn't crash. Suppose, for instance, that input unit C of the rose network is not stimulated and so it receives '0' input (maybe the rose network is shown a black-and-white photo of a rose and C is a red color detector). In that case we must recalculate the values of each of the output units for this new input vector $\langle 1, -1, 0, 1 \rangle$. Again we give the output unit E as an example and again we use (N) to calculate it:

Connection   *Weight*
A–E: $1 \times -0.25 = -0.25$
B–E: $-1 \times 0.25 = -0.25$
C–E: $0 \times 0.25 = 0$
D–E: $1 \times -0.25 = -0.25$
          Sum $= -0.75$

So the activation value of output unit E for the new degraded input vector $\langle 1, -1, 0, 1 \rangle$ (i.e. colorless rose appearance) is -0.75. Calculations for the remaining output units F, G, H go just as this one did, and yield the values:

E: -0.75
F: -0.75
G: 0.75
H: 0.75

Exercise 2   Verify the results for output units F, G, H.

Thus, the rose network transforms (or associates) the degraded input vector $\langle 1, -1, 0, 1 \rangle$ to the output vector $\langle -0.75, -0.75, 0.75, 0.75 \rangle$, and a comparison between results of normal versus degraded input:

normal: $\langle 1, -1, 1, 1 \rangle$
degraded: $\langle -0.75, -0.75, 0.75, 0.75 \rangle$

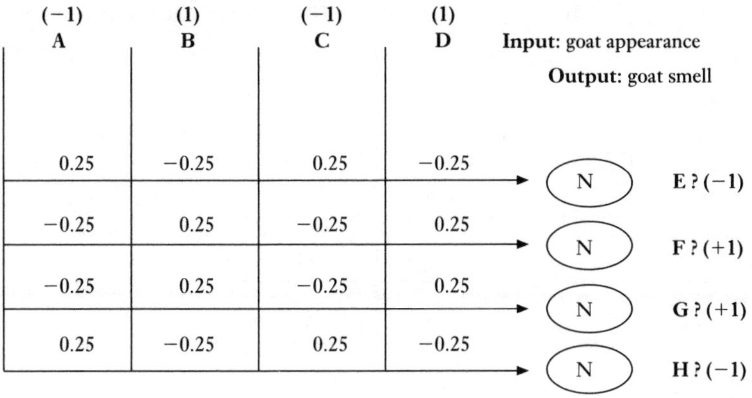

Figure 11.10 Goat network

reveals that although the numbers are different the pattern of signs is the same. As Rumelhart and McClelland (1986a: 35) put it: "the . . . pattern produced in response will have the activation of all the . . . units in the right direction [the right signs]; however, they will be somewhat weaker than they would be, had a complete . . . pattern been shown."

Superimposed networks

An important and to some, surprising, property of networks is their ability to simultaneously store associations between more than one pair of input–output vectors. To see this we construct a second network, along the same lines as the rose network, but one which associates the appearance of a goat with a goat smell (see figure 11.10; see also Rumelhart and McClelland, 1986a: 35). Again, we imagine that the activation given to the input nodes represents components of the way goats look, and the activation on the output nodes represents the way goats smell. As indicated by the numbers in parentheses, this network will transform the goat appearance input vector $\langle -1, 1, -1, 1 \rangle$ into the goat smell output vector $\langle -1, 1, 1, -1 \rangle$.

Exercise 3 Verify that for the input vector $\langle -1, 1, -1, 1 \rangle$ the goat network associates (computes) the output vector $\langle -1, 1, 1, -1 \rangle$. Hint: note that the 0.25 s always add up to 1, so check the signs.

Now, can we construct a single "rose and goat" network that will deliver the rose smell just for rose appearances, and goat smells just for goat appearances? (You

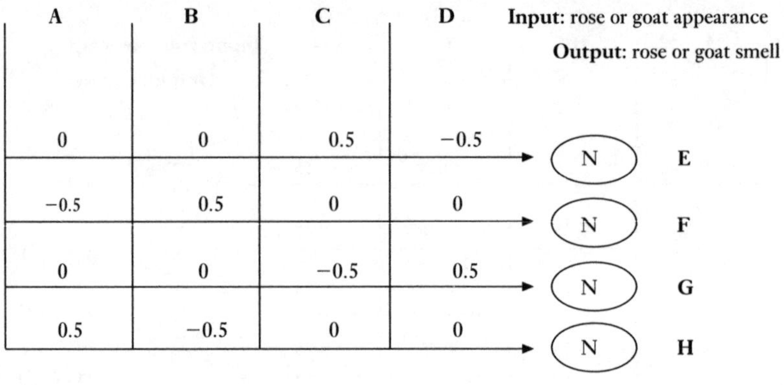

A	B	C	D	Input: rose or goat appearance
				Output: rose or goat smell
0	0	0.5	−0.5	N E
−0.5	0.5	0	0	N F
0	0	−0.5	0.5	N G
0.5	−0.5	0	0	N H

Figure 11.11   Rose and goat network

know we would not be doing this if the answer were not "yes".) The basic fact we will exploit is that two weight matrices, such as those embedded in the rose network and the goat network, can be *added together*, and that once they are added together, then the resulting matrix will produce the right output (no goaty-smelling roses). How do we add matrices? Just add their corresponding parts:

$$\begin{bmatrix} a & b \\ \\ c & b \end{bmatrix} + \begin{bmatrix} w & x \\ \\ y & z \end{bmatrix} = \begin{bmatrix} a+w & b+x \\ \\ c+y & d+z \end{bmatrix}$$

In the case of the rose network and the goat network we add the two matrices together and the resulting matrix and network is shown in figure 11.11 (see Bechtel and Abrahamsen, 1991: 49–50).

Computation

We now need to verify that the rose and goat network will not make a goat smell like a rose (nor vice versa). We give the network the goat appearance vector $\langle -1, 1, -1, 1 \rangle$ and see what we get as output. As usual we will compute the first output unit E in detail:

Connection   *Weight*
A–E: $-1 \times 0 = 0$
B–E: $1 \times 0 = 0$
C–E: $-1 \times 0.5 = -0.5$
D–E: $1 \times -0.5 = -0.5$
        Sum $= -1$

So far, so good, but both goat smell vectors and rose smell vectors begin with −1 (i.e. output unit E has −1 as output value for both vectors), so to make sure we are on the right track we should compute an output unit that is distinctive to goat smells. As we saw, for roses, F = −1, but for goats F = 1; what do we get from the rose and goat network for the goat appearance vector?

Connection	Weight
A–F: -1×-0.5	$= 0.5$
B–F: 1×0.5	$= 0.5$
C–F: -1×0	$= 0$
D–F: 1×0	$= 0$
	Sum $= 1$

So the value of output unit F, for the goat appearance input vector is 1, which is correct.

Exercise 4   Verify that the rose and goat network gives just goat smells for goat appearances, and rose smells for rose appearances.

Technical digression   There are certain limitations on vectors that such a network can store simultaneously, having to do in part with the number of units, the relationship between the input vectors which the network must keep separate, and even the type of learning algorithm used. What must the relationship between vectors be in order for an associative network to learn those vectors without interference? The vectors must be "orthogonal." Two vectors V1, V2 are *orthogonal* if they are at right angles to each other, that is, if their inner (dot) product is = 0. For instance let V1 = ⟨−1, 1, 1, −1⟩ and V2 = ⟨1, 1, 1, 1⟩; then they are orthogonal if the sum of the products of V1 and V2 = 0, i.e. if -1×1 (= −1) + 1×1 (= 1) + 1×1 (1) + -1×1 (= −1) = 0, which it does. In a system of n dimensions (units) there can be at most n mutually orthogonal vectors.

Recurrent networks

So far in this section we have reviewed just feedforward networks, networks where activation flows from inputs to outputs without looping back. By incorporating such loops the network can recycle activation (think of this as forming a brief memory – recall Hebb's reverberating circuits from chapter 3), and so allows the network to model some phenomena that evolve over time. There are many possible ways of feeding activation back into a network, even if we

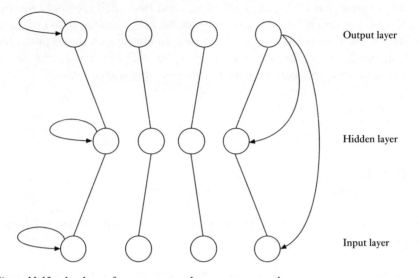

Figure 11.12   A schema for unaugmented recurrent networks

restrict ourselves to three-layer networks. For instance, different units in a given layer could loop back to a variety of different layers. Or we may require that all units in a layer be connected back to the same layer. We will say an "unaugmented (three-layer) recurrent network" is one where either: (1) a higher layer loops back to a lower layer or (2) a given layer loops back to itself (see figure 11.12).

We will say an "augmented (three-layer) recurrent network" is one which contains a separate augmenting layer of units, which feeds back into the (a) hidden, or (b) input layer. (Sometimes this distinction is ignored in the terminology of the literature.) One influential augmented recurrent network is that of Elman (1990a, 1990b, 1992) which contains what he calls a "context" layer, and which loops out from the hidden layer with fixed (unmodifiable) connections, and then loops back to the hidden layer with modifiable connections (see figure 11.13).

The effect of this augmenting "context" layer is to store activation for one time step, and so to function as a brief memory. By receiving information from the context layer the hidden layer has a record of previous activity; input to the hidden units at time t + 1 includes information from time t as well; input at time t + 2 includes information from time t + 2, t + 1, and t. A recurrent network can use this information to carry out tasks that are extended in time – if there are sequential dependencies in the data the network can find them.

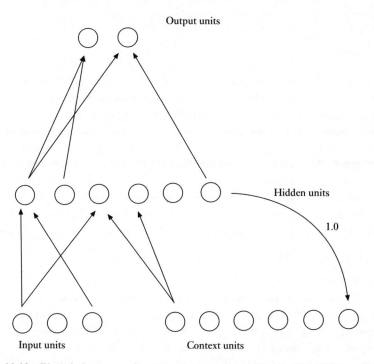

Figure 11.13 Elman's (augmented) recurrent network architecture (from Elman, 1990b: 349, figure 1; reproduced by permission of the MIT Press)

Recurrent networks are trained with the same algorithms (usually back-propagation, as with NETtalk) as feedforward three-layer networks. Elman (1990a) demonstrates how recurrent networks can find sequential regularities in a variety of domains.

Letter prediction
For example, Elman constructed a recurrent network composed of 6 input units, 20 hidden units, 6 output units, and 6 context units. He then constructed a list of letters based on the following principles:

1 First, the three consonants **b, d, g** were combined in *random* order to obtain a 1,000-letter sequence.
2 Then, each of these consonants was replaced, using the following rules, which in effect introduce the vowel **a** after **b**, the vowels **ii** after **d**, and the vowels **uuu** after **g**:

b → ba
d → dii
g → guuu

This produced a string of consonants and vowels such as: **diibaguuubadi-idiiguu.** . . . Now, since the order of the original consonants was random, no learning machine could predict where they will occur, so error should be high on each consonant. But the three rules that introduce the vowel sequences **a, ii, uuu** are completely predictable. That is, once any consonant **b, d, g** is found in the string, the machine should be able to learn what vowels follow it, as well as the number of the vowels. And that is just what the recurrent network did. After 200 training sessions through the original sequence it was presented with a new sequence that obeyed the same three vowel rules. As expected, it made random errors on the consonants, but predicted the vowels as well as their numbers.

Letter-in-word prediction
Elman also modified the string of consonants and vowels to form 15 words (with no breaks between them). Some 200 sentences, each consisting of 4 to 6 of these words, were constructed and strung together to form a string of 1,270 words, with each word broken down into letters yielding a stream of 4,963 letters. A recurrent network of 5 input units, 20 hidden and context units, and 5 output units was trained on 10 complete presentations of this sequence, which was too few for the network to memorize the whole sequence. Nevertheless, the errors it made indicated it had begun to recognize repeating sequences of letters in word-like groups. The network would make high errors at the beginning of a word (it would not know what word was coming next), but once it recognized the beginning of the word it would get better and better at predicting what word it was that began with that letter (see figure 11.14). Finally, Elman extended the network to recognizing the parts of speech of words in simple sentences, and eventually to words in embedded clauses in complex sentences.

11.3 Learning and Training

Typically, in connectionist networks, the notion of learning (or "training") has fairly restricted application. The overall architecture of the network is not affected (but see below), the activation passing rules are not affected, nor is the interpretation of the units or vectors. Basically, what "experience"

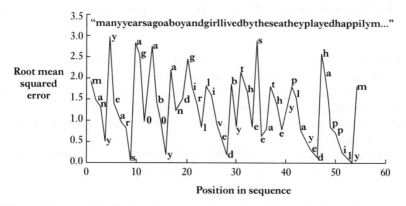

The error for a network trained on phoneme prediction. Error is high at the beginning of a word and decreases as the word is processed.

Figure 11.14 Error in letter-in-word prediction task (from Elman, 1990a: 194, figure 6; reproduced by permission of the author)

can affect is the values of the connection weights. With that said, we should note that some weight changes can be equivalent to architectural changes. For instance, if a weight is set at 0, that is functionally equivalent to not having a connection.

(1) One way of categorizing learning procedures is in terms of the training paradigm they use (see Rumelhart and Zipser, 1986: 161):

Regularity detector: in this paradigm there is a population of stimulus patterns and each stimulus pattern is presented with some probability. The system is supposed to discover statistically salient features of the input population. There is no a priori set of categories into which the patterns are to be classified; rather, the system must develop its own featural representation of the input stimuli which captures the most salient features of the population.

Auto associator: in this paradigm a set of patterns are repeatedly presented and the system is supposed to store the patterns. Then, later, parts of one of the original patterns or possibly a pattern similar to one of the original patterns is presented, and the task is to retrieve the original pattern through a kind of pattern completion procedure.

Pattern associator: this paradigm is a variant on the auto-association paradigm. A set of pairs of patterns are repeatedly presented. The system is to learn that when one member of the pair is presented it is supposed to produce the other.

Classification paradigm: the classification paradigm also can be considered a variant on the previous paradigms. In this case there is a fixed set of categories into which the stimulus patterns are to be classified. There is a training session in which the system is presented with the stimulus patterns along with the categories to which each stimulus belongs. The goal is to learn to correctly classify the stimuli so that in the future when a particular stimulus or a slightly distorted version of one of the stimuli is presented, the system will classify it properly. Perceptrons were early examples of machines in this paradigm.

(2)   Another way of categorizing learning procedures is in terms of whether they use a "teacher" or not – if they do they are called "supervised," if not they are called "unsupervised." In between is "forced learning," where one manipulates the content of the input stimuli, rather than adjust weights in virtue of output. We will focus here on supervised learning, but first a few words on unsupervised learning.

Unsupervised learning

In unsupervised learning there is no target output that the network is trained to approximate. One well-studied form of unsupervised learning is "competitive learning." Competitive learning detects regularities in the input population by developing internal representations of salient patterns (see figure 11.15). Competitive learning networks are hierarchically arranged layers of units with excitation between layers and inhibition within clusters of units at each layer. As the system learns, units come to respond to the same stimuli over time and different stimuli come to have different units respond to them.

Supervised learning

Supervised learning involves giving the network a sequence of *training pairs* consisting of an input vector and a target vector. The input vector is applied and the network computes the output on that input. The training algorithm compares the actual output with the target output and then adjusts the relevant connection weights according to some specific rule. Different training procedures use different rules.

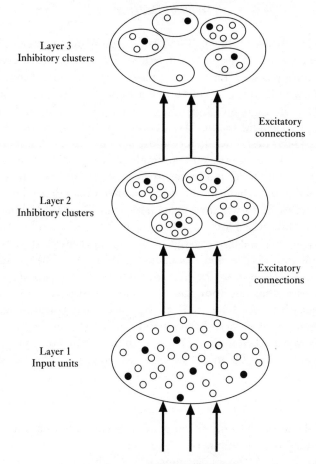

Layer 3
Inhibitory clusters

Excitatory
connections

Layer 2
Inhibitory clusters

Excitatory
connections

Layer 1
Input units

INPUT PATTERN

The architecture of the competitive learning mechanism. Competitive learning takes place in a context of sets of hierarchically layered units. Units are represented in the diagram as dots. Units may be active or inactive. Active units are represented by filled dots, inactive ones by open dots. In general, a unit in a given layer can receive inputs from all of the units in the next lower layer and can project outputs to all of the units in the next higher layer. Connections between layers are excitatory and connections within layers are inhibitory. Each layer consists of a set of clusters of mutually inhibitory units. The units within a cluster inhibit one another in such a way that only one unit per cluster may be active. We think of theconfiguration of active units on any given layer as representing the input pattern for the next higherlevel. There can be an arbitrary number of such layers. A given cluster contains a fixed number of units, but different clusters can have different numbers of units.

Figure 11.15   The architecture of a competitive learning mechanism (from Rumelhart and McClelland, 1986: 163, figure 2; reproduced by permission of the MIT Press)

Hebbian learning

As we noted in chapter 3, Hebb (1949) proposed the influential idea that when two connected neurons are active together, the strength of the connection between them increases.[1] This remark raises two questions: First, when this idea is applied to learning or training in a network, is it "supervised" learning or not? Second, how much would this strength increase, and what would it depend on? Turning to the first question, when two arbitrary units are involved, as Hebb described it, the adjustment in "weight" is made without "supervision." But in the case of a simple associator the second (B) "cell" would be the output node, and by adjusting connections to it, one would be in effect "supervising" it, because the weight change would depend on its output. So, for the networks we will investigate here, we will regard Hebbian learning as a species of supervised learning. Turning now to the second question, there are a variety of proposals for making Hebb's idea precise, and we will use the following one (see Bechtel and Abrahamsen, 1991: 48ff, 72ff): weight change is equal to the activation of the first unit times the activation of the second unit times a learning rate (how fast the system will change its weights). In simple associative networks, such as we have been considering, the first unit will be an input unit, and the second unit will be an output unit. Often the learning rate is taken to be a fraction with the number of input units in the denominator, and 1 in the numerator. So our working Hebbian learning rule is this:

(H)
    (1)   Find the product of: an input unit, a connected output unit, and a learning rate (1/number of input units).
    (2)   Add this to the previous connection weight.
    (3)   The result is the new connection weight.

Consider, for instance, a simple network (figure 11.16). We want to train this network, using rule (H), to distinguish one pair of input vectors from another pair of input vectors by responding to the first with a 1, to the second with a 0. To fix ideas, we will assume the first pair of vectors codes female faces, the second pair codes male faces:

Female pair (output = 1)
Vector 1: $\langle 1, -1, -1, 1 \rangle$
Vector 2: $\langle 1, 1, 1, 1 \rangle$

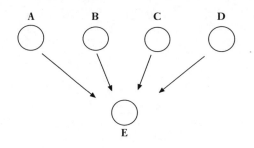

Figure 11.16 Face network

Male pair (output = 0)
Vector 3: ⟨1, −1, 1, −1⟩
Vector 4: ⟨−1, −1, 1, 1⟩

Can we train the "face network" to distinguish these two groups of faces? To train the network is to adjust the connection strengths in such a way that given a female face vector the network will respond with a 1, and given a male face vector the network will respond with a 0. For each vector there are four connection weights to consider and according to (H) we must train each connection by following these two steps: (a) first, find the product of input activation (input vector), desired output activation (either 1 for female or 0 for male), and the learning rate (1/number of input units = 1/4 = 0.25). Then (b) add this to the previous connection strength – this will be the new weight.

Vector 1

Let's start our training on vector 1, the first female vector, by training the first connection A–E. Remember, the categorization we want it to learn in this case is vector 1: ⟨1, −1, −1, 1⟩, output = 1 (see figure 11.17).

(H applied)
    (i)   Find the product of: input unit A, a connected output unit E, learning rate (1/4). Input unit A gets activation 1 from vector 1, the connected output unit E gets target activation 1, and the learning rate is 0.25. So the product is: $1 \times 1 \times 0.25 = 0.25$.
    (ii)   Add this to the previous connection weight 0.
    (iii)   The result is the new connection weight $0 + 0.25 = 0.25$.

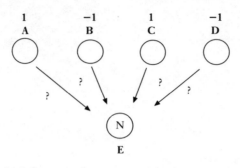

Figure 11.17   Untrained face network

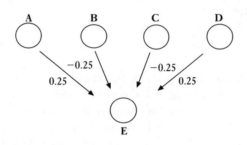

Figure 11.18   Face network trained on first vector

So the result of training the face network on vector 1 is to assign to the first connection the weight 0.25. If we repeat this style of calculation for the remaining connections we get:

Connection	Old weight	New weight
A–E: $1 \times 1 \times 0.25 + 0 =$		0.25
B–E: $-1 \times 1 \times 0.25 + 0 =$		−0.25
C–E: $-1 \times 1 \times 0.25 + 0 =$		−0.25
D–E: $1 \times 1 \times 0.25 + 0 =$		0.25

So our face network is now trained on the first vector (see figure 11.18).

Vector 2

We now train the face network in the same way on vector 2. The only difference is that at step (b) there will now be a previous connection strength, the weights resulting from learning vector 1. Remember, the categorization we want the network to learn now is vector 2: $\langle 1, 1, 1, 1 \rangle$. Notice that they are all

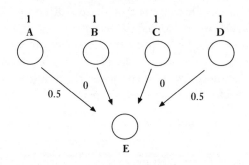

Figure 11.19   Face network trained on the second vector

the same. Notice also that the existing weights in the network are all the same (0.25) except for sign. So we should expect that the results of training on vector 2 will be differences of adding or subtracting 0.25, and this is right. Let's do the first weight to see this.

(H applied)

    (i)   Find the product of: input unit A, a connected output unit E, learning rate (1/4). Input unit A gets activation 1 from vector 2, the connected output unit E get target activation 1, and the learning rate is 0.25. So the product is: $1 \times 1 \times 0.25 = 0.25$,

   (ii)   Add this to the previous connection weight 0.25,

  (iii)   The result is the new connection weight $0.25 + 0.25 = 0.5$.

So the result of training the face network on vector 2 is to assign the first connection the weight 0.5. We repeat this style of calculation for the remaining connections and get:

Connection   *Old weight*   *New weight*
A–E: $1 \times 1 \times 0.25 = 0.25 + 0.25 \ = 0.5$
B–E: $1 \times 1 \times 0.25 = 0.25 + -0.25 = 0$
C–E: $1 \times 1 \times 0.25 = 0.25 + -0.25 = 0$
D–E: $1 \times 1 \times 0.25 = 0.25 + 0.25 \ = 0.5$

So our face network is now trained on the second vector (see figure 11.19).

Vectors 3 and 4

We now want to train the face network on vectors 3 and 4, the male faces. This turns out to be surprisingly easy. Notice that the target activation of the output unit is 0 in both cases. This means that there will be no change with these vectors, because in (H) we multiplied the input and learning rate by the output and that is 0, and anything multiplied by 0 is 0. So the increase is 0 and the previous weight remains the same – the face network trained for the second vector is our final face network. This completes the first training cycle; we made one pass through each of the input-output pairs.

Computation

We now want to see if the trained network will do what it was trained to do – will it recognize a female and male vector?

Vector 2
First let's see what it outputs when we give it the second female vector, vector 2: $\langle 1, 1, 1, 1 \rangle$. Using (N) we get: sum (input × weight): $1 \times 0.5 + 1 \times 0 + 1 \times 0 + 1 \times 0.5 = 1$. Which is correct. The face network, after one training cycle, correctly categorized vector 2 as 1 – female.

Vector 4
Next let's see what it outputs when we give it the second male vector, vector 4: $\langle -1, -1, 1, 1 \rangle$. Using (N) we get: sum (input × weight): $-1 \times 0.5 + -1 \times 0 + 1 \times 0 + 1 \times 0.5 = 0$. Which is correct. The face network, after one training cycle, correctly categorized vector 4 as 0 – male.

Exercise 5   Verify that the network categorizes vectors 1 and 3 correctly.

Technical digression   What are the limitations of the Hebb rule for learning vectors in an associative network? A linear associator trained by the Hebb rule will learn only orthogonal vectors without interference. As we noted in an earlier digression, two vectors are orthogonal when their inner product equals 0; that is, if we multiply the vectors and sum these products, that sum will be 0. If you try to teach a linear associator a new non-orthogonal vector, its performance will degrade – it will do worse on ones it used to perform correctly on.

Delta learning

With Hebbian learning, weights are set as a function of input activation and target output activation (plus learning rate, but that is constant for a network). There is no feedback from the discrepancy in performance between what the network *is* doing and what it *should be* doing. There is no opportunity for error to have an instructive effect. Here we take error to be the difference between the target output activation and the actual output activation:

(E)   Error = target activation − actual activation (of output unit).

Delta learning utilizes this information by increasing weights on connections when a output unit should be on, but it is off, and by decreasing weights on connections when an output unit should be off, but it is on. When the weight is right (has the right effect) it is left alone. The informal rule for delta learning is this:

(D)
(1)   find the error (E).
(2)   find the product of: the input activation × error × the learning rate.
(3)   add this to the previous weight.
(4)   The result is the new weight.

We will apply this learning procedure to the face network. We will use the following vectors with the following output values:

Input vectors	*Output*
V1: $\langle 1, -1, 1, -1 \rangle$	1
V2: $\langle 1, 1, 1, 1 \rangle$	1
V3: $\langle 1, 1, 1, -1 \rangle$	−1
V4: $\langle 1, -1, -1, 1 \rangle$	−1

Recall that the network started with each weight at 0.

Trial 1 (Vector 1)

As before, we now calculate the change in value of the first weight in the network, the connection A–E, when giving the network vector V1 to learn to associate with 1. Applying (D) to this connection, we get:

(D applied)
(i)   Find the error (E). This is the difference between what the output unit should produce and what is does produce. It should produce a 1. What does it produce? For that we need to use (N) again. The output is the sum of the products of input activation times weights. But

weights are all 0 to start with. So the products are all 0, so the sum is 0 – it produces 0. So the error is the difference between 1 and 0, i.e. 1.

(ii)   Find the product of: the input activation, the error, and the learning rate. The input activation is 1, the error is 1 and the learning rate is 0.25. So the product of these is $1 \times 1 \times 0.25 = 0.25$. So the result is $0 + 0.25 = 0.25$.

(iii) Add this to the previous weight. The previous weight was 0, so the result is 0.25.

(iv)   The result, 0.25, is the new weight.

So we know that the new weight on the first connection, A–E, is 0.25. We now need to do the same thing for the remaining connections. As can be seen, all of the numbers are the same except for sign (B–E and D–E are "–"). So the resulting weights for the first trial, vector 1, are:

A–E: 0.25
B–E: –0.25
C–E: 0.25
D–E: –0.25

Exercise 6   Verify these results for the last three connections.

Trial 2 (Vector 2)

We apply (D) to the second vector ⟨1, 1, 1, 1⟩ in the same way, starting with the first connection A–E:

(D Applied)

(i)   Find the error. According to (E) this is the difference between what the output unit should produce and what is does produce. it should produce a 1. What does it produce? For that we need to use (N) again: the output is the sum of the products of input activation times weights: $1 \times 0.25, 1 \times –0.25, 1 \times 0.25, 1 \times –0.25 = 0.25 + –0.25 + 0.25 + –0.25 = 0$. So the actual output is 0. So the error is $1 – 0$, i.e. again it is 1.

(ii)   Find the product of: the input activation, the error, and the learning rate. The input activation is 1, the error is 1 and the learning rate is 0.25. So the product of these is $1 \times 1 \times 0.25 = 0.25$. So the result is $0 + 0.25 = 0.25$.

(iii) Add this to the previous weight. The previous weight was 0.25, so the result is 0.5.

(iv) The result, 0.5, is the new weight.

The result of performing the same calculations on the remaining connections yields the new weights:

A–E: 0.5
B–E: 0
C–E: 0.5
D–E: 0

Exercise 7 Verify these last three calculations.

Trial 3 (Vector 3)

The result of performing the same calculations on the third vector yields the new weights (remember that the target output value is −1 in this case):

A–E: 0
B–E: −0.5
C–E: 0
D–E: 0.5

Trial 4 (Vector 4)

The result of performing the same calculations on the fourth vector yields the new weights (remember that the target output value is −1 in this case):

Cycle 1 Weights
A–E: −0.5
B–E: 0
C–E: 0.5
D–E: 0

Exercise 8 Verify the calculations for trials 3 and 4.

This completes the first cycle of training (one cycle of training is one training trial on each input–output pair), and we have trained the network for each of vectors 1–4. One could continue to train the network for more cycles. For

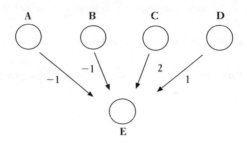

Figure 11.20 Delta-trained network after 20 cycles

instance, after 20 cycles the network has the weights (shown in figure 11.20; see also Haberland, 1994: 185):

Computation

We can verify that this network will give the right outputs for each of the four vectors. Consider, for instance, vector 3: $\langle 1, 1, 1, -1 \rangle$. This should give the output -1. Does it?

(N applied)
  Sum $(1 \times -1, 1 \times -1, 1 \times 2, -1 \times 1) = -1 + -1 + 2 + -1 = -1$.

The network gives the right output for vector 3 as input.

Exercise 9 Verify the correctness of the network for vectors 1, 2, 4.

> **Technical digression** How does delta learning overcome inadequacies of Hebbian learning? If the vectors are not orthogonal, but are linearly separable, then the Hebb rule will not learn them, but the delta rule can. If vectors are not linearly separable, the delta rule will still do the best it can – it will converge on the minimum of error. What are the limitations on delta learning? The delta rule will learn vectors only if they are linearly independent. The delta rule will not learn vectors that are not linearly separable. Hidden layers are needed for that, and the generalized delta rule (generalized to hidden layers) is needed for hidden layers.

Back Propagation (generalized delta rule)
The delta rule will not work if there is a hidden layer, since it can apply only to direct connections from input to output. In this case, the generalized delta

rule, also known as Back-propagation of Error (or "Backprop"), is required. As far as the output units are concerned, Backprop works pretty much the same way as the delta rule – the weight changes on the connections between the hidden units and the output units are proportional to the error on the output units. However, for the connections between the input units and the hidden units, there is no target activation, so there is no error signal that e.g. the delta rule could use. So how can we calculate the error on the hidden units in order to reduce it? This is exactly what Backprop does: it propagates the amount of error back though the network. The error on the hidden units is calculated in proportion to the error on the output units and to the strength of the connections between the hidden units and the output units. This is a way to determine the contribution of lower-layer units to the error of the output layer (see Suggested reading).

Technical digression   The XOR problem, introduced in chapter 4, is a good example of a problem with a solution that is not linearly separable. As we saw, the two-dimensional space of XOR cannot be partitioned by a single straight line (see figure 4.13 again). This is because two dissimilar inputs ⟨0, 0⟩ and ⟨1, 1⟩ require similar output, namely 0. By introducing a hidden layer the problem can be solved. The hidden layer unit(s) show how the structure of the input is transformed. The two dissimilar inputs are transformed into a similar pattern ⟨0, 0⟩. This property of networks with hidden layers proves to be important in many cognitive tasks (which often involve linearly inseparability) by transforming the input space into a linearly separable problem.

11.4   Representation(s)

Connectionists and non-connectionists alike mostly agree that to account adequately for human cognitive capacities we will have to see cognition as, in part, involving the "manipulation" (creation, transformation, and elimination) of *representations*, and as a consequence, connectionist models of cognitive capacities will have to simulate these processes. As we noted in part II, this raises two questions when applied to connectionist models:

(Q1)   What sorts of representations do connectionist models "manipulate" (create, transform, eliminate)

(Q2)   How do these connectionist representations represent what they do – what determines just what they represent?

The first question (Q1) was called *the problem of representations* [with an "s"], and the second question (Q2) was called *the problem of representation* [without an "s"]. An answer to (Q1) would reveal the (1) structure and (2) important features of the major schemes of connectionist representation. An answer to (Q2) would have to tell us (a) under what conditions something is a representation, i.e. represents something, and (b) what determines exactly what it represents.

Q1: Varieties of connectionist representations

There are a variety of proposals in the connectionist literature as to the nature of the representations they manipulate (create, transform, delete). The matter is complicated by an unstable terminology, so for perspicuity we adopt the following conventions (again, we will have to be lax, especially when reporting the views of others, since not everyone speaks this way):

Some terminology

Local (punctate) representations: the activation of an individual unit represents an element in its domain, e.g. a particular concept, property, or individual.

Quasi-distributed representations: a pattern of activation among sets of individual units represents an element in its domain, and units do not participate in other representations.

(Fully) distributed representations: a pattern of activation among sets of individual units represents an element in its domain, and units do participate in other representations.

Local representations

The basic idea behind local representations is that a specific unit is dedicated to a specific "concept." We saw this in NETtalk's input units, where a single unit was dedicated to a single letter. Such schemes are intuitive and simple; they are explicit and easy to understand. But they have grave defects as cognitive models, and are unrealistic as directly implemented in neural hardware.

Problems with local representations

As representations directly implemented in neural hardware, the first problem is *neural death*: losing one hundred thousand neurons a day is bound to zap an occasional concept, yet we rarely wake up without the concept of, say, grandmother. As Feldman (1989: 75) notes, this objection can be met by distributing the representation over as few as 3 or 4 units.[2] The second problem is that there are *not enough neurons* to represent everything including concepts and relations between them. For instance, the visual system is sensitive to at least six dimensions of information and if it were able to resolve even only ten values for each dimension at the narrowest level of one million (10^6) points, it would require 10^{12} neurons – too many (see Feldman, 1989). A final problem is fitting in a new concept. This requires finding a node with all the right pre-existing relations, or else resetting all the relevant relations in the network. This is (often) a biologically and computationally questionable procedure (see Rumelhart and McClelland, 1986a, chapter 3).

Distributed representations

Suppose we agree that despite their intuitive appeal, local representations are neurologically implausible and computationally inadequate, and that we should recruit more units into conceptual representations. An example of this was the output units of NETtalk where the representation of phonemes was distributed over many distinctive feature units and the same distinctive feature units participated in representing many phonemes.

Technical digression: *A simple scheme and its problems*: consider a simple case: the problem of representing the position of a dot on a plane (or a bug in the visual field). We have two groups of units available, one represents a position along the X axis, the other a position along the Y axis. We might represent the location of dot 2 thus as in figure 11.21.

The position of dot 2 can be represented by the pair of vectors: $\langle X: 0100 \rangle$, $\langle Y: 1000 \rangle$. If we want to represent dot 3 as well, we must complicate the vectors as in figure 11.22.

This gives us: $2 = \langle x: 0001 \rangle$, $\langle y: 0010 \rangle$; $3 = \langle x: 0001 \rangle$, $\langle y: 0010 \rangle$.

The binding problem

But how do we distinguish the representation of 2 and 3 in (figure 11.22) from 2′ and 3′ in figure 11.23? Here $2′ = \langle: 0001 \rangle$, $\langle y: 0010 \rangle$, which is the

Continued

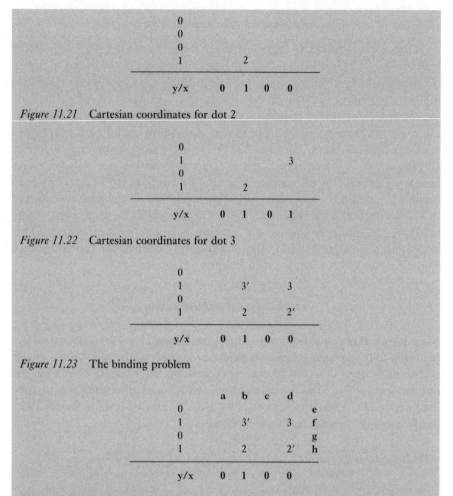

Figure 11.21 Cartesian coordinates for dot 2

Figure 11.22 Cartesian coordinates for dot 3

Figure 11.23 The binding problem

Figure 11.24 Conjunctive coding

same as 3 (or look at values on the diagonal). The occurrence of such "crosstalk" is called *the binding problem*: how to bind the positions together as in figure 11.22, so as to avoid the ghosts (2′, 3′) in figure 11.23.

Solution 1: conjunctive coding

One solution is to assign a unit to *each pair of possible combinations of X and Y*, as in figure 11.24. Thus dot 2 is at the node (b, h) whereas its ghost, 2′, is at node (d, f). Mutatis mutandis for dot 3 and its ghost, 3′. This would solve the binding problem for this simple case, but it quickly becomes computationally expensive.

If we operationally define the accuracy of a representational system as: the number of different encodings that are generated as a dot moves a standard distance across the plane – then with conjunctive coding the accuracy of getting a specific point is proportional to the square root of the number of points (see Rumelhart and McClelland, 1986a, 90). We can do much better.

Solution 2: coarse coding

One promising technique involves "coarse coding." Using this method, several units are given over to the input field in a kind of overlapping tiling. Is it better to use a few large zones or many small ones? Intuition, perhaps, suggests the latter, but in fact the former is more efficient. This is because accuracy is related to the number of zones (n) and to their radius (r): $a = n \times r$ ("=" is "proportional"). So increasing the radius of the zones increases the accuracy of the representation (see Rumelhart and McClelland 1986a: 91). This type of representation works best if points (of features in general) being detected are widely spaced. If they are close together, they risk being coded by the same group of units. There is a resolution-accuracy trade-off.

Microfeatures

As we will see in chapter 12, according to Smolensky (1988a), connectionist models operate between the classical conceptual level (e.g., frames) and the neural level. He calls this the "subconceptual" level. This is the level of the "intuitive processor." At this level, "representations are complex patterns of activity over many units. Each unit participates in many such patterns" (1988a, 6). The patterns as a whole have a conceptual interpretation or semantics, but not the units that make them up: "these units do not have a conceptual semantics: they are *subconceptual*" (p. 6). What, then, is their semantic role? There is at present no general answer, since each model adopts its own procedure for relating the activation patterns to a conceptual interpretation. There are some general strategies that are actually employed. One is just to borrow categories from some high-level conceptual description of the domain, such as assigning phonetic or graphic features to nodes. Another is to analyze the representations developed by hidden units during training using multidimensional scaling, hierarchical cluster analysis, etc.

Regarding the first method, notice that the high-level description of the domain of the model can be commonsensical. For instance:

> The connectionist representation of *coffee* is the representation of *cup with coffee* minus the representation of *cup without coffee*. . . . What remains, in fact, is a pattern of activity with active features such as brown liquid with flat top surface, brown liquid with curved sides and bottom surface, brown liquid contacting porcelain, hot liquid, and burnt odor. This represents *coffee*, in some sense – but *coffee in the context of cup*. (1988a: 16)

Smolensky later diagrams these as in figure 11.25.

Returning to the second method, analyses of hidden units suggest that networks can develop representations of categories that are in some sense "in the stimulus," but are not presented explicitly. They are a kind of hidden invariant of the sort discovered in the analysis of the hidden units in NETtalk.

So far we have described connectionist representations as local (punctate) or distributed and we have noted that they can be local with respect to some information (NETtalk: letters and distinctive features) and distributed with respect to others (NETtalk: words and phonemes). There are other possibilities as well (see figure 11.26).

Type 1: Examples of this type are Smolensky's "coffee story" we just reviewed. Certain patterns represent, say, a cup and constituent nodes represent microfeatures of that concept. The input and output layers of NETtalk go here too.

Type 2: An example of this might be the hidden layer of NETtalk where activation patterns represent vowels and consonants, but individual nodes have no interpretation.

Type 3: An example of this type is the propositional network to be discussed in chapter 13. Patterns represent propositions, but the constituent nodes have no particular semantic values.

Type 4: An example of this type might be recurrent networks, where representations are ordered in time in an attempt to capture the idea of occupying different structural relations. Here also might be Smolensky's "tensor product" representations.

Representation of *cup with coffee*	
Units	Microfeatures
●	upright container
●	hot liquid
○	glass contacting wood
●	porcelain curved surface
●	burnt odor
●	brown liquid contacting porcelain
○	oblong silver object
●	finger-sized handle
●	brown liquid with curved sides and bottom

Representation of *cup without coffee*	
Units	Microfeatures
●	upright container
○	hot liquid
○	glass contacting wood
●	porcelain curved surface
○	burnt odor
○	brown liquid contacting porcelain
○	oblong silver object
●	finger-sized handle
●	brown liquid with curved sides and bottom

Representation of *coffee*	
Units	Microfeatures
○	upright container
●	hot liquid
○	glass contacting wood
○	porcelain curved surface
●	burnt odor
●	brown liquid contacting porcelain
○	oblong silver object
○	finger-sized handle
●	brown liquid with curved sides and bottom

Figure 11.25   Coffee vectors (from Smolensky, 1991b: 208–9, figures 2–4; reproduced by permission of Kluwer Academic/Plenum Publishers)

Some advantages of distributed representations

Distributed representations are advertised as having a number of advantages over local representations in connectionist models. We will return to these in the next two chapters, but for now it is helpful to have an idea of these properties since they form some of the motivation for investigating connectionist

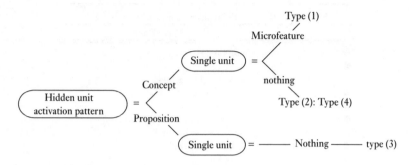

Figure 11.26 Types of connectionist representations (from Ramsey, 1992: 261, figure 8.1; reproduced by permission of Oxford University Press)

mechanisms in the first place. The most commonly mentioned advantages are: content addressability, pattern completion, (spontaneous) generalization, fault tolerance, graceful degradation, and improved relearning. These are not independent notions. "Content addressability," as we saw in chapter 6, contrasts with location addressability – the idea is that we store material in memory according to its representational content, not in some (arbitrary) address. We can access this remembered information with probes that are similar (in content) to the desired information. "Pattern completion" refers to the ability of systems with distributed representations to correctly recognize partial inputs. "Spontaneous generalization" refers to the ability of systems to raise the activation of nodes that are related to the target nodes. In this way the more specific feature "generalizes" to more general ones. "Fault tolerance" refers to the property of such systems to ignore false or misleading input information and still come up with the right answer, or the best fit. "Graceful degradation" refers to the fact that the system can be damaged in various ways and it will not just crash; rather its overall performance degrades along various general dimensions, such as speed and/or accuracy. Finally, "improved relearning" refers to the fact that if such a system is damaged, for example by injecting a high amount of noise into it, then retrained, it can relearn the set much faster than it did originally, and it will even improve its performance on items omitted from the retraining – i.e. the retraining tends to "generalize."

Q2: the nature of connectionist representation

Typically we find talk of three bearers of representation: input units, output units, hidden units; and three styles of acquiring representational force: programmer-specified, learned, and innate. The case of programmer-specified representation is relatively uninteresting, since it simply pushes the problem of the nature of representation back one step: how (and what) does the programmer's representation represent? However, when it is clear what the interpretation of the units is intended to be, the interest of the exercise is to see what the model does with the information given to it. Looking more closely at how the behavior of the model can be interpreted tells us something about the intended conception of representation the machine is being endowed with. Programmer-specified semantics, then, ultimately is just a stand-in for either learned or innate semantics. More interesting are cases of learned representations – where the machine develops its own representation of the stimuli (either through discovery, unsupervised, or through supervision). Typically the input units and the output units have their semantics specified by the programmer, and the hidden units get trained.

11.5   Generic Connectionism

We have reviewed some basic ideas in connectionist machines: units, activation, connections, weights, computation, and learning. From these samples we can see that connectionist networks share certain features, and differ in certain features, and it would be useful to try to specify these similarities and differences. We will adopt the trick of collecting common themes as answers to general questions about such networks.

Ten questions

I   Static features

Architecture
  Units
  1   How many units are there?
  Connections
  2   What is the pattern (geometry, "spatial" layout) of connections?
  3   Which connections are excitatory, which are inhibitory (if any)?
  4   What is the direction of the flow of activation?

Representation
   5   What do individual units at each layer represent, if anything?
   6   What do groups of units at each layer represent, if anything?

II   Dynamic features

Computation
   7   How does the network compute its output from its input?

Programming
   Units
   8   What are the "activation passing" rules (including thresholds and decay, if any)?
   Connections
   9   What are the weights on the connections?

Learning/training
   10   What is the procedure by which weights, and/or thresholds, are changed?

Generic connectionist machine

   1   A network of connected computing units.
   2   Each connection has a strength or weight.
   3   Each unit has a rule for passing on some activation value.
   4   Certain units are input units, and their (possibly joint) activation represents the input.
   5   Certain units are output units, and their (possibly joint) activation represents the output.
   6   Data/information is in the activation of units and the connection weights.
   7   There are learning algorithms for modifying the connection weights.
   8   Computation involves arithmetic operations on activation levels and connection strengths.

Notes

1   An earlier version can be found in James (1890).
2   The probability of losing any two neurons from a given group is one in ten million. That's a lot of days.

Study questions

Basic notions and terminology

What are the three functional parts of a unit?

What are "fan in" and "fan out"?

What is it to program a network?

What is the rule for activation passing called "Net"?

What is an "input vector"?

What is an "output vector"?

Say what computation is in the above two terms.

Given a network and an input vector, be able to use (N) to calculate an output vector.

Think about how a network accommodates defective input.

Think about how a single network can carry more than one association of patterns.

Learning and training

What are the main types of learning?

What is the rule (three parts) for "Hebbian" learning?

Given a network, an input vector, and an output, be able to calculate the weight assignment using the Hebb rule (H).

Given a network, an input vector and an output, be able to calculate the weight assignment using the Delta rule (D).

Representations

What are local representations?

What are quasi-distributed representations?

What are (fully) distributed representations?

What three problems do local representations have?

What advantages are distributed representations supposed to have?

How are connectionist representations supposed to be about what they are about?

Generic connectionism

What are the two "static" aspects of a generic connectionist machine?

What are the three "dynamic" aspects of a generic connectionist machine?

How is occurrent knowledge stored in a network?

How is dispositional knowledge stored in a network?

Suggested reading

General

See Schneider (1987) on connectionism as a paradigm shift. Anderson (1995) is a good survey introduction to connectionist networks. Two clear and useful introductions to connectionist machines with accompanying diskettes for running simulations are McClelland and Rumelhart (1988) and Caudill and Butler (1993): volume 1 covers the construction and training of basic networks, volume 2 covers the same with respect to advanced networks. For more recent diskettes see Plunkett and Elman (1997), and McLeod et al. (1998). McClelland and Rumelhart (1988), Levine (1991), Caudill and Butler (1993), and McLeod et al. (1998) survey a variety of architectures, including the ones we have discussed.

Basic notions

An early important article on connectionism (which made the label stick) was Feldman and Ballard (1982). Probably the most influential general discussion of connectionist (also called "parallel distributed") models to date is Rumelhart and McClelland (1986), vol. 1. Chapter 2: the general framework for parallel distributed processing is a good introduction to basic notions. Rumelhart (1989) is an excellent summary article of most of this material. Other good surveys of basic connectionism can be found in Wasserman (1989), chapter 1, Clark (1989), chapter 5, Churchland (1990), Quinlan (1991), chapter 2, Bechtel and Abrahamsen (1991), chapters 1–3, Haberland (1994), chapter 6, Bechtel (1994), Stillings et al. (1995), chapter 2.10, and Elman et al. (1996), chapter 2. Ballard (1997) is more technical, but it gives very useful details. For more on recurrent networks and language see Elman (1992).

Learning and training

Rumelhart and McClelland (1986a), vol. 1, chapter 5, on competitive learning nicely introduces this type of learning and contains an interesting historical discussion as well.

Chapter 8: Learning internal representations by error propagation, of the same book introduced back-propagation, the generalized delta rule, and places it in historical perspective. Hinton (1992) is a concise, authoritative survey of some main supervised and unsupervised training techniques.

Some mathematics

Rumelhart and McClelland (1986a) chapter 9: An introduction to linear algebra in parallel distributed processing, is a comprehensive introduction to just that. Shorter discussions can be found in Wasserman (1989), appendix B: Vector and matrix operations, and in Levine (1991), appendix 2: Difference and differential equations in neural networks, and Caudill and Butler (1993), volume 1, appendix D.

Representations

The first and most influential general discussion of distributed representations can be found in Rumelhart and McClelland (1986a), chapter 3: Distributed representations. See Nadel et al. (1986) and Feldman (1989) for discussion of the neurobiology of representation. A more philosophical introduction to connectionist representations can be found in Sterelny (1990), chapter 8. An extensive philosophical discussion can be found in Cussins (1990). Smolensky (1990) is a brief but authoritative overview. A critical appraisal of connectionist representation can be found in van Gelder (1991), Goschke and Koppelberg (1991), and Ramsey (1992).

Anthologies

Some representative anthologies on connectionism include Nadel et al. (1989), Morris (1989), Horgan and Tienson (1991), Ramsey, Stich, and Rumelhart (1991), Dinsmore (1992), Davis (1992), Clark and Lutz (1995), and MacDonald and MacDonald (1995).

12

The Connectionist Computational Theory of Mind

12.1 Introduction

In Part II we motivated the generic computational theory of mind (CTM) by putting computational constraints on the earlier representational theory of mind (RTM). We formulated it as:

(CTM)
1 Cognitive states are *computational relations* to *mental representations* which have content.
2 Cognitive processes (changes in cognitive states) are *computational operations* on these *mental representations*.

We also noted that we get a *digital* computational theory of mind by adding further specifically digital constraints to (CTM), and we considered two: the first involved specifying digital *architecture* (memory and control), the second involved specifying digital *representions*. We turn now to the issue of finding the analog of the DCTM for connectionist architectures, and exploring the associated theory of mind.

12.2 The Connectionist Computational Theory of Mind

The easiest approach is to get a *connectionist* computational theory by adding further specifically connectionist constraints to (CTM). Again it is natural to consider architecture and representation – the computational architecture and representations must be connectionist. The DCTM and the CCTM certainly have different styles of operation (they even have different mathematics), but CCTM contains *analogs* of the following DCTM features:

1 CCTM models contain *symbols*: nodes and vectors of nodes.
2 CCTM models are *programmed*: by setting the activation passing rules, connection strengths and thresholds, if any.
3 *Occurrent data*: are vectors of activated nodes.
4 *Dispositional data*: are stored in connection strengths.
5 *Computation* is vector transformation.

This should lead us to expect that a connectionist *computational* theory of mind is a real possibility. Is it more – is it an actuality? It seems not yet. Many observers would agree with Tienson's (1991) assessment that: "nothing has emerged as what could be called *a*, let alone *the*, connectionist conception of cognition . . . [which] would have to tell us what kind of network activity constitutes mental activity, and why. So far connectionism has not told us how to answer such questions" (1992: 2). And Smolensky, one of the most distinguished architects of connectionism, thinks its progress as a framework for modeling cognition is roughly Aristotelian: "what we have are interesting techniques and promising suggestions . . . we are somewhere approximating Aristotle's position in the intellectual history of this new computational approach. If there are any connectionist enthusiasts who think that we can really model cognition from such a position, they are, I fear, sadly mistaken" (1991b: 287).

However, using CTM as our model, we can formulate a preliminary version of the basic connectionist computational theory of mind as follows:

(B-CCTM)
1 Cognitive states are *computational relations* to *mental representations* which have content.
2 Cognitive processes (changes in cognitive states) are *computational operations* on these *mental representations*.
3 The computational architecture and representations (mentioned in 1 and 2) must be connectionist.

We made an effort, while introducing the DCTM, to motivate it in terms of, among other things, the mind–body problem. We delimited the domain of the theory roughly to cognitive states and processes, then we said something about what a certain class of these cognitive states were, according to the DCTM (the so-called "propositional attitudes"). The connectionist computational theory of mind is much less developed than its digital predecessor. Many issues remain unresolved at present. For instance, it is debatable whether or not CCTM offers a distinctive perspective on the mind–body problem, as some have suggested.[1] And it is debatable how much of the language of thought hypothesis can be transferred to CCTM. If this idea does extend to connectionist models, then we would have a connectionist analog of (DCTM) from chapter 8:

(CCTM)

1   Cognitive states are *computational relations* to *computational mental representations* (in the language of thought) which have content.
2   Cognitive processes (changes in cognitive states) are *computational operations* on these *computational mental representations* (in the language of thought).
3   The computational architecture and representations (mentioned in 1 and 2) are *connectionist*.

We will now explore some of the motivations for, and distinctive features of, the CCTM.

12.3   Motivations for the CCTM

Motivations for pursuing CCTM models come from two major quarters, similarities between network and human performance, and similarities between networks and human brains.

Human performance

Recall from our earlier discussion of Jets and Sharks, and NETtalk, that each model exhibited some human-like performance characteristics:

Jets and Sharks

This model was able to:

1   retrieve the specific characteristics of particular individuals ("exemplars");
2   extract central tendencies of classes of objects from stored knowledge of particular individuals ("exemplars");
3   fill in plausible default values.

NETtalk

1 acquired stress more quickly and accurately than phonemes;
2 followed a learning "power law" (i.e. learning plotted as error on double logarithmic scales is almost a straight line);
3 exhibited the feature that spaced practice (alternating old and new words) was more effective than continuous practice (a feature of human skill learning known since Ebbinghaus);
4 generalized its pronunciation fairly reliably to new words, and the more the network had learned, the better its performance was;
5 degraded gradually ("gracefully") in its overall performance, when damaged with random weights;
6 relearned items after damage quicker than it originally learned them;
7 revealed, upon hierarchical cluster analysis (on the average letter to sound activity levels of the hidden units) that vectors for vowels clustered together as opposed to consonants. Furthermore, within the vowel and consonant categories, similar vowels (and to some extent consonants) clustered together.

The brain

Another line of consideration in favor of CCTM models is to emphasize the *similarities* between CCTM models and the brain. The argument goes like this:

1a Models of mind/brain are to be preferred to models of mind or brain only, or
1b Models of minds should approximate or accommodate models of brains.
2 CCTM models of mind can also model gross structure and functioning of brains reasonably well.
3 So, CCTM is to be preferred.

The reasoning here is at odds with the DCTM assumption that one can study and understand the mind (software) completely independently of the brain (hardware). CCTM is more inclined to see mental phenomena as closely related to neural phenomena, and although connectionist models are not neural models, they mimic (or can be made to mimic) gross structural and functional features of the brain. So the CCTM strategy is to argue that insofar as DCTM hardware fails to reflect the gross structure and functioning of the brain, it is to be considered less seriously as a potential model of our brain-based cognition. And insofar as one shares this assumption, one will be moved by the preceding considerations.

The brain: structure

There are a number of structural similarities between CCTM models and brains:

1   units are like neurons;
2   connections (and weights) are like axons, dendrites, and synapses;
3   brains, and some CCTM models, are organized into layers;
4   brains probably learn by adjusting synaptic strengths, as some CCTM models do;
5   brains exhibit parallel excitation and inhibition, as some CCTM models do.

The brain: functioning

There are a number of functional similarities between CCTM models and the brain:

(1)   *Massively parallel*   Brain processing, like CCTM models, seems to be massively parallel in its processing. One argument for why this must be so goes as follows: neurons in the brain send a signal (do a flip-flop) in about $1/1,000$ second, a computer does it in about $1/100,000,000$ second – a million times faster. So if the brain worked by following a serial program it could only run about 100 instructions in $1/10$th of a second – which is about the time it takes for a brain to perform such fundamental operations as visual recognition and language understanding. But no program for these tasks can be written in 100 steps. Rumelhart and McClelland put it as follows: "Whereas basic operations in our modern serial computers are measured in the nanoseconds, neurons operate at times measured in the milliseconds – perhaps 10s of milliseconds. Thus, the basic hardware of the brain is some 10^6 times slower than that of serial computers. Imagine slowing down our conventional AI programs by a factor of 10^6. More remarkable is the fact that we are able to do very sophisticated processing in a few hundred milliseconds. Clearly, perceptual processing, most memory retrieval, much of language processing, much intuitive reasoning, and many other processes occur in this time frame. That means that these tasks must be done in no more than 100 or so serial steps. This is what Feldman (1985) calls the *100-step program constraint*. Moreover, note that individual neurons probably don't compute very complicated functions. It seems unlikely that a single neuron computes a function much more complex than a single instruction in a digital computer" (1986a, vol. 1: 130–1). This constraint is often called the "100 step rule."

(2) *Content addressability* The brain, like CCTM models, uses fragments of the information (content) to recover it – it is content-, not location-, addressable.

(3) *Distributed memory* In a brain, like in a CCTM model, it doesn't seem that each memory has a specific location. Rather, information is distributed over many parts of the brain and each part of the brain can participate in storing many pieces of information (recall the work of Lashley reviewed in chapter 3). One estimate is that between 700,000 and 7,000,000 neurons participate in storing a single memory trace, while another estimate is that it is about 1,000. We saw that in NETtalk about 20 percent of the hidden units participated in each coding.

(4) *Graceful degradation* Damage to a brain, like damage to CCTM models, produces a graded impairment of performance – nothing specific may go wrong, but the overall functioning of the system will not be as good.

(5) *Non-acute sensitivity to noise and defective input* The brain, like CCTM models, seems to process noisy and defective inputs effortlessly – recall the behavior of the rose network when its input was defective.

As we will see in chapter 13, these functional virtues are not uncontroversial.

12.4 A Bit of History: Connectionism and Associationism

We have presented the basic ingredients of connectionist machines, how they are organized, compute, and are trained. As we noted earlier, it is possible to see such models as the most recent development in a line of thinking dating back many centuries: classical associationism (chapter 1), Pavlov and conditioned reflexes (chapter 2), Lashley and Hebb (chapter 3), perceptrons (chapter 4), and Pandemonium (chapter 6). We now want to look in more detail at the relationship between connectionism and associationism.

One has to be struck at least by the geometrical similarity between early associationist networks and some connectionist networks. Compare again James's (1890) total recall (see figure 1.6(a) above), with Rumelhart and McClelland (1986a; see figure 12.1):

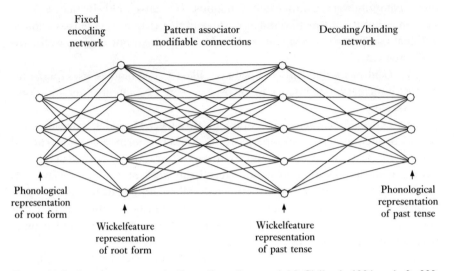

Fixed
encoding
network

Pattern associator
modifiable connections

Decoding/binding
network

Phonological
representation
of root form

Wickelfeature
representation
of root form

Wickelfeature
representation
of past tense

Phonological
representation
of past tense

Figure 12.1   Past tense network (from Rumelhart and McClelland, 1986, vol. 2: 222, figure 1; reproduced by permission of the MIT Press)

What might be the relationship between them in general? If we compare the "generic associationism" of our first chapter with the "generic con-nectionism" of chapter 11, it looks as if the former is a special case of the latter, in the sense that we could design a connectionist network to have many of the following representational and associative capacities. For instance, we could let the input nodes be sensory transducers processing sensations (think of NETtalk's letter detectors). We could let hidden units encode ideas, and we could let output units affect behavior (think of NETtalk's articulatory features). Connection strengths could then be set to capture similarities (or contrasts) between sensations, between ideas, or between sensations and ideas. Such associations (connection strengths) could record contiguity in space and (say, in a recurrent network) time. We might even think of the clus-tering of hidden units in NETtalk (chapter 10) in terms of similarity as a case of association. Cause and effect might be harder to handle, but only Hume embraced it, and only before he analyzed it away in terms of contiguity and succession.

Are there any differences between associationist and connectionist machines besides the generality and flexibility of the latter? Bechtel suggests that: "for the British associationists, the most common basis for association was similar-ity of the idea or spatial or temporal contiguity in the presentation of ideas. The primitives out of which these networks were built were tied directly to sensations. . . . The network of connections postulated by PDP theorists is quite different. None of the units in the network are directly sensory inputs or motor outputs, but many other units are only remotely connected to them" (1985: 57). Bechtel's observations might lead to differences that are only a matter of degree. For Bechtel, connectionism focuses on the center of the process between input and output, whereas associationists continued theorizing out to the periphery. Yet he gives no examples of this difference from either literature, and it is hard to see why it would be impossible in principle to extend connectionist models to the periphery.

There seem to be at least two linked differences between some connectionist models and association networks. First, in associationist networks, what get associated are *ideas*, and associations are built up by strengthening the "pathways" (connections) between these ideas. In *local* connectionist networks such as Jets and Sharks, the analogy holds up because the analog of an idea in such a connectionist network is a *node*, connection strengths are the analog of associations, and connectionist principles of learning primarily modify connection strengths. But in *distributed* connectionist networks the analog of ideas is a group or *vector* of nodes, and there are no connections or modifications of connection strengths between vectors – only connections between their constituent nodes. In other words, there are no unreduced vector-to-vector principles that could serve as the analog in these systems for idea-to-idea associations. Second, in generic associationism, ideas were *copies* of sensations and this was, as we saw, an important feature of the epistemology of associationism. However, since connections have weights not equal to 1, information is not *copied* between input and, say, hidden units.

12.5   Interpreting Connectionism: PTC

To begin with, we should note that there is no agreed-upon cognitive interpretation of connectionist formalism, nor of its philosophical implications. McLaughlin nicely summarizes the situation as follows: "While some maintain that connectionism may well show folk psychology to be false, others claim that connectionism may afford our best hope of vindicating folk psychology. While some hold that connectionism accords with a quasi-instrumentalistic approach to intentional ascriptions, others claim that it accords with a robust intentional realism. While some claim that connectionism allows us to jettison the view that cognitive processes are operations on syntactically structured mental representations, others claim that it offers our best hope for an account of cognitive operations on representations. While some claim that connectionism is congenial to unconscious processes of association, others hold that it lends support to the Cartesian idea that cognitive states are conscious, and holds promise of allowing cognitive science to eschew unconscious processes altogether" (1993: 164). This is not an encouraging list for anyone looking for consensus, and rather than pursue these various possibilities we will instead set out one comprehensive and coherent interpretation of connectionist formalism in psychological, neurological, and philosophical terms. Smolensky (1988a, 1989) offers a sketch of such an interpretation. He calls it the "proper treatment of connectionism" (PTC).

Levels of analysis

Human cognitive capacities can be analyzed at a minimum of three levels.

Conceptual

The first level is the "*conceptual*" (or "*symbolic*") level. At this level, cognitive structures are analyzed into familiar conceptual units, such as are captured by words or data structures we encountered in SHRDLU (see chapter 5): "put" "pyramid" "in" "box." Such symbol structures have traditional semantic interpretation and are operated on by symbol manipulation techniques in virtue of their form or shape.

Subconceptual

The second level is the *subconceptual* (or *subsymbolic*) level. This consists of entities that are the constituents of conceptual-level descriptions. *Subconcepts* (also called *microfeatures*) correspond to units (nodes) and *concepts* correspond to groups, patterns, or vectors of nodes. Since cognitive categories are realized in connectionist systems as patterns or vectors of activation, there are two sorts of constituency relations: there can be pattern–subpattern relations (subset), and there can be pattern–node relations (membership). The first is a concept–concept relation, the second is a concept–microfeature relation. These are both "part–whole" relations, but they are different, as illustrated in figure 12.2 (we ignore for now the question: what is the principled difference between a concept and a subconcept/microfeature?).

Neural

The third level is the *neural* level. This consists of the structure and operation of the nervous system as studied by neuroscience.

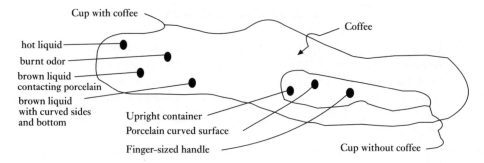

Figure 12.2   Two types of conceptual constituency in connectionist concepts

Knowledge and information processing style

There are two importantly different kinds of knowledge and information processing embedded in cognitive capacities.

Conscious rule application

The first kind of knowledge is conscious rule application.[2] Here explicit rules in some "linguistic" system (natural languages, programming languages, logical or mathematical notation) are applied to a concept-level task domain such as science or the law. Typically, such knowledge is the shared result of social and institutional practices, but this is not essential to its distinctive cognitive character. Such conscious rule application is typical of novice learners who might repeat to themselves such things as: turn, step, swing (tennis), or: "i" before "e" except after "c" (spelling).

Intuitive knowledge

The second kind of knowledge is intuitive knowledge – such as perception, (native) language understanding and skilled or practiced movement. Such knowledge is exercised in a distinctive fluid way and is not introspectively available (recall Fodor's "modules" or "input systems").

It is natural to see *conscious rule application* as cognitive capacities exercised at the *conceptual level*, and it is natural to see *intuitive processing* as cognitive capacities exercised at the *subconceptual level*. And we should see both these capacities as realized or instantiated at the *neural level*.

The level of connectionist models

We can now raise the question of where to situate connectionist models with respect to these two distinctions. Let's turn to the first distinction. According to Smolensky, the proper treatment of connectionism places connectionist *between* neurological models and traditional symbolic models – it involves subsymbolic modeling (the numbers in parentheses are Smolensky's 1988a originals):

(11)

> The fundamental level of the subsymbolic paradigm, the subconceptual level, lies between the neural and conceptual levels.

This level of analysis is more abstract than neurology (though it respects general features of neural architecture), but more faithful to the dynamics of cognition than traditional symbolic modeling, in the same way that quantum mechanics is more faithful to the dynamics of physical particles than classical mechanics; classical mechanics gives only an imprecise and approximate account of phenomena which quantum theory gives a precise and accurate account of. Let's look at these three levels in more detail.

Symbolic (conceptual) paradigm

The conceptual level, with its conscious rule interpreter, is the natural domain of the *symbolic paradigm*. This paradigm is concerned with "cultural" knowledge, such as science or the law, formulated in natural and scientific languages with explicit rules of inference applying to them. The theory of effective procedures, Turing machines, and programs for von Neumann computers provide models of how people process such knowledge, and execute such instructions:

(3)
(a)   Rules formulated in language can provide an effective formalization of cultural knowledge.
(b)   Conscious rule application can be modeled as the sequential interpretation of such rules by a virtual machine called the conscious rule interpreter.
(c)   These rules are formulated in terms of the concepts consciously used to describe the task domain – they are formulated at the conceptual level. (1988a: 4–5)

The symbolic paradigm holds that:

(4a,b)
(a)   The programs running on the intuitive processor consist of linguistically formalized rules that are sequentially interpreted.
(b)   The programs running on the intuitive processor are composed of elements, that is, symbols, referring to essentially the same concepts as the ones used to consciously conceptualize the task domain. (1988a: 5)

For instance, if we look at the examples from SHRDLU (see chapter 5) we see that data and instructions are formulated in commonsense terms such as PYRAMID and MOVE. These together comprise:

(4)
   The unconscious rule interpretation hypothesis: The programs running on the intuitive processor have a syntax and semantics comparable to those running on the conscious rule interpreter.   (1988a: 5)

The *computational style* of the symbolic paradigm is characterized by *discreetness* and *seriality*. On the symbolic paradigm there are:

(24)
(a)   Discrete memory locations, in which items are stored without mutual interaction.
(b)   Discrete memory storage and retrieval operations, in which an entire item is stored or retrieved in a single atomic (primitive) operation.
(c)   Discrete learning operations, in which new rules become available for use in an all-or-none fashion.
(d)   Discrete learning operations, in which conclusions become available for use in an all-or-none fashion.
(e)   Discrete categories, to which items either belong or do not belong.
(f)   Discrete production rules, with conditions that are either satisfied or not satisfied, actions that either execute or do not execute.

In the symbolic paradigm the above levels of cognition are analogized to levels of computer systems and, as with computer systems, it is not a part of the symbolic paradigm to say exactly how the symbolic level is implemented at the neural level (see figure 12.3). However, Smolensky rejects these claims for at least the following reasons:

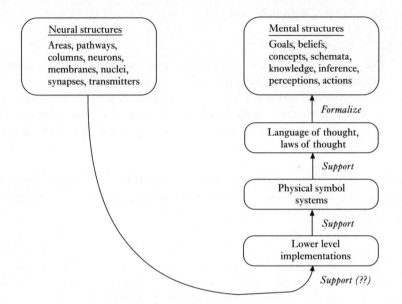

Figure 12.3 Neural and mental structures in the symbolic paradigm (from Haugeland, 1997: 235, figure 9.1; reproduced by permission of the MIT Press)

(5)

(a) Actual AI systems built on hypothesis (4) seem too brittle, too inflexible, to model true human expertise.

(b) The process of articulating expert knowledge in rules seems impractical for many important domains (e.g., common sense).

(c) Hypothesis (4) has contributed essentially no insight into how knowledge is represented in the brain.   (1988: 5)

Subsymbolic paradigm vs. symbolic paradigms

Smolensky's focus is on intuitive processes such as "perception, practiced motor behavior, fluent linguistic behavior . . . in short, practically all skilled performance." Connectionist models, construed on the subsymbolic paradigm, are precise and accurate descriptions of these processes, whereas symbolic models are not. This leads to Smolensky's alternative subsymbolic proposal:

(7)

The intuitive processor has a certain kind of connectionist architecture (which abstractly models a few of the most general features of neural networks).   (1988a: 6)

Smolensky elaborates the contrast. First, (4a) contrasts with:

(8a)

> *The connectionist dynamical system hypothesis*: The state of the intuitive processor at any moment is precisely defined by a vector of numerical values (one for each unit). The dynamics of the intuitive processor are governed by a differential equation. The numerical parameters in this equation constitute the processor's program or knowledge. In learning systems, these parameters change according to another differential equation.   (1988a: 6)

Second, (4b) contrasts with:

(8b)

> *The subconceptual unit hypothesis*: The entities in the intuitive processor with the semantics of conscious concepts of the task domain are complex patterns of activity over many units. Each unit participates in many such patterns.   (1988: 6)

Finally there is:

(8c)

> *The subconceptual level hypothesis*: Complete, formal and precise descriptions of the intuitive processor are generally tractable not at the conceptual level, but only at the subconceptual level.
>
> (1988a: 6–7)

These are summarized as (8), which is "the cornerstone of the subsymbolic paradigm"   (1988a: 7)

(8)

> *The subsymbolic hypothesis*: The intuitive processor is a subconceptual connectionist dynamical system that does not admit a complete, formal, and precise conceptual-level description.   (1988a: 7)

As Smolensky notes later (section 2.4), this feature precludes subconceptual models from implementing conceptual models – assuming that implementation carries with it the properties of being complete, formal and precise.

Finally, the computational style of the symbolic paradigm illustrated in (24) is contrasted with the *computational style* of the subsymbolic paradigm, which is *statistical* and *parallel*:

(25)

(a) Knowledge in subsymbolic computation is formalized as a large set of soft [statistical] constraints.

(b) Inference with soft constraints is a fundamentally parallel process.

(c) Inference with soft constraints is fundamentally non-monotonic.[3]

(d) Certain subsymbolic systems can be identified as using statistical inference.

In sum, in the *symbolic* paradigm, constraints are discrete and hard, inference is logical and serial. In the *subsymbolic* paradigm constraints are continuous and soft, inference is statistical and parallel.

Subsymbolic vs. neural

Smolensky rejects the idea that connectionist models are neural models:

(6)

> *The neural architecture hypothesis*: The intuitive processor for a particular task uses the same architecture that the brain uses for that task.
>
> (1988a: 5)

The reason for this is the loose correspondence between properties of the cerebral cortex and connectionist systems (see figure 12.4). Note that among the "negative" correspondences are some which are due to the model not being directly implemented in hardware, and others involve choices of features that could just as well have been made more neurologically faithful. There are further discrepancies Smolensky does not list, such as problems with negative weights, and problems with the biological machanisms of back-propagation. We return to this in chapter 13.

Relations between models and paradigms

According to PTC (proper treatment of connectionism), *brain* structure and functioning is (in principle of course) exactly characterized by the neural level of description. *Intuitive processing* is (again, in principle) exactly characterized by connectionist models at the subconceptual level of description – the level of nodes, vectors of nodes, and weighted connections. But what about *conscious rule application* and the *conceptual* level in general? Here matters are darker and more controversial. On the one hand, as we noted earlier, vectors of nodes are used to construct concepts such as CUP out of nodes with subconceptual interpretations. So it would seem that connectionist networks at a higher level of

Relations between the neural
and subsymbolic architectures

Cerebral cortex		Connectionist dynamical systems
State defined by continuous numerical variables (potentials, synaptic areas, . . .)	+	State defined by continuous numerical variables (activations, connection strengths)
State variables change continuously in time	+	State variables change continuously in time
Inter-neuron interaction parameters changeable; seat of knowledge	+	Inter-unit interaction parameters changeable; seat of knowledge
Huge number of state variables	+	Large number of state variables
High interactional complexity (highly non-homogeneous interactions)	+	High interactional complexity (highly non-homogeneous interactions)
Neurons located in 2 + 1 − d space	−	Units have no spatial location
have dense connectivity to nearby neurons;	−	uniformly dense
have geometrically mapped connectivity to distant neurons	−	connections
Synapses located in 3-d space;	−	Connections have no spatial location
locations strongly affect signal interactions		
Distal projections between areas have intricate topology	−	Distal projections between node pools have simple topology
Distal interactions mediated by discrete signals	−	All interactions non-discrete
Intricate signal integration at single neuron	−	Signal integration is linear
Numerous signal types	−	Single signal type

Figure 12.4 Neural vs. subsymbolic levels (from Smolensky, 1988a: 9, table 1; reproduced by permission of Cambridge University Press)

description (vectors of nodes) should give (in principle) an exact description of our concept-level cognition – our actual cognitive activity. On the other hand, we have the whole concept-level apparatus of natural language, mathematical notation, etc. Concept-level activity with these systems seems to be exactly described by the traditional symbolic representational schemes of AI (see chapter 7) running on traditional symbolic architectures such as vNMs or PSs. But something has to give; the two styles of modeling are not compatible. Traditional symbolic models conform to (24) (see above), while connectionist models conform to [25].

Hybrid theory

One popular suggestion is that perhaps a "hybrid theory" – one which used the symbolic paradigm for conscious rule application and the subsymbolic paradigm for intuitive processing – could be faithful to both. But as Smolensky (1988a, section 6) notes, the proposal has many problems. For instance: (1) how would the two theories communicate? (2) How would the hybrid system evolve with experience – from conscious rule application to intuition? (3) How would the hybrid system elucidate the fallibility of actual human rule application? (4) And how would the hybrid system get us closer to understanding how conscious rule application is achieved neurally?

PTC

In the light of these problems, and the failure of the symbolic paradigm to implement the subsymbolic paradigm, Smolensky opts for the opposite, and construes the subsymbolic as basic, and the symbolic as approximate and ultimately derivative. The PTC solution is to say that the higher level of description in terms of natural language or traditional "symbolic" representational schemes is only *approximate* – it only approximately describes our actual cognitive activity; in just the way that classical macro-physics only approximately describes what micro-physics exactly describes. This is illustrated in figure 12.5.

Approximate implementation

What is this relation of "approximation" exactly? We do not know for the general case, but Smolensky gives a particular example – of how a production system might be implemented (approximately) on connectionist systems capable of intuitively processing language. According to Smolensky (1988a, section 6) here is how it might go. First, language competence is intuitive

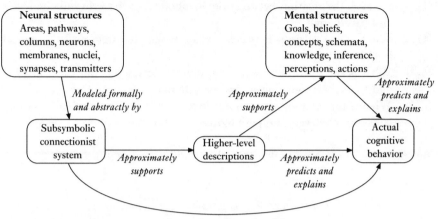

Figure 12.5 Neural and mental structures in the subsymbolic paradigm (from Haugeland, 1997: 237, figure 9.2; reproduced by permission of the MIT Press)

knowledge, so we assume that the connectionist system has linguistic competence. Then this competence can be used to encode linguistic expressions as patterns of activity. These can be stored in connectionist memories. Since some of these expressions can be rules, we can use these rules to solve problems sequentially. For example, we can store in the connectionist memory a set of productions of the form:

A (conditions) → B (action)

Then, given input A, connectionist pattern completion calls up the whole production. By operation of the production rule we get B, then as output the connectionist system executes B. Smolensky concludes:

(16)

> The competence to represent and process linguistic structures in a native language is a competence of the human intuitive processor; the subsymbolic paradigm assumes that this competence can be modeled in a subconceptual connectionist dynamical system. By combining such linguistic competence with the memory capabilities of connectionist systems, sequential rule interpretation can be implemented.   (1988a: 12)

There is certainly more to be said and more questions to be answered:

(Q1)   What is the relation between the symbolic and the subsymbolic levels and paradigms?

(Q2)   What is the relation between the symbolic paradigm and the neural level?

(Q3)   What is the relation between conscious rule application, the symbolic, and the subsymbolic levels and paradigms?

(Q4)   What is the relation between intuitive processing, the symbolic, and the subsymbolic levels and paradigms?

But pursuing these would take us further than we can presently go.

Consciousness, cognition, and content

The picture we have so far is of (ideal) connectionist models as exact models of conscious rule application at the connectionist conceptual level (vectors of nodes), and as exact models of intuitive processing at the connectionist subsymbolic level (nodes). But we do not yet have a general account of what makes a state of the network (or brain) a conscious state or even a cognitive state. And since cognitive states are representational, we also need an account of the nature (and acquisition) of representational states.

Consciousness

According to PTC, a necessary, but not a sufficient condition on consciousness is this:

(17)

> *Consciousness*:   The contents of consciousness reflect only the large-scale structure of activity patterns: subpatterns of activity that are extended over spatially large regions of the network and that are stable for relatively long periods of time.   (1988a: 17)

Of course this is pretty vague both spatially and temporally, and a necessary condition alone is not completely satisfactory. We want to know what properties make these large-scale, stable patterns into something conscious – remember the "hard problem" of consciousness (see chapter 9).

Cognition

Since subsymbolic principles are neither concept-level nor neural-level principles, in what sense do these models embody principles of *cognition* rather than just principles of neuroscience? What distinguishes those dynamical systems that are cognitive from those that are not? According to PTC:

(19)

> *A cognitive system*:   A necessary condition for a dynamical system to be cognitive is that, under a wide variety of environmental conditions, it maintains a large number of goal conditions. The greater the repertoire of goals and variety of tolerable environmental conditions, the greater the cognitive capacity of the system.   (1988a: 15)

Smolensky says that "only complexity" distinguishes a cognitive system from a thermostat or a river. This raises a number of important questions: What does (19), as only a necessary condition, tell us? Is having cognition a matter of degree – does the thermostat have a low level of cognition? Or is cognition either present or not, but the *amount* of cognition varies with the degree of complexity? And if we agree to call these systems "cognitive" what is the connection between the "cognitive" and the pre-theoretic notion of the "mental"?

The idea that cognition is related to goal satisfaction across a wide variety of environmental conditions goes back at least to Newell and Simon (1976) and their discussion of physical symbol systems (see also the Coda to this book). The difference is that Newell and Simon explicitly mention only "intelligence," not cognition: "we measure the intelligence of a system by its ability to achieve stated ends in the face of variations, difficulties, and complexities posed by the task environment." And as we noted in our discussion of the Turing test (chapter 9), ordinary usage inclines us to be more liberal in attributing "intelligence" to machines and more specifically their behavior, than "thoughtfulness" or "cognition."

The emergence of cognition

What is the relationship between the subsymbolic level and the neural level that creates or defines cognition in particular or mental states in general? At one point Smolensky tantalizingly remarks: "It is likely that connectionist models will offer the most significant progress of the past several millennia on the mind/body problem" (1988a: 3), but he does not elaborate on that idea. The view of the PDP (parallel distributed processing) group of connectionist researchers is that cognition (and perhaps mentality in general) emerges out of the interaction of neural elements, and although the new emergent level has distinct features that require some new concepts and vocabulary to describe, understanding this cognitive level involves understanding how it emerges: "We understand that new and useful concept emerges at different levels or organization. We are simply trying to understand the essence of cognition as a property emerging from the interaction of connected units in networks. We certainly believe in emergent phenomena in the sense of *phenomena which could never be understood or predicted by a study of the lower-level elements in isolation.* . . . The whole is different than the sum of its parts. There are nonlinear interactions among parts. This does not, however, suggest that the nature of the lower-level elements is irrelevant to the higher level of organization – on the contrary *the higher level is, we believe, to be understood primarily through the study of the interactions among lower-level units*" (Rumelhart and McClelland, 1986a: 128; emphasis added). Of course, the claim that cognition emerges from lower-level interactions does not tell us exactly what this "emergent" relationship is. In what sense are these new, higher-level, emergent phenomena not understandable or predicable from lower-level facts alone, yet they are to be understood primarily in terms of these lower-level phenomena? And how does "emergence" compare to other proposals as to the relationship between mind and body, such as identity or supervenience? These are all questions that need further work.

Content

How do states of a subsymbolic system get their content: their meanings and truth conditions? According to PTC:

(22)

> *Subsymbolic semantics*:   A cognitive system adopts various internal states in various environmental conditions. To the extent that the cognitive system meets its goal conditions in various environmental conditions, its internal states are *veridical representations* of the corresponding environmental states, with respect to the given goal conditions.
>
> (1988a: 15)

The fact that a subsymbolic system can generate veridical representations of the environment is a result of extracting information from the environment and internally coding it in its weights through a learning procedure.

SCDS and content

Where do concept-level cognitive structures get their semantic interpretations, and how are they organized in connectionist systems? As we have seen, in some systems such as Jets and Sharks and NETtalk (see chapter 10), the semantics is just assigned by the network's designer, usually to the input and output layers, and then through training, the hidden layers (if it has them) may form some semantically interpretable patterns. On analogy with our earlier discussion of what the frog's eye tells the frog's brain, we can formulate a Simple Connectionist Detector Semantics:

(SCDS)

Units, and sets of units, represent what activates them (or activates them sufficiently).

If we imagine evolution to be a kind of "programmer assignment" of meaning, we can think of the sensory and motor nodes as having genetically determined representational potential (semantics), and innate connection strengths can be seen as reflecting genetic dispositions to respond to recurring environmental configurations. On this view the system picks up and codes certain statistical regularities in the environment, forms categories from these regularities, and then uses these categories to act more or less successfully on the world. With additional experience, the system tunes its connections to adapt to new circumstances and to be more accurate in its interactions with familiar ones. Clark (1993: 190) characterizes connectionist machines as ones whose "basic mode of operation involves: some kind of statistically driven learning, the development of distributed representations, superpositional storage techniques and context sensitive representation and retrieval." Smolensky's PTC exemplifies these characteristics.

12.6   Taxonomizing Architectures (II)

Earlier we taxonomized computational architectures along the dimensions of *memory* and *control* (see our earlier discussion in chapter 6 for an explanation of terms relating to those dimensions). We have now seen that computational models can be contrasted also on the basis of *representations*. A representation is *(fully) distributed* if (1) more than one element (flip-flop, node, etc.) encodes it, and (2) that element encodes other representations. A representation is *quasi-distributed* if it satisfies just condition (1) above; that is, more than one element encodes it, but not the second. A representation is *local* if just one element encodes it. A representation is *semantically effectual* if the transition principles of the machine are defined over states that receive semantic interpretation, it is *not semantically effectual* otherwise. As Smolensky puts it: "Perhaps the fundamental contrast between the paradigms pertains to semantic interpretation of the formal models. In the symbolic approach, symbols (atoms) are used to denote the semantically interpretable entities (concepts); these same symbols are the objects governed by symbol manipulations in the

	Control	Memory	Representation
TM	Localized	Indirect	– Quasi-distributed – Semantically effectual
VNM	Localized	– Direct – Form-addressable	– Quasi-distributed – Semantically effectual
PS	Distributed	– Direct – Content-addressable	– Quasi-distributed – Semantically effectual
Pandemonium	Distributed	– Direct – Content-addressable	– Local (?) – Semantically effectual
Connectionist	Distributed	– Direct – Content-addressable	– Distributed – Not semantically effectual

Figure 12.6   A taxonomy of architectures

rules that define the system. The entities that are semantically interpretable are *also* the entities governed by the formal laws that define the system. In the subsymbolic paradigm, this is no longer true. The semantically interpretable entities are *patterns of activation* over large numbers of units in the system, whereas the entities manipulated by formal rules are the individual activations of cells in the network. The rules take the form of activation-passing rules, which are essentially different in character from symbol-manipulation rules" (1989: 54). As we have already noted, in a (distributed) connectionist system, concept-level interpretation is assigned at the level of patterns or vectors of activation, whereas the transition principles are stated at the node and connection levels (activation-passing rules, connection weights). But in traditional digital machines, the level of conceptual interpretation and the level of transition to the next state are the same – the program level. SHRDLU, for instance, puts a pyramid in the box because it executes the command: PUT(IN(BOX, PYRAMID)). Here we see the object of semantic interpretation (think of BOX, PYRAMID, PUT) causing the machine to carry out the action and move into the next program state. Adding this dimension gives us an expanded taxonomy that includes connectionist architectures (see figure 12.6).

These assignments are rough, but there seems to be something to the idea that going from TMs to connectionist machines involves a fragmentation of control, memory, and representation. As we move from left to right in the figure, global properties emerge from the interaction of local elements (more democracy, less autocracy), and other important properties such as fault tolerance and graceful degradation can be seen to piggyback on lower-level features – especially distributed control and representation. As Dennett puts it, in a slightly different context: "Notice what has happened in the progression from the von Neumann architecture to such . . . architectures as production systems and (at a finer grain level) connectionist systems. There has been what might be called a shift in the balance of power. Fixed, pre-designed programs, running along railroad tracks with a few branch points depending on the data, have been replaced by flexible – indeed volatile – systems whose subsequent behavior is much more a function of complex inter-actions between what the system is currently encountering and what it has encountered in the past" (1991: 269). We will return to these features in the next chapter.

Appendix
Connectionism and Turing's Unorganized Machines

Alan Turing's work (ca. 1948), published posthumously in 1969, on what he called *unorganized machines* – "machines which are largely random in their con-struction" – is only beginning to become widely known (see Copeland and Proudfoot, 1996). Turing had three types of such machines, what he called "A-type," "B-type," and "P-type." The technical details of, and differences between, these types of machine need not concern us here. What is of inter-est is their general character and the role Turing envisaged them playing in the future study of intelligence.

A-type unorganized machines

These were characterized by Turing using figure 12.7. In this simple machine there are five units, connected to just two other units, as indicated in the table on the left and the diagram on the right. Each unit is either *on* or *off*. The activation-passing rule is this: multiply the inputs and subtract from 1, i.e. the new value = (input 1 × input 2) − 1. There is a central clock which synchro-nizes all activation-passing. The result of giving each unit a 0 or a 1 is shown in the bottom chart. For instance, on the first condition, unit 1 = 1, because its input units (#2, #3) have the values: #2 = 1, #3 = 0. Applying the activation-

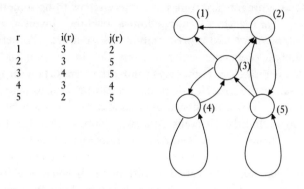

r	i(r)	j(r)
1	3	2
2	3	5
3	4	5
4	3	4
5	2	5

A sequence of five possible consecutive conditions for the whole machine is:

1	1	1	0	0	1	0
2	1	1	1	0	1	0
3	0	1	1	1	1	1
4	0	1	0	1	0	1
5	1	0	1	0	1	0

Figure 12.7   A-type unorganized machine (from Turing, 1948/69: 10; Ince, 1992: 114)

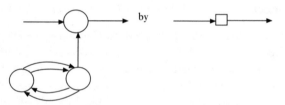

Figure 12.8   B-type circuit (from Turing, 1948/69: 11; Ince, 1992: 115)

passing rule we get: $1 \times 0 = 0$, $1 - 0 = 1$. So unit 1 should get the value 1, which it does. Regarding A-type machines and the brain Turing commented: "A-type unorganized machines are of interest as being about the simplest model of a nervous system with a random arrangements of neurons" (1948/69: 8; Ince, 1992: 120). Here we see Turing clearly envisioning these as potential abstract neural models.

B-type unorganized machines

These were simply A-type machines where each connection, each arrowed line in the diagram, is replaced with the circuit shown in figure 12.8. The result of

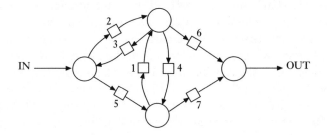

Figure 12.9   Schematic B-type machine (from Turing, 1948/69: 15; Ince, 1992: 119)

replacing all A-type connections with B-type connections results in a B-type machine, as in Turing's illustration (see figure 12.9).

Regarding B-type machines and the brain Turing commented: "This is a particular case of a very general property of B-type machines . . . viz. that with suitable initial conditions they will do any required job, given sufficient time and provided the number of units is sufficient. In particular, for a B-type unorganized machine with sufficient units one can find initial conditions which will make it into a universal machine with a given storage capacity" (1948/69: 9; Ince, 1992: 119). Here we have the idea that the brain might start out with a random set of connections and then with suitable training it might evolve into a universal Turing machine, which we have seen as a candidate for cognitive architecture. Sadly, he did not even sketch how he foresaw such a development unfolding.

P-type machines

P-type machines were the basis for Turing's experiments on learning. Turing clearly thought that human learning was in part based on pleasure and punishment (hence "P-type systems"):[4] "The training of the human child depends largely on a system of rewards and punishments, and this suggests that it ought to be possible to carry through the organizing with only two interfering inputs, one for 'pleasure' . . . and the other for 'pain' or "punishment." One can devise a large number of 'pleasure-pain' systems" (1948/69: 17; Ince, 1992: 121).

The general character of such "P-type" systems is as follows: "The P-type machine may be regarded as an LCM [logical computing machine, i.e. Turing machine] without a tape, and whose description is largely incomplete. When a configuration is reached, for which the action is undetermined, a random choice for the missing data is made and the appropriate entry is made in the description, tentatively, and is applied. When a pain stimulus occurs all tentative entries are canceled, and when a pleasure stimulus occurs they are all made permanent" (1948/69: 10; Ince, 1992: 122). So the machine is configured by allowing pain to erase a tentative configuration and pleasure to keep (reinforce?) it. Turing also anticipated recent simulations of connectionist machines on digital machines: "When some electronic machines are in actual operation I hope that they will make this [testing various training procedures' "methods of education"] more feasible. It should be easy to make a model of any particular machine that one wishes to work on within such a UPCM [Turing's acronym for a universal practical computing machine – today's digital computer] instead of having to work with a paper machine as at present. If also one decided on quite definite "teaching policies" these could also be programmed into the machine. One would then allow the whole system to run for an appreciable period, then break in as a kind of "inspector of schools" and see what progress has been made. One might also be able to make some progress with unorganized machines more like the A-type and B-types. The work involved with these is altogether too great for pure paper-machine work" (1948/69: 11; Ince, 1992: 125). Again, we can appreciate how far ahead of his time Turing was, and we have to acknowledge him as the inventor of the Turing machine, an important developer of the modern register machine, and an anticipator of connectionist machines and their training.

Notes

1   Thagard (1986), and Smolensky (1988a), thesis (1i), propose that connectionism might offer a new perspective on the mind–body problem. But since connectionist machines abstract from substance (they could be realized in neurons or silicon), it is difficult to see how connectionism per se could offer any help on the mind–body problem.
2   Or, as Smolensky often terms it, conscious rule "interpretation." This is standard in computer science, but outside it gives the impression that "interpreting" the rule is like "interpreting" the law.
3   "Monotonic" means *constantly increasing*. Traditional deductive inferences are monotonic because the set of conclusions drawn from given premises always grows, never shrinks. But in non-monotonic reasoning, conclusions can be *subtracted*, given additional evidence.
4   Let's not forget that 1948 was during the heyday of behaviorism, and his paper of 1950 introduced the "Turing Test," with its clearly behaviorist leanings.

Study questions

Motivations for the CCTM

What are some motivations from human performance?

What are some motivations from the brain?

A bit of history: connectionism and associationism

What are some similarities between associationist networks and connectionist networks?

What are some differences?

Is associationism a special case of connectionism?

Interpreting connectionism: PTC

What three levels at which the mind-brain can be described does Smolensky distinguish?

How might we represent "cup with coffee" in a connectionist model?

What two sorts of constituents do connectionist representations have?

What two kinds of cognitive capacities ("knowledge") does Smolensky distinguish?

What theses constitute the "proper treatment of connectionism" (PTC)?

How does PTC conceive of the relation between the subconceptual and the neural levels?

How does PTC conceive of the relation between the subconceptual and the conceptual levels (for both conscious rule application and intuitive processing)?

What is one necessary condition on a system for it to be cognitive?

What is one necessary condition on a pattern of activity for it to be a conscious state?

In what two ways might a connectionist network get its semantics – its representational capacities?

What would a detector semantics for a connectionist network look like?

Taxonomizing architectures (II)

What are the main dimensions along which we have taxonomized architectures?

What is the distinction between being semantically effectual (SE) and being semantically ineffectual (SI)?

How exactly does the difference between being SE and SI distinguish digital from connectionist machines?

In what sense is there a spectrum along which we can place computers from Turing machines to connectionist machines?

Suggested reading

Motivation for the CCTM

The classical advertisement of connectionism is Rumelhart and McClelland (1986a), volume 1, Part I.

A bit of history: connectionism and associationism

See Valentine (1989) and Walker (1990) for survey discussions of the history of connectionism in relation to earlier developments in psychology. In addition to Bechtel (1985), scattered discussions of associationism and connectionism can be found in Rumelhart and McClelland (1986a), and in Ramsey (1992).

Interpreting connectionism

The central statement of PTC is to be found in Smolensky (1988a). A shorter presentation can be found in Smolensky (1989). For further elaboration of PTC see the commentaries to the original publication in Smolensky (1988a), as well as Smolensky's extensive replies in the same issue, Rosenberg (1990a, b), Mills (1990), and van Gelder (1992). Clark (1993) is a book-length review of the strengths and weakness of connectionist models.

Consciousness, cognition, and content

For a survey of issues surrounding emergence see Beckermann et al. (1992). For more discussion of cognition as adaptability to the environment see Copeland (1993b), chapter 3, especially 3.6. See Ramsey (1992) for more on SCDS.

Taxonomizing architectures

See van Gelder (1997), section 5, for a more general taxonomy, one that is different from ours.

Turing's unorganized machines

See also Copeland (1998), and Copeland and Proudfoot (1999).

13

Criticisms of the Connectionist Computational Theory of Mind

13.1 Introduction

Sometimes what seems to be enough smoke to guarantee a robust fire is actually just a cloud of dust from a passing bandwagon.

(Dennett, 1991: 257)

In this chapter we review a number of issues that pose prima facie problems for the CCTM, as well as some connectionist responses. These should be taken as provisional, since connectionism is still a young theory, with much potential for development.

13.2 Differences: The CCTM and the Brain

It was obvious from the beginning of connectionism that CCTM models were indirectly related to real brains (see again our discussion of Smolensky's PTC in chapter 12). Still, it might be useful to note some further differences, if only of emphasis and selection, that might help guide us in making inferences from CCTM models to brains.

Neurons and units

Crick and Asanuma (1986: 367–71), for instance, note the gross similarity between some connectionist units and neurons: "they have multiple inputs, some sort of summation rule, a threshold rule, and a single output which is usually distributed to several other units." But they add as a note of caution:

"If the properties of real neurons present useful gadgets to neural modelers, they should not be mixed together in combinations that never occur together." One common proposal is that it is *groups* of (real) neurons that correspond to a unit, but they note, "this might be acceptable to neuroscientists if it were carefully stated how this group might be built out of more or less real neurons, but this is seldom if ever done." They go on to claim that brains do not always behave like connectionist models by listing a number of "devices loved by [CCTM] theorists which, if interpreted literally, are not justified by the available experimental evidence":

1   units that excite some units and inhibit others;
2   units that accept excitation from one unit only and whose output produces inhibition in one unit only;
3   units that connect to all other units of the same type;
4   units that can, by themselves, fire other units.

We should also recall (see chapter 9) the wide variety of types of neurons found in the brain, whereas typically a given CCTM model contains only one type, and add this to the above list:

5   CCTM models usually contain one sort of unit, whereas brains contain main sorts of neurons.

Chemistry

1   We noted at the end of chapter 3 that brains use neurotransmitters and neuromodulators which "allow cells to change their function enabling a neural network to switch its overall mode of activity dramatically" (Arbib, 1995: 6). CCTM models do not use any analog of these.

Geometry

1   As we saw (chapters 10, 11) many connectionist models come with distinct functionally defined layers (as many as you like). But brains seem to have a much more complicated physical geometry of layers, connections, and projections which probably serve computational roles not duplicated in existing models. For instance, there is the vertical

columnar organization of the cortex, with extensive connections within a single layer.
2   And we should not forget (see chapters 3, 8) the areas of the brain which appear at least partially dedicated to certain kinds of computations, such as Broca's and Wernicke's areas.

Learning

1   The brain doesn't seem to need so much repetition or supervision.
2   There don't seem to be biological mechanisms for, say, back-propagation, which in CCTM models is performed by the host computer.

Scale

There are also, of course, differences of scale, and although these are in principle surmountable, the differences are staggering. For instance, Churchland estimates that there are 10^{11} nonsensory neurons in the brain, and each neuron makes an average 10^3 synaptic connections (1989, chapter 9).

Activation vectors: Supposing there are about one thousand brain subsystems, that gives each subsystem 10^8 dimensions (units) to work with – one vector of 10^8 units can code an entire book. How many vectors can be constructed from 10^8 units? If each unit can take on (a modest estimate) 10 different values, then there are $10^{100,000,000}$ distinct activation vectors to work with. To appreciate this number, Stephen Hawking (1988) estimates that "there are something like $[10^{80}]$ particles in the region of the universe we can detect." And remember, this was the number of activation vectors for only *one* of the *thousand* postulated subsystems.

Weights and connections: If each neuron averages 10^3 connections, then each subsystem contains 10^{11} connections, and each of these can have any one of the $10^{10,000,000,000}$ vector interpretations.

This means that the brain commands enormous potential for making many fine distinctions in representational content. It should be noted that one could of course *design* a network for the purpose of mimicking the brain, but it is more interesting if such a design is the byproduct of trying to get the cognition right because that would suggest that brain architecture is not accidentally related to cognitive architecture.

13.3   CCTM: The Lures of Connectionism

Fodor and Pylyshyn (1988) (hereafter FP) cite about a dozen popular reasons for favoring connectionist (CCTM) architectures over what they call "classical" architectures or "conventional models" (DCTM), most of which we have just surveyed (1988: 51–4):

Eleven lures
1   Rapidity of cognitive processes in relation to neural speeds: the "hundred step" constraint.
2   Difficulty of achieving large-capacity pattern recognition and content-based retrieval in conventional architectures.
3   Conventional computer models are committed to a different etiology for "rule-governed" behavior and "exceptional" behavior.
4   DCTM's lack of progress in dealing with processes that are nonverbal or intuitive.
5   Acute sensitivity of conventional architectures to damage and noise.
6   Storage in conventional architectures is passive.
7   Conventional rule-based systems depict cognition as "all-or-none."
8   Continuous variation in degree of applicability of different principles in CCTM models.
9   Nondeterminism of human behavior is better modeled by CCTM.
10   Conventional models fail to display graceful degradation.
11   Conventional models are dictated by current technical features of computers and take little or no account of the facts of neuroscience.

Fodor and Pylyshyn want to show that these usual reasons given for preferring connectionism are invalid, and that they all suffer from one or other of the following defects:

Fodor's fork
1   These reasons are directed at properties *not essential* to classical cognitive architectures, or
2   these reasons are directed at the *implementation* or neural level, not the cognitive level.

The lures: five groups

FP group the usual reasons for favoring connectionist architectures under five categories, and they reply to each category in turn.

1. Parallel computation and the issue of speed (implementation)

There are two targets embedded in this section. The *first* target of objection is the "100-step" rule of Feldman and Ballard (1982). As Feldman (1989: 1) formulates the rule: "The human brain is an information processing system, but one that is quite different from conventional computers. The basic computing elements operate in the millisecond range and are about a million times slower than current electronic devices. Since reaction times for a wide range of tasks are a few hundred milliseconds, the system must solve hard recognition problems in about a hundred computational steps. The same time constraints suggest that only simple signals can be sent from one neuron to another." FP read the 100-step rule as something like the following argument in enthymatic form:

(P1)   Neurons fire in a few milliseconds.
(P2)   Relevant cognitive tasks take place in hundreds of milliseconds.

(C)   So, algorithmic analyses of these tasks should contain only hundreds of steps.

FP's reply to this argument is: "In the form that it takes in typical Connectionist discussions, this issue is irrelevant to the adequacy of Classical *cognitive* architecture. The '100 step constraint,' for example, is clearly directed at the implementation level. All it rules out is the (absurd) hypothesis that cognitive architectures are implemented in the brain in the same way as they are implemented on electronic computers" (1988: 54–5). But a CCTM partisan could say that if hardware is the mechanism of causation and if the hardware is constrained to operate in a few milliseconds, then the physical states that realize mental states can succeed each other at no *faster* rate than the sequence of realized computational states allows. The proprietary physical description of the nervous system has it firing in tens of milliseconds, so the relevant neural states cannot causally succeed each other at a faster rate. Thus, the instantiations of computations cannot succeed each other at a faster rate either. So computations are limited to 100 serial steps. Claiming that this is "implementation" does not change this fact.

The *second* issue involves the conclusion that "an argument for a network of parallel computers is not in and of itself either an argument against a classical architecture or an argument for a connectionist architecture" (1988: 56). This is because: "Although most algorithms that run on the VAX are serial, at the implementation level such computers are 'massively parallel'; they quite literally involve simultaneous electrical activity throughout almost the entire device" (1988: 55). "Classical architecture in no way excludes parallel execution of multiple symbolic processes . . . see . . . Hillis (1985)" (1988: 55–6). But a CCTM partisan could make two responses. *First*, the sense in which a VAX is "massively parallel" is not the same as the sense in which a connectionist machine is; the electrical activity spreading through a VAX is not like the spread of activation in a connectionist network in that it does not contribute directly to defining the entities that get semantic interpretation. *Second*, the messages being passed by Hillis' Connection machine are much more complex than connectionist machines, which usually pass degrees of activation between 0 and 1.

2. *Resistance to noise and physical damage (implementation)*

FP begin by noting: "Distribution over units achieves damage-resistance only if it entails that representations are also neurally distributed. However, neural distribution of representations is just as compatible with Classical architectures as it is with Connectionist networks. In the Classical case all you need are memory registers that distribute their contents over physical space" (1988: 52). There are two important differences between the damage resistance of connectionist and classical models. *First*, recall that distributed representations have two critical properties, and the classical analog only realizes the first of them:

(DIST)
(i)   R is a distributed representation if and only if
       R is instantiated in many units,
(ii) each unit that instantiates R instantiates numerous other representations
       at the same time.

Second, the way classical architectures get damage resistance is by redundancy – by storing multiple replicas throughout the machine. But a connectionist architecture does not get its resistance to noise and damage by scattering replicas around the network. To see the difference note that *each* scattered replica in a classical model can be knocked out by knocking out a single bit in each one, leaving all the other memories of the system intact. But in a connectionist model, because of (DIST ii) above, zapping units that store one piece of information will also zap units that participate in storing other pieces of information.

3. *"Soft" constraints, continuous magnitudes, stochastic mechanisms, and active symbols (not essential?)*

FP begin by noting that "One can have a Classical rule system in which the decision concerning which rule will fire resides in the functional architecture and depends on continuously varying magnitudes. Indeed, this is typically how it is done in practical 'expert systems' which, for example, use a Bayesian mechanism in their production-system rule interpreter. The soft or stochastic nature of rule-based processes arises from the interaction of deterministic rules with real-valued properties of the implementation, or with noisy inputs or noisy information transmission" (1988: 54). One glaring difference between these and connectionist systems is that these systems read and follow Bayesian probability equations. But reading and following Bayesian probability equations does not make the system "depend on a continuously varying magnitude" in the same way as connectionist systems, which use continuously varying activation values and weights. FP also suggest that the current problems classical psychological models have "with graceful degradation may be a special case of their general unintelligence: they may simply not be smart enough to know what to do when a limited stock of methods fails to apply" (1988: 54). But this does not seem to be the *way* connectionist networks handle defective input; these systems also get spontaneous completion and generalization as automatic consequences of the same architectural features that cause them to gracefully degrade.

4. *Explicitness of rules (not essential)* ·

FP comment here: "You *can* attack Connectionist architectures by showing that a cognitive process is rule *ex*plicit since, by definition, connectionist architecture precludes the sorts of logico-syntactic capacities that are required to encode rules and the sorts of executive mechanisms that are required to apply them" (1988: 57). It is not clear why connectionist models are "by definition" incompatible with explicit rules. Smolensky (1988, section 6) suggests a way in which a connectionist network might emulate a production system.

5. *On "brain-style" modeling (implementation)*

FP's next point is: "There is reason to be skeptical about whether the sorts of properties listed above [biological facts about neurons and neural activities] are reflected in any more-or-less direct way in the structure of the system that carries out reasoning. . . . The point is that the structure of 'higher levels' of a system are rarely isomorphic, or even similar, to the structure of 'lower levels' of a system . . . assumptions about the structure of the brain have been adopted in an all-too-direct manner as hypotheses about cognitive architecture" (1988: 58–60). It is not clear what the force of these observations is supposed to be. The main point of "brain-style" modeling is simply that *other things being equal* we should prefer a theory that is closer to one we can implement in neurons than one we cannot.

FP conclude their paper by saying that "many of the arguments for connectionism are best construed as claiming that cognitive architecture is *implemented* in a certain kind of network (of abstract 'units'). Understood this way, these arguments are neutral on the question of what the cognitive architecture is" (1988: 60–1).

General comments: the five groups

Notice that we get classical architectures to exhibit properties 1–5 by *complicating* these models – they do not emerge naturally from the intrinsic architecture. Furthermore, it would seem that not all the original eleven lures get covered by the replies (in particular 2, 4, 6), and these are all related to the parallel distributive character of connectionist architecture. Finally, there seem to be lures that are not listed, such as spontaneous generalization, prototype extraction, recovering from lesions, facilitated relearning, and human-like learning. The issue of a CCTM advantage in learning is taken up in McLaughlin and Warfield (1994). After surveying a number of studies of DCTM style learning, as well as comparisons to back-propagation with respect to speed and accuracy, they conclude that: "There is currently no justification whatsoever for the claim that connectionist architecture is better suited than classical architecture is to modeling pattern recognition capacities and the acquisition of such capacities by learning" (1994: 392).

General comments: implementation

The FP strategy of countering lures 1, 3, 5, 7–11 with the second branch of Fodor's fork (let's call these the "I-lures") could backfire. The reason is that according to FP, disputes about cognitive architecture are disputes about processes at the representational level – at the level of representational states of the organism (which encode states of the world). Psychological explanation deals with representational states. When we look at the I-lures we find a list of prima facie good-making *psychological* properties which FP are going to account for at the *implementational* level, not at the level of cognitive architecture, that is, not as a part of their cognitive theory. So we can offer Fodor and Pylyshyn an alternative to "Fodor's fork," namely:

The Classical Choice
Either it must be shown that these properties are not really cognitive (this requires argument), or they are cognitive but do not receive cognitive (algorithmic and representational) explanations.

It is possible to choose either, but neither seems attractive and connectionism is not forced to make this choice, since it allows the phenomena to be cognitive and to receive a cognitive explanation. And finally, let's not forget what an achievement a theory of "only implementation" would be for connectionism, and how badly classical theories need one. Classical theories without an account of implementation are cognitive theories with no conception of how they could be realized in, and so be true of, brains – our brains. This is like a biological theory of life with no conception of how it could be true of organisms. An implementation theory is not a luxury to classicism – without it classicism is a theory of computers and angels, not humans and related organisms. Or look at it another way: if some authors are right that classicism is like traditional chemistry, and connectionism implements classicism, then as McLaughlin aptly puts it: "if connectionism implements classicism, connectionism gets to be quantum mechanics and classicism only gets to be chemistry. If there were a Nobel Prize in psychology, an account of how a connectionist network in the brain implements a classical cognitive architecture would surely win it" (1993: 184).

13.4   CCTM and the Chinese Gym

Like the Chinese room, Searle's (1991) Chinese gym is supposed to be a counterexample to the proposal that the difference between standard digital computational theory of mind and connectionist models makes a difference to the force of the Chinese room argument: "The parallel 'brainlike' character of the processing, however, is irrelevant to the purely computational aspect of the process" (1990: 28): There are really two separate arguments here, one having to do with extending the Chinese room argument to the Chinese gym, and one having to do with the computational power of parallel and serial machines.

The Chinese gym argument

Searle (1980) had argued that the Chinese room shows that computation is not constitutive of, nor sufficient for, cognition, mind, intentionality, etc. So if the brainlike character of connectionist models is irrelevant to their computational properties, then connectionist programs (as well as digital programs) are not constitutive of, nor sufficient for, cognition, mind, intentionality, etc. As Searle put it: "Imagine I have a Chinese gym: a hall containing many monolingual English speaking men. These men would carry out the same operations as the nodes and synapses in connectionist architectures . . . no one in the gym speaks a word of Chinese, and there is no way for the system as a whole to learn the meanings of any Chinese words. Yet with the appropriate adjustments, the system could give the correct answers to Chinese questions" (1990b: 28). "You can't get semantically loaded thought contents from formal computations alone, whether they are done in serial or in parallel; that is why the Chinese room argument refutes strong AI in any form" (1990b: 28). Searle does not actually describe the simulation in the Chinese gym in the way that he describes the simulation in the Chinese room. Nodes are people, but what are the activation levels, activation–passing rules, connections, connection strengths, what is vector multiplication, and how is input converted into output? It is not clear what in the gym would correspond to these features of connectionist models, and since these are crucial, the analogy is extremely weak, unlike the situation with the Chinese room and digital machines.

But let's suppose we have a plausible model of a connectionist machine. What is the argument? Perhaps this:

(1)   The Chinese gym models a connectionist machine.
(2)   The Chinese gym does not speak/understand Chinese.

(3)   So, the connectionist machine does not speak/understand Chinese.

This argument would seem to have the form:

(1)   M models P.
(2)   M doesn't have property F.

(3)   So, P doesn't have property F.

But as Searle himself has often insisted, arguments of this form are invalid – consider:

(1)   M models P (lactation).

(2)   M doesn't have property F (it does not produce milk).

(3)   *So, P doesn't have property F (it does not produce milk).

Hence, Searle can't *conclude* that because the Chinese gym doesn't speak/understand Chinese, the connectionist model doesn't speak/understand Chinese.

The "serial–parallel" arguments

Searle seems to present two considerations (arguments?) on behalf of the conclusion that "parallel processing does not afford a way around the Chinese room argument" (1990b: 28).

(A)   *Connectionist programs run on serial machines*:   ". . . because parallel machines are rare, connectionist programs are usually run on traditional serial machines. Parallel processing, then, does not afford a way around the Chinese room argument" (1990b: 28).

(B)   *The (weak) equivalence of serial and parallel machines*:   "Computationally, serial and parallel systems are equivalent: any computation that can be done in parallel can be done in serial. If the man in the Chinese room is computationally equivalent to both, then if he does not understand Chinese solely by virtue of doing the computations, neither do they" (1990b: 28).

These two arguments appear to have the form:

(A)   Connectionist programs are usually run on traditional serial machines.

(C)   So, the Chinese room argument extends to parallel connectionist machines.

(B)   Any function that can be computed on a parallel machine can also be computed on a serial machine.

(C)   So, the Chinese room argument extends to parallel connectionist machines.

Suppose (A) and (B) were true without qualification – what would the arguments show about (C)? Nothing, because strong AI was the claim that an "appropriately programmed computer" has cognition, and all (A) and (B) show at most is the weak equivalence of a serial and a parallel machine. But machines running different programs can compute the same functions. So the argument would not establish its conclusion even if the assumptions were true without qualification. But they are not true without qualification.

Regarding (A)   There are at least three layers in play in connectionist modeling:[1]
Level 1:   Discrete, serial approximations of continuous, parallel models (run on digital, serial computers – as with Jets and Sharks).

These approximate:

Level 2:   Continuous, parallel models of continuous, parallel phenomena.

These exactly model:

Level 3:   Continuous, parallel phenomena themselves.

Some connectionist models are discrete and these can be simulated by being run on a serial digital machine, but most are continuous, and what run on a serial digital machine are discrete approximations of them (see Jets and Sharks again, chapter 10). Connectionists assume that important psychological properties (such as how and what the network learns) of the original continuous model will be preserved by the digital approximation. The important point is that psychologically relevant properties of connectionist models being simulated on serial digital machines are properties at the level of the virtual connectionist model, not properties of the underlying serial digital machine. One cannot infer from properties of the one to properties of the other – as far as the model is concerned, there is nothing lower.

Regarding (B)   What Searle seems to have in mind here is the computational equivalence of a collection of Turing machines running in parallel and a single (serial) Turing machine. It has been proven that for any computation that can be carried out by TMs running in parallel there is a single TM that can carry out that computation. But connectionist machines are not TMs running in parallel, so nothing follows from this.

Conclusion

Searle's discussion treats connectionism as if it is just another style of strong AI, another "implementation" of programs that won't do the job anyway. But two things should be kept in mind. *First*, many connectionists (see Smolenksy, 1988a; Rumelhart, 1989) do not view connectionism as a theory of implementation of standard programs. So if cognitive architecture matters to cognition, connectionist cognitive architecture might make a difference. *Second*, connectionists rarely propose to *duplicate* cognition by *simulating* or *modeling* it. Although connectionists such as Smolensky (1988a) claim that their models are more abstract than neurons, and so the *models* might be realizable in other material, they are free to agree with Searle that only certain kinds of stuff will duplicate cognition. This is an important difference between classical and connectionist theories: connectionists model cognitive activity as abstracted from the details of neural activity, and it is natural for them to insist that real brains (or their equivalent) are necessary for there to be cognitive activity. It is less natural for classical theorists to take this stand because their theories are no more related to real neural structures than a microwave oven. It might be objected that this is equivalent to denying that connectionists need believe in strong AI, and so Searle's argument against it would be irrelevant to them. Quite so, but it points to an alternative position between Searle's and strong AI, that substance + program = cognition, or more figuratively, the substance provides the 'stuff' of cognition and the program provides the 'form' – shaping it into various thought structures.

13.5 CCTM and Propositional Attitudes

So far, in our discussion of the CTM (that includes both the DCTM and the CCTM) we have been assuming a number of theses:

(R) There really are the so-called propositional attitudes (**R**ealism with respect to the attitudes).

(C) Central features of the attitudes are given to us in our commonsense folk psychology.

(N) The (scientific) Nature of the attitudes will be given to us by cognitive science.

On this plausible picture, commonsense folk psychology is used to identify the attitudes as a subject matter for cognitive science, and cognitive science then goes on to give us a refined, scientific account of their nature (think of how common sense picks out water as that clear tasteless liquid, etc., so that science can go on and tell us that the clear tasteless liquid is H_2O). But the stance comprising these three theses together is not completely stable nor uncontroversial. For instance, one could be a realist about the attitudes (R) and think folk psychology picks them out (C), but deny that it is the job of cognitive science to explain them (perhaps they are no more a natural scientific kind of object than armchairs are):

(J)   The Job of cognitive science is to explain cognition, and the attitudes will not make an appearance in this account.

Or one could be realistic about the attitudes (R), believe it is the job of cognitive science to account for them (N), but think that there could or will be a conflict between (C) and (N), and (N) will or should win:

(S)   The central features of the attitudes must be discovered by Science, not given to us in our commonsense folk psychology.

Or more radically, one could be an eliminativist and deny (R), deny that there are propositional attitudes at all – like witches and vital forces, they are figments of a false commonsense folk theory:

(E)   There really are no propositional attitudes (Eliminativism with respect to the attitudes).

Our purpose in raising these issues is not to resolve them, but to set the stage for an interesting on-going dispute concerning the implications of the CCTM with regard to realism vs. eliminativism of the attitudes.

It has seemed to some that our ordinary notion of propositional attitudes endows each of them with certain features, such as being constituted by concepts, being semantically evaluable as true or false (fulfilled or not fulfilled, etc.), being discrete, and being causally effective. Digital machines seem eminently well suited to house such states, and so their existence seems to support the DCTM over the CCTM. But matters may even be worse. Some contend that the CCTM cannot accommodate commonsense folk propositional attitudes, and hence we are in the position that if connectionism were true, then such attitudes would not exist – eliminativism. Connectionists, if this is right, must either show that the attitudes do not really have all these features, or that connectionist models can accommodate these features after all.

DCTM, propositional attitudes and folk psychology

We earlier outlined a conception of the DCTM according to which each propositional attitude is some specific computational relation to a representation. We summarized this playfully by saying that the representation was stored in the appropriate "box" – e.g. *believing* that red wine is healthy would involve storing a mental representation to the effect that wine is healthy (e.g. RED WINE IS HEALTHY) in the *belief box*. As we noted, each computational state so understood has a cluster of important properties:

1   they are constituted, in part, by *category* terms (e.g. WINE);
2   they are *semantically interpretable*: they are about something, true or false, etc.;
3   they are *functionally discrete* in that deleting one representation does not affect other representations (think back on predicate logic, semantic networks, and frames);
4   they play a *causal role* in the production of other attitudes and eventually output.

These features also seem to characterize commonsense notions of the attitudes, e.g. belief:

1   beliefs are constituted, in part, by *concepts*;

The following are called "propositional modularity" (Ramsey, Stich, and Garon, 1991):

2   beliefs are *semantically interpretable*: they are about something, true or false, etc.;
3   beliefs are *functionally discrete* in that deleting one does not affect other beliefs;[2]
4   beliefs play a *causal role* in the production of other attitudes and eventually behavior.

Ramsey et al. (1991), note that the causal role attitudes play is particularly rich and satisfies what, adapting Clark (1993: 194), is called the "equipotency condition":

Equipotency condition: A person has two particular belief-desire pairs which *could* cause a certain action (or other belief-desire), but on a particular occasion only one *in fact* does.

They illustrate this with a pair of examples. To take one, suppose our ambition is to explain why Alice went to her office on a particular occasion. Suppose that she wants to read her e-mail and she wants to talk to her research assistant, and she believes she can do both of these (only) in her office: "commonsense psychology assumes that Alice's going to her office might have been caused by either one of the belief–desire pairs, or by both, and that determining which of these options obtains is an empirical matter" (Ramsey et al., 1991: 99). For example, Alice might decide that on this occasion she only has time to check her e-mail, and so not talk to her RA, even though she wants to. This is easily modeled in the DCTM by having the program access one data structure but not another, thus satisfying the equipotency condition.

CCTM, propositional attitudes, and folk psychology

We earlier outlined a conception of the CCTM according to which network representations have a cluster of important features:

1   they are *distributed*;
2   they are *context sensitive* (see "the coffee story" again in chapter 12);
3   they are *subsymbolic* at the level of units and activation passing;
4   they are *cognitive* constituents of models of cognitive phenomena.

Now, the question arises of whether the CCTM can reconstruct the folk notion of a propositional attitude in the way that the DCTM apparently can. Some authors, such as Davies (1991), see the commitment to *conceptually* and causally structured representations forming a "language of thought" as a part of commonsense understanding of the attitudes, and goes on to conclude that due to the context-sensitivity of connectionist symbols: "Networks do not exhibit syntax and causal systematicity of process; the commonsense scheme is committed to syntax and causal systematicity of process; therefore connectionism is opposed to the commonsense scheme" (1991: 251). Other authors, such as Ramsey et al. (1991), emphasize the *propositional* level, but also argue that the CCTM cannot reconstruct the folk notion of a propositional attitude. We will focus on this latter argument. To make their case they start with a small network "A" (see figure 13.1).[3] They encoded the propositions shown in figure 13.2 on the input layer and used back-propagation to train the network to differentiate the true from the false ones on the output node.

Training terminated when the network consistently output greater than 0.9 for the true propositions and less than 0.1 for the false ones. The resulting

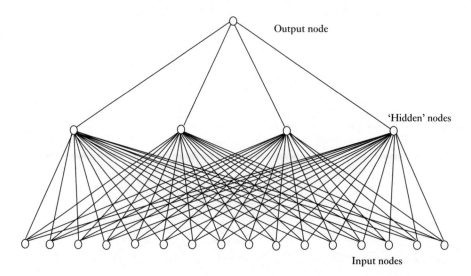

Figure 13.1 The structure of network "A" (from Ramsey et al., 1991: 107, figure 4)

Proposition	Input	Output
1 Dogs have fur.	11000011 00001111	1 true
2 Dogs have paws.	11000011 00110011	1 true
3 Dogs have fleas.	11000011 00111111	1 true
4 Dogs have legs.	11000011 00111100	1 true
5 Cats have fur.	11001100 00001111	1 true
6 Cats have paws.	11001100 00110011	1 true
7 Cats have fleas.	11001100 00111111	1 true
8 Fish have scales.	11110000 00110000	1 true
9 Fish have fins.	11110000 00001100	1 true
10 Fish have gills.	11110000 00000011	1 true
11 Cats have gills.	11001100 00000011	0 false
12 Fish have legs.	11110000 00111100	0 false
13 Fish have fleas.	11110000 00111111	0 false
14 Dogs have scales.	11000011 00110000	0 false
15 Dogs have fins.	11000011 00001100	0 false
16 Cats have fins.	11001100 00001100	0 false

Added proposition

17 Fish have eggs.	11110000 11001000	1 true

Figure 13.2 Table of propositions and coding (from Ramsey et al., 1991: 107, figure 3)

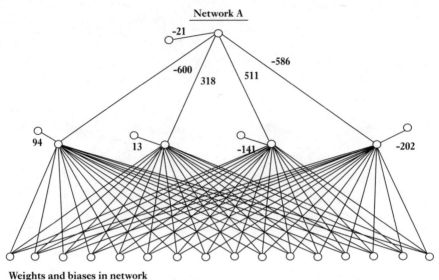

Figure 13.3   Weights in network "A" (from Ramsey et al., 1991: 108, figure 6)

stable assignment of weights is shown in figure 13.3. The authors also trained the network on an additional proposition and noted that *all* the weights changed slightly and some even changed dramatically (see figure 13.4).

With these results in place Ramsey et al. give two kinds of argument relating connectionism and folk psychology.

The holism argument (HA)
(1) Folk psychological attitudes are propositionally modular.
(2) So folk psychological attitudes are discrete states playing distinctive causal roles.
(3) Networks such as "A" are "holistic," i.e. they have no discrete states playing the distinctive causal role of folk psychological attitudes.
(4) So networks do not contain folk psychological attitudes.

Here is what Ramsey et al. (1991) say: "In the connectionist network . . . there is no distinct state or part of the network that serves to represent any particular proposition. The information encoded in network A is stored holistically and distributed throughout the network. . . . It simply makes no sense to ask

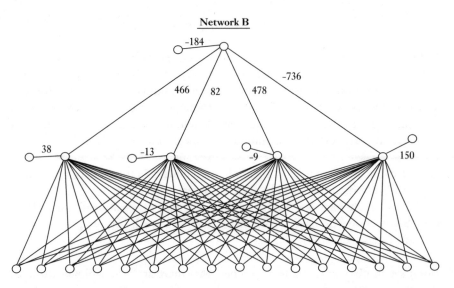

Figure 13.4   Weights in network "B" (from Ramsey et al., 1991: 110, figure 9; figures 13.1–13.4 are reprinted by permission of Ridgeview Publishing Co.)

whether or not the representation of a particular proposition plays a causal role in the network's computation" (ibid.: 108–9). They go on: "commonsense psychology seems to presuppose that there is generally some answer to the question of whether a particular belief or memory played a causal role in a specific cognitive episode. But if belief and memory are subserved by a connectionist network like ours, such questions seem to have no clear meaning" (ibid., 109).

The natural kinds argument (NKA)
(1)   Folk propositional attitude states are psychological natural kinds.
(2)   States of networks that encode propositional attitudes are not natural kinds.
(3)   So networks do not contain folk propositional attitudes.

Here is what Ramsey et al. (1991) say: "The moral here is that . . . there are *indefinitely* many connectionist networks that represent the information that dogs have fur just as well as network A does. . . . From the point of view of the connectionist model builder, the class of networks that might model a cognitive agent who believes that dogs have fur is not a genuine kind at all, but simply a chaotically disjunctive set. Commonsense psychology treats the class of people who believe that dogs have fur as a psychologically natural kind; connectionist psychology does not" (ibid.: 111).

Eliminativism

If the above arguments are correct, then there is nothing in a connectionist network of the sort just considered that has the last three features of a commonsense propositional attitude (propositional modularity) – being a discrete, semantically interpretable and causally productive state of the system. If we also subscribe to thesis [C] above, then it follows that there is nothing in a connectionist network corresponding to propositional attitudes:

(1) If connectionism is true, then folk psychological attitudes are not propositionally modular (see HA, NKA above).
(2) Folk psychological attitudes, if they exist, are propositionally modular.
(3) So, if connectionism is true, then: [E] There really are no propositional attitudes (repeated).

But it seems obvious to many researchers that there are propositional attitudes (beliefs, desires, intentions, etc.), so the above argument appears to be a *reductio ad absurdum* of connectionism:

(4) There really are propositional attitudes.
(5) So, connectionism is false.

As Ramsey et al. put it: "In these models there is nothing with which propositional attitudes of commonsense psychology can plausibly be identified" (ibid.: 116). "*If* connectionist hypotheses of the sort we shall sketch turn out to be right, so too will be eliminativism about propositional attitudes" (ibid.: 94). There are of course a number of ways friends of connectionism and/or folk psychology could respond to this discussion. The original argument has three steps, and replies can be directed at any of these steps.

I.   Connectionism and propositional modularity

This reply tries to show that connectionist models, contra Ramsey et al., do have states with the last three central features of attitudes, i.e. that propositional modularity is preserved in connectionist models, though it is not obvious to casual inspection at the units and weights level of description. Ramsey et al. (1991) anticipate three ways in which connectionists might argue that this is the case:

1. *Connectionist*:   A belief (that P) is a particular *pattern* of activation.

Ramsey et al. *reply*   Particular patterns of activation are brief and transitory phases in the time course of a network, but beliefs (and other propositional attitudes) are relatively stable and long-lasting cognitive states, so beliefs (and other propositional attitudes) are not patterns of activation.

Recall that we earlier distinguished occurrent beliefs from standing beliefs and we identified occurrent beliefs with patterns of activation. This objection argues that standing beliefs are not patterns of activation as well. But it does not show that occurrent beliefs are not patterns of activation.

2. *Connectionist*:   A belief (that P) is a *disposition* to produce a particular pattern of activation.

This avoids the endurance problem since such dispositions can be long-term, and a disposition can exist even if the activity does not, just as we can believe something even when not thinking about it at the moment.

Ramsey et al. *reply*   Dispositions are not the right sort of enduring states to be beliefs (and other propositional attitudes), they are not discrete causally active states, as required. In particular, recall the equipotency condition rehearsed earlier, where Alice might have gone to her office to see her assistant, but actually went on this occasion to check her e-mail: "It is hard to see how anything like these distinctions can be captured by the dispositional account in question. . . . In a distributed connectionist system like network A, however, the dispositional state that produces one activation pattern is functionally inseparable from the dispositional state that produces another" (Ramsey et al. 1991, 115–16). One thing to note about this argument is that it rests on the inability to see how to map folk psychology on to connectionist networks. It is not a direct argument against the proposal, and so it is closer to the next and final objection.

3. *Connectionist*:   A belief (that P) is a *still to be discovered* property of the system – some covert functionally discrete system of propositional encoding.

Ramsey et al. *reply*   This, of course, might be true, but we must be given some reason to suppose so, or it just begs the question.

Clark's (1990) strategy is to show that analogs of beliefs (and other propositional attitudes) exist in connectionist networks, but at higher levels of description. Clark argues that "distributed, subsymbolic, superpositional connectionist models are actually more structured than Ramsey et al. think, and hence visibly compatible with the requirements of propositional modularity.

To this end we might question the choice of units-and-weights description as the sole description of a network of the purposes of a scientific psychology" (1990: 90). Clark takes NETtalk as his example, and in particular Sejnowski and Rosenberg's hierarchical cluster analysis (HCA) of the activation of the hidden layers which yielded a coherent semantic interpretation of the weight space in terms of vowels and consonants. Clark's proposal is basically that (standing) beliefs might be revealed in a complicated enough system (maybe network "A" was not complicated enough) by a technique such as HCA. As he notes, Ramsey et al. purport to "argue directly from distributed, subsymbolic storage and representation to eliminativism. The mere possibility of a cluster analysis turning out as I've suggested shows that there is no direct inference of the kind claimed" (1990: 94).

II.   Challenging eliminativism

This reply tries to show that the inference to non-existence does not follow, that lacking the property of "propositional modularity" is not sufficient for saying that propositional attitudes do not exist in the system. We clearly want to draw distinction between being *mistaken* about the features of something and showing the thing *doesn't exist*. We saw in chapter 3 that some famous Greeks thought the brain is a radiator for the blood and that we think with our heart, and some famous medievals viewed thinking as taking place in the hollow spaces in the brain, yet we assume that they were *wrong* about the brain (and the heart), not that brains and hearts (as they conceived them) *don't exist*. This could be because either:

1   the principles that allow one to infer the non-existence of the attitudes from the falseness of the description of propositional modularity are defective (*wrong principles*);
2   not all three features are actually true of propositional attitudes (*commonsense is wrong*);
3   not all three features constitute the commonsense conception propositional attitudes (*commonsense is misdescribed*).

We take these up in turn.

1.   Wrong principles
This is the step that Stich and Warfield (1995) challenge, thereby rejecting the Ramsey et al. conclusion to eliminativism. They see the problem as this: there is no plausible way to bridge the gap between the fact that connectionism makes folk psychology *mistaken* about the attitudes, to the conclusion that connec-

tionism shows the *non-existence* of the attitudes. They propose and reject two principles to underwrite the inference to eliminativism. First, there is:

(DTR)

The *Description Theory of Reference.* Theories contain terms that refer to entities in virtue of satisfying some (perhaps weighted) set of descriptions associated with each term.

So if nothing in a connectionist network fits the description of a modular propositional attitude, then the network does not contain them.

Reply: Stich and Warfield reply that the dominant view in the philosophy of language now is that the description theory is false, and that its rival, the "historical-causal chain" theory "will prove to be the correct account of the reference of most theoretical terms" (1995: 406). On this rival account, terms get their reference in virtue of historical-causal chains leading back to the entities they refer to (though mental terms are rarely discussed by the authors cited), and it is not necessary for speakers or thinkers to know a correct description of the thing referred to (maybe everything one knows about, say, Julius Caesar is wrong). If this is the way propositional attitude terms work, then discovering that there is no state which can be described in terms of modular propositional attitudes will not show that the system does not have propositional attitudes – just that propositional attitudes do not have those described properties, and that we were mistaken. However, it is still controversial that "most theoretical terms" work this way, since some at least seem to be introduced by description. Moreover, the work on theoretical terms has mostly been restricted to physics and biology – there is no guarantee psychological (mental) terms will be as well behaved. Finally, it is not clear we want to assimilate folk psychological notions to theoretical terms in science.

(CP)

Constitutive Properties Some properties are constitutive of, or essential for, being the thing it is. If nothing in the system has those properties, then the thing those properties constitute does not exist in that system.

For instance, having 79 protons (having the atomic number 79) is one of the constitutive properties of being gold, and if we find something with 92 protons, we know it is uranium, not gold in disguise. Likewise, if no state of a connectionist network is constituted by the three properties of being a modular propositional attitude, then the system does not contain commonsense propositional attitudes.

Reply: Stich and Warfield reply, *first*, that it is very difficult to make a case that certain properties rather than others are constitutive of something – just thinking they are is not enough. *Second*, Quine and others have impressively questioned the whole idea that there are constitutive properties, or in the linguistic mode, that there are properties that are "analytically" connected to referring terms – properties that the referents must have for the term to refer to them. The weight of tradition is against such an idea and "if there are philosophers who choose to follow this path, we wish them well. But we don't propose to hold our breath until they succeed" (1990: 409). But we might add that the presence or absence of essential features is controversial, and not much of this work has been carried out in the domain of psychological (mental) notions.

What should we conclude regarding eliminativism so far? It is clear that by showing that two specific principles (DTR), (CP) do not get one from mistakenness to non-existence, one has not shown that no principle will do so. Therefore it is ironic that Stich and Warfield do not consider the principle (below) on which Ramsey et al. (1991) based their original argument. As Ramsey et al. (1991) note, the philosophy of science has not formulated any principle for deciding these cases of mistake vs. non-existence, so it is basically a judgment call, but:

(DFD)
"if the posits of the new theory strike us as *deeply* and *fundamentally different* from those of the old theory . . . then it will be plausible to conclude that the theory change has been a radical one, and that an eliminativist conclusion is in order."   (ibid.: 96; emphasis added)

This does seem reasonable on the face of it, so it looks like connectionist networks contain no "modular" propositional attitudes. What should we conclude concerning eliminativism? Could connectionist models lack "modular" states and still have propositional attitudes? We still have two responses to consider.

2.   Commonsense is wrong
Ramsey et al. (1991) contend that all three features of propositional modularity are part of our folk notion of the attitudes, and Smolensky (1995), for one, finds only the first two in the models he investigates. Stich and Warfield comment that if Smolensky's future work does not uncover the third feature, causal role, then his constructions "will not count as an adequate response to Ramsey et al.'s challenge". But if one were to *deny* that causal role is either (a)

part of the folk notion of the attitudes, or (b) a part of the attitudes (*simpliciter*), then the Ramsey et al. challenge would have to be modified.

3. Commonsense wrongly described

Clark (1993 following 1991) favors this third response, and proposes "to reject outright the idea that folk psychology is necessarily committed to beliefs and desires being straightforwardly causally potent . . . there are other ways . . . in which a construct can have explanatory value – ways which do not require that it be identified with any specific underlying scientific essence" (1993: 211). His strategy here is to replace causal demands on networks with "explanatory" demands, then to argue that connectionist *explanations* of behavior in terms of propositional attitudes can be given which satisfy the equipotency condition. However, it is not so clear that commonsense psychology does not embrace the doctrine of particular causal roles.

The score

We have rehearsed a dispute regarding the status of propositional attitudes in connectionist models. The arguments are supposed to show that connectionism is false because it entails that there are no propositional attitudes as commonly understood (when it seems that there are). We have seen that each argument has its strengths and weaknesses. It seems presently to be a draw – neither side has established its case. The crucial issue seems to be the distinctive causal vs. explanatory role of the attitudes, and that issue is not yet resolved.

13.6 CCTM Detector Semantics

Earlier, when discussing the neuro–logical tradition in cognitive science (chapter 4), we formulated simple detector semantics (SDS) for such systems as the frog's visual system, and sketched various problems with it. Then, in discussing the CCTM, we formulated Simple Connectionist Detector Semantics:

(SCDS)

Units, and set of units, represent what activates them (or activates them sufficiently)

We continue the same strategy here, seeing how connectionist representations fare with respect to the various problems we set out earlier. As we will see, SCDS faces serious obstacles, both as to its *correctness* and as to its *completeness*.

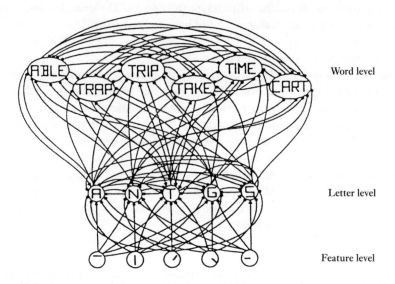

Word level

Letter level

Feature level

Figure 13.5   Letter recognition network (from McClelland and Rumelhart, 1981: 380, figure 3; reproduced by permission of the American Psychological Association)

The right-cause or "depth," and the no-cause problems

Recall that the right-cause or "depth" problem is the problem of picking out the link in the causal chain that is the one the representation is about. The "no-cause problem" is the problem of accounting for the semantics of representations when there are no (relevant) causes.

Right cause

Consider first McClelland and Rumelhart's influential (1981) model of letter recognition in 1,179 four-letter words (see figure 13.5).

First, there is a node for each word, a node for each letter in each of the four positions, and a node for each letter feature. Next, the nodes are collected into three levels: a feature level, a letter level, and a word level. Finally, there are two-way excitation and inhibition connections between nodes. Adjacent levels can have excitatory and inhibitory connections, but within-level connections are inhibitory. The (considerable) interest of the system lies not in its connection to the world, for as McClelland and Rumelhart admit, the model "obviously skirts several fundamental issues about the lower levels of processing" (1981: 383), but in its subsequent behavior after being tweaked by the relevant stimuli. McClelland and Rumelhart note two things: first, "each feature is detected with some probability p . . . [which will] . . . vary with the visual quality of the display" (1981: 381). Second, "we identify nodes according to the units [in the stimuli] they detect" (1981: 379).

There are no real output nodes in this model. Rather, the output is read off of the results of temporally integrating the pattern of activation on all nodes in accordance with a particular rule. This gives the *response strength*: "each cycle for which output is requested, the program computes the probability that the correct alternative is read out and the probability that the incorrect alternative is read out, based on the response strength" (1981: 407).

What about letter and word nodes – the "hidden" units? These are activated as a function of the activation of each of the nodes connected to them. Consider the letter "T"; it is activated by the simultaneous activation of a center vertical edge detector and an upper horizontal edge detector, focused on the same area of the "retina."[4] So what activates the "T" node is the joint (temporal and spatial) activation of the vertical and horizontal edge detectors. The same goes for word nodes, but in spades. In this case the node is activated by four letter-position node pairs such as: "T" in the first position, "A" in the second position, "K" in the third position, "E" in the fourth position, for "TAKE."

By (SCDS) these nodes are all about what activates them, and what activates them is earlier nodes. But what we want the theory to say, what is correct, is that letter nodes detect letters *in the world*, and word detectors detect words *in the world*. What is being detected are letter and words *our there*, not earlier nodes in the flow of information. The theory in which the model is embedded must find a way of handling the transitivity of "activates" – it must find the right cause of the node's activation. This the *right cause* problem for connectionist systems.

Similarly for Rumelhart and McClelland's (1986b) past tense learner, except that here the A units represent word roots ad the B units represent past tense forms, both in their Wickelfeature representations. Fixed decoding networks convert these from and to phonological representations. The intended interpretation of the representations is clearly auditory (Rumelhart and McClelland do not say how the network was stimulated, but most likely it was from a keyboard). The components of each Wickelfeature are complex, and Rumelhart and McClelland engineered them to some extent for computational expediency. However, the basic point is that the features they are made from mark 10 points on four "sound" dimensions: (1) interrupted consonants vs. continuous consonants vs. vowels; (2) stops vs. nasals, fricatives vs. sonorants, high vs. low; (3) front, middle back; (4) voiced vs. unvoiced, long vs. short (see figure 13.6).

| | | Place | | | | | |
| | | Front | | Middle | | Back | |
		V/L	U/S	V/L	U/S	V/L	U/S
Interrupted	*Stop*	b	p	d	t	g	k
consonant	*Nasal*	m	–	n	–	N	–
Cont. consonant	*Fric.*	v/D	f/T	z	s	Z/j	S/C
	Liq/SV	w/l	–	r	–	y	h
Vowel	*High*	E	i	O	^	U	u
	Low	A	e	I	a/α	W	*/o

Key: N = ng in *sing*; D = th in *the*; T = th in *with*; Z = z in *azure*; S = sh in *ship*; C = ch in *chip*; E = ee in *beet*; i = i in *bit*; O = oa in *boat*; ^ = u in *but* or schwa; U = oo in *boot*; u = oo in *book*; A = ai in *bait*; e = e in *bet*; I = i_e in *bite*; a = a in *bat*; α = a in *father*; W = ow in *cow*; * = aw in *saw*; o = o in *hot*.

Figure 13.6 Features in Wickelfeatures (from Rumelhart and McClelland, 1986a, vol. 2: 235, table 5; reproduced by permission of the MIT Press)

The question is: what are nodes which are dedicated to picking up such features, actually picking up? "Voiced" has to do with the vibration of the vocal cords, but "front," "middle," and "back" have to do with the place of articulation in the mouth. Are these nodes shape-of-the-mouth detectors? Or should the causal chain go back only to the feature of the sound (if there is one) that these configurations of the mouth produce?[5]

No cause

As we noted earlier, the limiting case of the right-cause problem is the "no-cause" problem – how can we represent things which do not cause tokenings of representations? These include logical notions, such as XOR, abstract entities such as numbers, sets, and so forth, future entities such as our great-great grandchildren, and perhaps even social roles such as being the mayor of New York. Consider the XOR network of linear threshold units represented in figure 13.7. This model has a hidden ("internal") unit without which XOR could not be computed, but there is no obvious interpretation to be assigned to them at all, let alone a detector semantics. Its meaning is more a function of the role it plays in the network than what turns it on.

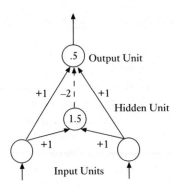

Input Units

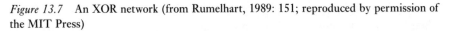

Figure 13.7 An XOR network (from Rumelhart, 1989: 151; reproduced by permission of the MIT Press)

The misrepresentation (disjunction) problem

The next problem, as we saw in our discussion of what the frog's eye tells the frog's brain (chapter 4), was made famous by Fodor as the *disjunction problem*. For connectionist systems it might go like this. Suppose we define a "T" detector as a node that is on just when it is exposed to the letter "T."[6] However, like all devices it occasionally gets things wrong – it occasionally fires when it gets, say, an "I." But now our T detector is functioning like an I detector, which is to say it is overall a T-or-I detector. Thus it would seem that misrepresentation is impossible; a potential case of misrepresentation is converted by the theory into the veridical representation of a disjunction. Not at all what we wanted.

The entailment problem

Another problem for connectionist detector semantics is specifying the semantic relationships *between* representations. We saw before that complex representational systems approximating human cognition will exhibit at least some logical entailments, and the problem is to capture these relations in a network. This is the entailment problem for connectionist systems. Notice that, say, NETtalk can be said to capture at least some primitive relations: it represents "a" as a vowel in the sense that if an "a"-unit is turned on, activation will spread to its hidden "vowel-units" and turn them on. But just as we saw for semantic networks earlier, the problem is to control this spread insofar is it is supposed to track just inference.

The representing-as, "spread" or "qua" problem

It is important to distinguish two aspects of detector semantics representations. One is related to what thing in the world the representation is *of* or *about*. Consider again from chapter 4 what the frog's eye tells the frog's brain. Presumably a normally functioning frog in its natural habitat has representations that are *of* or *about* bugs. That is, as a matter of historical fact, the things that turn on the frog's bug detector in the wild are *bugs*. The other aspect of a representation is *how* it represents that thing – what it represents the thing *as*. Settling this is what we called (chapter 4) the "spread" or "qua" problem. The authors speak of a "small object (3 degrees or less)" and a "fly-sized object, 1 degree large." Clearly these do *not have to be* bugs. To us (so to speak) the frog's "bug" representation might be indistinguishable from a "small dark blob moving erratically" representation. We might know what a system's representation is *of*, what object(s) in the world it is tracking, and still not know what it represents it to be – what it is represented *as*. It is also important to keep in mind that a representation can depict something *as* having one property, but not depict it as having another, even though all the things it detects (or even all things) that have the first property also have the second. Taking an example from Dretske (1986a), an electric eye in an elevator door might detect the presence of things at the door, but even though only people (or redheads) use the elevator, we would not say it is a people (or redhead) detector.[7] Detector semantics seems well suited to answer questions regarding what the system is representing – what the representations are representations-*of*. How do we account for representation-*as* in a connectionist system with detector semantics? Perhaps we saw the beginnings of an answer in the rose and goat networks of chapter 11. There we assigned to each node a psychophysical "dimension" such as color, shape, smell, or texture, and we allowed levels of activation to represent points on these dimensions: red color, oval shape, fragrant smell, rough texture, etc. This vector, then, would not only be caused by (and so *of*) a rose, or goat, but it would represent it *as* red, oval, fragrant, etc., that is, as a *rose*.

Conclusion

Where does this leave us? Let's call a semantics for a system *derivative* if it requires another system, which already has a semantics, to give the first system its semantics. Let's call the semantics of a system *non-derivative* if no other semantical system is required. Digital computers typically have derivative semantics; human thought has, in general, non-derivative semantics.[8] We are in the position that very few connectionist models have a non-derivative semantics even for input layers of nodes. This leaves us without a non-derivative semantics for most of the nodes or patterns of activation in connectionist networks, and whatever semantics they get is derivative – given to them via labels from the programmer. But of course the programmer's representational system is the kind of cognitive capacity connectionists are trying to model, so it won't do to presuppose such capacities in the modeling.

13.7   CCTM Problems and Prospects

CCTM models share some of the problems with the DCTM, including the problems of consciousness and qualia, but they also currently have various specific liabilities including the following:

1   They have trouble with temporally extended processes (e.g., language production and comprehension, proofs).
2   They have trouble with highly structured processes (e.g., language production and comprehension, proofs).
3   They have scaling-up problems – what works with small numbers of units and a small domain does not readily extend to larger ones.
4   The semantics of the individual nodes and vectors is unclear – what are they about, and how do they get their aboutness.
5   The semantics of complex representations is unclear – how is the semantics of a complex expression related to the semantics of its constituents and their relations, i.e., are they compositional?

Notes

1   Recall that models do not model every aspect of what they model – a model of the solar system might be made out of brass.
2   Though changing one might affect others – learning that Reno, Nevada, is west of Los Angeles, California, might change one's beliefs about the geography of California and Nevada.
3   They actually call it "a connectionist model of memory" and usually refer to its contents as "information" not "beliefs." However, if it is not a model of connectionist belief, it is irrelevant to the issue of the attitudes.
4   If they were not "focused" on the same area of the "retina," then the simultaneous presentation of "|" and "—" would activate the "T" detector even though separately they do not constitute a "T."

5   Answering these questions involves hard, and to some extent unresolved problems in acoustic and articulatory phonetics. Detector semantics is partly an empirical issue – that's part of its attraction.
6   The phrase "just when" includes the idea of causation – this is a causal theory.
7   What a thing actually detects doesn't exhaust its representational potential – we must count what it *would* detect in the right (that's the hard part) counterfactual circumstances.
8   A qualification may be required for thinking in a public language where what the words are about is fixed by the linguistic community, or experts in the linguistic community.

Study questions

The brain

What are some major differences between typical connectionist models and the brain? [**hint**: neurons vs. units, chemistry, geometry, learning, scale]

Lures of connectionism

What is "Fodor's fork"?

What is the "100–step rule" lure? Is it inessential or implementation?

Why do people believe it?

What is Fodor and Pylyshyn's reply?

How should we assess that reply?

What is the "resistance to noise and damage" lure? Is it inessential or implementation?

What is Fodor and Pylyshyn's reply?

How should we assess that reply?

What is the "soft constraints" lure? Is it inessential or implementation?

What is Fodor and Pylyshyn's reply?

How should we assess that reply?

What is the "explicitness of rules" lure? Is it inessential or implementation?

What is Fodor and Pylyshyn's reply?

How should we assess that reply?

What is the "brain-style modeling" lure? Is it inessential or implementation?

What is Fodor and Pylyshyn's reply?

How should we assess that reply?

Were there any "lures" of connectionism not covered by Fodor and Pylyshyn's five groups? What are some examples?

What is the "classical choice" offered to Fodor and Pylyshyn?

What are some of the main problem areas for connectionist models?

The Chinese gym

What is Searle's Chinese gym situation?

What is Searle's Chinese gym argument?

What is a problem with it?

What is Searle's "serial" argument?

What problem does it have?

What is Searle's "parallel" argument?

What problem does it have?

Propositional attitudes

What are "realism" and "eliminativism" with respect to the propositional attitudes?

What are propositional attitudes, according to the DCTM?

What four features do propositional attitudes have, according to the DCTM?

What four features do propositional attitudes have, according to commonsense?

What is the "equipotency condition" on the attitudes?

What four features do representations have, according to the CCTM?

What is "propositional modularity"?

What is the "holism" argument?

What is the "natural kinds" argument?

What are the two major strategies for replying to these arguments?

Detector semantics

What is simple connectionist detector semantics (SCDS)?

What is the "right-cause" problem for (SCDS)?

What is the "no-cause" problem for (SCDS)?

What is the "misrepresentation (disjunction)" problem for (SCDS)?

What is the "entailment" problem for (SCDS)?

What is the "representation-as" problem for (SCDS)?

Can connectionist networks compute XOR? How?

Problems and prospects

What are some problems that the CCTM shares with the DCTM?

What are some distinctive problem areas for the CCTM?

Suggested reading

CCTM and the brain

For basics on neurons see selected readings for chapter 3, and Arbib (1995). Kosslyn (1983), chapter 2, is a semi-popular introduction to connectionist computation and the brain. For more on neurons and connectionist networks see Crick and Asanuma (1986), Schwartz (1988), Churchland (1989; 1990, section 1.4), Copeland (1993b), chapter 10.5, McLeod et al. (1998), chapter 13, and Dawson (1998), chapter 7.IV. For a recent discussion of biologically realistic network models of brain functioning see Rolls and Treves (1998), and for a recent discussion of connectionist neuroscience see Hanson (1999).

Lures of connectionism

The most influential statement of the "lures" of connectionism is probably Rumelhart and McClelland (1986a), chapter 1. These are also discussed in Bechtel and Abrahamsen (1991), chapter 2 and passim. Connectionism as implementation vs. cognition is discussed by Chater and Oaksford (1990). See McLaughlin (1993), and McLaughlin and Warfield (1994) for a more recent defense of classical architectures.

Chinese gym

Churchland and Churchland (1991) reply in passing to the Chinese gym argument, but see Copeland (1993a; 1993b, chapter 10.6) and Dennett (1991) for a more sustained discussion. Both Smolensky (1988a) and Franklin and Garzon (1991) speculate that "neural networks may be strictly more powerful than Turing machines, and hence capable of solving problems a Turing machine cannot." We return to this issue in the next chapter.

Propositional attitudes

Our presentation of the CCTM and eliminativism follows the discussion in Ramsey, Stich, and Garon (1991), Clark (1990; 1993, chapter 10), and Stich and Warfield (1995). See Smolensky (1995) for another, more technically demanding, reponse to Ramsey, Stich, and Garon (1991) and propositional modularity. Our discussion is indebted to Braddon-Mitchell and Jackson (1996), chapters 3 and 14, and Rey (1997), chapter 7. The *locus classicus* for eliminativism in folk psychology is Churchland (1981). For a short introduction to issues in folk psychology see von Eckhardt (1994) and Churchland (1994) and the many references therein. For recent work see Greenwoood (1991), Christensen and Turner (1993), Stich (1996) chapter 3, and Carruthers and Smith (1996).

Detector semantics

See Fodor (1984, 1987, 1990) for more on the "disjunction" problem. See Dretske (1986a) and references therein for more on representation-as. See Ramsey (1992) for discussion of SCDS.

Problems and prospects

For an early survey of issues in the CCTM see Rumelhart and McClelland (1986a), chapters 1 and 26. General discussion of problems and prospects of connectionism can be found in Rumelhart and McClelland (1986a), chapter 4; Minsky and Papert (1969); the epilogue to the 1988 reprinting; Rosenberg (1990a,b); and Quinlan (1991), chapter 6. Some early empirical criticisms of connectionism are Massaro (1988) and Ratcliff (1990).

Coda: Computation for Cognitive Science, or What IS a Computer, Anyway?

C.1 Introduction

We have been assuming that for a computer model of the mind to be plausible, a computer must be viewed roughly and intuitively as a device with an architecture for executing procedures involving representations (of the world). More precisely, according to the computational theory of mind (CTM):

(CTM)
(a) Cognitive states are *computational relations* to *mental representations* which have content.
(b) Cognitive processes (changes in cognitive states) are *computational operations* on *mental representations* which have content.

In Part II we formulated the digital version of this, the DCTM, by putting digital restrictions on computational terms in the CTM. In Part III we formulated the connectionist version of this, the CCTM, by putting connectionist restrictions on the computational terms in the CTM.

Now we would like to formulate a more general view of a computer and computation – one that covers possible as well as actual devices. Suppose a machine fell to earth and we wanted to know if it was a computer – if it computed. What would we want to know about it? There are two broad ways of abstractly characterizing a computer and computation – by way of its *functioning* and by way of its *levels of description*. Each has its strengths and weaknesses. We will look at each briefly and then see if we can combine them into a better idea.

Terminological note   We will be going back and forth between the notions of a "computer" and "computation." This is not uncommon. For instance, dictionaries often define computers in terms of computation or vice versa: a computer is something that computes (see below), and computation is what computers do. This is, of course, inadequate in many ways: (1) computers do more than compute (they give off heat, their lights blink, etc.); (2) people compute, but people are not computers (even though thinking may be computation); and finally (3) it's circular. We have to break into the circle somewhere; we will break into it with the notion of a computer, but we could have broken into it with the notion of a computation.

C.2   Functional View of Computers

One place to start is with already-existing definitions, and there are two major sources of definitions of computers and computation: dictionaries and textbooks.

Dictionary

Here is a good sample:

Computer.   1. One who, or that which computes. [to compute, to determine by calculation] 2. A mechanical or electronic apparatus capable of carrying out repetitious and highly complex mathematical operations at high speeds.
     (*Random House Dictionary of the English Language*, unabridged edition: 303)

There are many problems with these definitions: the first suffers the above-mentioned problem of circularity, and the second rules out most or all people as capable of computation. Just think of non-calculating persons, or people who can't carry out repetitious and highly complex mathematical operations at any, let alone high, speeds.

Textbook

(Don't expect to understand this.)[1]

Definition 3.1   A (completed) computation by the program **P** on the machine **M** is a finite sequence: $L_0, m_0, L_1, m_1, \ldots, L_n, m_n$ of alternating labels of **P** and elements of **M**, where the label L_0 is contained in the start instruction

of **P**, the label L_n is contained in some halt instruction of **P**, and where for
$i < n$ we have either an instruction of the form: L_i: do F; go to L' belonging to
P, in which case $L_{i+1} = L'$ and $m_{F(mi)}$, or an instruction of the form: L_i: if P then
go to L' else go to L'' belonging to **P**, in which case $m_{i+1} = m_i$, and either $m_{P(mi)}$
$= T$ and $L_{i+1} = L'$ or $m_{P(mi)} = F$ and $L_{i+1} = L''$.   (Scott 1967: 193)

Problems with this definition include the fact that it depends on prior definitions of programs and machines, and in fact defines a computation in their
terms (and it makes a computer carrying out a computation equivalent to a
UTM).

Newell: physical symbol systems

One frequently mentioned notion of a computer is what Newell (1980, following Newell and Simon, 1976) calls a "(Physical) symbol system": "a broad
class of systems that is capable of having and manipulating symbols, yet is also
realizable within our physical universe . . ." (1980: 38). A (physical) symbol
system (SS) consists of five subsystems: memory, operators, control, input, and
output (see figure C.1).

The memory is composed of "symbol structures" or "expressions" of a specific type, with specific roles. There are ten operators (assign, copy, etc.) each
of which takes symbols as inputs and produces symbols as output; the process
is called an "operation" (see figure C.2).

Control governs the behavior of the system by taking an operation and its
attendant symbols as *active* and then executing ("interpreting") that operation
on those symbols. It then prepares for the next operation. The controls of this
machine are shown in figure C.3.

This machine is universal in the sense that it is equivalent to a universal
Turing machine: "If properly instructed through part of their input, [they]
can behave like any other machine . . . they can produce all the input–output
functions that can be produced by any machine, however defined" (1980: 52).
Regarding this type of machine, Newell goes on to advance what he calls the
"Physical symbol system hypothesis": "The necessary and sufficient condition
for a physical system to exhibit general intelligent action is that it be a physical symbol system" (1980: 72). (But that gets ahead of our story – we want to
know what a computer is.) One thing that is troubling about (physical) symbol
systems, of course, is that many computers are not such universal machines,
including all special purpose Turing Machines, and most pocket calculators.
Also, even if we allow less than universal sets of operations to appear in the
machine, the whole organization is very reminiscent of a von Neumann

SS: Example symbol system

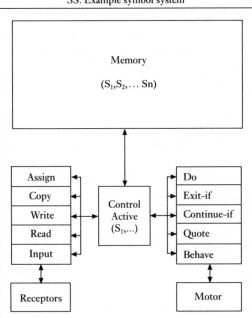

Figure C.1 Structure of a paradigmatic symbol system (from Newell, 1980: 45, figure 2; figures C.1–C.3 reproduced by permission of *Cognitive Science*)

machine, and so it looks as if it is just too specific in architecture to be a general characterization of a computer.

von Eckhardt

A more general but still somewhat commonsensical definition has been offered by von Eckhardt: "A computer is a device capable of automatically inputting, storing, manipulating, and outputting information in virtue of inputting, storing, manipulating, and outputting representations of that information. These information processes occur in accordance with a finite set of rules that are effective and that are, in some sense, in the machine itself (1993: 114). This is a vast improvement over the first definitions in that it recognizes that sophisticated number crunching is not essential to computation. It also recognizes the role of procedures and representations. However, it uses notions like "storing" and "manipulating" information that need explication and could easily, like the

Assign symbol S_1 to the same entity as symbol S_2	(assign S_1 S_2)
Produces S_1 with new assignment	
Copy expression E (create new symbol)	(copy E)
Produces newly created expression and symbol	
Write S_1 at role R_1, . . . in expression E	(write E R_1S_1 . . .)
Produces the modified expression	
nil is the same as doesn't exist	
Read symbol at role R of E	(read R E)
Produces the expression or nil	
Do sequence S_1 S_2 S_3 . . .	(do S_1 S_2 . . .)
Produces the expression produced by last S_1	
Exit sequence if the prior result is E	(exit-if E)
Produces prior expression	
Continue sequence if the prior result is E	(continue-if E)
Produces prior expression	
Quote the symbol S	(quote S)
Produces S without interpretation	
Behave externally according to expression E	(behave E)
Produces feedback expression	
Input according to expression E	(input E)
Produces new expression or nil	

Figure C.2   Operators of the symbol system (from Newell, 1980: 46, figure 3)

Newell definition, become too specific for computers in general. Also, the characterization needs to make it clear that the "rules" need not be explicitly stored in the memory of the machine as a program. We return to this issue in section C.4. In sum, as a characterization of the kind of device that might be like us, it is probably close to being an accurate reflection of the *standard digital* computational model of the mind. But it is too close: we are currently after something even more general, not just what is a computer – that it may resemble us – but what is a computer *simpliciter*?

C.3   Levels of Description View of Computers

So far we have been trying to get at the notion of a computer by abstracting or generalizing from the details of existing machines, but we seem not to be able to lose all vestiges of that specific architecture. Let's try another tack.

Interpret the active expression:

> If it is not a program:
> Then the result is the expression itself.

> If it is a program:
> Interpret the symbol of each role for that role;
> Then execute the operator on its inputs;
> Then the result of the operation is the result.

Interpret the result:

> If it is a new expression:
> Then interpret it for the same role.

> If it is not a new expression:
> Then use as symbol for role.

Figure C.3 The control operations of the symbol system (from Newell, 1980: 48, figure 4)

Fodor

A more abstract conception of a computer was proposed by Fodor: "it is feasible to think of . . . a system as a computer just so far as it is possible to devise some mapping which pairs physical states of the device with formulae in a computing language in such a fashion as to preserve desired semantic relations among the formulae. For example, we may assign physical states of the machine to sentences of the language in such a way that if $S_1 \ldots S_n$ are machine states, and if $F_1 \ldots F_n$ are the sentences paired with $S_1 \ldots S_{n-1}$, S_n, respectively, then the physical constitution of the machine is such that it will actually run through that sequence of states only if $F_1 \ldots F_{n-1}$ constitutes a proof of F_n" (1975: 73). Now that is definitely more abstract, but what does it amount to? First of all, what Fodor characterizes is a computation, not a computer, so let's just say a *computer* is something capable of a computation, as Fodor characterizes them. This said, the idea is that we can identify some states (S) of a machine as representational, and we can bring out this representational character by assigning sentences or "formulae" (F) to them (the "language of thought" for the machine):

S_1
|
F_1

The machine moves from representational state to representational state:

$$S_1 \rightarrow S_2 \rightarrow S_n$$
$$|$$
$$F_1$$

And to each of these subsequent representational states we assign a formula:

$$S_1 \quad \rightarrow \quad S_2 \quad \rightarrow \quad S_n$$
$$| \qquad\qquad | \qquad\qquad |$$
$$F_1 \quad \rightarrow \quad F_2 \quad \rightarrow \quad F_n$$

"P" \qquad\qquad "P → Q" \qquad "Q"

In this case the sequence of states constitutes a "proof" of "Q" from "P" and "if P then Q". This proposal says nothing about the state transitions of the machine other than that they respect the desired semantic relations between formulae, i.e., if "P" and "P → Q" are true, then "Q" must be true. Fodor also doesn't say why it is a part of the notion of a computer that its output should always preserve some desired semantic relation between formulae – especially when he illustrates this with the notion of a "proof," which is not a semantic notion at all, but a syntactic one (e.g. a string of formulae is a *proof* in an axiomatic system if it begins with an axiom and each subsequent formula is either an axiom or is the result of applying an inference rule to an axiom or a previously derived formula).

Marr

It was Marr's idea that computers (or "information processing devices" as he called them) could be understood at three different levels: "[below are] the different levels at which an information-processing device must be understood before one can be said to have understood it completely" (1982: 24). Marr continues: "Each of the three levels of description will have its place in the eventual understanding of perceptual information processing and of course they are logically and causally related . . . some phenomena may be explained at only one or two of them" (1982: 25).

Computational theory: What is the goal of the computation, and why is it appropriate, and what is the logic of the strategy by which it can be carried out?

Representation and algorithm: How can this computation be implemented? In particular, what is the representation for the input, and what is the algorithm for the transformation?

Hardware implementation: How can the representation and algorithm be realized?

Following Marr (who spoke of levels of analysis, not levels of description), we will insist that to be a computer, a device be describable at "hardware" and "algorithm" levels independently of the semantic relations between formulae. That is to say, we want to be able to describe the behavior of the machine in terms of the transitions it is making and why it is making them. However, it is not clear that the level of "computational theory" is actually a part of our conception of a computer, as opposed to part of a good strategy for discovering the computational character of a particular device.

   Dennett (1991: 276) relates Marr's levels to his own theory of "stances": the *intentional stance*, the *design stance* and the *physical stance* (though these may better be related to the three levels identified by Pylyshyn, see below). The idea behind these stances is, roughly, that taking a certain stance gives one predictive and explanatory leverage with respect to a system, or an "object" as Dennett puts it. In particular, adopting the *physical stance* towards an object involves determining "its physical constitution (perhaps all the way down to the microphysical level) and the physical nature of the impingements upon it, and using your knowledge of the laws of physics to predict the outcome for any input. . . . The strategy is not always practically available, but that it will always work *in principle* is a dogma of the physical sciences" (1987a: 16). This corresponds to Marr's level of *hardware implementation*. In adopting the *design stance* towards an object, "One ignores the actual (possibly messy) details of the physical constitution of an object, and, on the assumption that it has a certain design, predicts that it will behave *as it is designed to behave* under various circumstances. . . . Only the designed behavior is predictable from the design stance, of course" (ibid.: 16–17). This corresponds to Marr's level of *algorithm and representation*. Finally, adopting the *intentional stance* towards an object, as a first approximation, "consists of treating the object whose behavior you want to predict as a rational agent with beliefs and other mental states exhibiting what Brentano and others call *intentionality*" (ibid.: 15). As a second approximation: "first you decide to treat the object whose behavior is to be predicted as a rational agent; then you figure out what beliefs that agent ought to have, given its place in the world and its purpose. Then you figure out what desires it ought to have, on the same considerations, and finally you predict that this rational agent will act to further its goals in the light of its beliefs" (ibid.: 17). This corresponds to Marr's level of *computational theory*.

Pylyshyn

This idea, that computers are devices with three proprietary levels of description, has been canonized by Pylyshyn (1989: 57) as the "classical view," although he modifies the levels a bit. According to Pylyshyn, computers (and minds, if they are computers) must have at least the following three distinct levels of organization:

1 *The semantic level (or knowledge level)* At this level we explain why appropriately programmed computers do certain things by saying what they know, and what their goals are by showing that these are connected in certain meaningful or even rational ways.
2 *The symbol level* The semantic content of knowledge and goals is assumed to be encoded by symbolic expressions. Such structured expressions have parts, each of which also encodes some semantic content. The codes and their structures, as well as the regularities by which they are manipulated, are another level of organization of the system.
3 *The physical level* For the entire system to run, it has to be realized in some physical form. The structure and the principles by which the physical object functions corresponds to the physical level.

This captures to some extent Fodor's concern that computers are symbol systems whose *physical* description and *semantic* description go hand in hand (levels 2 and 3). And it captures Marr's concern that information processors have a level of description having to do with the *goals* of the system and its *rationality*. But the exact character of the second level is obscure. What, for instance, are "the regularities by which they [structured expressions] are manipulated"? Is this Marr's algorithmic level?

Fodor–Marr–Pylyshyn

Pulling the three proposals together, along with our complaints about them, yields a revised "levels of description" notion of a computer. We want it to have at least three levels of description: a *physical* level (hardware), a *structural* (formal syntactic) level (algorithmic), and a *semantic* level. Optionally, we also want to be able to evaluate the device from the point of view of its *goals* and the *rationality* of its strategies for achieving these:

(F–M–P)   is a *computer* if and only if there is, for X, a best correct:
(a)   *physical description* under which it moves from physical state to physical state in accordance with physical laws; and a correlated
(b)   *structural description* under which it moves from state to state in accordance with general structural principles;
(c)   *semantic description* under which its structurally specified states are semantically interpreted to be about something;
(d)   *rational description* (optional) under which its semantically interpreted states bear relations of rationality and coherence.

Our characterization of level (c) separates the semantic or representational character of certain states from the structure (form, syntax) at level (b), and purpose at level (d) – which is optional. That is, there is nothing inherently contradictory about an "irrational" computational device, though there would be little apparent point to designing one. The formulation is intended to be compatible with both "classical" and connectionist architectures in that the general structural principles alluded to in (b) could be the hardwiring or programs of "classical" machines, or rules for activation passing and connection strengths embodied in connectionist machines.

One worry about the levels of description view is that it leaves out any mention of what the device will *do*, yet our conception of computers seems to involve the idea that they can compute, and that seems to involve at least rudimentary processing capacities. But the main worry about levels of description views in some people's eyes (see chapter 9) is the complement of the functional view. Whereas the functional view threatened to be too narrow, the levels of description view threatens to be too broad – what will fail to be a computer? So it would seem that unless we can tighten up the notion of a "best description," we may have to allow planets to be computers computing their orbits, or (analog) watches to be computers computing the time. We return to this issue shortly.

C.4   Combined Functional–Descriptive
View of Computers

Some of the above worries about each species of definition of a computer can perhaps be met by combining the strong points of each into a single characterization. On this combined "functional-descriptive" view a computer is characterized as follows:

(F–D)   X is a *computer* if and only if
1   X is capable of:
   (a)   automatically inputting, storing, manipulating, and outputting information in virtue of;
   (b)   inputting, storing, manipulating, and outputting representations of that information;
   (c)   these information processes occur in accordance with a finite set of principles that are, in some sense, in the machine itself.

2   X has a best correct:
   (a)   *physical description* under which it moves from physical state to physical state in accordance with physical laws; and a correlated
   (b)   *structural description* under which it moves from state to state in accordance with general structural principles;
   (c)   *semantic description* under which its structurally specified states are semantically interpreted to be about something;
   (d)   *rational description* (optional) under which its semantically interpreted states bear relations of rationality and coherence.

Notice that our characterization of a computer has the virtue that it does not require or forbid it to be made out of any particular *kind of stuff*, but only requires that the stuff be causally sufficient to move the machine from state to state. Our characterization also does not require the machine to have any particular *architecture*, or to have any particular *operations* on representations. It is completely general up to its physicality. And if we understood what non-physical causation might be like, we could reformulate condition (a) in even more general terms:

2(a′)   *causal description* under which it moves from state to state in accordance with causal laws.

We now elaborate on this conception by distinguishing different kinds and levels of computation, such as hardwired vs. program-controlled.

C.5   Levels of Computation: Stabler

According to Stabler (1983), putative computational devices can come in levels or kinds, each of which corresponds to a sense in which (F–D) (1c) is true:

1   A system which simply *computes* a function F: here what matters is just that the system produces the right output for each given input.

2   A system which will (is hardwired to) *execute a program*, P, which computes a function F: here what matters is that the output is gotten from the input in a certain way, by going through certain intermediary steps (described by the instructions of a program).

3   A system which *uses a program*, P, to govern its execution of P which computes a function F: here what matters is that the steps be under that control of other program-states of the machine.

These levels form an "isa" hierarchy (see chapter 7) from level 3 to level 1 in the sense that any system that falls under level 3 falls under level 2, and any system that falls under level 2 falls under level 1, but not necessarily conversely.

Now let's turn to a more precise characterization of these levels:

Level 1

A system S *computes a function F* if and only if S realizes that function; i.e. if and only if there is a 1–1 mapping or encoding (a "realization function") from some set of symbols to physical states of the system so that, in the right circumstances (the machine is not "broken," etc.), the system will always, in virtue of causal laws that apply to it, go from one state s_i (initial), to another, s_f (final), where, for every pair of such states, the symbol associated with the final state (s_f) is a function F of the symbol associated with the initial state (s_i). (This seems to have been the conception Fodor had in mind.)

On this conception a system computes a function (e.g. computes the successor function from a number n to its successor n + 1) when the states of the system can be paired with symbols or formulae F_1, F_2, . . . (e.g., 0, 1, . . .) in such a way that when the system is in state s_i (e.g. state 23) and that state is associated by the realization mapping with a certain symbol F_{23} (e.g. "23") then the machine will move into state sf (e.g., state 24) and that state will have been associated by the realization mapping with symbol F_{24} (e.g., "24").

Stabler (1983: 402) notes that level 1 computational descriptions will be *too generous* in that suitably baroque mappings will allow any computation to be realized by any (suitably complex) system – everything will become a computer. For instance, imagine that we have a formula that correctly describes the motion of a planet. That is, if the planet is at location L_1 at time t_1, it will next be at location L_1 at time t_2, etc. Then there will be a mapping from the solutions of the equation to the time and location of the planet that is 1–1. The planet will be computing its orbit! Not at all what we want. The answer, he suggests, is to "impose quite definite constraints on the realization mapping." One possibility would be to take the "realization" relation seriously and require that some state of the physical system *be* the symbol of whatever "F" represents. It is a hard unsolved problem what these constraints might be, but it might be important if the claim that cognition is a species of computation is to be non-trivial. We do not want cognition to be computation just because everything is. We return to this issue at the end of this chapter.

Level 2

A system S *executes a program P (to compute a function F)* if and only if (i) P contains a sequence of instructions I, . . . I$_n$, which specify a sequence of functions FI, . . . FI$_n$, the composition of which is F; (ii) S computes F by computing the sequence of functions FI, . . . FI$_n$. On this conception sequences of instructions in the program map on to the state transitions of the system. A hand calculator might be an example of this.

Level 3

A system S *uses program P to govern its execution of P (to compute a function F)* if and only if (i) there is a 1–1 program realization function which maps the instructions of P on to states of S; (ii) there is a set of control states such that S computes FI$_i$ because it is in a control state which determines that FI$_i$ is computed. Were S in a different control state, S might have computed a different FI.

It is at levels 2 and 3 that the notion of "running a program" gets separated into two importantly different notions: operating *in accordance with* a program (level 2) vs. being *controlled by* a program (level 3). At level 3 a system must not only conform to the program's description (the instructions) of its computational steps, but those descriptions themselves *counterfactually control* subsequent steps of the process. So it will be much more difficult to find a (non-bizarre, see above) mapping under which an arbitrary physical system is running a specific program (level 3), than it will be to find some (non-bizarre, see above) mapping under which that object can be said to be described by that program (level 2). It is clear from Stabler's account as well that the program (software) is not distinct from the hardware in the *programmed machine*: "This terminology [the software level is 'above' the hardware level] is unfortunate, though, insofar as it suggests that the 'software' is something other than 'hardware,' something other than a physical part or feature of the system. These suggestions of the colloquial terms are incorrect. The present account makes clear the commitment to an actual physical and causally efficacious realization of any program used by any physical system" (1983: 393).

C.6 Digital and Connectionist Computers

Earlier we outlined two kinds of notions of a computer:[2] one in terms of *what a computer can do*, one in terms of the *levels of description* of the device. We then suggested a *combined view*, and finally we distinguished three kinds or levels of computation – computing a function, computing in accordance with a program, and computing using a program. It is sometimes said that connectionist models are an *alternative* to computational models of cognition, but this appears to be true only if one takes "computational" to be "digital," "serial," or even "von Neumann." Both "functionally" and "descriptively" a connectionist machine is a computer.

Functionally we characterized a computer as being *hardware* capable of *inputting, storing, "manipulating"*[3] (*computing*), and *outputting* information in accordance with *principles in the system*. There is a rough correspondence between aspects of a connectionist machine and traditional digital machines: the network configuration of nodes and connections is the hardware configuration and the activation-passing rules and connection strengths are its internal principles. The input vectors are its input, the output vectors are its output. Information is stored in the connection strengths. It manipulates (computes) by multiplying its inputs by its connection strengths and passing the activation on in accordance with its activation-passing rules. Probably the DCTM notion hardest to reconstruct in, and most alien to, CCTM is the notion of a program, interpreted as a series of instructions directing the course of some computation. Notice that with DCTM we distinguished the program being run from the algorithm the program encodes (two different programs can encode the same algorithm). But with CCTM changes in weights and/or activation-passing rules change both what it does and how it does it. The issue of individuating algorithms in CCTM (how much change is a change of algorithm) has not been settled.

Descriptively we characterized a computer as receiving a three-part description in terms of *symbolic, structural*, and *physical* levels. Clearly a connectionist machine can be described at those three levels as well: patterns of activation (vectors) that receive semantic interpretation are symbolic,

the organization of nodes and connections is structural, and the stuff out
of which it is made that determine its activation-passing properties and its
connection strength properties (e.g. the chemistry of a synapse or the
diameter of a neuron) are physical. We can summarize these observations as
follows:

Functional

hardware: nodes and connections
inputting: input vector
storing: connection strengths
manipulating / computing: vector multiplication
outputting: output vector
principles in the system: activation-passing rules, connection strengths,
   vector multiplication

Descriptive

symbolic: vectors
structural: activation-passing   rules,   connection   strengths,   vector
   multiplication
physical: nodes and connections

Digital computers as limiting cases of connectionist computers?

Given this similarity, it is not surprising that a digital machine can be seen
as just a limiting case, a very special and "unnatural" configuration, of a
connectionist machine: where the connections are limited to about four per
unit, where every unit passes on just two values of activation: 0, 1, etc.
That is, we build a system out of McCulloch and Pitts "neurons," and we
build McCulloch and Pitts "neurons" out of connectionist nodes by not letting
them do anything continuous and by regimenting their connections. For
instance:

Connections: limit to about 4
Activation passing: limit values to 0, 1
Logic gates: limit rules to Boolean functions: AND, NOT, etc.

Networks and Turing machines

The whole issue of the computational power of networks in comparison to Turing machines is at present very unclear. Hornik et al. (1989) showed that some connectionist machines (three-layer, feed-forward) can *approximate* a TM. On the other hand, there are still many connectionist machines whose computational power is unknown. And it is still an open question whether there are "algorithms" that a connectionist machine can compute that a Turing machine cannot. Franklin and Garzon (1991) report interesting results relating Turing machines to connectionist machines:

1 They give a careful characterization of what it means to implement a Turing machine using a connectionist machine.
2 They exhibit an effective procedure for building a (synchronous, binary, linear threshold) network that behaves exactly as a given Turing machine behaves.

Given the Church–Turing thesis (see chapter 6) that any computable function is Turing machine computable this shows that "any computable function can be computed via a suitable neural network" (1991: 127).

3 They prove the unsolvability of the "stability problem" for networks (will an arbitrary net stabilize on arbitrary inputs) as an analog of Turing's proof of the unsolvability of the "halting problem" for Turing machines (will an arbitrary Turing machine halt on arbitrary inputs?).

Finally, Siegelmann and Sontag (1992) proved that "one may simulate all . . . Turing machines by nets [recurrent networks] using only first-order (i.e. linear) connections and rational weights" (1992: 440). They go on to note that "a consequence of Theorem 1 is the existence of a universal processor net, which upon receiving an encoded description of a recursively computable partial function (in terms of a Turing Machine) and an input string, would do what the encoded Turing Machine would have done on the input string" (1992: 448). Siegelmann and Sontag go on to estimate that given Minsky's universal Turing machine (see chapter 6) with 4 letters and 7 control states, there exists "a universal net with 1,058 processors. . . . Furthermore, it is quite possible that with some care in the construction one may be able to drastically reduce this estimate" (1992: 449). Kilian and Siegelmann (1993) generalized the result of Siegelmann and Sontag from networks using a specific little-used activation-passing rule, to the common "sigmoid" rule found in many three-layer feedforward networks, such as NETtalk (see chapter 10): "We show that . . . there exists a universal architecture that can be used to compute any recursive function. . . . Our techniques can be applied to a much more general class of 'sigmoid-like' activation functions, suggesting that Turing universality is a relatively common property of recurrent neural network models" (1993: 137). The moral of all this is that we are gradually, but finally, getting a clearer picture of the computational power of connectionist models that will hopefully rival our understanding of traditional computational power.

C.7   Is Everything a Computer?

As Stabler noted, the constraints on realizations must be substantial in order to avoid the consequence that computation is everywhere, and so trivialize the claim that cognition is a species of computation. Earlier (see chapter 9) we reviewed Searle's "syntax arguments" against the view that the brain is a digital computer (what he called "cognitivism") in any interesting sense. Searle argued that everything is a computer, so it is trivial and uninteresting that a brain is a computer. We argued that these arguments stemmed, in part, from a faulty characterization of computation and computers. Now, with our current conception of a computer and Stabler's levels at hand, we can see more clearly one of the things that went wrong. At best Searle's conception is that an object is a computer if it has a level-2 description – i.e. can be described as computing some function. But as we noted there, to capture our pre-theoretic notion of a level-2 computer, restrictions must be put on the mapping from symbols to states. Searle can best be viewed here as forcing that issue, and implicitly denying that such constraints can be found. However, if we are interested in a conception of a computer that at least applies to *us*, and we are not hardwired for all our cognitive capacities (programs), then we will need at least a level-3, perhaps a level-4 device (a device capable of learning algorithms). It is much more difficult to find a level-3 description of a system than a level-2 description. For example, if the wall-WordStar example is to show that a wall can be "interpreted" as running WordStar, then the fact that the wall can be described as a WordStar realization must suffice to show that the wall is a computer. But that simply does not follow. The hierarchy of levels is inclusive from level 3 to level 2 to level 1, but not the reverse – i.e. something could receive a level-2 description without thereby satisfying a level-3 description. We traced the problem to the fact that when a program is running on a machine (level-3) the program states of the machine counterfactually control subsequent states of the machine. Searle has not shown that the wall has this property – he has only claimed that the wall can be described in terms of the steps of a program (level-2 executing a program). We should also note that Stabler's hierarchy only applies to condition (2b) – how about all the other conditions on being a computer, in particular (2c). Does the wall get a true semantic level of description? It looks as if it does not.

Notes

1 This definition is typical, and is repeated, for instance, in Clark and Cowell (1976).
2 We also noted, and rejected, definitions of computers such as Newell's in terms of being equivalent to universal Turing machines.
3 Notice that "manipulating" symbols does not entail operations *on* them, nor does it entail manipulating them with "rules" stored in the computer's memory. It only involves creating, changing or destroying symbols, and connectionist processes do all three of these.

Study questions

What in general is the "functional" view of a computer?

What is Newell's conception of a "physical symbol system"?

What is von Eckhardt's conception of a computer?

What in general is the "levels of description" view of a computer?

What is Fodor's conception of a computer?

What are Marr's three levels of description for an information processing device?

How do Marr's "levels" relate to Dennett's "stances"?

What is Pylyshyn's conception of a computer?

How did we put together Fodor, Marr, and Pylyshyn?

What is the combined functional–descriptive view of a computer?

What are Stabler's three levels of computation?

Why are connectionist machines computers?

Is everything a computer – Why, Why not?

Suggested reading

The material reviewed in this chapter is from the non-technical literature on computation. There is also a technical literature on computation from the perspective of mathematics, logic, and computer science, which is beyond the scope of this discussion.

Computation

See Newell and Simon (1972), and Newell and Simon (1976) for more on physical symbol systems. Von Eckhardt (1993), chapter 3: The computational assumption, and Glymour (1992), chapter 12: The computable, are good chapter-length non-mathematical introductions to the topic, as is Copeland (1996a). At a more technical level, Minsky (1967) and Davies (1958) are classic texts, and Boolos and Jeffrey (1989) relate computation to logic. There are many good contemporary texts on computation. One that has been used in cognitive science (see for instance Stabler, 1983) is Clark and Cowell (1976). Odifreddi (1989), chapter 1, is an excellent but lengthy (over 100 pages) survey of computability and recursiveness. See Hornik et al. (1989) for a proof that multilayer feedforward networks can approximate a universal Turing machine as close as one wishes, and Franklin and Garzon (1991) for a demonstration that "any computable function can be computed via a suitable neural net."

Is everything a computer?

Putnam (1988) and Searle (1990b, 1992, chapter 9) are the contemporary focus for the idea that the standard definition of a computer makes everything a computer. See Goel (1992), Chalmers (1996a), Chalmers (1996b), chapter 9, Copeland (1996a) and Harnish (1996) for further discussion.

Bibliography

Akmajian, A., Demers, R., Farmer, A., and Harnish, R. (1995), *Linguistics: An Intro-duction to Language and Communication*, 4th edn, Cambridge, MA: MIT Press.

Anderson, J. (1983), *The Architecture of Cognition*, Cambridge, MA: Harvard University Press.

Anderson, J. (1993), *Rules of the Mind*, Hillsdale, NJ: Lawrence Erlbaum.

Anderson, J. (1995), *Introduction to Neural Networks*, Cambridge, MA: MIT Press.

Anderson, J., and Bower, G. (1974), *Human Associative Memory*, New York: Hemisphere.

Anderson, J., and Rosenfeld, E. (eds) (1988), *Neurocomputing*, Cambridge, MA: MIT Press.

Anderson, J., and Rosenfeld, E. (eds) (1998), *Talking Nets: An Oral History of Neural Networks*, Cambridge, MA: MIT Press.

Angell, J. R. (1911), Usages of the terms mind, consciousness and soul, *Psychological Bulletin*, 8: 46–7.

Arbib, M. (ed.) (1995), *Handbook of Brain Theory*, Cambridge, MA: Bradford/MIT Press.

Aristotle, On memory and reminiscence. In R. McKeon (ed.) (1941), *The Collected Works of Aristotle*, New York: Random House.

Armstrong, D. M. (1999), *The Mind-Body Problem: An Opinionated Introduction*, Boulder, CO: Westview Press.

Aspry, W. (1990), *John von Neumann and the Origins of Modern Computing*, Cambridge, MA: MIT Press.

Aspry, W., and Burks, A. (eds) (1987), *Papers of John von Neumann on Computers and Computer Theory*, Cambridge, MA: MIT Press.

Atlas, J. (1997), On the modularity of sentence processing: semantical generality and the language of thought. In J. Nuyts and E. Pederson (eds) (1997), *Language and Conceptualization*, Cambridge: Cambridge University Press.

Augarten, S. (1984), *Bit By Bit: An Illustrated History of Computers*, New York: Ticknor and Fields.

Baars, B. (1986), *The Cognitive Revolution in Psychology*, New York: Guilford Press.

Bain, A. (1855), *The Senses and the Intellect*, 4th edn, New York: D. Appleton (1902).

Bain, A. (1859), *The Emotions and the Will*, 4th edn, New York: D. Appleton.

Baker, L. Rudder (1987), *Saving Belief*, Princeton, NJ: Princeton University Press.

Ballard, D. (1997), *An Introduction to Neural Computation*, Cambridge, MA: Bradford/MIT Press.

Bara, B. (1995), *Cognitive Science: A Developmental Approach to the Simulation of the Mind*, Hillsdale, NJ: Lawrence Erlbaum.

Barr, A., Cohen, P., and Feigenbaum, E. (eds) (1981), *The Handbook of Artificial Intelligence*, vols 1–3, Los Altos, CA: William Kaufmann.

Barsalou, L. (1992), *Cognitive Psychology: An Overview for Cognitive Scientists*, Hillsdale, NJ: Lawrence Erlbaum.

Barwise, J., and Etchemendy, J. (1999), *Turing's World 3.0: An Introduction to Computability Theory*, Cambridge: Cambridge University Press.

Baumgartner, P., and Payr, S. (eds) (1995), *Speaking Minds: Interviews with Twenty Eminent Cognitive Scientists*, Princeton, NJ: Princeton University Press.

Beakley, B., and Ludlow, P. (eds) (1992), *The Philosophy of Mind: Classical Problems, Contemporary Issues*, Cambridge, MA: Bradford/MIT Press.

Beatty, J. (1995), *Principles of Behavioral Neuroscience*, Dubuque: Brown and Benchmark.

Bechtel, W. (1985), Contemporary connectionism: are the new parallel distributed processing models cognitive or associationist? *Behaviorism*, 13(1): 53–61.

Bechtel, W. (1994), Connectionism. In S. Guttenplan (ed.), *A Companion to the Philosophy of Mind*, Cambridge, MA: Blackwell.

Bechtel, W., and Abrahamsen, A. (1991), *Connectionism and the Mind*, Cambridge, MA: Blackwell.

Bechtel, W., and Graham, G. (eds) (1998), *A Companion to Cognitive Science*, Cambridge, MA: Blackwell.

Beckermann, A., Flohr, H., and Kim, J. (eds) (1992), *Emergence or Reduction? Essays on the Prospects of Nonreductive Physicalism*, New York: Walter de Gruyter.

Bever, T. (1992), The logical and extrinsic sources of modularity. In M. Gunnar and M. Maratsos (eds) (1992), *Modularity and Constraints in Language and Cognition*, Hillsdale, NJ: Lawrence Erlbaum.

Block, H. (1962), The Perceptron: a model for brain functioning. I, *Review of Modern Physics* 34: 123–35. Reprinted in Anderson and Rosenfeld (1988).

Block, N. (1978), Troubles with functionalism. In C. W. Savage (ed.) (1978), *Perception and Cognition: Issues in the Foundations of Psychology*, Minneapolis: University of Minnesota Press.

Block, N. (ed.) (1981), *Readings in the Philosophy of Psychology*, vol. 1, Cambridge, MA: Harvard University Press.

Block, N. (1983), Mental pictures and cognitive science, *Philosophical Review*, 90: 499–541.

Block, N. (1986), Advertisement for a semantics for psychology. In French et al. (1986).

Block, N. (1990), The computer model of the mind. In D. Osherson and E. Smith (eds) (1990), *An Invitation to Cognitive Science*, vol. 3: *Thinking*, Cambridge, MA: Bradford/MIT Press.

Block, N. (1994), Consciousness, Qualia. In S. Guttenplan (ed.) (1994), *A Companion to the Philosophy of Mind*, Cambridge, MA: Blackwell.

Block, N. (1995), On a confusion about a function of consciousness, *The Behavioral and Brain Sciences*, 18: 227–47. Reprinted in Block et al. (1997).

Block, N., Flanagan, O., and Guzeldere, G. (eds) (1997), *The Nature of Consciousness*, Cambridge, MA: Bradford/MIT Press.

Block, N., and Fodor, J. (1972), What psychological states are not, *Philosophical Review*, April: 159–81.

Block, N., and Segal, G. (1998), The philosophy of psychology. In A. C. Grayling (ed.) (1998), *Philosophy 2*, Oxford: Oxford University Press.

Bobrow, D., and Collins, A. (eds) (1975), *Representation and Understanding*, New York: Academic Press.

Bobrow, D., and Winograd, T. (1979), An overview of KRL, a Knowledge Representation Language, *Cognitive Science*, 1: 3–46.

Boden, M. (1977), *Artificial Intelligence and Natural Man*, New York: Basic Books.

Boden, M. (ed.) (1990), *The Philosophy of Artificial Intelligence*, Oxford: Oxford University Press.

Boolos G., and Jeffrey, R. (1989), *Computability and Logic*, 3rd edn, Cambridge: Cambridge University Press.

Boring, E. et al. (1939), *Introduction to Psychology*, New York: John Wiley.

Boring, E. (1951), *A History of Experimental Psychology*, 2nd edition, New York: Appleton, Century, Crofts.

Bower, G. (1975), Cognitive psychology: an introduction. In W. Estes (ed.), *Handbook of Learning and Cognitive Processes*, New York: Wiley.

Bower, G., and Clapper, J. (1989), Experimental Methods in cognitive science. In Posner (1989).

Brachman, R. (1979), On the epistemological status of semantic networks. In Findler (1979).

Brachman, R., and Levesque, H. (eds) (1985), *Readings in Knowledge Representation*, San Mateo, CA: Morgan Kaufman.

Braddon-Mitchell, D., and Jackson, F. (1996), *Philosophy of Mind and Cognition*, Oxford: Blackwell.

Brand, M., and Harnish, R. (eds) (1986), *The Representation of Knowledge and Belief*, Tucson: University of Arizona Press.

Brink, F. (1951), Excitation and conduction in the neuron (ch. 2), Synaptic mechanisms (ch. 3). In S. S. Stevens, *Handbook of Experimental Psychology*, New York: Wiley.

Broadbent, D. (1957), A mechanical model for human attention and immediate memory, *Psychological Review*, 64: 205–15.

Broadbent, D. (1958), *Perception and Communication*, New York: Pergamon.

Bruner, J., Goodnow, J., and Austin, G. (1956), *A Study of Thinking*, New York: Wiley.

Burge, T. (1979), Individualism and the mental. In P. French et al. (eds) (1979), *Contemporary Perspectives in the Philosophy of Language*, Minneapolis: University of Minnesota Press.

Burks, A., Goldstine, H., and von Neumann, J. (1946), Preliminary discussion of the logical design of an electronic computing instrument. In Aspry and Burks (1987).

Cajal, R. y (1909), *New Ideas on the Structure of the Nervous System in Man and Vertebrates*, Cambridge, MA: Bradford/MIT Press.

Carnap, R. (1937), *The Logical Syntax of Language*, London: Routledge and Kegan Paul.

Carpenter, B., and Doran, R. (1977), The other Turing machine, *Computer Journal*, 20(3): 269–79.

Carpenter, B., and Doran, R. (eds) (1986), *A. M. Turing's ACE Report of 1946 and Other Papers*, Cambridge, MA: MIT Press.

Carruthers, P., and Smith, P. (eds) (1996), *Theories of Theories of Mind*, Cambridge: Cambridge University Press.

Caudill, M., and Butler, C. (1993), *Understanding Neural Networks*, vols 1 and 2, Cambridge, MA: Bradford/MIT Press.

Chalmers, D. (1992), Subsymbolic computation and the Chinese room. In Dinsmore (1992).

Chalmers, D. (1995a), On implementing a computation, *Minds and Machines*, 4: 391–402.

Chalmers, D. (1995b), The puzzle of conscious experience, *Scientific American*, 273: 80–6.

Chalmers, D. (1995c), Facing up to the problem of consciousness, *Journal of Consciousness Studies*, 2(3): 200–19. Reprinted in Cooney (2000).

Chalmers, D. (1996a), Does a rock implement every finite-state automaton? *Synthese*, 108: 309–33.

Chalmers, D. (1996b), *The Conscious Mind*, Oxford: Oxford University Press.

Chater, N., and Oaksford, M. (1990), Autonomy, implementation and cognitive architecture: a reply to Fodor and Pylyshyn, *Cognition*, 34: 93–107.

Cherniak, E., and McDermott, D. (1985), *Introduction to Artificial Intelligence*, Reading, MA: Addison Wesley.

Chisley, R. (1995), Why everything doesn't realize every computation, *Minds and Machines*, 4: 403–20.

Chomsky, N. (1959), Review of Skinner, *Verbal Behavior*, *Language*, 35: 26–58.

Christensen, S., and Turner, D. (eds) (1993), *Folk Psychology and the Philosophy of Mind*, Hillsdale, NJ: Lawrence Erlbaum.

Church, A. (1936), An unsolvable problem of elementary number theory, *American Journal of Mathematics*, 58: 345–63. Reprinted in Davis (1965).

Churchland, P. M. (1981), Eliminative materialism and propositional attitudes, *Journal of Philosophy*, 78: 67–90.

Churchland, P. M. (1988), *Matter and Consciousness*, rev. edn, Cambridge, MA: Bradford/MIT Press.

Churchland, P. M. (1989), On the nature of explanation: a PDP approach. In P. M. Churchland (1989), *A Neurocomputational Perspective*, Cambridge, MA: Bradford/MIT Press. Reprinted with some changes in Haugeland (1997).

Churchland, P. M. (1990), Cognitive activity in artificial neural networks. In D. Osherson and E. Smith (eds) (1990), *An Invitation to Cognitive Science*, vol. 3, Cambridge, MA: Bradford/MIT Press.

Churchland, P. M. (1994), Folk psychology (2). In Guttenplan (1994).

Churchland, P. M., and Churchland, P. S. (1991), Could a machine think? *Scientific American*, 262(1): 32–7.

Churchland, P. S. (1986), *Neurophilosophy*, Cambridge, MA: Bradford/MIT Press.

Churchland, P. S., and Sejnowski, T. (1992), *The Computational Brain*, Cambridge, MA: Bradford/MIT Press.

Clark, A. (1989), *Microcognition*, Cambridge, MA: Bradford/MIT Press.

Clark, A. (1990), Connectionist minds, *Proceedings of the Aristotelian Society*: 83–102. Reprinted in MacDonald and Macdonald (1995).

Clark, A. (1991), In defense of explicit rules. In Ramsey, Stich, and Rumelhart (1991).

Clark, A. (1993), *Associative Engines*, Cambridge, MA: Bradford/MIT Press.

Clark, K., and Cowell, D. (1976), *Programs, Machines and Computability: An Introduction to the Theory of Computing*, New York: McGraw-Hill.

Clark, A., and Lutz, R. (eds) (1995), *Connectionism and Context*, Berlin: Springer Verlag.

Cognitive Science Society (eds), *Proceedings of the Annual Conference of the Cognitive Science Society*, Hillsdale, NJ: Lawrence Erlbaum (annual).

Cognitive Science 1978: Report of the State of the Art Committee to the Advisors of the Alfred P. Sloan Foundation, October 1, 1978. Reprinted in Machlup and Mansfield (1983).

Cohen, J., and Schooler, J. (eds) (1996), *Scientific Approaches to Consciousness*, Hillsdale, NJ: Lawrence Erlbaum.

Collins, A., and Smith, E. (eds) (1988), *Readings in Cognitive Science*, San Mateo, CA: Morgan Kaufman.

Cooney, B. (2000), *The Place of Mind*, Belmont, CA: Wadsworth.

Copeland, J. (1993a), The curious case of the Chinese gym, *Synthese*, 95: 173–86.

Copeland, J. (1993b), *Artificial Intelligence: A Philosophical Introduction*, Oxford: Blackwell.

Copeland, J. (1996a), What is computation? *Synthese*, 108: 335–59.

Copeland, J. (1996b), The Church–Turing thesis. In J. Perry and E. Zalta (eds), *The Stanford Encyclopedia of Philosophy* [http://plato.stanford.edu].

Copeland, J. (1997), The broad conception of computation, *American Behavioral Scientist*, 40(6): 690–716.

Copeland, J. (1998), Turing's O-machines, Searle, Penrose and the brain, *Analysis*, 58(2): 128–38.

Copeland, J., and Proudfoot, D. (1996), On Alan Turing's anticipation of connectionism, *Synthese*, 108: 361–77.

Copeland, J., and Proudfoot, D. (1999), Alan Turing's forgotten ideas in computer science, *Scientific American*, April: 99–103.

Corsi, P. (1991), *The Enchanted Loom: Chapters in the History of Neuroscience*, Oxford: Oxford University Press.

Cowan, J., and Sharp, D. (1988), Neural nets and artificial intelligence. Reprinted in Graubard (1988).

Crane, T. (1995), *The Mechanical Mind*, New York: Penguin.

Crevier, D. (1993), *AI: The Tumultuous History of the Search for Artificial Intelligence*, New York: Basic Books.

Crick, F. (1994), *The Astonishing Hypothesis: The Scientific Search for the Soul*, New York: Touchstone/Simon and Schuster.

Crick, F., and Asanuma, C. (1986), Certain aspects of the anatomy and physiology of the cerebral cortex. In J. McClelland and D. Rumelhart (eds) (1986), *Parallel Distributed Processing*, vol. 2, Cambridge, MA: Bradford/MIT Press.

Cummins, R. (1986), Inexplicit information. In Brand and Harnish (1986).

Cummins, R. (1989), *Meaning and Mental Representation*, Cambridge, MA: Bradford/MIT Press.

Cummins, R. (1996), *Representations, Targets, and Attitudes*, Cambridge, MA: Bradford/MIT Press.

Cummins, R., and Cummins, D. (eds) (1999), *Minds, Brains and Computers: The Foundations of Cognitive Science*, Oxford: Blackwell.

Cussins, A. (1990), The connectionist construction of concepts. In Boden (1990).

D'Andrade, R. (1989), Cultural cognition. In Posner (1989).

Davies, M. (1991), Concepts, connectionism and the language of thought. In Ramsey, Stich, and Rumelhart (1991).

Davies, M. (1995), Reply: consciousness and the varieties of aboutness. In C. MacDonald and G. MacDonald (eds) (1995), *Philosophy of Psychology: Debates on Psychological Explanation*, Cambridge, MA: Blackwell.

Davis, M. (1958), *Computability and Unsolvability*, New York: McGraw-Hill.

Davis, M. (ed.) (1965), *The Undecidable*, Hewlett, NY: Raven Press.

Davis, S. (ed.) (1992), *Connectionism: Theory and Practice*, Oxford: Oxford University Press.

Dawson, M. (1998), *Understanding Cognitive Science*, Oxford: Blackwell.

Dennett, D. (1978a), Skinner skinned. In *Brainstorms*, Montgomery, VT: Bradford Books.

Dennett, D. (1978b), Towards a cognitive theory of consciousness. In *Brainstorms*, Montgomery, VT: Bradford Books.

Dennett, D. (1985), Can machines think? In M. Shafto (ed.) (1985), *How We Know*, New York: Harper and Row.

Dennett, D. (1987a), *The Intentional Stance*, Cambridge, MA: Bradford/MIT Press.

Dennett, D. (1987b), Fast thinking. In *The Intentional Stance*, Cambridge, MA: Bradford/MIT Press.

Dennett, D. (1991), *Consciousness Explained*, London: Penguin.

Dennett, D. (1995), *Darwin's Dangerous Idea*, London: Penguin.

Descartes, R. (1641), *Meditations*. In E. Haldane and G. Ross (1931), *Philosophical Works of Descartes*, vol. 1, Cambridge: Cambridge University Press. Reprinted by Dover Publications (1955).

Descartes, R. (1649), *Passions of the Soul*. In E. Haldane and G. Ross (1931), *Philosophical Works of Descartes*, vol. 1, Cambridge: Cambridge University Press. Reprinted by Dover Publications (1955).

Devitt, M. (1989). A narrow representational theory of mind. In S. Silvers (ed.) (1989), *ReRepresentations*, Dordrecht: Kluwer.

Devitt, M. (1991), Why Fodor can't have it both ways. In Loewer and Rey (1991).

Devitt, M. (1996), *Coming to Our Senses*, Cambridge: Cambridge University Press.

Dinsmore, J. (ed.) (1992), *The Symbolic and Connectionist Paradigms*, Hillsdale, NJ: Lawrence Erlbaum.

Dretske, F. (1981), *Knowledge and the Flow of Information*, Cambridge, MA: Bradford/MIT Press.

Dretske, F. (1986a), Aspects of representation. In Brand and Harnish (1986).

Dretske, F. (1986b), Misrepresentation. In R. Bogdan (ed.) (1986), *Belief: Form, Content and Function*, Oxford: Oxford University Press.

Dretske, F. (1993), Conscious experience, *Mind*, 102: 263–83.

Dretske, F. (1995), *Naturalizing the Mind*, Cambridge, MA: Bradford/MIT Press.

Dreyfus, H. (1972/9), *What Computers Can't Do*, rev. edn, New York: Harper and Row.

Dreyfus, H., and Dreyfus, S. (1988), Making a mind vs. modeling the brain: artificial intelligence back at a branchpoint. Reprinted in Graubard (1988).

Dunlop, C., and Fetzer, J. (1993), *Glossary of Cognitive Science*, New York: Paragon House.

Ebbinghaus, H. (1885), *Memory: A Contribution to Experimental Psychology*, Columbia Teacher's College [1913].

Edelman, G. (1989), *The Remembered Present: A Biological Theory of Consciousness*, New York: Basic Books.

Elman, J. (1990a), Finding structure in time, *Cognitive Science*, 14: 213–52.

Elman, J. (1990b), Representation and structure in connectionist models. In G. Altman (ed.) (1990), *Cognitive Models of Speech Processing*, Cambridge, MA: Bradford/MIT Press.

Elman, J. (1992), Grammatical structure and distributed representations. In Davis (1992).

Elman, J. (1993), Learning and development in neural networks: the importance of starting small, *Cognition*, 48(1): 71–99.

Elman, J. et al. (1996), *Rethinking Innateness*, Cambridge, MA: Bradford/MIT Press.

Eysenck, M., and Keane, M. (1990), *Cognitive Psychology: A Student's Handbook*, Hillsdale, NJ: Lawrence Erlbaum.

Fancher, R. E. (1979), *Pioneers of Psychology*, New York: W. W. Norton.

Feigenbaum, E., and Feldman, E. (eds) (1963), *Computers and Thought*, New York: McGraw-Hill. Reissued (1995) Cambridge, MA: Bradford/MIT Press.

Feldman, J. (1989), Neural representation of conceptual knowledge. In Nadel et al. (1989).

Feldman, J., and Ballard, D. (1982), Connectionist models and their properties, *Cognitive Science*, 6: 205–54.

Field, H. (1977), Logic, meaning and conceptual role, *Journal of Philosophy*, July: 379–409.

Fikes, R., and Nilsson, N. (1971), STRIPS: a new approach to the application of theorem proving to problem solving, *Artificial Intelligence*, 2: 189–208.

Findler, N. (ed.) (1979), *Associative Networks*, New York: Academic Press.

Finger, S. (1994), *Origins of Neuroscience: A History of Explorations into Brain Function*, Oxford: Oxford University Press.

Flanagan, O. (1991), *The Science of the Mind*, 2nd edn, Cambridge, MA: Bradford/MIT Press.

Flanagan, O. (1992), *Consciousness Reconsidered*, Cambridge, MA: Bradford/MIT Press.

Fodor, J. (1975), *The Language of Thought*, Cambridge, MA: Harvard University Press.

Fodor, J. (1980a), Methodological solipsism considered as a research strategy in cognitive science, *The Behavioral and Brain Sciences*, 3(1): 63–73. Reprinted in Fodor (1981b).

Fodor, J. (1980b), Commentary on Searle, *The Behavioral and Brain Sciences*, 3: 431–2.

Fodor, J. (1981a), The mind-body problem, *Scientific American*, 244(1): 114–23.

Fodor, J. (1981b), *RePresentations*, Cambridge, MA: Bradford/MIT Press.

Fodor, J. (1983), *Modularity of Mind*, Cambridge, MA: Bradford/MIT Press.

Fodor, J. (1984), Semantics, Wisconsin style, *Synthese*, 59: 231–50. Reprinted in Fodor (1990).

Fodor, J. (1985), Precis of *The Modularity of Mind*, *The Behavioral and Brain Sciences*, 8: 1–6. Commentary on Fodor (1985), *The Behavioral and Brain Sciences*, 8: 7–42. Reprinted in Fodor (1990).

Fodor, J. (1986), The Modularity of Mind, and Modularity of Mind: Fodor's Response. In Z. Pylyshyn and W. Demopolous (eds) (1986), *Meaning and Cognitive Structure*, Norwood, NJ: Ablex.

Fodor, J. (1987), *Psychosemantics*, Cambridge, MA: Bradford/MIT Press.

Fodor, J. (1989), Why should the mind be modular? In G. Alexander (ed.), *Reflections on Chomsky*, Oxford: Blackwell. Reprinted in Fodor (1990).

Fodor, J. (1990), *A Theory of Content*, Cambridge, MA: Bradford/MIT Press.

Fodor, J. (1991), Replies. In Loewer and Rey (1991).

Fodor, J. (1994), *The Elm and the Expert*, Cambridge, MA: Bradford/MIT Press.

Fodor, J. (1998), *In Critical Condition*, Cambridge, MA: Bradford/MIT Press.

Fodor, J., and Lepore, E. (1991), Why meaning (probably) isn't conceptual role, *Mind and Language*, 4. Reprinted in S. Stich and T. Warfield (eds) (1994), *Mental Representation: A Reader*, Oxford: Blackwell.

Fodor, J., and Lepore, E. (1992), *Holism: A Shopper's Guide*, Cambridge, MA: Blackwell.

Fodor, J., and Pylyshyn, Z. (1988), Connectionism and cognitive architecture: a critical analysis. In S. Pinker and J. Mehler (eds), *Connections and Symbols*, Cambridge, MA: Bradford/MIT Press.

Forster, K. (1978), Accessing the mental lexicon. In E. Walker (ed.) (1978), *Explorations in the Biology of Language*, Cambridge, MA: Bradford/MIT Press.

Franklin, S., and Garzon, M. (1991), Neural computability. In O. Omidvar (ed.) (1991), *Progress on Neural Networks*, vol. 1, Norwood, NJ: Ablex.

Frege, G. (1979), *Begriffsschrift*. Trans. T. Bynym (1979) as *Concept Script*, Oxford: Oxford University Press.

Frege, G. (1892), On sense and reference. Reprinted in Harnish (1994).

Frege, G. (1918), The thought: a logical inquiry, *Mind* 65: 289–311. Reprinted (with correction) in Harnish (1994).

French, P. et al. (eds) (1986), *Midwest Studies in Philosophy*, X, Minneapolis: University of Minnesota Press.

French, R. (1990), Subcognition and the Turing test, *Mind*, 99: 53–65.

Gall, F. (1835), *On the Functions of the Brain* and of Each of Its Parts, 6 volumes, Boston, MA: Marsh, Capen, and Lyon.

Gandy, R. (1988), The confluence of ideas in 1936. In R. Herken (ed.) (1988), *The Universal Turing Machine: A Half Century Survey*, Oxford: Oxford University Press.

Gardner, H. (1985), *The Mind's New Science*, New York: Basic Books.

Garfield, J. (ed.) (1987), *Modularity in Knowledge Representation and Natural Language Understanding*, Cambridge, MA: Bradford/MIT Press.

Garfield, J. (ed.) (1990), *Foundations of Cognitive Science*, New York: Paragon House.

Gazzaniga, M. (ed.) (1995), *The Cognitive Neurosciences*, Cambridge, MA: Bradford/MIT Press.

Gazzaniga, M., and LeDoux, J. (1978), *The Integrated Mind*, New York: Plenum Press.

Geschwind, N. (1979), Specialization of the human brain. In *The Brain*, San Francisco: Freeman.

Glymour, C. (1992), *Thinking Things Through*, Cambridge, MA: Bradford/MIT Press.

Gödel, K. (1931), [trans. from the original German as] "On formally undecidable propositions of Principia Mathematica and related systems. In Davis (1965).

Goel, V. (1992), Are computational explanations vacuous? *Proceedings of the 14th Annual Conference of the Cognitive Science Society*, Hillsdale, NJ: Lawrence Erlbaum.

Goldberg, S., and Pessin, A. (1997), *Gray Matters: An Introduction to the Philosophy of Mind*, Armonk, NY: M. E. Sharpe.

Goldman, A. I. (1993a), The psychology of folk psychology, *The Behavioral and Brain Sciences*, 16(1): 15–28.

Goldman, A. I. (1993b), Consciousness, folk psychology, and cognitive science, *Consciousness and Cognition*, 2: 364–82.

Goldman, A. I. (ed.) (1993c), *Readings in Philosophy and Cognitive Science*, Cambridge, MA: Bradford/MIT Press.

Goldman, A. I. (1993d), *Philosophical Applications of Cognitive Science*, Boulder, CO: Westview Press.

Goschke, T., and Koppelberg, S. (1991), The concept of representation and the representation of concepts in connectionist models. In Ramsey, Stich, and Rumelhart (1991).

Graubard, S. (ed.) (1988), *The Artificial Intelligence Debate: False Starts, Real Foundations*, Cambridge, MA: MIT Press.

Greenwood, J. (ed.) (1991), *The Future of Folk Psychology*, Cambridge: Cambridge University Press.

Gross, C., Rocha-Miranda, C., and Bender, D. (1972), Visual properties of neurons in the inferotemporal cortex of the macaque, *Journal of Neurophysiology*, 35: 96–111.

Gross, M., and Lentin, A. (1970), *Introduction to Formal Grammars*, New York: Springer-Verlag.

Guttenplan, S. (ed.) (1994), *A Companion to the Philosophy of Mind*, Oxford: Blackwell.

Güzeldere, G. (1997), The many faces of consciousness: a field guide. In Block et al. (1997).

Haberland, K. (1994), *Cognitive Psychology*, Boston: Allyn and Bacon.

Halliday, M. A. K. (1970), Functional diversity in language as seen from a consideration of modality and mood in english, *Foundations of Language*, 6: 322–61.

Hameroff, S., et al. (eds) (1996), *Toward a Science of Consciousness: The First Tucson Discussions and Debates*, Cambridge, MA: Bradford/MIT Press.

Hanson, S. (1999), Connectionist neuroscience: representational and learning issues of neuroscience. In Lepore and Pylyshyn (1999).

Harlow, H. (1953), Mice, monkeys, men and motives, *Psychological Review*, 60: 23–32.

Harman, G. (1982), Conceptual role semantics, *Notre Dame Journal of Formal Logic*, 23(2): 242–56.

Harman, G. (1987), (Non-solipsistic) conceptual role semantics. In Lepore (1987).

Harnish, R. (ed.) (1994), *Basic Topics in the Philosophy of Language*, Englewood Cliffs NJ: Prentice-Hall.

Harnish, R. (1995), Modularity and speech acts, *Pragmatics and Cognition*, 3(1): 2–29.

Harnish, R. (1996), Consciousness, cognitivism and computation: a reply to Searle, *Conceptus*, 29 Nr. 75: 229–49.

Harnish, R., and Farmer, A. (1984), Pragmatics and the modularity of the language system, *Lingua*, 63: 255–77.

Hartley, D. (1749), *Observations on Man*. Reprinted New York: Garland (1971).

Hatfield, G. (1992), Descartes' physiology and psychology. In J. Cottingham (ed.) (1992), *The Cambridge Companion to Descartes*, Cambridge: Cambridge University Press.

Haugeland, J. (ed.) (1981), *Mind Design*, Cambridge, MA: Bradford/MIT Press.

Haugeland, J. (1985), *Artificial Intelligence: The Very Idea*, Cambridge, MA: Bradford/MIT Press.

Haugeland, J. (ed.) (1997), *Mind Design II*, Cambridge, MA: Bradford/MIT Press.

Hawking, S. (1988), *A Brief History of Time*, New York: Bantam Books.

Hayes, P. (1979), The naive physics manifesto. In D. Mitchie (ed.) (1979), *Expert Systems in the Electronic Age*, Edinburgh: Edinburgh University Press.

Hayes, P. (1980), The logic of frames. In D. Meting (ed.), *Frame Conceptions and Understanding*, Berlin: de Gruyter. Reprinted in Webber and Nilsson (1981).

Hebb, D. O. (1949), *The Organization of Behavior*, New York: Wiley.

Hebb, D. O. (1972), *A Textbook of Psychology*, 3rd edn, Toronto: W. B. Saunders.

Heims, S. (1980), *John von Neumann and Norbert Wiener*, Cambridge, MA: MIT Press.

Hernstein, R., and Boring, E. (eds.) (1966), *A Source Book in the History of Psychology*, Cambridge, MA: Harvard University Press.

Hewitt, C. (1971), Procedural embedding of knowledge in PLANNER. In *Proceedings of the Second Joint Conference on Artificial Intelligence*, pp. 167–82, London: British Computer Society.

Hewitt, C. (1990), The challenge of open systems. In D. Partridge and Y. Wilks (eds) (1990), *The Foundations of AI: A Sourcebook*, Cambridge: Cambridge University Press.

Hilgard, E. (1987), *Psychology in America*, New York: Harcourt Brace Jovanovich.

Hillis, D. (1985), *The Connection Machine*, Cambridge, MA: Bradford/MIT Press.

Hinton, G. (1992), How neural networks learn from experience, *Scientific American*, September.

Hirschfeld, L., and Gelman, S. (eds) (1994), *Mapping the Mind: Domain Specificity in Cognition and Culture*, Cambridge: Cambridge University Press.

Hirst, W. (ed.) (1988), *The Making of Cognitive Science: Essays in Honor of George A. Miller*, Cambridge: Cambridge University Press.

Hobbes, T. (1651), *Leviathan*. Reprinted Indianapolis: Bobbs-Merrill (1958).

Hodges, A. (1983), *Alan Turing: The Enigma*, New York: Simon and Schuster.

Hofstadter, D. (1979), *Gödel, Escher, Bach*, New York: Basic Books.

Hofstadter, D. (1981), The Turing test: a coffee house conversation. In D. Hofstadter and D. Dennett (eds) (1981), *The Mind's I*, New York: Basic Books.

Hopcroft, J., and Ullman, J. (1969), *Formal Languages and Their Relation to Automata*, New York: Addison Wesley.

Horgan, T. (1994), Computation and mental representation. In S. Stich and T. Warfield (eds) (1994), *Mental Representation*, Cambridge, MA: Blackwell.

Horgan, T., and Tienson, J. (eds) (1991), *Connectionism and the Philosophy of Mind*, Dordrecht: Kluwer Academic.

Hornik, K. et al. (1989), Multilayer feedforward networks are universal approximators, *Neural Networks*, 2: 359–66.

Horst, S. (1996), *Symbols, Computation and Intentionality; A Critique of the Computational Theory of Mind*, Berkeley: University of California Press.

Hubel, D., and Wiesel, T. (1979), Brain mechanisms of vision. In *The Brain*, San Francisco: Freeman.

Hume, D. (1739), *A Treatise of Human Nature*, Oxford: Oxford University Press (1880).

Hunt, M. (1993), *The Story of Psychology*, New York: Doubleday.

Ince, D. (ed.) (1992), *Mechanical Intelligence: Collected Works of A. M. Turing*, Amsterdam: North-Holland.

Jackson, F. (1986), What Mary didn't know, *Journal of Philosophy*, 83: 291–5.

Jacob, P. (1997), *What Minds Can Do*, Cambridge: Cambridge University Press.

James, W. (1890), *The Principles of Psychology*, New York: Dover.

James, W. (1892), *Psychology (Briefer Course)*, New York: Holt.

Jeffrey, R. (1991), *Formal Logic: Its Scope and Limits*, 3rd edn, New York: McGraw-Hill.

Johnson-Laird, P. (1988), *The Computer and the Mind: An Introduction to Cognitive Science*, Cambridge, MA: Harvard University Press.

Kandel, E., Schwartz, J., and Jessell, T. (1995), *Essentials of Neural Science and Behavior*, Norwalk: Appleton and Lange.

Karmiloff-Smith, A. (1992), *Beyond Modularity: A Developmental Perspective on Cognitive Science*, Cambridge, MA: Bradford/MIT Press.

Kent, E. (1981), *The Brains of Men and Machines*, Peterborough, NH: BYTE/McGraw-Hill.

Kilian, J., and Siegelmann, H. (1993), On the power of sigmoid neural networks, *Proceedings of the Sixth ACM Workshop on Computational Learning Theory*, 137–43. New York: Association for Computing Machinery.

Kim, J. (1993), *Supervenience and the Mind*, Cambridge: Cambridge University Press.

Kim, J. (1994), Supervenience. In Guttenplan (1994).

Kim, J. (1996), *Philosophy of Mind*, Boulder, CO: Westview.

Klahr, D., Langley, P., and Neches, R. (eds) (1987), *Production System Models of Learning and Development*, Cambridge, MA: Bradford/MIT Press.

Kobes, B. (1990), Individualism and artificial intelligence. In J. Tomberlin (ed.) (1990), *Philosophical Perspectives*, 4, Atascadero, CA: Ridgeview.

Kosslyn, S. (1980), *Image and Mind*, Cambridge, MA: Harvard University Press.

Kosslyn, S., and Koenig, O. (1992), *Wet Mind*, New York: Free Press.

Kurzweil, R. (1990), *The Age of Intelligent Machines*, Cambridge, MA: Bradford/MIT Press.

Kurzweil, R. (1999), *The Age of Spiritual Machines*, New York: Penguin Books.

Lackner, J., and Garrett, M. (1972), Resolving ambiguity: effects of biosing context in the unattended ear, *Cognition*, 1: 359–72.

Laird, J., Newell, A., and Rosenbloom, P. (1987), Soar: an architecture for general intelligence, *Artificial Intelligence*, 33(1): 1–64.

Lashley, K. (1923), The behavioristic interpretation of consciousness, *Psychological Review*, 30: 329–53.

Lashley, K. (1929), *Brain Mechanism and Intelligence*, Chicago: Chicago University Press.

Lashley, K. (1951), The problem of serial order in behavior. In L. Jeffress (ed.), *Cerebral Mechanisms in Behavior*, New York: Wiley.

Leahey, T. (1992), *A History of Psychology*, 3rd edn, Englewood Cliffs, NJ: Prentice-Hall.

Lehman, J., Laird, J., and Rosenbloom, P. (eds) (1998), A gentle introduction to Soar: an architecture for human cognition. In Scarborough and Sternberg (1998).

Lepore, E. (ed.) (1987), *New Directions in Semantics*, New York: Academic Press.

Lepore, E. (1994), Conceptual role semantics. In Guttenplan (1994).

Lepore, E., and Loewer, B. (1986), Solipsistic semantics. In French et al. (1986).

Lepore, E., and Pylyshyn, Z. (eds) (1999), *What is Cognitive Science?*, Oxford: Blackwell.

Lettvin, J. et al. (1959), What the frog's eye tells the frog's brain. Reprinted in W. McCulloch (1965).

Levine, D. (1991), *Introduction to Neural Cognitive Modeling*, Hillsdale, NJ: Lawrence Erlbaum.

Levine, J. (1983), Materialism and qualia: the explanatory gap, *Pacific Philosophical Quarterly*, 64: 354–61.

Lindsay, P., and Norman, D. (1972), *Human Information Processing: An Introduction to Psychology*, New York: Academic Press.

Lisker, L., and Abramson, A. (1964), A cross-language study of voicing of initial stops: acoustical measurements, *Word*, 20: 384–422.

Loewer, B., and Rey, G. (eds) (1991), *Meaning in Mind*, Oxford: Blackwell.

Lormand, E. (1994), Qualia! (now playing at a theater near you), *Philosophical Topics*, 22(1 and 2): 127–56.

Luger, G. (ed.) (1995), *Computation and Intelligence*, Cambridge, MA: Bradford/MIT Press.

Lycan, W. (ed.) (1990), *Mind and Cognition*, Oxford: Blackwell.

Lycan, W. (1997), Consciousness as internal monitoring. In Block et al. (1997).

McClamrock, R. (1995), *Existential Cognition: Computational Minds in the World*, Chicago: University of Chicago Press.

McClelland, J. (1981), Retrieving general and specific information from stored knowledge of specifics. *Proceedings of the Third International Conference of the Cognitive Science Society*, Berkeley, 1981.

McClelland, J., and Rumelhart, D. (1981), An interactive activation model of context effects in letter perception: Part I. An account of basic findings, *Psychological Review*, 88(5): 375–407.

McClelland, J., and Rumelhart, D. (1988), *Explorations in Parallel Distributed Processing*, Cambridge, MA: Bradford/MIT Press.

McCorduck, P. (1979), *Machines Who Think*, San Francisco: W. H. Freeman.

McCulloch, G. (1995), *The Mind and Its World*, London: Routledge.

McCulloch, W. (1965), *Embodiments of Mind*, Cambridge, MA: MIT Press.

McCulloch, W., and Pitts, W. (1943), A logical calculus of the ideas immanent in nervous activity. Reprinted in W. McCulloch (1965), and in Anderson and Rosenfeld (1998).

McDermott, D. (1976), Artificial intelligence meets natural stupidity, SIGART Newsletter, 57. Reprinted in Haugeland (1981).

McDermott, D. (1986), A critique of pure reason. Research Report YALEU/CSD/RR no. 480.

MacDonald, C., and MacDonald, G. (eds) (1995), *Connectionism: Debates on Psychological Explanation*, vol. 2, Oxford: Blackwell.

McGinn, C. (1982), The structure of content. In A. Woodfield (ed.) (1982), *Thought and Object*, Oxford: Oxford University Press.

McGinn, C. (1991), *The Problem of Consciousness*, Cambridge, MA: Blackwell.

Machlup, F., and Mansfield, U. (eds) (1983), *The Study of Information: Interdisciplinary Messages*, New York: Wiley.

McLaughlin, B. (1993), The connectionism/classicism battle to win souls, *Philosophical Studies*, 71:163–90.

McLaughlin, B., and Warfield, T. (1994), The allure of connectionism reexamined, *Synthese*, 101: 365–400.

McLeod, P., Plunkett, K., and Rolls, E. (1998), *Introduction to Connectionist Modelling of Cognitive Processes*, Oxford: Oxford University Press.

McTeal, M. (1987), *The Articulate Computer*, Oxford: Blackwell.

Maloney, J. C. (1989), *The Mundane Matter of the Mental Language*, Cambridge: Cambridge University Press.

Marcel, A., and Bisiach, E. (eds) (1988), *Consciousness in Contemporary Science*, Oxford: Oxford University Press.

Marr, D. (1977), Artificial intelligence – a personal view. Reprinted in Haugeland (1981).

Marr, D. (1982), *Vision*, San Francisco: Freeman.

Marx, M., and Hillix, W. (1963), *Systems and Theories in Psychology*, New York: McGraw-Hill.

Massaro, D. (1988), Some criticisms of connectionist models of human performance, *Journal of Memory and Language*, 27: 213–34.

Metropolis, N. et al. (eds) (1980), *A History of Computing in the Twentieth Century*, New York: Academic Press.

Mill, J. S. (1829), *The Analysis of the Phenomena of the Human Mind*, London: Baldwin and Cradock.

Mill, J. S. (1843), *A System of Logic*. Reprinted London: Longmans (1967).

Miller, G. (1951), *Language and Communication*, New York: McGraw-Hill.

Miller, G. (1956), The magical number seven, plus or minus two: some limits on our capacity for processing information, *Psychological Review*, 63: 81–97. Reprinted in Miller (1967).

Miller, G. (1967), *The Psychology of Communication*, New York: Basic Books.

Miller, G., Galanter, E., and Pribram, K. (1960), *Plans and the Structure of Behavior*, New York: Holt, Rinehart, and Winston.

Mills, S. (1990), Connectionism and eliminative materialism, *Acta Analytica*, 6: 19–31.

Minsky, M. (1966), Artificial intelligence. In *Information*, San Francisco: W. H. Freeman (originally published in *Scientific American*).

Minsky, M. (1967), *Computation: Finite and Infinite*, Englewood Cliffs, NJ: Prentice-Hall.

Minsky, M. (1975), A framework for representing knowledge. In P. Winston (ed.) (1975), *The Psychology of Computer Vision*, New York: McGraw-Hill. Reprinted in Collins and Smith (1988). Selections reprinted in Haugeland (1997).

Minsky, M., and Papert, S. (1969), *Perceptrons*, Cambridge, MA: MIT Press. Expanded edn 1988.

Moody, T. (1993), *Philosophy and Artificial Intelligence*, Englewood Cliffs: Prentice-Hall.

Morris, R. (1989), *Parallel Distributed Processing: Implications for Psychology and Neurobiology*, Oxford: Oxford University Press.

Mylopoulos, J., and Levesque, H. (1984), An overview of knowledge representation. In M. Brodie et al. (eds) (1984), *On Conceptual Modeling*, New York: Springer-Verlag.

Nadel, L., et al. (1986), The neurobiology of mental representation. In Brand and Harnish (1986).

Nadel, L., Cooper, L., Culicover, P., and Harnish, R. (eds) (1989), *Neural Connections, Mental Computation*, Cambridge, MA: Bradford/MIT Press.

Nagel, T. (1974), What is it like to be a bat?, *Philosophical Review*, 83: 435–50.

Nagel, T. (1993), What is the mind-body problem? In *Experimental and Theoretical Studies in Consciousness*, New York: Wiley.

Neisser, U. (1967), *Cognitive Psychology*, New York: Appleton, Century, Crofts.

von Neumann, J. (1945), First draft of a report on the EDVAC. In Aspry and Burks (1987).

Newell, A. (1973), Production systems: models of control structures. In W. Chase (ed.), *Visual Information Processing*, New York: Academic Press.

Newell, A. (1980), Physical symbol systems, *Cognitive Science*, 4(2): 135–83. Reprinted in D. Norman (ed.) (1981), *Perspectives in Cognitive Science*, Norwood, NJ: Ablex.

Newell, A. (1983), Reflections on the structure of an interdiscipline. In Machlup and Mansfield (1983).

Newell, A. (1990), *Unified Theories of Cognition*, Cambridge, MA: Harvard University Press.

Newell, A., Rosenbloom, P., and Laird, J. (1989), Symbolic structures for cognition. In Posner (1989).

Newell, A., and Simon, H. (1972), *Human Problem Solving*, Englewood Cliffs, NJ: Prentice-Hall.

Newell, A., and Simon, H. (1976), Computer science as an empirical inquiry, *Communications of the ACM*, 19(3): 113–26. Reprinted in Haugeland (1997).

Nietzsche, F. (1887), *On the Genealogy of Morals*, trans. (1967), New York: Vintage Books.

Nilsson, N. (1965), *Learning Machines*, New York: McGraw-Hill. Reissued with an introduction by T. Sejnowski as *The Mathematical Foundations of Learning Machines*, San Mateo, CA: Morgan Kaufman (1990).

Norman, D. (1981), What is cognitive science? In D. Norman (ed.) (1981), *Perspectives on Cognitive Science*, Norwood, NJ: Ablex.

Norman, D., and Rumelhart, D. (1975), *Explorations in Cognition*, San Francisco: Freeman.

Odifreddi, P. (1989), *Classical Recursion Theory*, Amsterdam: North Holland.

O'Keefe, J., and Nadel, L. (1978), *The Hippocampus as a Cognitive Map*, Oxford: Oxford University Press.

Osherson, D., et al. (eds) (1990, 1995), *An Invitation to Cognitive Science*, vols 1–3; (1998) vol. 4, Cambridge, MA: Bradford/MIT Press, 1st, 2nd edns.

Papert, S. (1988), One AI or many? Reprinted in Graubard (1988).

Partridge, D. (1996), Representation of knowledge. In M. Boden (ed.) (1996), *Artificial Intelligence*, New York: Academic Press.

Pavlov, I. (1927), *Conditioned Reflexes*, Oxford: Oxford University Press. Reprinted by Dover Books.

Pavlov, I. (1928), *Lectures on Conditioned Reflexes* (trans. W. Horsley Gant), New York: Liveright.

Penrose, R. (1989), *The Emperor's New Mind*, New York: Penguin Books.

Pessin, A., and Goldberg, S. (eds) (1996), *The Twin Earth Chronicles*, New York: M. E. Sharpe.

Plunkett, K., and Elman, J. (1997), *Exercises in Rethinking Innateness*, Cambridge, MA: Bradford/MIT Press.

Pohl, I., and Shaw, A. (1981), *The Nature of Computation*, Rockville, MD: Computer Science Press.

Posner, M. (ed.) (1989), *Foundations of Cognitive Science*, Cambridge, MA: Bradford/MIT Press.

Post, E. (1943), Formal reductions of the general combinatorial problem, *American Journal of Mathematics*, 65: 197–268.

Putnam, H. (1960), Minds and machines. In S. Hook (ed.) (1960), *Dimensions of Mind*, New York: New York University Press. Reprinted in Putnam (1975a).

Putnam, H. (1967), The nature of mental states. Reprinted in Putnam (1975a). Originally titled "Psychological Predicates" and published in W. Capitain and D. Merrill (eds) (1967), *Art, Mind, and Religion*, Pittsburgh: University of Pittsburgh Press.

Putnam, H. (1975a), *Philosophical Papers*, vol. 2, Cambridge: Cambridge University Press.

Putnam, H. (1975b), The meaning of meaning. Reprinted in Putnam (1975a), and in Harnish (1994).

Putnam, H. (1981), Brains in a vat. In *Reason, Truth and History*, Cambridge: Cambridge University Press.

Putnam, H. (1988), *Representation and Reality*, Cambridge, MA: Bradford/MIT Press.

Pylyshyn, Z. (1979), Complexity and the study of artificial and human intelligence. Reprinted in Haugeland (1981).

Pylyshyn, Z. (1983), Information science: its roots and relations as viewed from the perspective of cognitive science. In Machlup and Mansfield (1983).

Pylyshyn, Z. (1984), *Computation and Cognition*, Cambridge, MA: Bradford/MIT Press.

Pylyshyn, Z. (1989), Computing in cognitive science. In Posner (1989).

Quinlan, P. (1966), *Semantic Memory*, Report AFCRL-66-189, Bolt Beranek and Newman, Cambridge, MA.

Quinlan, P. (1968), Semantic memory. In M. Minsky (ed.) (1986), *Semantic Information Processing*, Cambridge, MA: MIT Press. Reprinted in Collins and Smith (1988).

Quinlan, P. (1991), *Connectionism and Psychology*, New York: Harvester-Wheatsheaf.

Ramsey, W. (1992), Connectionism and the philosophy of mental representation. In S. Davis (ed.) (1992), *Connectionism: Theory and Practice*, Oxford: Oxford University Press.

Ramsey, W., Stich, S., and Garon, J. (1991), Connectionism, eliminativism, and the future of folk psychology. In Ramsey, Stich, and Rumelhart (1991). Also in Greenwood (1991). Reprinted in MacDonald and Macdonald (1995), and Stich (1996).

Ramsey, W., Stich, S., and Rumelhart, D. (eds) (1991), *Philosophy and Connectionist Theory*, Hillsdale, NJ: Lawrence Erlbaum.

Ratcliff, R. (1990), Connectionist models of recognition memory: constraints imposed by learning and forgetting functions, *Psychological Review*, 97(2): 285–308.

Rey, G. (1986), What's really going on in Searle's Chinese room?, *Philosophical Studies*, 50: 169–85.

Rey, G. (1997), *Contemporary Philosophy of Mind*, Oxford: Blackwell.

Rich, E. (1983), *Artificial Intelligence*, New York: McGraw-Hill.

Rolls, E., and Treves, A. (1998), *Neural Networks and Brain Function*, Oxford: Oxford University Press.

Rosenberg, J. (1990a), Connectionism and cognition, *Acta Analytica*, 6: 33–46. Reprinted in Haugeland (1997).

Rosenberg, J. (1990b), Treating connectionism properly: reflections on Smolensky, *Psychological Research*, 52: 163–74.

Rosenblatt, F. (1958), The perceptron: a probabilistic model for information storage and organization in the brain, *Psychological Review*, 63: 386–408. Reprinted in J. Anderson and E. Rosenfeld (eds) (1988).

Rosenblatt, F. (1962), *Principles of Neurodynamics*, Washington, DC: Spartan Books.

Rosenthal, D. (1986), Two concepts of consciousness, *Philosophical Studies*, 49: 329–59.

Rosenthal, D. (1997), A theory of consciousness. In Block et al. (1997).

Rumelhart, D. (1989), The architecture of mind: a connectionist approach. In Posner (1989). Reprinted in Haugeland (1997).

Rumelhart, D., and McClelland, J. (eds) (1986a), *Parallel Distributed Processing*, vols 1 and 2, Cambridge, MA: Bradford/MIT Press.

Rumelhart, D., and McClelland, J. (1986b), On learning the past tenses of English verbs. In Rumelhart and McClelland (1986a), vol. 2, ch. 17.

Rumelhart, D., and Zipser, D. (1986), Feature discovery by competitive learning. In Rumelhart and McClelland (1986a), vol. 1, ch. 5.

Russell, B. (1918), The philosophy of logical atomism, *The Monist*. Reprinted (1985) La Salle, IL: Open Court.

Scarborough, D., and Sternberg, S. (eds) (1998), *An Invitation to Cognitive Science*, vol. 4, Cambridge, MA: Bradford/MIT Press.

Schank, R., and Abelson, R. (1977), *Scripts, Plans, Goals and Understanding*, Hillsdale, NJ: Lawrence Erlbaum. Chs 1–3 reprinted in Collins and Smith (1988).

Schneider, W. (1987), Connectionism: is it a paradigm shift for psychology?, *Behavior Research Methods, Instruments, and Computers*, 19: 73–83.

Schwartz, J. (1988), The new connectionism: developing relations between neuroscience and artificial intelligence. In Graubard (1988).

Scott, D. (1967), Some definitional suggestions for automata theory, *Journal of Computer and System Sciences*, 1: 187–212.

Seager, W. (1999), *Theories of Consciousness*, New York: Routledge.

Searle, J. (1969), *Speech Acts*, Cambridge: Cambridge University Press.

Searle, J. (1979), What is an intentional state? *Mind*, January: 74–92.

Searle, J. (1980), Minds, brains and programs, *Behavioral and Brain Sciences*, 3: 417–24. Reprinted in Haugeland (1997).

Searle, J. (1983), *Intentionality*, Cambridge: Cambridge University Press.

Searle, J. (1990a), Consciousness, explanatory inversion, and cognitive science, *Behavioral and Brain Sciences*, 13(4): 585–642.

Searle, J. (1990b), Is the brain a digital computer?, *Proceedings of the American Philosophical Association*, 64(3): 21–37. Incorporated into Searle (1992), ch. 9.

Searle, J. (1991), Is the brain's mind a computer program?, *Scientific American*, 262(1): 26–31.

Searle, J. (1992), *The Rediscovery of the Mind*, Cambridge, MA: Bradford/MIT Press.

Searle, J. (1997), *The Mystery of Consciousness*, New York: New York Review.

Sechenov, L. (1863), *Reflexes of the Brain*. Excerpted in R. Hernstein and E. Boring (eds) (1965), *A Source Book in the History of Psychology*, Cambridge, MA: Harvard University Press.

Segal, G. (1996), The modularity of theory of mind. In P. Carruthers and P. Smith (eds) (1996), *Theories of Mind*, Cambridge: Cambridge University Press.

Seidenberg, M., et al. (1982), Automatic access to the meanings of ambiguous words in context, *Cognitive Psychology*, 14: 489–537.

Sejnowski, T., and Rosenberg, C. (1987), Parallel networks that learn to pronounce English text, *Complex Systems*, 1: 145–68.

Selfridge, O. (1959), Pandemonium: a paradigm for learning. In D. Blake et al. (eds), *Proceedings of the Symposium on the Mechanization of Thought Processes*, National Physical Laboratory, London: HMSO.

Selfridge, O., and Neisser, U. (1960), Pattern recognition by machine, *Scientific American*, August: 60–8.

Shannon, C., and Weaver, W. (1949), *The Mathematical Theory of Communication*, Urbana: University of Illinois Press.

Shear, J. (ed.) (1997), *Explaining Consciousness: The Hard Problem*, Cambridge, MA: Bradford/MIT Press.

Shepherd, G. (1991), *Foundations of the Neuron Doctrine*, Oxford: Oxford University Press.

Shepherd, G. (1994), *Neurobiology*, 3rd edn, Oxford: Oxford University Press.

Sherrington, C. (1906), *The Integrative Action of the Nervous System*, reprinted (1973), New York: Arno Press.

Shortliff, E. H. (1976), *Computer-based Medical Consultants: MYCIN*, New York: North-Holland.

Siegelmann, H., and Sontag, E. (1992), On the computational power of neural nets, *Proceedings of the Fifth ACM Workshop on Computational Learning Theory*, 440–449.

Skinner, B. F. (1938), *The Behavior of Organisms*, Englewood Cliffs, NJ: Prentice-Hall.

Skinner, B. F. (1957), *Verbal Behavior*, Englewood Cliffs, NJ: Prentice-Hall.

Skinner, B. F. (1976), *About Behaviorism*, New York: Knopf.

Smith, L. (1986), *Behaviorism and Logical Positivism*, Stanford, CA: Stanford University Press.

Smolensky, P. (1988a), On the proper treatment of connectionism, *Behavioral and Brain Sciences*, 11: 1–23. *Peer commentary*: 23–58. *Author's replies*: 59–74.

Smolensky, P. (1988b), *Lectures on Connectionist Cognitive Modeling* (unpublished manuscript).

Smolensky, P. (1989), Connectionist modelling: neural computation, mental connections. In Nadel et al. (1989). Reprinted in Haugeland (1997).

Smolensky, P. (1990), Representation in connectionist networks. In D. Memmi and Y. Visetti (eds) (1990), *Intellectica* (Special issue 9–10) *Modeles Connexionists*.

Smolensky, P. (1991a), Connectionism, constituency, and the language of thought. In Loewer and Rey (1991).

Smolensky, P. (1991b), The constituent structure of connectionist mental states: a reply to Fodor and Pylyshyn. In Horgan and Tienson (1991).

Smolensky, P. (1995), On the projectable predicates of connectionist psychology: a case for belief. In MacDonald and MacDonald (1995).

Squire, L., and Kosslyn, M. (eds) (1998), *Findings and Current Opinion in Cognitive Neuroscience*, Cambridge, MA: Bradford/MIT Press.

Stabler, E. (1983), How are grammars represented?, *Behavioral and Brain Sciences*, 6: 391–421.

Staugaard, Jr., A. (1987), *Robotics and AI*, Englewood Cliffs, NJ: Prentice-Hall.

Sterelny, K. (1990), *The Representational Theory of Mind*, Oxford: Blackwell.

Sternberg, S. (1970), Memory-scanning: mental processes revealed by reaction-time experiments, *American Scientist*, 57: 421–57.

Stich, S. (1978), Autonomous psychology and the belief desire thesis, *The Monist*, 61: 573–90.

Stich, S. (1983), *From Folk Psychology to Cognitive Science*, Cambridge, MA: Bradford/MIT Press.

Stich, S. (1991), Narrow content meets fat syntax. In Loewer and Rey (1991).

Stich, S. (1996), *Deconstructing the Mind*, Oxford: Oxford University Press.

Stich, S., and Warfield, T. (1995), Reply to Clark and Smolensky: do connectionist minds have beliefs? In MacDonald and MacDonald (1995).

Stillings, N., et al. (1995), *Cognitive Science: An Introduction*, 2nd edn, Cambridge, MA: Bradford/MIT Press.

Stone, J. (1972), Morphology and physiology of the geniculo-cortical synapse in the cat: the question of parallel input to the striate cortex, *Investigative Ophthalmology*, 11, 338–46.

Sutherland, N. S. (ed.) (1989), *The International Dictionary of Psychology*, New York: Continuum.

Tarski, A. (1969), Truth and proof, *Scientific American*, June: 63–77.

Tennant, H. (1981), *Natural Language Processing*, New York: Petrocelli.

Thagard, P. (1986), Parallel computation and the mind-body problem, *Cognitive Science*, 10: 301–18.

Thagard, P. (1996), *Mind: An Introduction to Cognitive Science*, Cambridge, MA: Bradford/MIT Press.

Thagard, P. (ed.) (1998), *Mind Readings*, Cambridge, MA: Bradford/MIT Press.

Thorndike, E. (1911), *Animal Intelligence*, New York: Hafner.
Thorndike, E. (1929), *Human Learning*, New York: Johnson Reprint Corporation.
Tienson, J. (1991), Introduction. In Horgan and Tienson (1991).
Tremblay, J.-P., and Sorensen, P. (1984), *An Introduction to Data Structures and Their Applications*, 2nd edn, New York: McGraw-Hill.
Turing, A. (1936/7), On computable numbers, with an application to the *entscheidungs-problem*, *Proceedings of the London Mathematical Society*, Series 2, 42: 230–65. Reprinted in Davis (1965).
Turing, A. (1946), Proposal for development in the mathematics division of an automatic computing engine (ACE). Reprinted in Carpenter and Doran (1986).
Turing, A. (1948), Intelligent machinery. In B. Meltzer and D. Michie (eds) (1969), *Machine Intelligence*, 5: 3–23, New York: Academic Press. Reprinted in Ince (1992).
Turing, A. (1950), Computing machinery and intelligence, *Mind*, 236. Reprinted in Haugeland (1997), and in Ince (1992).
Valentine, E. (1989), Neural nets: from Hartley and Hebb to Hinton, *Journal of Mathematical Psychology*, 33: 348–57.
van Gelder, T. (1991), What is the "D" in "PDP"? A survey of the concept of distribution. In Ramsey, Stich, and Rumelhart (1991).
van Gelder, T. (1992), The proper treatment of cognition. In *Proceedings of the 14th Annual Conference of the Cognitive Science Society*, Hillsdale, NJ: Erlbaum.
van Gelder, T. (1997), Dynamics in cognition. In Haugeland (1997).
Verschure, P. (1992), Taking connectionism seriously. In *Proceedings of the 14th Annual Conference of the Cognitive Science Society*, Hillsdale, NJ: Erlbaum.
von Eckhardt, B. (1993), *What is cognitive science?* Cambridge, MA: Bradford/MIT Press.
von Eckhardt, B. (1994), Folk psychology (1). In Guttenplan (1994).
Walker, S. F. (1990), A brief history of connectionism and its psychological implications, *AI and Society*, 4: 17–38.
Waltz, D. (1982), Artificial intelligence, *Scientific American*, October.
Wang, H. (1957), A variant of Turing's theory of calculating machines, *Journal of the Association of Computing Machinery*, 4: 63–92.
Warner, H. (1921), *A History of Association Psychology*, New York: Charles Scribner's Sons.
Wasserman, P. (1989), *Neural Computing: Theory and Practice*, New York: Van Nostrand Reinhold.
Watson, J. B. (1913), Psychology as the behaviorist views it, *Psychological Review*, 20: 158–77.
Webber, B., and Nilsson, N. (eds) (1981), *Readings in Artificial Intelligence*, San Mateo, CA: Morgan Kaufman.
Weiskrantz, L. (1988), Some contributions of neuropsychology of vision and memory to the problem of consciousness. In A. Marcel and E. Bisiach (eds) (1988), *Consciousness in Contemporary Science*, Oxford: Oxford University Press.
White, R. (2000), Some basic concepts of computability theory. In B. Cooney (ed.), *The Place of Mind*, Belmont, CA: Wadsworth.

Whitehead, A. N., and Russell, B. (1910–13), *Principia Mathematica*, vols 1–3, Cambridge: Cambridge University Press. 2nd edn (1925).

Wilks, Y. (1977), Natural language understanding systems with the A. I. paradigm: a survey and some comparisons. In Zampoli (1977).

Wilson, F. (1992), Association, ideas, and images in Hume. In P. Cummins and G. Zoeller (eds) (1992), *Minds, Ideas and Objects*, Atascadero, CA: Ridgeview.

Wilson, R., and Keil, F. (eds) (1999), *The MIT Encyclopedia of the Cognitive Sciences*, Cambridge, MA: MIT Press.

Winograd, T. (1972), *Understanding Natural Language*, New York: Academic Press.

Winograd, T. (1973), A procedural model of language understanding. In R. Shank and K. Colby (eds) (1973), *Computer Models of Thought and Language*, San Francisco: Freeman.

Winograd, T. (1975), Frame representations and the declarative/procedural controversy. In Bobrow and Collins (1975).

Winograd, T. (1977), Five lectures on artificial intelligence. In Zampolli (1977).

Winograd, T. (1980), What does it mean to understand language?, *Cognitive Science*, 4: 209–41.

Winograd, T. (1983), *Language as a Cognitive Process*, Reading, MA: Addison-Wesley.

Winston, P. (1977), *Artificial Intelligence*, Reading, MA: Addison Wesley.

Woods, W. (1975), What's in a link? In Bobrow and Collins (1975). Reprinted in Collins and Smith (1988).

Young, R. M. (1970), *Mind, Brain and Adaption in the Nineteenth Century*, Oxford: Oxford University Press.

Zampoli, A. (ed.) (1977), *Linguistic Structures Processing*, New York: North-Holland.

Index